S0-ABQ-715

3765

Fundamentals of
ASSEMBLY LANGUAGE
PROGRAMMING
Using the IBM PC and Compatibles

Richard C. Detmer

Northwest Missouri State University

D. C. Heath and Company

Lexington, Massachusetts   Toronto

To my wife Carol
and my daughters
Kristina and Laura

Acquisitions Editor: J. Carter Shanklin
Developmental Editor: Katherine Pinard
Production Editor: Marret McCorkle
Designer: Cornelia Boynton
Production Coordinator: Lisa Arcese
Cover: Nancy Lindgren

Trademark Acknowledgments:
IBM is a registered trademark of International Business Machines, Inc. Microsoft is a registered trademark of Microsoft Corporation. Codeview is a registered trademark of Microsoft Corporation.

Copyright © 1990 by D. C. Heath and Company.

All rights reserved. No part of this publication may be reproduced or transmitted in any form or by any means, electronic or mechanical, including photocopy, recording, or any information storage or retrieval system, without permission in writing from the publisher.

Published simultaneously in Canada.

Printed in the United States of America.

International Standard Book Number: 0–669–18206–0

Library of Congress Catalog Card Number: 89–84585

10   9   8   7   6   5   4   3   2

Preface

Individual users have different perceptions of computers. For example, someone playing an action game may view the computer as a weapons control unit used to fire missiles at an outer space invader, but a student using a word processing program to prepare a term paper views the computer as a typewriter, a spelling checker, or a typist, and an owner of a small business using an accounts-receivable program considers the computer a bookkeeper that keeps records of sales and prepares monthly bills.

A computer programmer often sees a computer as an instrument to create new applications software for the game player, the student, and the small-business owner. A high-level language programmer's image of the computer is provided by the language compiler, which gives the impression that the computer stores object types like INTEGER, REAL, and ARRAY OF CHAR in named memory locations, calculates values of expressions, calls procedures, executes while loops, and so forth. An assembly language programmer works more closely with the computer hardware itself, storing data in memory and registers and giving detailed instructions to the central processing unit.

To program effectively, assembly language programmers must understand certain fundamental principles. These apply to almost all computers and assemblers. *Fundamentals of Assembly Language Programming Using the IBM PC and Compatibles* teaches these fundamental concepts:

- Basic computer architecture: memory, CPU, I/O devices, operating system software, and applications software
- Representation of data in a computer in numeric formats and as character strings
- The functions of an assembler, including translation of assembly language mnemonics to machine instructions and of symbols to memory references
- Instructions to operate on 2's complement integers
- Instructions to manipulate individual bits
- Instructions for branching and looping
- Instructions to handle strings of characters
- Coding of subroutines: parameter passing, local variables, and preserving the environment for the calling procedure
- Use of macros
- Implementation of program designs in assembly language

IBM PC computers (or compatibles) and the Microsoft Macro Assembler are used as the means to teach these concepts.

By giving students a firm understanding of these principles, *Fundamentals of Assembly Language Programming* prepares them to program more effectively in any programming language, to pursue advanced studies in computer design and architecture, or to learn more about system details that are specific to IBM PC computers and PC-DOS.

Text Organization and Content

The material in this book has been class-tested for five semesters in a one-semester assembly language class. The minimal prerequisite for this class is a good course in a structured high-level language; most students have taken a "CS 1" course using Pascal or Modula-2. The assembly language course covers Chapters 1–7 and 9 thoroughly; I consider the material in these chapters the most important topics for an assembly language course. In most semesters portions of Chapters 8, 10, 11, and 12 have also been included. There has never been enough time for Chapters 13 or 14, although well-motivated students have covered one or both independently.

The material in Chapters 8 and 11 can be covered any time after Chapter 3. In my experience, most students need to think about addressing modes and the assembly process repeatedly. Consequently, almost every chapter before Chapter 8 introduces a new addressing mode; Chapter 8 completes the logical framework and provides new applications. From Chapter 3 on, information about the assembly process and instruction formats is given, but Chapter 11 tells the whole story.

Prerequisites

This book assumes that the student has had the experience of programming a computer in a structured, high-level language such as Pascal or Modula-2. The student should also know how to write a logical design for a program, as a step prior to writing code. This book uses pseudocode to express program logic.

It is assumed that the student has previously used microcomputers and has an introduction to the IBM PC or compatible microcomputer and the PC-DOS or MS-DOS operating system that he or she will use.

Style and Pedagogy

The text primarily teaches by example. A complete assembly language program is presented very early, in Chapter 3, and its components are carefully explained at a level that the student is able to understand. Subsequent chapters include many examples of assembly language code along with appropriate explanations of new or difficult concepts.

The text uses numerous figures and examples. Many series of "before" and "after" examples are given for instructions.

Exercises appear at the end of each section. Short-answer exercises reinforce understanding of the material just covered, and programming exercises offer an opportunity to apply the material to assembly language programs.

Debugging Utilities

The PC-DOS and MS-DOS operating systems come with the DEBUG utility, which allows the programmer to trace the execution of machine language programs. The Microsoft Macro Assembler comes with the CodeView debugging utility. Appendix E presents short tutorials on the use of DEBUG and CodeView.

In my teaching experience, students have little difficulty grasping the concepts of machine-level program execution without a debugger and there rarely seems to be enough time to cover essential topics in an assembly language course. Debuggers are sometimes used to input data for an assembly language program. This is not necessary with this text since the Instructor's Guide includes a disk with input/output procedures that are easily called by macros in assembly language programs. Listings of this software are also included in appendixes at the end of this book.

Debuggers are sometimes used for modifying executable code. If this is done, it is very easy to forget to revise the assembly language source code, or to make a change to the source code that is different from that made to the executable code. It is my conviction that good programs in any programming language result from good designs. If a program fails to execute correctly, the programmer should check to see whether the design is correct and that the source code faithfully implements the design.

The Intel Family of Microprocessors

The primary job of an assembler is to translate assembly language statements into machine instructions to be executed by the processor, in this instance the Intel 8088 microprocessor contained in the IBM PC (or the Intel 8086, which uses indentical instructions). The code in this book is written for the Microsoft Macro Assembler, but it should require almost no changes to be translated with other 8088 assemblers. Since the focus of this book is fundamental concepts, no attempt is made to cover all the options available with the Microsoft Macro Assembler.

Coverage of 80286 and 80386 Processors   The Microsoft Macro Assembler will also translate assembly language for Intel 80186, 80286, and 80386 processors. The assembly language is essentially the same since these processors execute all 8086/8088 instructions, plus additional instructions. Appendix C describes some of the additional capabilities of Intel 80286 and 80386 microprocessors.

Coverage of the 8087 Math Coprocessor   Chapter 14 discusses how to program using the Intel 8087 math coprocessor and contrasts doing arithmetic with and without the coprocessor. The Intel 80287 and 80387 coprocessors execute the same instructions as the 8087, plus more.

Instructors's Guide and Software Disk

Supplementary materials for this book include an Instructor's Guide with a software disk. The Instructor's Guide contains teaching tips and solutions to many exercises. The software disk contains files to define and use the input/output macros described in Chapter 3: the "header file" IO.H contains macro definitions, IO.ASM contains source code for the procedures called by the input/output macros, and IO.OBJ is an assembled version of IO. ASM. The software disk also contains EXAMPLE.ASM, the example program used in Chapter 3. Listings of this software are included in Appendixes F and G.

Acknowledgments

I would like to thank my students at Northwest Missouri State University who patiently used manuscript versions of the book, all the good folks at D. C. Heath who put up with my strong opinions, and Karin Ellison, who convinced me to go with D. C. Heath.

I would also like to express my appreciation to those who reviewed the book: Robert Borschat, South Dakota State University; Ronald Curtis, Canisius College; Virginia Eaton, Northeast Louisiana University; Tom Fenyo, DeAnza College; Joe Grimes, California Polytechnic State University; Roy Levow, Florida Atlantic University; James F. Peters, Kansas State University; Robert Sterling, Tidewater Community College—Virginia Beach; and Gene Waters, Arizona State University.

R. C. D.

CONTENTS

To the Student

Why should you learn to program in assembly language? Perhaps the most important reason is that an assembly language programmer learns to understand the computer as it really is, without applications programs or a high-level language compiler distorting the view. This can make you a better programmer in a high-level programming language, prepare you for other courses that study the computer hardware, or give you a basis for learning more about a particular computer system.

There are several reasons for actually programming in assembly language. Assembly language code usually executes very rapidly. Some programming tasks need to be implemented in assembly language just for this speed. Sometimes part of a program is written in a high-level language, and critical sections are coded in assembly language procedures that are then called from the high-level program. In addition, programs that must access specific memory locations or input/output device addresses are difficult or impossible in most high-level languages. However, these can be implemented in assembly language. In other words, assembly language programs give execution speed and hardware access that is often lacking in high-level language programs.

What can you expect in an assembly language course? An assembly language programmer sees the computer at its hardware level. You will learn how data are represented for storage in a computer. You will study a particular computer system, how memory is addressed, and what instructions are executed by its central processing unit. You will find out how an assembler translates an assembly language source program into machine code to be executed by the hardware.

It often takes many assembly language instructions to do the same job as a single high-level language statement. Consequently assembly language programs tend to be long and to require a lot of attention to detail. It is very important that you make a logical design for an assembly language program *before* you begin to write assembly language code. Hours of work can be saved by designing a program before implementing it in a programming language; this is especially true with assembly language since it is so easy to get lost in the details of the code. If your program doesn't work after you eliminate the syntax errors flagged by the assembler, first check to be sure that your design is correct, and then check to be sure you have faithfully implemented your design.

The assembly language programmer is responsible for reserving memory space for data to be stored. Sometimes data can be referenced by name, but other times it cannot. The format in which data are stored depends on the use that will be made of it. For example, strings to be printed are stored in a different format than integers to be used in arithmetic calculations. Although a "write" procedure in a high-level language will take care of converting the value of an integer variable to printable character codes, it will be your job in an assembly language program to convert data from one format to another when necessary.

You will be expected to learn how a computer's arithmetic instructions work. A computer operates on binary data, which is easily converted into hexadecimal (base 16) notation. Many inexpensive calculators are capable of manipulating hexadecimal values. You may find one a valuable investment.

In summary, you may occasionally find studying assembly language difficult or tedious, but your reward will be a much better understanding of how computers work.

CHAPTER 1

Representing Data in a Computer

When you program in a high-level language (like Pascal or Modula-2) you use variables of different types (such as integer or character); once you have declared variables, you don't have to worry about how the data are represented in the computer. In assembly language, however, you must be more concerned with how data are stored. Often you have the job of converting data from one representation to another. Sometimes an "unusual" representation is used directly in assembly language code. This chapter covers some common ways that data are represented in a microcomputer. Chapter 2 discusses why the microcomputer's physical components are important to the assembly language programmer. Chapter 3 illustrates how to write and execute an assembly language program.

------- 1.1 --

Binary and Hexadecimal Numbers

A computer uses **bits** (binary digits, each an electronic state representing zero or one) to denote values. We represent such **binary** numbers using the digits 0 and 1 and a base 2 place-value system. This binary number system is like the decimal system except that the positions (right to left) are 1's, 2's, 4's, 8's, 16's (and higher powers of 2) instead of 1's, 10's, 100's, 1000's, 10000's (powers of 10). For example, the binary number 1101 can be interpreted as the decimal number 13,

$$1 \quad\quad 1 \quad\quad 0 \quad\quad 1$$
$$\text{one } 8 + \text{one } 4 + \text{no } 2 + \text{one } 1 \; = \; 13$$

Binary numbers are so long that they are awkward to read and write. For instance, it takes the eight bits 11111010 to represent the decimal number 250, or the fifteen bits 111010100110000 to represent the decimal number 30000. The **hexadecimal** (base 16) number system represents numbers using about one-fourth as many digits as the binary system. Conversions between hexadecimal and binary are so easy that **hex** can be thought of as shorthand for binary. The hexadecimal system requires sixteen digits. The digits 0, 1, 2, 3, 4, 5, 6, 7, 8 and 9 are used just as in the decimal system; A, B, C, D, E and F are used for the decimal numbers 10, 11, 12, 13, 14 and 15, respectively. Either uppercase or lowercase letters can be used for the new digits.

The positions in hexadecimal numbers correspond to powers of 16. From right to left, they are 1's, 16's, 256's, etc. The value of the hex number 9D7A is 40314 in decimal since

$$
\begin{array}{rcl r l}
9 & \times & 4096 & 36864 & [\,4096 = 16^3\,] \\
+\ 13 & \times & 256 & 3328 & [\,\text{D is } 13,\ 256 = 16^2\,] \\
+\ 7 & \times & 16 & 112 & \\
+\ 10 & \times & 1 & 10 & [\,\text{A is } 10\,] \\
& & & = 40314 &
\end{array}
$$

Figure 1.1 shows equivalent values in decimal, hexadecimal, and binary systems for small numbers. It is worthwhile to memorize this table or to be able to construct it very quickly.

Figure 1.1 Decimal, Hexadecimal, and Binary Numbers.

Decimal	Hexadecimal	Binary
0	0	0
1	1	1
2	2	10
3	3	11
4	4	100
5	5	101
6	6	110
7	7	111
8	8	1000
9	9	1001
10	A	1010
11	B	1011
12	C	1100
13	D	1101
14	E	1110
15	F	1111

A hexadecimal number can be converted to its equivalent binary form simply by substituting four bits for each hex digit. The bits are those found in the third column of Figure 1.1, padded with leading zeros, as needed. For example,

$$3B8E2_{16} = 11\ 1011\ 1000\ 1110\ 0010_2 \quad .$$

The subscripts 16 and 2 are used to indicate the base of the system in which a number is written; they are usually omitted when there is little chance of confusion. The extra spaces in the binary number are inserted just to make it more readable. Note that in the hex to binary conversion above, the rightmost hex digit 2 was converted to 0010, with leading zeros included. It was not necessary to insert leading zeros when converting 3, the leftmost hex digit, although it would have been correct since leading zeros do not change the value of a binary number.

To convert binary numbers to hexadecimal format, use the opposite steps: break the binary number into groups of four bits, starting from the right, and substitute the corresponding hex digit for each group of four bits. For example,

$$1011011101001101111 = 101\ 1011\ 1010\ 0110\ 1111 = 5BA6F$$

You have seen how to convert a binary number to an equivalent decimal number. However, instead of converting a long binary number directly to decimal, it is faster to convert it to hex, and then convert the hex number to decimal.

Again using the above 19-bit-long number,

$$1011011101001101111_2$$
$$= 101\ \ 1011\ \ 1010\ \ 0110\ \ 1111$$
$$= 5BA6F_{16}$$
$$= 5 \times 65536 + 11 \times 4096 + 10 \times 256 + 6 \times 16 + 15 \times 1$$
$$= 375407_{10}$$

An even easier way to convert hexadecimal numbers to equivalent decimal numbers is to use a calculator that allows entry of hex digits and that does conversion between bases with one or two keystrokes. Such calculators can do arithmetic directly in hex as well as decimal, and often have a full range of other functions available. They are moderately priced (many under $20) and are a worthwhile investment for an assembly language student especially since they make it easy to convert decimal numbers to hexadecimal. (No calculator is needed to convert the hexadecimal result to binary.) One warning: many of these calculators use seven segment displays and display the lowercase letter b so that it looks almost like the numeral 6. Other characters may also be difficult to read.

If you have no hex calculator available, or if the battery dies at an awkward moment, here is an algorithm for converting a decimal number to its hex equivalent. It produces the hex digits of the answer in order, right to left. The algorithm is expressed in pseudocode—this is the way that algorithms and program designs will be written in this book.

until decimal_number = 0 loop

    divide decimal_number by 16, getting quotient and remainder;
    remainder (in hex) is the next digit (right to left);
    decimal_number := quotient;

end until;

As an example, the algorithm is traced for the decimal number 5876:

- Since this is an **until** loop, the controlling condition is not checked until the body has been executed the first time.
- Divide 16 into 5876 (decimal_number).

```
        367  quotient     the new value for decimal_number
    16) 5876
        5872
           4  remainder    the rightmost digit of the answer
                                             Result so far:  4
```

- 367 is not zero. Divide it by 16.

$$\begin{array}{r} 22 \\ 16\overline{)367} \\ 352 \\ \hline 15 \end{array}$$

22 quotient   the new value for decimal_number

15 remainder   the second digit of the answer

Result so far: F4

■ 22 is not zero. Divide it by 16.

$$\begin{array}{r} 1 \\ 16\overline{)22} \\ 16 \\ \hline 6 \end{array}$$

1 quotient   the new value for decimal_number

6 remainder   the third digit of the answer

Result so far: 6F4

■ 1 is not zero. Divide it by 16.

$$\begin{array}{r} 0 \\ 16\overline{)1} \\ 0 \\ \hline 1 \end{array}$$

0 quotient   the new value for decimal_number

1 remainder   the fourth digit of the answer

Result so far: 16F4

■ 0 is zero, so the **until** loop terminates. The answer is $16F4_{16}$.

The **octal** (base 8) number system is used with some computer systems. Octal numbers are written using digits 0 through 7. Most calculators that do hex arithmetic also handle octal values. It is easy to convert a binary number to octal by writing the octal equivalent for each group of three bits, or to convert from octal to binary by replacing each octal digit by three bits. To convert from decimal to octal, one can use an algorithm that is the same as for decimal to hex except that you divide by 8 instead of 16 at each step.

Exercises 1.1

Complete the table below by supplying the missing two forms for each number.

	Binary	Hexadecimal	Decimal
1.	100	_____	_____
2.	10101101	_____	_____
3.	1101110101	_____	_____

	Binary	Hexadecimal	Decimal
4.	11111011110	_____	_____
5.	10000000001	_____	_____
6.	_____	8EF	_____
7.	_____	10	_____
8.	_____	A52E	_____
9.	_____	70C	_____
10.	_____	6BD3	_____
11.	_____	_____	100
12.	_____	_____	527
13.	_____	_____	4128
14.	_____	_____	11947
15.	_____	_____	59020

1.2

Character Codes

Letters, numerals, punctuation marks, and other characters are represented in a computer by assigning a numeric value to each character. Several schemes for assigning these numeric values have been used. The system commonly used with microcomputers is the American Standard Code for Information Interchange (abbreviated **ASCII** and pronounced "ask-ee").

The ASCII system uses seven bits to represent characters, so that values from 000 0000 to 111 1111 are assigned to characters. This means that 128 different characters can be represented using ASCII codes. The ASCII codes are usually given as hex numbers from 00 to 7F or as decimal numbers from 0 to 127.[*] The inside front cover has a complete listing of ASCII codes. Using this table, you can check that the message

---

[*] Some computers, including the IBM PC and compatible systems, use an extended character set, additionally assigning characters to hex numbers 80 to FF (decimal 128 to 255). Extended character sets will not be used in this book.

Computers are fun.

can be coded in ASCII, using hex numbers, as

43 6F 6D 70 75 74 65 72 73 20 61 72 65 20 66 75 6E 2E
C o m p u t e r s   a r e   f u n .

Note that a space, even though it is invisible, has a character code (hex 20).

Numbers can be represented using character codes. For example, the ASCII codes for the date October 23, 1970 are

4F 63 74 6F 62 65 72 20 32 33 2C 20 31 39 37 30
O c t o b e r   2 3 ,   1 9 7 0

with the number 23 represented using ASCII codes 32 33, and 1970 represented using 31 39 37 30. This is very different from the binary representation in the last section, where $23_{10} = 10111_2$ and $1970_{10} = 11110110010_2$. Computers use both of these representations for numbers: ASCII for input and output, and binary for internal computations.

The ASCII code assignments seem to be rather arbitrary, but there are certain patterns. The codes for uppercase letters are contiguous, as are the codes for lowercase letters. The codes for an uppercase letter and the corresponding lowercase one differ by exactly one bit. Bit 5 is 0 for an uppercase letter and 1 for the corresponding lowercase letter; other bits are the same. (Bits in assembly language are numbered right to left, starting with 0 for the rightmost bit.) For example,

- uppercase M codes as $4D_{16} = 1001101_2$
- lowercase m codes as $6D_{16} = 1101101_2$.

The printable characters are grouped together from 20_{16} to $7E_{16}$. (A space is considered a printable character.) Numerals 0, 1, ... , 9 have ASCII codes 30_{16}, 31_{16}, ... , 39_{16}, respectively.

The characters from 00_{16} to $1F_{16}$, along with $7F_{16}$ are known as **control characters**. For example, the ESC key on an ASCII keyboard generates a hex 1B code. (The abbreviation ESC stands for Extra Services Control but most people say "escape.") The ESC character is often sent to a peripheral device in combination with other characters to turn on a special feature such as double-width printing on a printer. Since such character sequences are not standardized, they will not be covered in this book.

The two ASCII control characters that will be used the most frequently in this book are $0D_{16}$ and $0A_{16}$, for carriage return (CR) and line feed (LF), respectively. The $0D_{16}$ code is generated by an ASCII keyboard when the Return or Enter key is pressed. When sent to an ASCII display, it causes the cursor to move to the beginning of the current line, without going down to a new line. When carriage return is sent to most ASCII printers, it causes the print head to move to the beginning of the line. The line feed code $0A_{16}$ causes an ASCII display to move the cursor straight down, or causes most printers to roll the paper up one line, in both cases without going to the beginning of the new line. To display a message and move to the beginning of a new line, it is necessary to send the message characters plus CR and LF characters to the screen or printer. This may be an annoying requirement as you program in assembly language, but you also have the option of not using CR or LF characters when you want to either leave the cursor on a line after prompting for input or to piece together a line using several output instructions.

Lesser used control characters include form feed ($0C_{16}$), which causes many printers to jump to the top of a new page; horizontal tab (09_{16}), which is generated by the Tab key on the keyboard; backspace (08_{16}), generated by the Backspace key; and delete ($7F_{16}$), generated by the Delete key. Notice that the Backspace and Delete keys do not generate the same codes. The bell character (07_{16}) causes an audible signal to be generated when it is output to the display. A good programming practice is to sound the bell only when really necessary.

Many large computers use a code representation for characters called Extended Binary Coded Decimal Information Code (abbreviated EBCDIC and pronounced ib-SEE-dick or eb-SEE-dick). The EBCDIC system will be used in this book only as an example of an alternative coding scheme, when translation from one coding system to another is discussed in Chapter 7.

Exercises 1.2

1. Each of the following hexadecimal numbers can be interpreted as representing a decimal number or a pair of ASCII codes. Give both interpretations.

   (a) 2A45   (b) 7352   (c) 2036   (d) 106E

2. Find the ASCII codes for the characters in each of the following strings. Don't forget spaces and punctuation. Carriage return and line feed are shown by CR and LF, respectively (written together as CRLF so that it will be clear that there is no space character between them).

   (a) January 1 is New Year's Day.CRLF

   (b) George said, "Ouch!"

   (c) R2D2 was C3P0's friend.CRLF   ["0" is the numeral zero]

   (d) Your name?   [put two spaces after the question mark]

   (e) Enter value: [put two spaces after the colon]

3. What would be displayed if you output each of the following sequences of ASCII codes to a computer's screen?

    (a) 62 6C 6F 6F 64 2C 20 73 77 65 61 74 20 61
         6E 64 20 74 65 61 72 73

    (b) 6E 61 6D 65 0D 0A 61 64 64 72 65 73 73 0D
         0A 63 69 74 79 0D 0A

    (c) 4A 75 6E 65 20 31 31 2C 20 31 39 34 37 0D 0A

    (d) 24 33 38 39 2E 34 35

    (e) 49 44 23 3A 20 20 31 32 33 2D 34 35 2D 36 37 38 39

1.3

2's Complement Representation for Signed Integers

So far two ways to represent numbers have been described—by using binary integers (often expressed in hex), and the other by using ASCII codes. With ASCII, a negative integer could be expressed simply by coding the minus sign. For example, the ASCII codes for the four characters –817 are 2D, 38, 31 and 37. To express the decimal number –817 in binary, you could use the fact that

$$817_{10} = 331_{16} = 1100110001_2$$

and write –817 as –331 in hex, or –1100110001 in binary. Since bits, not minus signs, are what are actually stored in the computer, it is not obvious how to represent the minus sign. The **2's complement** system is an excellent scheme for storing signed integers in binary; it is discussed in this section.

When an integer is represented in 2's complement form, the number of bits to be used, that is, the length of the representation, must be decided in advance. In a computer with an 8088 processor, numbers are usually stored using 8 bits, 16 bits, or 32 bits. For 8088 applications, a group of 8 bits is called a **byte**, 16 bits (two bytes) is called a **word** and 32 bits (four bytes) is called a **doubleword**. (These terms are not universal. Each has been defined differently for other computer systems.) Since each of the sixteen patterns of four bits corresponds to a hex digit, it is easy to show the contents of a byte with 2 hex digits, a word with 4 hex digits, or a doubleword with 8 hex digits.

To represent a positive integer in 2's complement form, simply write it in binary with enough leading zeros to make it the chosen length. As an example, the word-length representation for 1116_{10} is 0000 0100 0101 1100, or 04 5C using hex digits grouped two per byte. The same number in doubleword length is 00 00 04 5C. Using a hex calculator you can easily do the conversion from decimal to hex and add leading zeros. This gives the 2's complement form of a positive integer.

A positive number must have a leading (leftmost or high order) 0 bit in its 2's complement representation. A leading 1 bit is reserved to indicate a negative number. The rest of a negative number is not just the bit pattern for the corresponding unsigned number.

A hex calculator also makes it easy to convert a negative decimal number to 2's complement form. For instance, if the decimal display shows –565 and the convert to hex key is pressed, a typical calculator will display FFFFFFFDCB (perhaps with a different number of leading F's). For a word-size representation, ignore all but the last four hex digits; the answer is FD CB or 1111 1101 1100 1011 in binary. The doubleword representation is FF FF FD CB, which is almost too long to write in binary.

The 2's complement representation of a negative number can also be found without a calculator. One method is to first express the unsigned number in hex, and then subtract this hex number from 10000_{16} to get the word-length representation, or from 100000000_{16} to get the doubleword-length representation. The number you subtract from is, in hex, a 1 followed by the number of 0's in the length of the representation—four for word-length, eight for doubleword-length. In binary, the number of zeros is the length of the representation in binary. This binary number is a power of two, and subtraction is sometimes called "taking the complement," so this operation is the source of the term "2's complement."

The word-length representation of the decimal number –76 is found by first converting the unsigned number 76 to its hex equivalent 4C, then by subtracting 4C from 10000.

$$1\ 0\ 0\ 0\ 0$$
$$-\ 4\ C$$

Since you cannot subtract C from 0, you have to borrow 1 from 1000, leaving FFF.

$$\begin{array}{r} ^1 \\ F\ F\ F\ 0 \\ -\ 4\ C \\ \hline F\ F\ B\ 4 \end{array}$$

After borrowing, the subtraction is easy. The units digit is

$$10_{16} - C_{16} = 16_{10} - 12_{10} = 4 \text{ (in decimal or hex)},$$

and the digit in the 16's position is

$$F_{16} - 4 = 15_{10} - 4_{10} = 11_{10} = B_{16}.$$

It is not necessary to convert the hex digits to decimal to subtract them if you learn the addition table for single hex digits.

The operation of subtracting a number from 1 followed by an appropriate number of 0's is called **taking the 2's complement**, or complementing the number. Thus "2's complement" is used both as the name of a representation system, and as the name of an operation. The operation of taking the 2's complement can be accomplished with a hex calculator by pressing the change sign key.

Since a given 2's complement representation is a fixed length, obviously there is a maximum size number that can be stored in it. For a word, the largest positive number stored is 7F FF, since this is the largest 16-bit number that has a high-order bit of 0 when written in binary. Positive numbers written in hex can be identified by a leading hex digit of 0 through 7. The hex number 7FFF is 32767 in decimal. Negative numbers are distinguished by a leading bit of 1, corresponding to hex digits of 8 through F.

Once the sign of a 2's complement representation is determined, it is not too difficult to find the corresponding decimal number. To convert a positive 2's complement number to decimal, just treat it like any unsigned binary number and convert it by hand or with a hex calculator. For example, the word-length 2's complement number 0D 43 represents the decimal number 3395.

Note that if you take the 2's complement of a number and then take the 2's complement of the result, you get back to the original number. In general, for word size and any number N,

$$N = 10000 - (10000 - N).$$

For example, using the word-length 2's complement value F39E

$$10000 - (10000 - F39E) = 10000 - C62 = F39E$$

This says again that the 2's complement operation corresponds to negation. Because of this, if you start with a bit pattern representing a negative number, the 2's complement operation can be used to find the unsigned number corresponding to it.

The word-length 2's complement number E9 73 represents a negative value since the sign bit (leading bit) is 1 (E = 1110). Taking the complement finds the corresponding unsigned number.

$$10000 - E973 = 168D = 5773_{10}.$$

This means that the decimal number represented by E9 73 is –5773.

The word-length 2's complement representations with a leading 1 bit range from 80 00 to FF FF. These convert to decimal as follows:

$$10000 - 8000 = 8000 = 32768_{10},$$

so 80 00 is the representation of –32768. Similarly

$$10000 - FFFF = 1,$$

so FF FF is the representation of –1. Recall that the largest positive decimal integer which can be represented as a word-length 2's complement number is 32767; the range of decimal numbers which can be represented in word-length 2's complement form is –32768 to 32767.

Using a calculator to convert a negative 2's complement representation to a decimal number is a little tricky. For example, if you start with the word-length representation FF 30 and your calculator displays 10 hex digits, you must enter the ten-hex-digit version of the number FFFFFFFF30 with six extra leading F's. When you push the convert-to-decimal button(s), your calculator should display –208.

------- **Exercises 1.3** ---

1. Find the word-length 2's complement representation of each of the following decimal numbers:

   (a) 845
   (b) 15000
   (c) 100
   (d) –10
   (e) –923

2. Find the doubleword-length 2's complement representation of each of the following decimal numbers:

   (a) 3874
   (b) 1000000
   (c) –100
   (d) –55555

3. Find the decimal integer that is represented by each of these word-length 2's complement numbers:

   (a) 00 A3
   (b) FF FE
   (c) 6F 20
   (d) B6 4A

4. Find the decimal integer that is represented by each of these doubleword-length 2's complement numbers:

(a) 00 00 F3 E1
(b) FF FF FE 03
(c) 98 C2 41 7D

5. Find the range of decimal integers that can be stored in 2's complement form in a byte.

6. Find the range of decimal integers that can be stored in 2's complement form in a doubleword.

1.4

Addition and Subtraction of 2's Complement Numbers

One of the reasons that the 2's complement representation scheme is commonly used to store signed integers in computers is that addition and subtraction operations can be easily and efficiently implemented in computer hardware. This section discusses addition and subtraction of 2's complement numbers, and introduces the concepts of carry and overflow, which will be needed later.

To add two 2's complement numbers, simply add them as if they were unsigned binary numbers. Here are some examples using word size representations. The decimal version of each problem is given to the right.

First, two positive numbers are added:

```
  0A 07          2567
+ 01 D3        +  467
  0B DA          3034
```

The answer is correct in this case since $BDA_{16} = 3034_{10}$.

Next, a positive number and a negative number are added:

```
  02 06            518
+ FF B0        + (–80)
1 01 B6            438
```

This time there appears to be a problem with the answer since it will not even fit in a word. However, if you ignore the extra "1" on the left, the word 01 B6 is the 2's complement representation of the decimal number 438.

Now two negative numbers are added:

```
    FF  E7            (-25)
 +  FF  F6         + (-10)
  1 FF  DD            -35
```

Again the sum in hex is too large to fit in two bytes, but if you discard the extra 1, then FF DD is the correct 2's complement representation of -35.

Each of the last two additions have a **carry** that transfers a digit out of the usual high-order position into the next position to the left and that results in an "extra" digit. The remaining digits give the correct 2's complement representation. The last four digits are not always the correct sum. Consider the addition of the following two positive numbers:

```
    48  3F          18495
 +  64  5A        +25690
    AC  99          44185
```

There was no carry (out of the high-order digit), but the representation is plainly incorrect since AC 99 represents the *negative* number -21351. You see intuitively that the problem arose because the decimal sum 44185 is bigger than the maximal value 32767 that can be stored in the two bytes of a word.

Here is another example showing a wrong answer, this time resulting from adding two negative numbers.

```
    E9  FF           (-5633)
 +  8C  F0        + (-29456)
  1 76  EF           -35089
```

This time there is a carry, but the remaining four digits 76 EF cannot be the right answer since they represent the *positive* number 30447. Again, you can intuitively see that a problem will arise because -32768 is the most negative number that can be stored in a word.

In the above "incorrect" examples, **overflow** occurred. Computer hardware can detect overflow as it performs addition, and the sum will be correct if there is no overflow. The computer actually performs addition in binary, of course, and the process is logically a right-to-left pairwise addition of bits, very similar to the procedure that humans use for decimal addition. As the computer adds a pair of bits, sometimes a carry (of 1) into the next column to the left is generated. This carry bit is added to the sum of these two bits, and so on. The column of particular interest is the leftmost one; the sign position. There may be a carry *into* this position and/or a carry *out* of this position, into the "extra" bit. This "carry out" (into the extra bit) is what was called just "carry" above and was seen as the extra hex "1." Figure 1.2 identifies when overflow does or does not occur. The table can be summarized by saying that overflow occurs

Figure 1.2 Overflow in Addition.

Carry into Sign Bit?	Carry out of Sign Bit?	Overflow?
no	no	no
no	yes	yes
yes	no	yes
yes	yes	no

when the number of carries into the sign position is different from the number of carries out of the sign position.

Each of the above addition examples is now repeated, but this time in binary. The carry digits are written above the columns they are carried into.

```
                111
  0000 1010 0000 0111        0A 07
+ 0000 0001 1101 0011      + 01 D3
  0000 1011 1101 1010        0B DA
```

This example has no carry into the sign position and no carry out, so there is no overflow.

```
1 1111 11
  0000 0010 0000 0110        02 06
+ 1111 1111 1011 0000      + FF B0
1 0000 0001 1011 0110      1 01 B6
```

This example has a carry into the sign position and a carry out, so there is no overflow.

```
1 1111 1111 11    11
  1111 1111 1110 0111        FF E7
+ 1111 1111 1111 0110      + FF F6
1 1111 1111 1101 1101      1 FF DD
```

Again, there is both a carry into the sign position and a carry out, so there is no overflow.

```
1          1111 11
  0100 1000 0011 1111        48 3F
+ 0110 0100 0101 1010      + 64 5A
  1010 1100 1001 1001        AC 99
```

Overflow does occur in this addition since there is a carry into the sign position, but no carry out.

```
1      1    11  111
  1110 1001 1111 1111           E9 FF
+ 1000 1100 1111 0000        +  8C F0
1 0111 0110 1110 1111        1  76 EF
```

There is also overflow in this addition since there is a carry out of the sign bit, but no carry in.

Subtraction of numbers in 2's complement form is done by simply subtracting the two numbers as unsigned numbers, if possible. However, if the second number is larger than the first, append an extra leftmost 1 to the first number. For example, for the decimal subtraction 195 – 618 = –423,

```
  00 C3
- 02 6A
```

is changed to

```
  1 00 C3
-   02 6A
    FE 59
```

The hex digits FE 59 do represent –423. The extra 1 that had to be appended to do the above subtraction is called a **borrow**.

Overflow is also defined for subtraction. You can see that overflow will occur in a given subtraction if you know that the difference is going to be outside of the decimal range –32768 to 32767 and the wrong answer is generated. To detect overflow procedurally, as a computer would, turn a subtraction problem into an addition problem, that is, take the complement of the second number and then add. If overflow occurs in the new addition problem, then it occurs in the original subtraction problem.

Exercises 1.4

Perform each of the following operations on word-size 2's complement numbers. For each, find the specified sum or difference. Determine whether overflow occurs. For a sum, determine if there is a carry. For a difference, determine if there is a borrow. Check your answers by converting the problem to decimal.

1. 00 3F + 02 A4
2. 1B 48 + 39 E1
3. 6C 34 + 50 28
4. 7F FE + 00 02
5. FF 07 + 06 BD
6. 2A 44 + D9 CC
7. FF E3 + FC 70
8. FE 00 + FD 2D
9. FF F1 + 80 05
10. 8A D0 + EC 78
11. 9E 58 – EB BC
12. EB BC – 9E 58
13. EB BC – 79 1C
14. 79 1C – EB BC

1.5

Other Systems for Representing Numbers

Sections 1.2 and 1.3 presented two commonly used systems for representing numbers in computers: strings of character codes (often ASCII) and 2's complement forms. This section introduces three additional systems for representing numbers: 1's complement, binary coded decimal (BCD), and floating point. The 1's complement system is an alternative scheme for representing integers; it is used in a few computer systems, but not the 8088. Binary coded decimal and floating point forms are used in 8088 computers, as well as other systems. They will be discussed more fully when the appropriate instructions for manipulating data in these forms are covered. The primary reason for introducing them here is to illustrate that there are many alternative representations for numeric data, each valid when used in the correct context.

Representation of numbers in the **1's complement** system is similar to that for the 2's complement. A fixed length is chosen for the representation and a positive integer is simply the binary form of the number, padded with one or more leading zeros on the left to get the desired length. To take the negative of the number, each bit is "complemented"–each zero is changed to one and each one is changed to zero. This operation is sometimes referred to as taking the 1's complement of a number. Although it is easier to negate an integer using 1's complement than 2's complement, the 1's complement system has several disadvantages, the most significant being that it is harder to design circuitry to add or subtract numbers in this form. There are two representations for zero (why?), an awkward situation. Also, a slightly smaller range of values can be represented; for example, –255 to 255 for an 8-bit length, instead of –256 to 255 in a 2's complement system.

The byte-length 1's complement representation of the decimal number 97 is just the value 0110 0001 in binary (61 in hex). Changing each 0 to 1 and

Figure 1.3 Binary Coded Decimal Representation.

Decimal	BCD Bit Pattern
0	0000
1	0001
2	0010
3	0011
4	0100
5	0101
6	0110
7	0111
8	1000
9	1001

each 1 to 0 gives 1001 1110 (9E in hex), the byte-length 1's complement representation of −97.

There is a useful connection between taking the 1's complement and taking the 2's complement of a binary number. If you take the 1's complement of a number and then add 1, you get the 2's complement. This is often easier to do by hand than the subtraction method presented in Section 1.3.

In **binary coded decimal** (BCD) schemes, each decimal digit is coded with a string of bits with fixed length, and these strings are pieced together to form the representation. Most frequently four bits are used for each decimal digit; the choices for bit patterns are shown in Figure 1.3. Only these ten bit patterns are used.

One BCD representation of the decimal number 926708 is

1001 0010 0110 0111 0000 1000.

Using one hex digit as shorthand for four bits, and grouping two hex digits per byte, this BCD representation can be expressed in three bytes as 92 67 08. Notice that the BCD representation in hex looks just like the decimal number.

Often BCD numbers are encoded using some fixed number of bytes. For purposes of illustration, assume a four-byte representation. For now, the question of how to represent a sign will be ignored; without leaving room for a sign, eight binary coded decimal digits can be stored in four bytes. Given these choices, the decimal number 3691 has the BCD representation 00 00 36 91. Notice that the doubleword 2's complement representation for the same number would be 00 00 0E 6B, and that the ASCII codes for the four numerals are 33 36 39 31.

It is not as efficient for a computer to do arithmetic with numbers in a BCD format as with 2's complement numbers. It is usually very inefficient to do arithmetic on numbers represented using ASCII codes. However, ASCII codes are the only method so far for representing a number that is not an integer. For example, 78.375 can be stored as 37 38 2E 33 37 35. Floating point representation systems allow for nonintegers to be represented, or at least closely approximated.

Floating point schemes store numbers in a form that corresponds closely to scientific notation. The example below shows how to convert the decimal number 78.375 into **IEEE single format** which is 32 bits long. (IEEE is the abbreviation for the Institute of Electrical and Electronics Engineers.) This format was one of several sponsored by the Standards Committee of the IEEE Computer Society and approved by the IEEE Standards Board and the American National Standards Institute (ANSI).

First 78.375 must be converted to binary. In binary, the positions to the right of the radix point (it is not appropriate to say *decimal* point for the "." in a binary number) correspond to negative powers of two (1/2, 1/4, 1/8, etc.), just as they correspond to negative powers of 10 (1/10, 1/100, etc.) in a decimal number. Since 0.375 is $3/8 = 1/4 + 1/8$, $0.375_{10} = 0.011_2$. The whole part 78 is 100 1110 in binary, so

$$78.375_{10} = 1001110.011_2$$

Next this is expressed in binary scientific notation with the mantissa written with 1 before the radix point.

$$1001110.011_2 = 1.001110011 \times 2^6$$

The exponent is found exactly as it is in decimal scientific notation, by counting the number of positions the radix point must be moved to the right or left to produce the mantissa. The notation here is really mixed; it would be more proper to write 2^6 as 10^{110}, but it is more convenient to use the decimal form. Now the floating point number can be pieced together:

- left bit 0, for a positive number (1 means negative)
- 1000 0101, for the exponent. This is the actual exponent, 6, plus a **bias** of 127, with the sum, 133, in 8 bits.
- 00111001100000000000000, the fraction expressed *with the leading 1 removed* and padded with zeros on the right to make 23 bits

The entire number is then

0 10000101 00111001100000000000000.

Regrouping gives

0100 0010 1001 1100 1100 0000 0000 0000,

or

42 9C C0 00

in hex.

This example worked out easily because 0.375, the noninteger part of the decimal number 78.375, is a sum of negative powers of 2. Most numbers are not as nice, and usually a binary fraction is chosen to closely approximate the decimal fraction. Techniques for choosing such an approximation are not covered in this book.

To summarize, the following steps are used to convert a decimal number to IEEE single format:

1. The leading bit of the floating point format is 0 for a positive number and 1 for a negative number.

2. Write the unsigned number in binary.

3. Write the binary number in binary scientific notation $f_{23} . f_{22} ... f_0 \times 2^e$, where $f_{23} = 1$. There are 24 fraction bits, but it is not necessary to write trailing 0's.

4. Add a bias of 127_{10} to the exponent e. This sum, in binary form, is the next 8 bits of the answer, following the sign bit. (Adding a bias is an alternative to storing the exponent as a signed number.)

5. The fraction bits $f_{22} f_{21} ... f_0$ form the last 23 bits of the floating point number 19. The leading bit f_{23} (which is always 1) is dropped.

Computer arithmetic on floating point numbers is usually much slower than with 2's complement integers. However the advantages of being able to represent nonintegral values or very large or small values often outweigh the relative inefficiency of computing with them.

Exercises 1.5

Express each of the following decimal numbers as a word-length 1's complement number.

1. 175

2. −175

3. −43

4. 43

Use BCD to encode each of the following decimal numbers in four bytes. Express each answer in hex digits, grouped two per byte.

5. 230

6. 1

7. 12348765

8. 17195

Use IEEE single format to encode each of the following decimal numbers in floating point.

9. 175.5   10. -1.25

11. -11.75 12. 45.5

1.6

Chapter Summary

All data are represented in a computer using electronic signals. These can be interpreted as patterns of binary digits (bits). These bit patterns can be thought of as binary numbers. Numbers can be written in decimal, hexadecimal, or binary forms.

For representing characters, most microcomputers use ASCII codes. One code is assigned for each character, including non-printable control characters.

Integer values are represented in a predetermined number of bits in 2's complement form; a positive number is stored as a binary number (with at least one leading zero to make the required length), and the pattern for a negative number can be obtained by subtracting the positive form from a 1 followed by as many 0's as are used in the length. A 2's complement negative number always has a leading 1 bit. A hex calculator, used with care, can simplify working with 2's complement numbers.

Addition and subtraction are easy with 2's complement numbers. Since the length of a 2's complement number is limited, there is the possibility of a carry, a borrow, or overflow.

Other formats in which numbers are stored are 1's complement, binary coded decimal (BCD) and floating point.

CHAPTER 2

Parts of a Computer System

The basic components of a computer vary from one system to another. This chapter discusses how the hardware of a particular class of microcomputers, the IBM PC and compatible systems, affects the assembly language programmer. The subsequent chapters are concerned with using assembly language to program these "personal computers" or "PCs."

───── 2.1 ────────────────────────────────────

PC Hardware: Memory

A practical computer system consists of **hardware** and **software**. The major hardware components of a typical microcomputer system are a central processing unit chip (CPU), memory chips, a keyboard for input, a monitor to display output, and one or more disk drives to store programs and data. Software refers to the programs that the hardware executes.

The **memory** in an IBM PC or compatible microcomputer is logically a collection of "slots" each of which can store one byte of instructions or data. Each byte of memory has a numeric label called its **address**; for a PC, these start at 00000 and can be as large as the unsigned number $FFFFF_{16}$. An address can always be expressed as five hex digits. Figure 2.1 shows a logical picture of the possible memory in a PC. Since $FFFFF_{16} = 1,048,575_{10}$ a PC can contain up to 1,048,576 bytes of memory, one megabyte. In practice, the user memory in most PCs is limited to addresses from 00000 to $9FFFF_{16}$, which is 640 kilobytes of memory (640K where 1K is 2^{10} or 1024 bytes). This limitation is placed by the operating system used on most PCs. Some PCs have less than 640K bytes of memory, but large computer systems and some microcomputer systems have several megabytes of memory.

Physically a PC's memory consists of **integrated circuits** (ICs). Many of these "chips" provide **random access memory** (RAM) that can be written to or read from by program instructions. The contents of RAM chips are lost when the computer's power is turned off. Other ICs are **read only memory** (ROM) chips, which permanently retain their contents, and which can be read from but not written to.

A PC's memory can be visualized as a collection of **segments**. A segment is 64K bytes long and starts on an address that is a multiple of 16. This means that one segment starts at address 00000, another (overlapping the first) starts at address 16 (00010_{16}), another starts at address 32 (00020_{16}), and so on. Notice that the starting address of a segment ends in 0 when written in hex. The **segment number** of a segment consists of the first four hex digits of its address.

Instead of using its five-hex-digit address, a byte of memory can be referenced by a segment that contains it, followed by an **offset** from the beginning

Figure 2.1 Logical Picture of PC Memory.

Figure 2.2 Locating a Byte by its Segment and Offset.

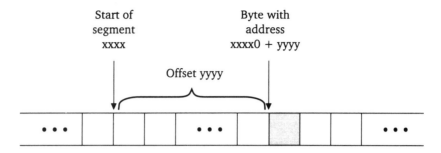

of the segment. The offset is the distance from the first byte of the segment to the byte being addressed. In hex an offset is between 0000 and $FFFF_{16.}$ (Note that $FFFF_{16}$ is 64K – 1.) The notation for such a segment-offset address is the four-hex-digit segment number followed by a colon (:), followed by the four-hex-digit offset. Figure 2.2 shows how a byte is located by its offset within a segment.

The notation 18A3:5B27 refers to the byte that is 5B27 bytes from the beginning of the segment starting at address 18A30. Add the starting address and the offset to get the five-hex-digit address.

18A30	starting address of segment 18A3
+ 5B27	offset
1E557	five-hex-digit address

One byte may be referenced by many segment:offset combinations. For example, another pair that also references the byte at address 1E557 is 17F2:6637 since

17F20	starting address of segment 17F2
+ 6637	offset
1E557	five-hex-digit address

Although each byte of memory has a five-hex-digit address, in the actual programming of the 8088 processor it is often convenient to think of a four-hex-digit offset as an address. This replacement is possible because the data for a program is typically stored in a memory segment whose segment number stays fixed for a given program, with the result that a particular data item can be located by its offset within the **data segment**. Similarly, program instructions are stored in the **code segment** and a particular instruction can be "addressed" by its offset within this memory segment.

In summary, a PC uses numbers from 00000_{16} to $FFFFF_{16}$ to address bytes of memory. Each of these bytes can also be referenced by many segment:offset combinations. When a memory segment is known, a byte of memory can be located using just a four-hex-digit offset.

Find the five-hex-digit address that corresponds to each segment:offset pair below:

1. 2B8C:8D21   2. 059A:7A04

3. 1234:5678   4. 1235:5688

5. 0001:0000   6. 0000:0001

7. F000:FFFF   8. 00FF:FF00

9. 3BAC:90DF   10. 400D:D09A

——— 2.2 ——————————————————————————————

PC Hardware: The CPU

The IBM PC and compatible microcomputer systems use the Intel 8088, a microprocessor made by Intel Corporation. This integrated circuit executes over 200 different instructions. Much of this book will be concerned with using these instructions to implement programs. Besides the 8088, Intel also makes an 8086 microprocessor, which executes the same instruction set as the 8088, and more powerful microprocessors such as the 80286 and 80386, which execute all the 8088 instructions, and more. Other microprocessors manufactured by Intel and competing companies have different instruction sets, but assembly language programming for them is similar to programming for the 8088. Comparable assembly language techniques are also applicable to many larger computer systems.

The 8088 chip has 14 **registers**, each an internal storage location which holds a 16-bit word. Typical instructions transfer data between these registers and memory or perform operations on data stored in the registers or in memory. All of these registers have names, and many of them have special purposes; the names and purposes are summarized below.

The AX, BX, CX, and DX registers are called **data registers** or **general registers**, and each has special purposes that will be described along with relevant instructions in later chapters. The AX register is sometimes known as the **accumulator** since it is the destination for many arithmetic results. As an example of an instruction using the AX register,

```
add    ax, 158
```

adds the decimal number 158 (converted to word-length 2's complement form) to the number already in AX, replacing the number originally in AX by the sum.

Each of the AX, BX, CX, and DX registers can be used as two independent 8-bit registers, a "high-order" half for the left eight bits and a "low-order" half for the right eight bits. The names for these register parts are AH, AL, BH, BL, CH, CL, DH, and DL. Here the "H" and "L" designate those parts of the registers that are high-order and low-order.

There are four **segment registers**, CS, DS, ES, and SS. The CS register contains the memory segment number of the code segment, the area of memory where the instructions currently being executed are stored. Since a segment is 64K long, the length of a program's collection of instructions is often limited to 64K; a longer program requires that the contents of CS be changed while the program is running. Similarly, DS contains the segment number of the data segment; this is the area of memory where most data is stored. The ES register contains the segment number of the **extra segment**, which can have multiple uses. Finally, SS contains the segment number of the **stack segment**, where a stack (discussed below) is maintained.

A **stack** is a data structure analogous to a stack of plates in a cafeteria. When a plate is placed on the stack, it goes on the top. The only plate that is normally removed is the one on the top. With the 8088, an area of memory serves as the stack, and words of memory are the plates. The SP register is the **stack pointer**, containing the offset of the top word on the stack. (The start of the segment is determined by the SS register.)

To place a new data word on the stack, the offset in SP is decremented by two bytes (one word) and the data word is stored at the address determined by the segment in SS and the offset in SP. To remove a word from the top of the stack, the value at the address determined by SS and SP is copied and then the offset in SP is incremented by two bytes. One common use for the stack is in procedure (subroutine) calls. The offset of the instruction following the procedure call is stored on the stack. When it is time to return from the procedure, this offset is retrieved from the stack. Procedures are discussed in Chapter 6.

Normally the only word in the stack segment that is accessed is the one at the top of the stack. However, the BP register is a **base pointer** that can also keep an offset in the stack segment and can be used in procedure calls, particularly when parameters are involved.

The registers SI and DI are **index registers**. They can be used to indicate memory addresses of the source and destination when strings of many characters are moved from one place to another in memory; SI stands for *source index* and DI stands for *destination index*. Since they are just 16 bits long, they cannot hold complete five-hex-digit addresses; instead they hold offsets in segments whose segment numbers are given by segment registers.

The **instruction pointer**, or IP register, cannot be directly accessed by an assembly language programmer. The CPU has to fetch instructions to be executed from memory, and IP keeps track of the offset of the next instruction to be fetched. The segment number for this code segment is given by the CS register. The 8088 actually fetches instructions to be executed later while it is still executing earlier instructions, making the assumption (usually correct) that the instructions to be executed next will follow sequentially in memory. If this assumption turns out to be wrong, for example in the case when a procedure call is executed, then the CPU throws out the instructions it has stored, sets IP to contain the offset of the procedure, (and perhaps modifies the contents of the CS register) and then fetches its next instruction from the new address.

The final register is called the **flag register** and has no name that is used in instructions. Some of its 16 bits are set by different instructions to indicate the outcome of execution of the instruction. Each of these bits is itself called a status bit, or a flag. Some of the flag register's 16 bits are named:

??	??	??	??	OF	DF	IF	TF	SF	ZF	??	AF	??	PF	??	CF	flag
15	14	13	12	11	10	9	8	7	6	5	4	3	2	1	0	bit

Bit 11 is the overflow flag (OF). It is, for example, set to 0 following an addition in which no overflow occurred, and to 1 if overflow did occur. Similarly, bit 0, the carry flag (CF), indicates the absence or presence of a carry out from the sign position after an addition. Bit 7, the sign flag, contains the left bit of the result after some operations. Since the left bit is 0 for a nonnegative 2's complement number and 1 for a negative number, SF indicates the sign. Bit 6, the zero flag (ZF) is set to 1 if the result of some operations is zero, and 0 if the result is nonzero (positive or negative). Bit 2, the parity flag, is set to 1 if the number of 1 bits in a result is even and to 0 if the number of 1 bits in the result is odd. Other flags will be described later when their use will be clearer.

As an example of how flags are set by instructions, consider again the instruction

```
add  ax, 158
```

This instruction affects AF, CF, OF, PF, SF, and ZF. Suppose that AX contains the word FF F3 prior to execution of the instruction. Since 158_{10} corresponds to the word 00 9E, this instruction adds FF F3 and 00 9E, putting the sum 00 91 in the AX register. It sets the carry flag CF to 1 since there is a carry, the overflow flag OF to 0 since there is no overflow, the sign flag SF to 0 (the leftmost bit of the sum 00 91), and the zero flag ZF to 0 since the sum is not zero. The parity flag PF is set to 0 since 0000 0000 1001 0001 contains three 1 bits, an odd number. The AF flag will be discussed in Chapter 13 (decimal arithmetic).

In summary, the 8088 CPU executes a variety of instructions, using its 14 internal registers for operands, results of operations, and for keeping track of segments and offsets. The registers are listed in Figure 2.3.

Figure 2.3 8088 Registers.

Name	Use/Comments
AX	accumulator, general use; high-order byte AH and low-order byte AL
BX	general use; high-order BH and low-order BL
CX	general use; high-order CH and low-order CL
DX	general use; high-order DH and low-order DL
CS	gives segment where instructions currently being executed are located
DS	gives data segment
ES	gives extra segment
SS	gives stack segment
SP	stack pointer;offset to top of stack in the stack segment
BP	base pointer; offset of reference point in the stack segment
SI	source index; offset to source in string moves
DI	destination index; offset to destination
IP	instruction pointer; offset in code segment of next instruction to be fetched
flags	collection of flags, or status bits

—— **Exercises 2.2** ——————————————————————————————————————

1. Suppose that the data segment register DS contains the segment number 23D1 and that an instruction fetches a word at offset 7B86 in the data segment. What is the five-hex-digit address of the word that is fetched?

2. Suppose that the data segment register DS contains the segment number 014C and that an instruction fetches a word at offset 15FE in the data segment. What is the five-hex-digit address of the word that is fetched?

3. Suppose that the stack segment register SS contains the segment number 2000 and that the stack pointer register SP contains the offset 087A. What is the five-hex-digit address of the top of the stack?

4. Suppose that the stack segment register SS contains the segment number 0F00 and that the stack pointer register SP contains the offset 9E14. What is the five-hex-digit address of the top of the stack?

5. For each **add** instruction below, assume that AX contains the given contents before the instruction is executed, and give the contents of AX as well as the values of the CF, OF, SF, and ZF flags after the instruction is executed:

	AX Before	Instruction
(a)	00 45	add ax, 45
(b)	FF 45	add ax, 45
(c)	00 45	add ax, -45
(d)	FF 45	add ax, -45
(e)	FF FF	add ax, 1
(f)	7F FF	add ax, 100

2.3

PC Hardware: Input/Output Devices

A CPU and memory make a computer, but without input devices to get data or output devices to display or write data the computer is not usable for many purposes. Typical **I/O devices** are a keyboard for input, a monitor to display output, and a disk drive for data and program storage.

An assembly language programmer can look at I/O devices in several different ways. At the lowest level, each device uses a collection of addresses or **ports** in the I/O address space. There are 64K port addresses in the 8088 architecture, and a typical I/O device uses three to eight ports. These addresses are distinct from ordinary memory addresses. The programmer uses instructions that output data or commands to these ports, or input data or status information from them. Such programming is very tedious and the resulting programs are difficult to reuse with different computer systems.

Because of the problems with low-level programming of I/O devices, programmers commonly use procedures that do the "busywork" of communicating with the devices, giving them a higher-level, more logical view of the devices. Many such routines are still fairly low-level, such as procedures to display a single character on the monitor or those to get a single character from the keyboard. A higher-level procedure might print a string of characters on a printer.

An assembly language programmer may write input/output procedures, using knowledge of I/O ports and devices. Some computers have input/output procedures built into ROM. Many operating systems (discussed below) also provide input/output procedures.

———— 2.4 ————————————————————————————————

PC Software

Without software, computer hardware is virtually useless. **Software** refers to the programs or procedures that are executed by the hardware. This section discusses different types of software.

PC Software: The Operating System

A general-purpose computer system needs an **operating system** to enable it to run other programs. The IBM PC usually runs the operating system known as PC-DOS; compatible systems use very similar operating systems called MS-DOS. (DOS stands for **disk operating system**.) All of these operating systems were developed by Microsoft Corporation; IBM customized PC-DOS to work on the IBM PC, and other hardware manufacturers have customized the versions of MS-DOS that run on their hardware. One reason that customization is required is that the operating system uses software routines permanently programmed into ROM chips and these routines vary from system to system. In this book the PC-DOS and MS-DOS operating systems will collectively be called DOS.

It is not the purpose of this text to provide detailed instruction on DOS. However, an overview of the variety of services provided by DOS is appropriate. When no application program is running, DOS usually displays a **A>** or **C>** prompt to show that it is ready to process a command. The letter that appears identifies the default disk drive, the drive which is assumed to be the source of needed files unless a command or program specifically says otherwise. Commands for DOS can be entered in either uppercase or lowercase letters. Some commands recognized by DOS are **resident**, that is, in memory whenever the prompt is displayed; these are carried out as soon as the command is entered. For example, the resident command

        A>cls

clears the screen and

        A>dir

displays a directory or catalog of the files on the default disk. Another resident command **del** is used to delete one or more files from the default disk; for example,

        C>del program1.asm

removes the file PROGRAM1.ASM from the C disk.

Transient commands are not kept in memory, but are programs that are stored on disk. When the user enters a command that is not resident, DOS checks the disk for a program whose name corresponds to the command. If it finds one, it loads the program (copies it from disk to memory) and starts it executing.

One of the convenient features of DOS is that a user can easily enlarge the set of commands at his or her disposal by adding new programs to a disk. Transient commands provided with the operating system are sometimes called **utilities**. An example of a DOS utility is

```
A>chkdsk
```

This utility reports on the amount of space used and free on the A disk as well as the amount of memory contained in the PC being used. Utilities are also used to format a new floppy disk to prepare it for use, to copy one disk to another, and for many other purposes. The transient commands provided with DOS vary from version to version.

Section 2.3 mentioned that an assembly language program can access some DOS services for input and output operations. One such service waits for a key to be pressed on the keyboard and then puts the ASCII code for the character in the AL half of the AX register. Another takes the character that a programmer has loaded into the DL half of the DX register and displays it on the monitor. Functions are also provided for communicating with the printer or with the communications port that may be used for a modem connection. However, a large collection of DOS functions are for file management. These open and close files, read from or write to files, search for directory entries, and so on. One useful function terminates a program, returning to the DOS prompt. All these DOS services are useful to an assembly language programmer. Some DOS services are discussed in Chapter 10 (interrupts and input/output).

PC Software: Text Editors

A **text editor** is a program that allows the user to create or modify text files that are stored on disk. A text file is a collection of ASCII codes. Those text files of most interest in this book are assembly language source code files, files that contain assembly language statements.

Microsoft provides a text editor called EDLIN with PC-DOS or MS-DOS. The EDLIN editor is called a **line editor** since it treats a text file as a collection of lines. There are commands to modify lines, to delete lines, to insert new lines before an existing line, to list lines, and so on.

Most people find a **full-screen editor** easier to use than a line editor. A full-screen editor uses all or part of the monitor display as a "window" into the file. The user can move the window up or down (and sometimes left or right) to display different portions of the file. To make changes to the file, cursor control keys or a pointing device like a mouse are used to move the cursor to the place to be modified so that the changes can be entered.

Word processors are text editors that provide extra services for formatting and printing documents. For example, when one uses a text editor, usually the Return or Enter key must be pressed at the end of each line. However, a word processor usually wraps words automatically to the next line as they are typed, so that Return or some other key is used only at the end of a paragraph. The word processor places the words on each line within specified margins. Although it can sometimes be used as an editor to prepare an assembly language source code file, a word processor may store formatting information with the file along with the ASCII codes for the text. Such extra information may make the file unsuitable as an assembly language source code file. One way to check if a word processor is acceptable for assembly language programs is to use the DOS `type` command. For the file on the A disk named PROGRAM1.ASM, the command

```
A>type program1.asm
```

will display the file on the monitor. If no unusual characters are displayed, then the word processor is satisfactory for preparing assembly language programs.

PC Software: Language Translators and the Linker

Language translators are programs that translate a programmer's source code into a form that can be executed by the computer. They are usually not provided with the DOS operating system, although they are invoked in the same way as transient commands. Language translators can be classified as interpreters, compilers, or assemblers.

Interpreters directly decipher a source program. To execute a program, an interpreter looks at a single line of source code and follows the instructions of that line. A BASIC language program is often executed by an interpreter. Although the interpreter itself may be a very efficient program, those programs it has interpreted usually execute relatively slowly. An interpreter is generally convenient since it allows a program to be quickly changed and run. The interpreter itself is often a very large program.

Compilers start with source code and produce **object code,** which ordinarily consists of instructions to be executed by the intended CPU. The BASIC language is sometimes compiled, and high-level languages such as Pascal, Modula-2, FORTRAN, COBOL, and C are commonly compiled. The object code produced by a compiler must often be **linked** or combined with other object code to make a program that can be loaded and executed. For this purpose, Microsoft provides a utility called `link` with DOS. The number of steps involved in preparing a program for execution sometimes makes the process seem tedious. However, resulting compiled programs execute much more rapidly than interpreted programs and do not require an interpreter program to be loaded along with the program to be actually executed.

An **assembler** is used much like a compiler, but translates assembly language, rather than a high-level language like Pascal, into machine code. Often the resulting files must be linked to prepare them for execution. Because assembly language is closer to machine code than a high-level language, the job of an assembler is somewhat simpler than the job of a compiler. For example, the assembly language instruction cited in Section 2.2,

add ax, 158

is translated by the assembler into the three bytes 05 00 9E. The first byte 05 is the **op code** (operation code), which says to add the number contained in the next two bytes to the word already in the AX register. The word 00 9E is the 2's complement representation of 158_{10}.

Exercises 2.4

1. Microsoft operating systems come in several versions. The **ver** resident command reports what version of DOS is executing on a PC. Use this command to find out what version of DOS your system uses.

2. Find out what text editors are available for your system. Pick one and use it to create a short file. Practice making changes to the file. Use the **type** command to display the file on the monitor.

2.5

Chapter Summary

This chapter has discussed the hardware and software components that make up a PC microcomputer system.

The major hardware components are the CPU and memory. The CPU executes instructions and uses its internal registers for instruction operands and results, and to determine addresses of data and instructions stored in memory. Bytes of memory can be addressed by five-hex-digit numbers or by a four-hex-digit segment and a four-hex-digit offset within the segment.

An operating system is a vital software component. Microsoft PC-DOS or MS-DOS operating systems provide resident commands and also load and execute utilities or other programs stored on disk. An assembly language programmer may use software routines provided by DOS for interfacing with I/O devices.

Other important software programs are text editors and language translators.

CHAPTER 3

Using the Assembler

This chapter tells how to use the Microsoft Macro Assembler. The first part discusses the types and formats of statements that are accepted by the assembler. Then there is an example of a complete assembly language program, and directions on how it can be assembled, linked, and executed. The last portion of the chapter fills in details about constructs that have been illustrated in the example, laying the groundwork for programs in future chapters.

3.1

Assembly Language Statements

Each assembly language statement is entered on a single line of the source code file. A line may be up to 128 characters long, but it is good practice to limit a line to 80 characters so that it can be displayed on the monitor. Blank lines are acceptable and are useful to separate sections of code.

Because assembly language programs are far from self-documenting, it is important to use an adequate number of comments. Comments can be placed on any statement; a semicolon (;) begins the comment, which then extends until the end of the line. A comment can take an entire line or can follow other assembly language elements on a line.

There are three types of functional assembly language statements: instructions, directives, and macros. An **instruction** is translated by the assembler into bytes of object code (machine code) that will be executed at run time. Each instruction corresponds to one of the operations that can be executed by the 8088 CPU. The instruction

```
add   ax, 158          ; add 158 to contents of AX register
```

was used as an example in Chapter 2.

A **directive** tells the assembler to take some action. An action initiated by a directive does not result in machine instructions and often has no effect on the object code. For example, the assembler can produce a listing file showing the original source code, the object code and other information in addition to producing a file of object code. The directive

```
PAGE
```

tells the assembler to generate a page break in that listing file. The object code produced is the same with or without the **PAGE** directive.

A **macro** is a type of statement that is a shorthand designation for a sequence of other statements—instructions, directives, or even other macros. The assembler expands a macro to the statements it represents, and then assembles these new statements. Macros will appear in the example program later in this chapter.

A statement other than just a comment contains several components, including a **mnemonic**, which identifies the purpose of the statement, and three other fields: name, operand, and comment. These components must be in the following order:

[name]   mnemonic   [operand(s)]   [;comment]

The square brackets indicate that those items are optional in some statements; however, the name and operand fields may also be required in some statements.

Multiple operands are separated by commas; spaces can also be added. Sometimes a single operand has several components with spaces between them, making it look like more than one operand. The name, mnemonic, operand, and comment fields may start in any columns, but for readability it is important to follow a pattern of indentation and alignment of source code.

In the instruction

```
add    ax, 158
```

the mnemonic is **add** and the operands are **ax** and **158**. The assembler recognizes **add** as a mnemonic for an instruction that will perform some sort of addition. The operands provide the rest of the information that the assembler needs. The first operand **ax** tells the assembler that the word in the AX register is to be one of the values added, and that the AX register will be the destination of the sum. Since the second operand is a number (as opposed to another register designation or a memory designation), the assembler knows that it is the actual value to be added to the word in the AX register. The resulting object code is 05 9E 00, where 05 stands for "add the word immediately following this byte in memory to the word already in AX." The assembler takes care of converting the decimal number 158 to its word-length 2's complement representation 00 9E, the bytes of which are stored backwards in the object code.

One use for the name field is to symbolically label what will be, following assembly and linking of the program, an instruction's address in memory. Other instructions can then easily refer to the labeled instruction.

If the above **add** instruction needs to be repeatedly executed in a program loop, it could be coded with a label in the name field, as

```
add_loop:    add  ax, 158
```

The instruction can then be the destination of a **jmp** (jump) instruction, the assembly language version of a **goto**:

```
jmp    add_loop      ; repeat addition
```

High-level language loop structures like **while** or **for** are not available in assembly language, although they can be implemented using **jmp** and/or other instructions.

It's considered good coding practice to make a label descriptive. The label **add_loop** might help to clarify the assembly language code, identifying the first instruction of a program loop that includes an addition. Other times labels may parallel key words in a pseudocode design. A design with an **if** construct might be coded with labels **if_1** and **endif_1**.

Notice the colon (:) following the label. A colon is used with instructions or macros expanding to instructions, but is not used on the name field of a directive.

Labels and other names used in assembly language are formed from letters, digits and special characters. The special characters allowed are underscore (_), percent sign (%), question mark (?), dollar sign ($), at sign (@) and period (.). A name may not begin with a digit; **2_loop** is illegal. If a period is used it must be the first character; .loop is allowed but add.loop is not. Except for digits and the period, other characters may be used in any position. In this book the only special character used extensively will be an underscore, and for readability, it will not be used as a leading character. A name may have many characters, but only the first 31 characters are actually used. The Microsoft Macro Assembler will not allow instruction mnemonics, directive mnemonics, register designations, and other words that have a special meaning to the assembler to be used as labels.

Assembly language statements can be entered in either uppercase or lowercase letters. The assembler normally treats add_loop the same as ADD_LOOP, although it can be instructed to distinguish between them. Mixed-case code is easier for people to read than code written all in uppercase or lowercase, and all-uppercase code is especially difficult to read. This book will generally follow the convention of using lowercase source code except for directive mnemonics.

—— *Exercises 3.1* ——————————————————————————————

1. Name and describe the three types of assembly language statements.

2. For each combination of characters below, determine whether or not it is an allowable label (name). If not, give a reason.

   (a) repeat   (b) exit
   (c) more?   (d) ?more
   (e) 2much   (f) add
   (g) add_2   (h) add.2
   (i) this_is_the_end_of_the_program

—— 3.2 ——————————————————————————————————————

A Complete Example

This section presents a complete example of an assembly language program. It is easy to get lost in the details of assembly language, so a program design greatly aids coding in assembly language. This program will prompt for two numbers, then find and display their sum. The algorithm implemented by this program is

prompt for the first number;
input ASCII characters representing the first number;
convert the characters to a 2's complement word;
store the first number in memory;
prompt for the second number;
input ASCII characters representing the second number;
convert the characters to a 2's complement word;
add the first number to the second number;
convert the sum to a string of ASCII characters;
display a label and the characters representing the sum;

Figure 3.1 lists the complete program that implements this design. The parts are explained below.

Figure 3.1 A Complete Assembly Language Program.

```
INCLUDE io.h

cr              EQU     0dh    ; carriage return character
Lf              EQU     0ah    ; linefeed character

stack           SEGMENT STACK
                DW      100h DUP (?)
stack           ENDS

data            SEGMENT
number1         DW      ?
number2         DW      ?
prompt1         DB      'Enter first number:  ',0
prompt2         DB      cr,Lf,'Enter second number:  ',0
string          DB      40 DUP (?)
label1          DB      cr,Lf,'The sum is '
sum             DB      6 DUP (?)
                DB      cr,Lf,0
data            ENDS

code            SEGMENT
                ASSUME cs:code,ds:data

start:          mov     ax,SEG data      ; load data segment number
                mov     ds,ax

prompt:         output prompt1           ; prompt for first number
                inputs string,40         ; read ASCII characters
                atoi    string           ; convert to integer
                mov     number1,ax       ; store
```

Figure 3.1 Continued.

```
        output prompt2        ; prompt for second number
        inputs string,40      ; read ASCII characters
        atoi   string         ; convert to integer
        mov    number2,ax      ; store

        mov    ax,number1      ; first number to AX
        add    ax,number2      ; add second number

        itoa   sum,ax          ; convert to ASCII characters

        output label1          ; output label and sum

quit:   mov    al,0            ; return code 0
        mov    ah,4ch          ; DOS function to return
        int    21h             ; interrupt for DOS services

code    ENDS
        END    start
```

The Source Code

In the example program in Fig. 3.1, the statement

```
    INCLUDE io.h
```

is a directive. It instructs the assembler to copy the file IO.H into your program as the program is assembled.[*] The source file is not modified—it still contains just the INCLUDE directive, but for purposes of the assembly, the lines of IO.H are inserted at the point of the INCLUDE directive. In order to be included, this file should be on the same disk as your source program when the assembler is invoked.

The file IO.H contains mostly definitions for macros, which are described in detail in Section 3.6. There are also several directives in file IO.H. One of these instructs the assembler not to show the contents of the included file in a listing. Another tells the assembler to suppress listings of the statements into which a macro expands, resulting in a shorter program listing. The last statement in IO.H, the directive

```
    .LIST          ; begin listing
```

instructs the assembler to resume listing source statements. This statement is shown in the listing file, and will be the only statement from IO.H that will be seen in the listing.

---

[*] The files IO.H, IO.OBJ, and IO.ASM are written by the author of this book, and are available to the user.

The next two statements

```
cr          EQU     0dh     ; carriage return character
Lf          EQU     0ah     ; linefeed character
```

use the directive **EQU** to equate symbols to values. After an **EQU** directive, the symbol mentioned can be used as a synonym for the value in subsequent source code. Using names rather than numbers can make clearer source code. In this code, **cr** is being equated to the hexadecimal number 0D, which is the ASCII code for a carriage return character; **Lf** is given the hex value 0A, the ASCII code for a linefeed character. An uppercase **L** has been used to avoid confusion with the number 1.

The carriage return and linefeed characters referred to here are needed to skip to a new line of output, and are frequently used in defining data to be printed or displayed on a monitor.

In these **EQU** directives the assembler recognizes the values **0dh** and **0ah** as hexadecimal because each has a trailing **h**. Numeric values in an assembly language statement are in decimal unless otherwise indicated in the source code. Suffixes which mean types of values other than hex will be introduced in Section 3.4. A hexadecimal value must start with a digit, not one of the hex digits "a" through "f", so that the assembler can distinguish it from a name.

The statement

```
so      EQU     eh          ; eh is not a hex constant
```

would result in an error since the assembler would try to give **so** the value of a symbol **eh** which has not been previously defined. A legal alternative is

```
so      EQU     0eh         ; "shift out" control character
```

The bulk of the program is divided into three segments. Each of these is bracketed by **SEGMENT** and **ENDS** (end segment) directives.

```
segment_name    SEGMENT
                    .
                    .
                    .
segment_name    ENDS
```

The same segment name, chosen by the programmer, is used as the label with both directives. The example program of Fig. 3.1, uses **stack**, **data** and **code**, names that are descriptive of the purposes of the segments. Notice that there is no colon (:) following a segment name. The stack segment reserves space for a stack, the data segment reserves space for data (and also initializes some values), and the code segment contains instructions to be executed at run time.

The segments of the program will be assigned to memory segments when DOS loads the program for execution. The operand of the first segment directive

```
STACK
```

indicates to DOS that is a stack segment. The operating system will initialize the stack segment register SS to the segment number where this segment is loaded, and the stack pointer register SP to an offset at the end of the data area that is reserved in the stack segment.

The **SEGMENT** and **ENDS** directives for the data segment and the code segment have no operands in this example: the **ENDS** directive never has an operand, and although operands are used with **SEGMENT** directives in some applications, they will not be needed for most programs in this book.

The last statement of the program is the directive

        END   start

The **END** directive tells the assembler to stop processing source code statements. There is exactly one **END** statement in a source file and it is the last statement. The operand **start** identifies the first instruction to be executed in the program. When the program is loaded, the operating system will initialize the code segment register CS register to the segment containing this instruction, and will start the instruction pointer register IP at the offset of this instruction from the start of the segment.

The stack and data segments contain no instructions, only **DW** and **DB** directives. These directives are used to define one or more words (**DW**) or bytes (**DB**) of storage. In the stack segment,

        DW   100h DUP (?)

tells the assembler to reserve 100_{16}, that is 256_{10}, words of storage without initial values; the **DUP** operator says to repeat what comes after it, and (**?**) indicates undefined storage. The first directives in the data segment

        number1   DW   ?
        number2   DW   ?

each reserves a single word of storage in the data segment. The first word has the label **number1**, which will be associated with a word at offset 0000 from the beginning of the data segment, and the second word has the label **number2**, which will be associated with a word at offset 0002. The question mark (**?**) operand tells the assembler that no initial value is to be assigned.

The address identified with the label **prompt1** will have offset 0004 from the first of the data segment since four bytes have been used by the two words. Each of the **DB** directives

        prompt1   DB   'Enter first number: ',0
        prompt2   DB   cr,Lf,'Enter second number: ',0
        label1   DB   cr,Lf,'The sum is '
                            . . .
                    DB   cr,Lf,0

reserves multiple bytes of storage with initial values. In each case the operands give the initial values, and the assembler counts how many initial values there are to know how many bytes to reserve. When **DB** operands are strings of characters between apostrophes (`'`), the assembler uses the ASCII codes of the characters for the initial values. When an operand is a number, its value is coded in two hex digits. Since

```
Enter first number:
```

has 21 characters (including two trailing spaces), there are 22 bytes reserved by the first of these statements, with initial values

```
45 6E 74 65 72  .   .   . 3A 20 20 00    [ASCII codes]
 E  n  t  e  r  .   .   . :  SP SP  0     [source code]
```

The last of these three **DB** directives has no label, but it reserves and initializes three bytes of memory that will immediately follow the bytes from the previous directive. The initial values will be 0D, 0A and 00, where the first two values come from earlier equating `cr` to `0dh` and `Lf` to `0ah`.

The code segment begins with the directive

```
ASSUME  cs:code,ds:data
```

This directive tells the assembler that if an instruction uses a label that is in the code segment, the actual address of the operand should be calculated by using the CS segment register plus the offset of the label from the beginning of the code segment, and also to make the corresponding assumption for the DS segment register and labels in the data segment.

Recall that the DOS operating system takes care of initializing the CS segment register to the code segment because of the operand on the **END** directive. The operating system does not initialize the DS segment register to point at the start of the data segment. This job is left to the programmer. In this example, it is accomplished by the two instructions

```
start:      mov     ax,SEG data   ; load data segment number
            mov     ds,ax
```

Chapter 4 will discuss **mov** (move) instructions, which are similar to simple assignment statements in a high-level language. The statement

```
mov    ax,SEG data
```

copies the segment number of the data segment into the AX register, and

```
mov    ds,ax
```

copies it from the AX register to the DS segment register.

The assembly operator **SEG** tells the assembler to use the segment number for the data segment. **SEG** is not needed in this program since the assembler knows that **data** is the label on a **SEGMENT** directive, but its inclusion helps to document the program for the human reader. The actual segment number of the data segment cannot be determined until the program is loaded, at which time it is embedded in the program by DOS.

It may seem strange that two instructions were used instead of the single instruction

```
mov     ds,SEG data
```

but there is no one instruction that can load an "immediate mode" operand directly into a segment register. (Operand types are discussed in Section 3.5.)

The statements starting with label **prompt:** actually do something visible.

```
prompt:      output prompt1      ; prompt for first number
             inputs string,40    ; read ASCII characters
             atoi   string       ; convert to integer
```

Each of these three statements is a macro that expands to a series of statements following the macro definitions in IO.H. At run time, the **output** macro displays the ASCII characters in the data segment starting at label **prompt1**, continuing until a null character (00) is encountered. The null character serves to mark the end of the characters. The result is that

```
Enter first number:
```

is displayed on the monitor, and the cursor stays on the line following two trailing spaces. The label **prompt:** serves little purpose in this program, but could be used as the destination of a jump instruction if a similar program were to calculate many sums in a loop.

The **inputs** macro is used to input a string of characters from the keyboard. The first operand, **string**, gives the destination in the data segment for the ASCII codes which the keyboard generates. The second operand, **40**, limits the number of characters to be accepted. The Return or Enter key is used at execution time to mark the end of the characters entered; the CR code is not copied to the data segment.

Since the 8088 cannot easily do arithmetic on numbers in ASCII format, the character codes stored at **string** are converted to word-length 2's complement form for addition. The **atoi** (ASCII to integer) macro does this task. It scans ASCII codes in memory, beginning at the location given by the operand, skipping leading blanks, noting a plus or minus sign, and processing decimal digits until a trailing nondigit is encountered. The corresponding 2's complement value is stored in the AX register. The next instruction

```
mov     number1,ax           ; store
```

copies this word into the data segment to the word reserved at **number1**.

The next four statements take care of getting the second number. The carriage return and linefeed characters at the beginning of **prompt2** place it down a line on the monitor display. The number, in 2's complement form, is stored in the data segment at the word with label **number2**.

The comments on the instructions

```
mov     ax,number1      ; first number to AX
add     ax,number2      ; add second number
```

identify their functions. The first one copies the word stored in the data segment at **number1** back into the AX register, and the second one adds the word stored at **number2** to the word already in the AX register. It should be noted that the preceding instruction

```
mov     number2,ax
```

did not destroy the value of the second number that was in AX. Therefore the sum could be computed with one instruction

```
add     ax,number1
```

instead of the two which are used.

The sum in the AX register is in 2's complement form. The integer to ASCII macro **itoa** produces a six-character-long string of ASCII codes for the decimal version of a 2's complement number (with leading spaces for small numbers). For

```
itoa    sum,ax      ; convert to ASCII characters
```

the destination is the six bytes reserved in the data segment at **sum** and the source is the 2's complement word in the AX register.

The **output** macro is used again to display a label and the sum. The statement

```
output label1               ; output label and sum
```

will display bytes of memory reserved and defined by the three **DB** directives

```
label1      DB      cr,Lf,'The sum is '
sum         DB      6 DUP (?)
            DB      cr,Lf,0
```

When the statements of this **output** macro are executed, the previous **itoa** macro will have replaced the uninitialized bytes at **sum** by ASCII codes. The bytes from all three **DB** macros will be in contiguous memory, since within a segment, the order of the statements determines exactly the order of the resulting code. Starting at **label1** the **output** macro will move the cursor to a new line (**cr** and **Lf**), then display **The sum is** , then the six bytes of the sum, and finally move the cursor to another new line. The null byte in the third **DB** finally terminates the execution of the **output** macro.

The last three instructions of the program provide for clean termination of the program. They ask the DOS operating system, via an **int** (interrupt) instruction, to exit the program. The AH half of AX is used to hold the function code $4C_{16}$ corresponding to the particular DOS service requested, and the AL half is used to send a return code of zero, indicating no error.

```
quit:       mov     al,0        ; return code 0
            mov     ah,4ch      ; DOS function to return
            int     21h         ; interrupt for DOS services
```

The label `quit:` is not needed, but helps to document the code.

How to Assemble, Link, and Run a Program

The exact steps required to prepare a program for execution depend on how a particular PC is set up. If a PC has only a single floppy disk drive, the most convenient arrangement is to have a bootable disk containing the following files:

- COMMAND.COM (part of the operating system)
- a text editor program
- MASM.EXE (the Microsoft assembler)
- LINK.EXE (the Microsoft linker)
- IO.H (the definition file to be included)
- IO.OBJ (previously assembled procedures used by the input/output macros)
- the assembly language source code file.

.ASM is the usual file type (extension) for an assembly language source code file. Suppose that the source file for the example program is called EXAMPLE.ASM. The MASM program is executed to assemble the file EXAMPLE.ASM. Figure 3.2 shows a dialog with a PC, with user responses under-lined.* The response to the request for a source filename omitted the file type; [.ASM] says that MASM will assume the standard type. The Enter key was the only response given to

> Object filename [example.OBJ]:

thus accepting the assembler's choice of EXAMPLE.OBJ for the name of the object code file. The default choice for the source listing file is NUL.LST, a dummy file with nothing in it. Instead, the response of **example** told the assembler to produce a listing file named EXAMPLE.LST. Finally, an Enter response to the prompt

> Cross-reference [NUL.CRF]:

accepted the assembler's choice of discarding the cross-reference file. A short time after this fourth response, MASM displays the last three lines shown in Figure 3.2. In general, if there are errors in a source file, error messages will appear both on the monitor and in the listing file.

If EXAMPLE.ASM is assembled as shown above, the disk will contain two additional files, EXAMPLE.LST and EXAMPLE.OBJ. The listing file EXAMPLE.LST

---

* Different versions of MASM or LINK may generate other output than is shown in the examples in this section

Figure 3.2 Assembly of EXAMPLE.ASM.

```
A>masm
Microsoft (R) Macro Assembler Version 5.10
Copyright (C) Microsoft Corp 1981, 1988.  All rights reserved.

Source filename [.ASM]: example
Object filename [example.OBJ]:
Source listing  [NUL.LST]: example
Cross-reference [NUL.CRF]:

  47576 + 383009 Bytes symbol space free

      0 Warning Errors
      0 Severe   Errors

A>
```

Figure 3.3 Linking EXAMPLE.OBJ.

```
A>link

Microsoft (R) Overlay Linker  Version 3.61
Copyright (C) Microsoft Corp 1983-1987.  All rights reserved.

Object Modules [.OBJ]: example+io
Run File [EXAMPLE.EXE]:
List File [NUL.MAP]:
Libraries [.LIB]:

A>
```

is an ASCII file that can be printed or viewed on the monitor, but the object code file EXAMPLE.OBJ is not printable.

The final action needed to make the program executable is to link it with input/output procedures in IO.OBJ. Figure 3.3 illustrates interaction with the linker LINK. User input is again underlined. For object modules to be linked, the user responded

    example+io

This tells the linker to use object code from both EXAMPLE.OBJ and IO.OBJ. The linker's default choices were accepted for the next two responses: EXAMPLE.EXE for the name of the executable program file, and a dummy list file for the linker. (The linker's list file is different from the assembler's source listing file.) The final prompt asks for the name of a library of object code units. The null response (Enter only) told the linker that all the units needed are pre-

Figure 3.4. Execution of EXAMPLE.EXE.

```
A>example
Enter first number:    98

Enter second number:   -35

The sum is       63

A>
```

sent in EXAMPLE.OBJ and IO.OBJ. (If many separate object code units are being linked, it is easier to store some in a library than to list them all as object modules, separated by plus (+) signs. Multiple libraries can be specified.) If there are errors, messages will be displayed on the monitor; otherwise the linker simply returns to the DOS prompt.

After LINK is finished, the disk will contain the file EXAMPLE.EXE, the executable file for the program. This is then run by typing the name EXAMPLE in response to the DOS prompt. Figure 3.4 shows how a run might appear. The file EXAMPLE.EXE is not modified by executing it, so the program can be run many times without again using the assembler or linker.

The procedures in this section have assumed that all programs were on a single floppy disk, but one alternative is to keep MASM.EXE and LINK.EXE on a separate disk from the other files. This disk is put in a second floppy disk drive (the B drive), the source code disk is put in the A drive, and the assembler is executed with

```
A>b:masm
```

Similarly the linker is executed with

```
A>b:link
```

Responses to prompts remain the same as those previously given. This two-floppy-disk system will work even if a PC has only a single floppy disk drive because the DOS operating system will prompt for floppy disks to be switched in the drive as needed. A PC with a hard disk drive will work much as shown in this section, assuming that the files have been installed in appropriate subdirectories. However, the prompt with a hard disk system is usually C> instead of A>.

Exercises 3.2

1. What are the three segments used in the example program of Fig. 3.1? Which 8088 registers "point to" each of these segments at execution time?

2. Is the following statement true or false? Why? The words reserved by the directives

```
number1      DW      ?
number2      DW      ?
```

are contiguous in memory.

3. Identify three directives that appear in the example program.

4. Identify three macros that appear in the example program.

5. Identify three instructions that appear in the example program.

6. Suppose that EXAMPLE.ASM is assembled and linked according to the instructions in this section. What additional files will be generated?

Programming Exercises 3.2

1. Run the example program given in this section. Use a text editor to create the source code file EXAMPLE.ASM and then assemble, link, and execute it as shown. Run the program several times with different data.

2. Modify the example program given in this section to prompt for, input, and add three numbers. Call the source code file ADD3.ASM. Follow steps parallel to those of this section to assemble and link the program, producing ADD3.EXE. Run ADD3 several times with different data.

3. The instruction

```
sub     ax, label
```

will subtract the word at *label* from the word already in the AX register. Modify the example program to prompt for and input two numbers, then subtract the second number from the first. Call the source code file SUBTRACT.ASM. Follow steps parallel to those of this section to assemble and link the program, producing SUBTRACT.EXE. Run SUBTRACT several times with different data.

3.3

The Assembler Listing File

The listing file generated by MASM during assembly contains a wealth of information. Examination of the listing file can help to understand the assembly process.

Figure 3.5 shows a listing file for EXAMPLE.ASM. A **PAGE** directive (without operands) has been inserted in the source code to cause a page break before the code segment, and another form of the **PAGE** directive is at the beginning of the file. This form

PAGE *length, width*

has operand *length,* which specifies the number of lines to put on each page before a page break is automatically inserted, and operand *width,* which specifies how many columns wide to make the listing. Choosing a length of 39 lines ensures that the pages will fit on a page 8 1/2-inches long, leaving one-inch margins at top and bottom. Using 100 for the width keeps most assembly language statements on one line, even including the additional characters added by the assembler. The appropriate choices for length and width depend on the printer and paper size used to print the listing file. No **PAGE** directive is required.

The listing begins by echoing the **PAGE** and **INCLUDE** directives, and the last line of IO.H. The **C** in front of .**LIST** indicates that this line is associated with an **INCLUDE** file.

For each **EQU** directive the MASM assembler shows the value to which the symbol is equated as four hex digits. This listing shows **000D** for **cr** and **000A** for **Lf**.

The leftmost column for the rest of the listing shows the offset (distance) of each directive (except the **PAGE** directives) or of each instruction from the beginning of the segment that contains it. This offset is in bytes. The lines

```
0000                              stack          SEGMENT stack
0000    0100[                     DW             100h DUP (?)
            ????
                          ]


0200                              stack          ENDS
```

show that the 256 (100_{16}) words reserved in this segment start at an offset of 0000, and the segment ends at an offset of 0200 (512_{10} bytes). The notation

```
0100[
    ????
              ]
```

says that MASM is reserving 0100_{16} words without any initial value for the **DW**. The assembler uses **????** for an uninitialized word and **??** for an uninitialized byte; each question mark stands for one hex digit.

The data segment again starts at an offset of 0000. The line

```
0000    0000                      number1        DW        ?
```

shows an offset of **0000** since this statement is the first in the new segment. The assembler shows an initialized word with value **0000**. Other versions of MASM use the uninitialized word **????**. Since this word takes two bytes, the

Figure 3.5 Listing File.

```
Microsoft (R) Macro Assembler Version 5.10              8/10/88 22:11:42
                                                         Page     1-1

                              PAGE    45,100

                          C   INCLUDE io.h
                          C   .LIST             ; begin listing

= 000D                        cr      EQU  0dh   ; carriage return character
= 000A                        Lf      EQU  0ah   ; linefeed character

0000                          stack   SEGMENT STACK
0000  0100[                           DW   100h DUP (?)
        ????
      ]
0200                          stack   ENDS

0000                          data    SEGMENT
0000                          number1 DW   ?
0000                          number2 DW   ?
0002
0004  45 6E 74 65 72 20       prompt1 DB   cr,Lf,'Enter first number: ',0
      66 69 72 73 74 20
      6E 75 6D 62 65 72
      3A 20 00
001A  0D 0A 45 6E 74 65       prompt2 DB   cr,Lf,'Enter second number: ',0
      72 20 73 65 63 6F
      6E 64 20 6E 75 6D
      62 65 72 3A 20
      00
0033  0028[                   string  DB   40 DUP (?)
        ??
      ]
005B  0D 0A 54 68 65 20       label1  DB   cr,Lf,'The sum is '
      73 75 6D 20 69 73
      20
0068  0006[                   sum     DB   6 DUP (?)
        ??
      ]
006E  0D 0A 00                        DB   cr,Lf,0
0071                          data    ENDS
```

Figure 3.5 Continued.

```
Microsoft (R) Macro Assembler Version 5.10           8/10/88 22:11:42
                                                      Page     1-2

                                    PAGE
0000                                code    SEGMENT
                                            ASSUME  cs:code,ds:data

0000  B8 ---- R                     start:  mov     ax,SEG data    ; load data segment number
0003  8E D8                                 mov     ds,ax

0005                                prompt: output  prompt1        ; prompt for first number
                                            inputs  string,40      ; read ASCII characters
                                            atoi    string         ; convert to integer
002E  A3 0000 R                             mov     number1,ax     ; store

                                            output  prompt2        ; prompt for second number
                                            inputs  string,40      ; read ASCII characters
                                            atoi    string         ; convert to integer
005A  A3 0002 R                             mov     number2,ax     ; store

005D  A1 0000 R                             mov     ax,number1     ; first number to AX
0060  03 06 0002 R                          add     ax,number2     ; add second number

                                            itoa    sum,ax         ; convert to ASCII characters

                                            output  label1         ; output label and sum

0083  B0 00                         quit:   mov     al,0           ; return code 0
0085  B4 4C                                 mov     ah,4ch         ; DOS function to return
0087  CD 21                                 int     21h            ; interrupt for DOS services

0089                                code    ENDS
                                            END     start
```

Figure 3.5 Continued.

```
Microsoft (R) Macro Assembler Version 5.10                          8/10/88 22:11:42
                                                                       Symbols-1
Macros:

                N a m e                              Lines

ATOI. . . . . . . . . . . . . . . . . . .              12
INPUTC. . . . . . . . . . . . . . . . . .               5
INPUTS. . . . . . . . . . . . . . . . . .              13
ITOA. . . . . . . . . . . . . . . . . . .              15
M_ERROR . . . . . . . . . . . . . . . . .               9
OUTPUT. . . . . . . . . . . . . . . . . .              19

Segments and Groups:

                N a m e                Length   Align   Combine  Class

CODE. . . . . . . . . . . . . . . . . .  0089    PARA    NONE
DATA. . . . . . . . . . . . . . . . . .  0071    PARA    NONE
STACK . . . . . . . . . . . . . . . . .  0200    PARA    STACK

Symbols:

                N a m e                Type      Value   Attr

ATOI_PROC . . . . . . . . . . . . . . . L FAR    0000    External

CR. . . . . . . . . . . . . . . . . . . NUMBER   000D

INC_PROC. . . . . . . . . . . . . . . . L FAR    0000            External
INS_PROC. . . . . . . . . . . . . . . . L FAR    0000            External
ITOA_PROC . . . . . . . . . . . . . . . L FAR    0000            External

LABEL1. . . . . . . . . . . . . . . . . L BYTE   005B    DATA
LF. . . . . . . . . . . . . . . . . . . NUMBER   000A

NUMBER1 . . . . . . . . . . . . . . . . L WORD   0000    DATA
NUMBER2 . . . . . . . . . . . . . . . . L WORD   0002    DATA

OUT_PROC. . . . . . . . . . . . . . . . L FAR    0000            External

PROMPT. . . . . . . . . . . . . . . . . L NEAR   0005    CODE
PROMPT1 . . . . . . . . . . . . . . . . L BYTE   0004    DATA
```

Figure 3.5 Continued.

```
Microsoft (R) Macro Assembler Version 5.10              8/10/88 22:11:42
                                                        Symbols-2

PROMPT2 . . . . . . . . . . . . . . .   L BYTE  001A    DATA

QUIT . . . . . . . . . . . . . . . . .  L NEAR  0083    CODE

START . . . . . . . . .   L NEAR  0000    CODE
STRING. . . . . . . .     L BYTE  0033    DATA    Length = 0028
SUM . . . . . . . . .     L BYTE  0068    DATA    Length = 0006

@CPU . . . . . . . .      TEXT   0101h
@FILENAME . . . . .       TEXT   example
@VERSION . . . . . .      TEXT   510

   165 Source  Lines
   287 Total   Lines
    31 Symbols

47608 + 392753 Bytes symbol space free

    0 Warning Errors
    0 Severe Errors
```

assembler uses 0002 for the offset of the next statement.

```
0002    0000                              number2    DW    ?
```

Again two bytes are reserved, so the offset is 0004 for the next statement. The next two entries show the initial values assigned by the DB statements at prompt1 and prompt2.

```
0004    45 6E 74 65 72 20        prompt1    DB    'Enter first ...
        66 69 72 73 74 20
        6E 75 6D 62 65 72
        3A 20 20 00
001A    0D 0A 45 6E 74 65        prompt2    DB    cr,Lf,'Enter ...
        72 20 73 65 63 6F
        6E 64 20 6E 75 6D
        62 65 72 3A 20 20
        00
```

The offset for the statement after prompt1 can be calculated by taking its offset 0004 plus the number of bytes 22 (16_{16}) and finding the sum 001A. Similarly, the offset of the statement following prompt2 will be at 001A + 19 = 0033 since there are 25 bytes generated in the second prompt. The notation

```
0033    0028[
                ??
                                        ]
```

shows 28_{16} (40_{10}) uninitialized bytes (??) of storage. The remaining statements in the data segment illustrate no new concepts.

The assembly listing for the code segment shows, in hex, the machine code for instructions. The first byte of the machine code for each instruction is called its **opcode** (operation code). By looking at an opcode as the program executes, the 8088 knows what kind of operation is to be done and whether or not there are more bytes of the instruction. The machine code for a single instruction can be from one to six bytes long.

The line

```
0000  B8 ---- R            start:    mov    ax,SEG data    ; load ...
```

shows that this instruction starts at an offset of 0000 and has three bytes (six hex digits) of object code, starting with the opcode B8. To the 8088 the opcode B8 means that the next two bytes of the instruction are to be loaded into the AX register. The assembler shows these two bytes as ---- since their value is not known at assembly time. The notation R indicates that the operand SEG data represents a **relocatable** object, that is, the linker (and, in this case, the loader) will have to determine the value of the unknown bytes, putting it in the object code before execution actually begins.

The next instruction has an offset of 0003 since the first instruction takes three bytes.

```
0003    8E D8                              mov    ds,ax
```

The opcode 8E is used when the contents of a general register or a word in memory are to be copied to a segment register. The second byte has three fields

Name	Bits Long	Value
mod	2	11
sreg	3	011
r/m	3	000

The entries in the value column come from looking at the binary version 11011000 of D8. The mode value (mod = 11) tells the CPU that the source of the data to be moved is a register rather than a word in memory, the segment register value (sreg = 011) indicates that the destination register is DS, and register/memory value (r/m = 000) says that the source register is AX.

The offset for the next instruction will be 0005 since a total of five bytes have been used by the first two instructions. The next three statements are macros. The instructions for these macros are not shown because IO.H contains the directive .SALL, which tells MASM not to show macro expansions. The listing shows an offset of 002E for the **mov** instruction following the **output, inputs**, and **atoi** macros, so you can calculate that there are a total of 41 bytes of code generated from the three macros.

$$002E - 0005 = 29_{16} = 41_{10}$$

To see a listing for the macro expansions, either the .SALL directive can be removed from IO.H, or the directive

    INCLUDE io.h

can be followed by the directive .LALL, which causes macro expansions to be included in the program listing.

The next instruction

    002E   A3 0000 R   mov   number1,ax

and the instruction

    005A   A3 0002 R   mov   number2,ax

are identical except for the **mov** destinations. The opcode A3 means that a word is to be copied from AX to memory. The assembler shows the offsets of **number1** and **number2** in the data segment (**0000** and **0002**, respectively) as the destination addresses in the last two bytes of each instruction. At run time the actual address will be calculated as the sum of the offset and the contents of the segment register DS.

Using some MASM options, different segments in a program can be combined by the linker so that some may not start on actual 8088 memory segment boundaries. This requires that the linker adjust offsets to correspond to the actual memory segment boundaries. Consequently offsets are shown as relocatable (R) even though the distance of a label from the beginning of a program segment cannot be changed.

Not only are relocatable values subject to alteration before the instructions for a program are actually run, but MASM also does not show word-length values as they actually appear in the final code. The instruction

```
005A  A3 0002 R                           mov     number2,ax
```

in the listing seems to say that if the offset for **number2** is not adjusted then the machine code for this instruction will be A3 00 02. In fact, it will be A3 02 00, with the low-order byte of the word before the high-order byte. In general, the bytes of word-length values are stored backwards in instructions and in memory. The assembler listing shows the logical value, rather than the actual machine code.

Remaining statements from the code segment are assembled similarly. Chapter 11 (the assembly process) provides more details about formats of 8088 instructions and how they are assembled.

The final part of the assembly listing shows all the symbols that are used in the listing. The first few lines show all the macro names that are defined by including IO.H even though not all are used in this program. Then the segment names are shown. Some of the unfamiliar symbols are names of procedures that are called by the macros in IO.H.

Exercises 3.3

Answer the following questions by looking at the assembly listing in Figure 3.5.

1. What are the ASCII codes for characters in the string

   The sum is ⌴, where ⌴ stands for a blank space?

2. What is the offset of the label **sum** in the data section?

3. If the following statements

   ```
   extra     DW     5 DUP (?)
   label2    DB     'The End',cr,Lf
   ```

   were added immediately before

   ```
   data  ENDS
   ```

   what offsets and values would MASM show for them in the assembly listing? (Hint: The inside front cover (Hexadecimal/ASCII Conversion) may also be useful for this problem.)

4. What is the offset in the code segment of the label `quit`?

5. What object code does the assembler generate for the statement `int 21h`?

6. What object code does the assembler generate for the statement `int 33`? (Hint: The operand is in decimal.)

7. How many bytes of object code are generated by the `itoa` and `output` macros immediately preceding the label `quit`? (Hint: Look at the offset of the `add` before these two instructions and at the offset `quit`.)

3.4

Operands of DB and DW Directives

This section discusses operands used in DB and DW directives. Constant operands are written the same way in directives and in instructions. Numeric operands can be expressed in decimal, hexadecimal, binary, or octal notations. The assembler assumes that a number is decimal unless it has a suffix indicating another base or unless a `.RADIX` directive changes the default radix. (The `.RADIX` directive is not used in this book.) The suffixes that may be used are

Suffix	Base	Number System
H	16	hexadecimal
B	2	binary
O or Q	8	octal

Any of these suffixes can be coded in uppercase or lowercase. Octal is not used often, but when it is, "Q" is easier to read than "O" although either letter can be used to designate that the number is octal.

The directive

```
mask        DB          01111101b
```

reserves one byte of memory and initializes it to 7D. This is equivalent to

```
mask        DB          175q
```

since $175_8 = 7D_{16}$.

A numeric operand for a DB directive can be in the decimal range –255 to 255. An unsigned number from 0 to 255 (00 to FF) can be stored in a byte. A negative number from –128 to –1 is given its correct byte-length 2's complement form by a DB. A negative number from –255 to –129 is treated as if it were converted to word-length 2's complement form, with the high-order byte then thrown away.

For example,

```
negative    DB    -185
```

assigns an initial value of 47 to the byte it reserves since the word-length 2's complement version of –185 is FF 47.

In general it makes sense to restrict numeric operands for DB directives to –128 to 255. The comments in the following examples indicate the initial values of the bytes that are reserved.

```
byte1       DB    255      ; value is FF
byte2       DB    128      ; value is 80
byte3       DB    91       ; value is 5B
byte4       DB    0        ; value is 00
byte5       DB    -1       ; value is FF
byte6       DB    -91      ; value is A5
byte7       DB    -128     ; value is 80
```

The situation for DW directives is similar; the allowable range for a numeric operand is –65,535 to 65,535. Unsigned numbers from 0 to 65,535 (0000 to FFFF) will fit in a word. Negative numbers from –32,768 to –1 are converted to their correct word-length 2's complement form. Negative numbers from –65,535 to –32,769 are treated as if they are converted to four-byte-long 2's complement form, with only the last two bytes used to initialize storage. The following examples give the initial values reserved for the words.

```
word1       DW    65535    ; value is FFFF
word2       DW    32767    ; value is 7FFF
word3       DW    1000     ; value is 03E8
word4       DW    0        ; value is 0000
word5       DW    -1       ; value is FFFF
word6       DW    -1000    ; value is FC18
word7       DW    -32768   ; value is 8000
word8       DW    -40000   ; value is 63C0
```

For word8, –40000 has the four-byte 2's complement form

```
FF  FF  63  C0
```

the last two bytes of which are used.

As mentioned in the previous section, the bytes of a word are actually stored backwards so that, for example, the initial value of the word reserved for word6 above is 18FC. This book will concentrate on the logical rather than actual way that the bytes are stored.

The DB directive allows either character operands with a single character or string operands with many characters. Either apostrophes (') or double quotation marks (") can be used to designate characters or delimit strings. They must be in pairs, however. It is not legal to have an apostrophe on the left and double quotation marks on the right. A string delimited with apostrophes can contain double quotation marks, and one delimited with double quotation marks can contain apostrophes, so it is possible to have strings containing these special characters. In a string delimited by apostrophes, the MASM assembler also recognizes pairs of consecutive apostrophes as standing for a single apostrophe; this is similar to the handling of string delimiters by many high-level languages. Pairs of consecutive double quotation marks are treated similarly in strings delimited by double quotation marks.

Each of the following DB directives is legal.

```
char1       DB      'm'     ; value is 6D
char2       DB      "m"     ; value is 6D
string1     DB      'Joe'   ; value is 4A 6F 65
string2     DB      "Joe"   ; value is 4A 6F 65
string3     DB      "Joe's" ; value is 4A 6F 65 27 73
string4     DB      'Joe''s' ; value is 4A 6F 65 27 73
```

Notice that the string delimiters—the apostrophes or double quotation marks on the ends of the string—are not themselves coded.

Character operands can be used in DW directives. The ASCII code for a single character is placed in the low-order byte of the word and 00 is placed in the high-order byte. String operands can also be used, but they are limited to strings of two characters. The ASCII code for the first character is the value for the high-order byte and the code for the second character is the value for the low-order byte. Examples are

```
word9       DW      ' '     ; value is 0020
word10      DW      'OK'    ; value is 4F4B
```

There have already been examples of DB directives with multiple operands separated by commas. In a similiar way, the DW directive also allows multiple operands. For example, the directive

```
words       DW      10, 20, 30, 40
```

reserves four words of storage with initial values 00 0A, 00 14, 00 1E, and 00 28.

The DUP operator can be used to generate multiple bytes or words with known as well as uninitialized values. Its use is limited to DB, DW, and other directives that reserve storage. Several examples of the use of DUP with DW and DB follow.

■ The directive

```
table       DW      100 DUP(0)
```

reserves 100 words of storage, each word having value 0000. This can be an effective way of initializing an array.

- If one needs a string of 50 asterisks, then

```
stars        DB    50 DUP('*')
```

will do the job.

- If one wants 25 asterisks, separated by spaces,

```
stars_and_spaces     DB    24 DUP('* '),'*'
```

reserves these 49 bytes and assigns the desired initial values.

DUP operators can even be nested. To produce ASCII codes for

*****␣ ␣ ␣ ␣ ␣|||||␣ ␣ ␣ ␣ ␣

[five asterisks, five spaces (represented by ␣), five vertical bars, five spaces] repeated 40 times, use the DB directive

```
ssf  DB 40 DUP(5 DUP('*'),5 DUP(' '),5 DUP('|'),5 DUP(' '))
```

A programmer must exercise care to match parentheses in such an operand.

An operand of a DW, DB, or other statement can be an expression involving arithmetic or other operators. These expressions are evaluated by MASM at assembly time, not at run time, and the resulting value is used. It is usually not helpful to use an expression instead of the constant of equivalent value, but sometimes it can contribute to clearer code. The following directives are equivalent, each giving an initial hex value of 0090.

```
gross        DW    144
gross        DW    12*12
gross        DW    10*15 - 7 + 1
```

Recall that an offset takes a word of storage. The DW directive allows the programmer to assign an initial value that is the offset of some other area of storage. This is similar to having a pointer variable whose value is the address of some block of memory.

The statements

```
array        DB    100 DUP(?)
pointer      DW    OFFSET array
```

reserve 100 bytes of storage for **array**. One word is reserved for **pointer**, and it is initialized to the offset of **array** in the data area. If, for instance, the offset of **array** were 02F6, then the initial value assigned to the word reserved for **pointer** would be 02F6. The operator **OFFSET** is not required in this case, but its inclusion makes the code clearer.

Each symbol defined by a DB or DW directive is associated with a type: *byte* or *word*. The assembler notes this type and checks to be sure that symbols are used appropriately in instructions. For example, MASM will generate an error message if

```
char         DB    'x'
```

is used in the data segment and then

```
mov   AX,char
```

appears in the code segment—the AX register is a word long, but `char` is associated with a single byte of storage.

The Microsoft assembler has three additional directives for reserving storage, DD, DQ, and DT. The DD directive reserves and optionally initializes a *doubleword* (four bytes) of storage. The DQ is for *quadwords* (eight bytes). These two directives are useful in defining floating point or large integer values. The DT directive allocates ten bytes of storage; it is useful for initializing packed decimal or floating point values.

───── **Exercises 3.4** ─────

Find the initial values that MASM will generate for each DB and DW below.

1.	db1	DB	10110111b
2.	db2	DB	11011110b
3.	db3	DB	33q
4.	db4	DB	65q
5.	db5	DB	0abh
6.	db6	DB	7fh
7.	db7	DB	253
8.	db8	DB	108
9.	db9	DB	-73
10.	db10	DB	-145
11.	db11	DB	'D'
12.	db12	DB	'd'
13.	db13	DB	'John said, "help!"'
14.	db14	DB	'John''s program'
15.	db15	DB	5 DUP("<>")
16.	db16	DB	3 DUP(4 DUP('+'), 3 DUP('-'))
17.	db17	DB	'a' + 1

18. db18	DB	'Z' - 5
19. dw1	DW	1010001001011b
20. dw2	DW	1101111010010111b
21. dw3	DW	2274q
22. dw4	DW	736q
23. dw5	DW	0ffffh
24. dw6	DW	3d4eh
25. dw7	DW	1000
26. dw8	DW	-1000
27. dw9	DW	50000
28. dw10	DW	-50000
29. dw11	DW	'h'
30. dw12	DW	'3'
31. dw13	DW	'OK'
32. dw14	DW	'75'
33. dw15	DW	-5,-4,-3,-2,-1
34. dw16	DW	-10,10
35. dw17	DW	5 DUP(1)
36. dw18	DW	10 DUP(-1)
37. dw19	DW	100/2
38. dw20	DW	15*12 - 5

3.5

Operands of Instructions

There are many types of instruction operands: some are constants, some designate CPU registers, and some reference memory locations. There are several ways of referencing memory; the simpler ways will be discussed in this section while the more complex methods will be mentioned here but explained more fully in Chapter 8 (other addressing modes).

Many instructions have two operands. In general, the first operand gives the destination of the operation, although it may also designate one of the sources.

The second operand gives the source (or a source) for the operation, never the destination. For example, when

```
mov    al,'/'
```

is executed, the byte 2F (the ASCII code for /, the slash) will be loaded into the AL register half, replacing the previous byte. The second operand '/' specifies the constant source. When

```
add    ax,number1
```

is executed, AX gets the sum of the word designated by **number1** and the old contents of AX. The first operand AX specifies the source for one word as well as the destination for the sum; the second operand **number1** specifies the source for the second of the two words that are added together.

Figure 3.6 lists the addressing modes used by the Intel 8088 microprocessor. For each mode, the location of the data is given. When this location is in storage, it is called an **effective address** (EA); the 8088 calculates the actual address using this effective address and a segment register as discussed in Section 2.1.

In this section and those following, the first four of the modes shown in Figure 3.6 will be discussed. For each mode there will be examples showing assembly language instructions that result in the mode, along with a brief look at how the machine code looks for some of the examples.

For an **immediate mode** operand, the data to be used is built into the instruction before it is executed. The data is placed there by the assembler, linker, or loader, depending on the stage at which the value can be determined. The programmer writes an instruction including an actual value, or a symbol standing for an actual value. For a **register mode** operand, the data to be used is

Figure 3.6 Intel 8088 Addressing Modes.

Mode	Location of Data
immediate	in the instruction itself
register	in a register
direct	at a memory location whose effective address (EA) is built into the instruction
register indirect	at a memory location whose EA is in a register
based	at a memory location whose EA is calculated as the sum of the contents of a base register and a number built into the instruction
indexed	at a memory location whose EA is calculated as the sum of the contents of an index register and a number built into the instruction
based and indexed	at a memory location whose EA is calculated as the sum of the contents of a base register and the contents of an index register and (optionally) a number built into the instruction

in a register. To indicate a register mode operand, the programmer simply codes the name of the register. A register mode operand can specify a register as a destination, but an immediate mode operand cannot be a destination.

In each of the following examples the first operand is register mode and the second operand is immediate mode. The object code (as shown by the MASM listing) is in the second column.

Instruction			*Object Code*	
mov	al,	'/'	B0	2F
add	ax,	135	05	0087
mov	ax,	SEG data	B8	----

In the first example, the ASCII code 2F (for the slash) is the second byte of the instruction, and is placed there by the assembler. In the second example, the word-length 2's complement version of 135 is assembled into the instruction. As mentioned before, the MASM listing shows the logical value—the actual object code will be 05   87 00, with the high- and low-order bytes reversed. For the final example, MASM shows ---- since the segment number for **data** cannot be determined until the program is loaded. At the time the program is loaded the segment number will be inserted into the instruction, with the low-order byte first. The important thing is that when the program actually executes, the value for **SEG data** is built into the instruction—an immediate operand.

A **direct mode** operand uses data in memory. The effective address (offset) of that data is built into the instruction. Usually the programmer will code a symbol that is associated with a **DB** or **DW** directive in the data segment, or with an instruction in the code segment. The location corresponding to such a symbol will be relocatable; the MASM listing will show a logical location, and the actual value is usually put in the code by the linker.

Here are typical statements using direct mode operands:

```
mov    number1, ax
add    ax, number2
```

Assuming that **number1** and **number2** are labels of **DW** directives in the data segment, **number1** is a direct mode operand in the first example and **number2** is a direct mode operand in the second example. In both of these cases the assembler will show the offset of the label in the data segment, and the linker will adjust this address if necessary to get the machine code which will be executed.

On rare occasions the programmer may code a segment register and an actual offset for a direct operand; MASM allows the instruction

```
mov    bx,ds:0014h
```

which will load the BX register with the word that is 20 bytes beyond the beginning of the data segment. This address would not be relocatable.

A **register indirect** operand uses data in memory. However, the offset of that data is not built into the instruction; rather the instruction specifies a register

Figure 3.7 Register Indirect Addressing.

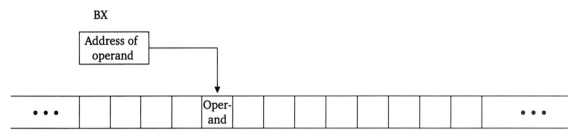

and when the instruction is executed the CPU uses the location at the offset contained in the register. The programmer codes a register indirect operand by putting a register name in square brackets: [ ].

Consider the following instructions whose operand modes are shown in the comments.

```
mov    bx,OFFSET table    ; register, immediate
mov    ax,[bx]            ; register, register indirect
```

The first instruction loads the address of `table` (that is, the offset of the first word reserved) into the BX register. The second instruction loads the value of the first word at `table` into the AX register because it loads the word that is at the address contained in the BX register. It is useful to think of **bx** as a pointer into memory and **[bx]** as the object that is pointed to. Figure 3.7 illustrates the situation.

Only four registers may be used for register indirect addressing: BX, BP, SI, and DI. The effective address for each of these except BP is an offset in the data segment; that is, the DS segment register is used to calculate the actual address at run time. When the BP register is used, the SS segment register is used to calculate the actual address.

With register indirect mode, the register acts like a pointer variable in a high-level language. The register contains the location of the data to be used in the instruction, not the data itself. When the size of the memory operand is ambiguous, the **PTR** operator must be used to give the size to the assembler.

For example, MASM will give an error message for

```
mov   [bx], 0     ; illegal -- size of destination is unknown
```

Either of

```
mov  BYTE PTR [bx], 0    ; legal, destination a byte in memory
```

or

```
mov  WORD PTR [bx], 0    ; legal, destination a word in memory
```

is acceptable. Other sizes can be specified with the **PTR** operator, but this book will use only **BYTE** and **WORD** sizes.

A few instructions have no operand. Many have a single operand. Sometimes an instruction with no operand requires no data or an instruction with one operand needs only one value. Other times the location of one or more operands is implied by the instruction and is not coded. For example, one 8088 instruction for multiplication is **mul**; it might be coded

```
mul    bh
```

Only one operand is given for this instruction; the other value to be multiplied is always in the AL register half. (This instruction will be explained more fully in the next chapter.)

The assembler allows the use of a location-counter operand **$** to represent the value of the offset of a statement as it is assembled. This may be used in instructions or directives.

One possible use of the location counter is shown in the following instruction.

```
jmp    $ - 5
```

Here control is transferred to the instruction five bytes prior to the **jmp** instruction. This technique is occasionally used when there is a reason to avoid a label on the target instruction. However, the above statement would more often be coded

```
jmp    repeat
```

where **repeat** is the label on the instruction five bytes before.

Here is an example showing use of the location-counter operand in a directive.

```
prompt            DB      cr, Lf, 'Enter a number:    '
prompt_length     EQU     $ - prompt
```

The value of **prompt_length** will be the difference of the offsets of the two statements. The first statement reserves 19 bytes of storage, so the offset of the second statement must be 19 larger than the first. Therefore the difference is 19, or 0013 in hex. This sort of code can save a programmer the trouble of counting bytes. The code section might then use a statement like

```
mov    dx,prompt_length
```

Note that **prompt_length** is an immediate operand in this **mov** instruction. It has the value 0013, which is assembled into the instruction. Notice that if the string is changed, no other code needs to be changed. This example also shows that a label in source code does not always imply a direct operand.

Identify the mode of each operand in the following instructions. Assume that the instructions are in a program also containing the code

```
cr          EQU         0dh

data        SEGMENT

value       DW          ?
string      DB          "Help!"
length      EQU         $ - string

data        ENDS
```

1. mov   value, 100
2. mov   cx, value
3. mov   dx, length
4. mov   bx, OFFSET string
5. mov   ah, cr

6. mov   ax, [si]
7. mov   [bx], cx
8. mov   string, '*'
9. add   value, 1
10. add   ax, [bx]

3.6

Input/Output Using Macros Defined in IO.H

In order to write useful programs, you need to be able to input and output data. Operating systems provide routines to aid in these tasks. A typical input routine might wait for a character to be pressed on the keyboard, and then return the ASCII code for that character in a register. An output routine might display at the terminal the characters in a string up to some terminating character like a dollar sign. It usually requires several instructions to use the I/O routines provided by DOS, and these routines are somewhat limited in what they can do.

High-level languages usually provide for input or output of numeric data in addition to character or string data. A numeric input routine in a high-level language usually accepts a string of character codes representing a number, converts the characters to a 2's complement or floating point form, and stores the value in a memory location associated with some variable name. Conversely, output routines of high-level languages start with a 2's complement or floating point number in some memory location, convert it to a string of characters that represent the number, and then output the string. Operating systems usually do not

Figure 3.8 Macros in IO.H.

Macro	Operands	Description
output	string [,length]	output a string of characters to the display up to a null character (00); optional length operand limits number of characters displayed so that null is not required
inputs	destination,length	input a string of up to (length −1) characters from the keyboard to the data area; Return key terminates input; CX gets count of characters
inputc	(none)	read one character from keyboard to register AL; Return is not used after the character
itoa	destination,source	convert a number in binary integer format at source (memory or register) to a six-character-long string at destination in data segment
atoi	source	convert a number in ASCII string format at source in data segment to word-length 2's complement form in the AX register

provide these services, so the assembly language programmer must code them.

The file IO.H provides a set of macro definitions that make it possible to do input, output, and numeric conversion fairly easily. Each macro looks much like an 8088 instruction, but actually expands to one or more instructions, including a call to an external procedure to do most of the work. The source code for these external procedures is in the file IO.ASM; already assembled versions are in IO.OBJ. These macros and procedures make assembly language programming simpler for beginners. However, an experienced assembly language programmer usually develops a similar collection of macros and/or procedures for input, output, and numeric conversion for a particular computer system, and then uses them repeatedly.

Figure 3.8 lists the macros defined in IO.H and briefly describes them. Additional explanation then follows. Source code listings for IO.H are in Appendex F; those for IO.ASM are contained in Appendix G. These macros will be used in programs in subsequent chapters. The code that actually does the work will be explained as the necessary instructions are presented, and the macro definitions will be used as examples in Chapter 12 (macros and conditional assembly).

The `output` macro is used to output a string of characters to the monitor. It has the format

```
output    string [,length]
```

In this format, the *string* operand references a location in the data segment. The *length* operand is optional, but if used, it may be an immediate (constant) operand, or it may reference a 16-bit register or a word of storage in the data segment. For a register or memory operand, the value of the word in the register or storage will be used for *length*.

The *length* operand determines the number of characters to be displayed. If the *length* operand is omitted, then the string must be terminated by a null character (00). All characters before the null byte will be displayed. Even if the *length* operand is used, a null character will terminate output of the string.

It is important that the area of the data segment referenced by *string* contain ASCII codes for characters that the monitor can display. Most of these will be printable characters, although it makes sense to include carriage return, line feed, and a few other special characters. If one attempts to use the `output` macro to display non-ASCII data (such as an integer in 2's complement form) there may be strange results. Usable ASCII codes can be generated at assembly time by DB directives with initial values given, at run time using the `itoa` macro, or by some other means. As illustrated in the example program of Figure 3.1, the `output` macro can display characters from several DB directives at the same time.

The `output` macro does not change any register contents, including the flag register.

The `inputs` macro is used to input a string of characters from the keyboard. It has the format

```
inputs    destination,length
```

In the macro `inputs` (<u>input s</u>tring), the first operand *destination* references a string of bytes in the data segment and the second references the length of that string. The destination string should be between 2 and 80 bytes long. The *length* operand is usually an immediate operand, but it may reference a register or word in the data segment containing a value to be used.

When the instructions of the `inputs` macro are executed, the computer waits for characters to be entered from the keyboard. The characters prior to pressing Return (or Enter) are stored sequentially at the destination address, followed by a null character (00). The carriage return character is not stored in the destination string. Register CX contains the number of characters actually read, not including the null. The computer beeps if more than (*length*) characters are typed before return is pressed.

As an illustration, suppose that the data segment contains

```
response   DB    20 DUP (?)
```

and the code segment contains

```
inputs response,20
```

If AbCd6(Return) is typed at execution time, then memory at **response** will contain the ASCII codes 41 62 43 64 36 00 plus 14 undefined characters. Register CX will contain 0005, the number of nonnull characters. No more than 19 characters can be read from the keyboard; no more than 20 characters (including the null character) will be stored at **response**.

As characters are typed, they will be displayed on the monitor. The Backspace key can be used to make corrections. When the Return key is pressed, both a carriage return and a linefeed will be displayed on the monitor and the cursor will move to the beginning of the next line.

The **inputs** macro affects only the destination area and the CX register. No other registers, including the flag register, are altered.

The **inputc** (input character) macro has no operand. It inputs a single character from the keyboard and stores its ASCII code in the AL register half. No Return is needed, although the ASCII code for the carriage return character might be the value in AL if the Return key is the one that is pressed. If the character is printable, it will be displayed on the monitor.

Both AH and AL are altered by **inputc**. The AH register half is set to 00, and the AL register half receives the ASCII code for the character. No other registers, including the flag register, are affected.

The **itoa** macro has the format

> **itoa** *destination,source*

The name **itoa** (integer to ASCII), describes the function of the macro. It takes a word-length source containing a 2's complement integer, and produces a string of exactly six ASCII characters representing the same integer in the decimal number system. The *source* operand is normally a register or memory operand, although an immediate operand will work. (Since an immediate operand is known at assembly time, a character string can be set up then—there is little reason to convert one to character format at run time.) The destination will almost always be a six-byte area of storage in the data segment reserved with a **DB** directive.

The string of characters produced will have leading blanks if the number has fewer than six characters. If the number is negative, a minus sign will immediately precede the digits. Since the decimal range for a word-length 2's complement number is –32768 to 32767, there is no danger of generating too many characters to fit in a six-byte field. A positive number will always have at least one leading blank.

The **itoa** macro alters only the six-byte area of memory that is the destination for the ASCII codes. No registers are changed, including the flag register.

The **atoi** (ASCII to integer) macro is in many ways the inverse of the **itoa** macro. It has only a single operand, the address of a string of ASCII character codes in storage, and it scans this area of memory for characters that represent a decimal number. If it finds characters for a decimal number in the range –32768 to 32767, then the word-length 2's complement form of the number is placed in the AX register.

The source string may contain any number of leading blanks. These are skipped by `atoi`. There may then be the ASCII code for – or the ASCII code for + (plus). A number is assumed positive if there is no leading sign. Codes for digits 0 through 9 must immediately follow the optional sign. Once a digit code is encountered, `atoi` continues scanning until any character other than a digit is encountered. Such a character terminates the scan.

Some problems may arise when the `atoi` macro is used. The macro may find no digit code; this would be the case if a space character were between a minus sign and the first digit of a number, or if the source string began with the code for a letter. The decimal number could be too large to store in word-length 2's complement form (outside the range –32,768 to +32,767). If any of these things occurs, a value of 0000 is placed in AX and the overflow flag OF is set to 1.

If `atoi` is able to successfully convert a string of ASCII characters, then the overflow flag OF is set to 0. In all cases, the SF, ZF, and PF flags are set according to the value returned in AX as follows:

- SF is 1 if the number is negative, and 0 otherwise
- ZF is 1 if the number is 0, and 0 if the number is nonzero
- PF reflects the parity of the number returned in AX

In addition, CF is 0; DF, IF and TF are unchanged; and AC is undefined. No registers other than AX and the flag register are changed.

The `atoi` macro will typically be used immediately after the `inputs` macro. The `inputs` macro produces a string of ASCII codes, including a trailing null character. When `atoi` is applied to this string, the null character serves as a terminating character for the scan. If atoi is applied to a string that comes from some source other than `inputs`, the programmer must ensure that it has some trailing nondigit character to stop `atoi` from scanning too far.

Exercises 3.6

---

1. (a) Given the data segment definition

    `response1     DB        10 DUP(?)`

    and the code segment macro

    `inputs    response1,10`

    what ASCII codes will be stored in the data segment if

    `578(return)`

    is typed at run time?

(b) If the macro

```
atoi        response1
```

follows the above **inputs** macro, what will be in the AX register, a what will be the values of the OF, SF, and ZF flags?

2. (a) Given the data segment definition

```
response2    DB          10 DUP(?)
```

and the code segment macro

```
inputs    response2,10
```

what ASCII codes will be stored in the data segment if

```
7-Up(return)
```

is typed at run time?

(b) If the macro

```
atoi        response2
```

follows the above **inputs** macro, what will be in the AX register, and what will be the values of the OF, SF, and ZF flags?

3. (a) Given the data segment definition

```
response3    DB          10 DUP(?)
```

and the code segment macro

```
inputs    response3,10
```

what ASCII codes will be stored in the data segment if

```
123456(return)
```

is typed at run time?

(b) If the macro

```
atoi        response3
```

follows the above **inputs** macro, what will be in the AX register, and what will be the values of the OF, SF, and ZF flags?

4. Suppose a program contains the data segment definitions

```
value4       DW          ?
        . . .
result4      DB          6 DUP(?)
             DB          ' sum',0dh,0ah,0
```

and the code segment macro

```
itoa      result4,value4
```

(a) Assuming that at run time the word referenced by `value4` contains FF1A, what codes will be placed in storage at `result4` by the `itoa` macro?

(b) If the `itoa` macro is followed by

```
output    result4
```

what will be displayed on the monitor?

(c) If the `itoa` macro is followed by

```
output    result4,9
```

what will be displayed on the monitor?

5. Suppose a program contains the data segment definitions

```
result5      DB        6 DUP(?)
             DB        ' total',0dh,0ah,0
```

and the code segment macro

```
itoa      result5,BX
```

(a) Assuming that at run time the BX register contains 1AFF, what codes will be placed in storage at `result5` by the `itoa` macro?

(b) If the `itoa` macro is followed by

```
output    result5
```

what will be displayed on the monitor?

(c) If the `itoa` macro is followed by

```
output    result5,6
```

what will be displayed on the monitor?

3.7

Chapter Summary

This chapter introduced 8088 assembly language as translated by the Microsoft MASM assembler.

An assembly language comment always starts with a semicolon. Other statements have the format

[name] mnemonic [operand(s)] [;comment]

The three types of assembly language statements are:

- instructions—each corresponds to a CPU instruction
- directives—tell the assembler what to do
- macros—expand into additional statements

An assembly language program is often written in three segments, stack, data, and code. To get an executable program, one must translate the program to object code using an assembler such as MASM and then link the program using a linker such as LINK.

DB or DW directives reserve bytes or words of storage and optionally assign initial values.

The simpler modes of instruction operands are:

- immediate—data built into the instruction
- register—data in a register
- direct—data in storage at an address in the instruction
- register indirect—data at an address in a register

Several macros for input and output are defined in the file IO.H. They call procedures whose assembled versions are in the file IO.OBJ. The macros are:

- output—to display a string on the monitor
- inputs—to input a string from the keyboard
- inputc—to input a single character from the keyboard
- atoi—to convert a string to a 2's complement number
- itoa—to convert a 2's complement number to a string

Basic Instructions

This chapter covers 8088 instructions used to transfer data from one location to another and instructions used for arithmetic with 2's complement numbers. It details what types of operands are allowed for the various instructions. Finally, it gives some methods for accomplishing equivalent operations even when the desired operand types are not allowed.

────── 4.1 ──

Transferring Data Between Locations

A main concept discussed in Chapter 4 is that of time efficiency. The length of time it takes an instruction to execute is measured in **clock cycles**. A standard PC operates at 4.77 MHz, that is, 4,770,000 cycles per second or about 210 nanoseconds per cycle. (A nanosecond is 10^{-9} seconds.) For each instruction, the number of 8088 clock cycles required for execution will be listed. Some 8088-based PCs operate at higher clock rates. Microcomputers using Intel microprocessors more powerful than the 8088 usually operate at higher clock rates and also require fewer clock cycles for some instructions. In general, instructions that access memory are much slower than instructions that use data in registers, so that frequently used data should be kept in registers when possible.

In some assembly language applications it is important to produce compact code—object code with as few bytes as possible—although, as the amount of memory included in computers has increased, this is not as critical as it once was. The number of bytes of object code required for various instructions will also be listed.

Most computer programs must copy data from one location to another. With 8088 assembly language programs, this job is done by the **mov** (move) instruction. Each **mov** instruction has the form

        mov   *destination, source*

and transfers a byte or a word from the *source* operand location to the *destination* operand location. The *source* location is not changed. A **mov** is similar to a simple assignment statement in a high-level language. For example, the assignment statement

        count := number

might correspond directly to

        mov   count,cx   ; count := number

assuming that the CX register contains the value of **number**. The analogy between high-level language assignment statements and **mov** statements cannot be carried too far; the assignment

        count := 3*number + 1

cannot be coded with a single **mov** instruction. Multiple instructions are required to evaluate the right-hand expression before the resulting value is copied to the destination location.

Another limitation of 8088 assembly language is that not all combinations of source and destination operand types are allowed. For instance,

```
mov   count,number      ; illegal for two memory operands
```

is not allowed if both **count** and **number** reference memory locations. Figure 4.1 lists the allowable forms of the **mov** instruction by operand type. The Intel 8088 address mode nomenclature (summarized in Figure 3.6) is used in Figure 4.1, as well as some new terminology. Here the notation **register 8** refers to a register half (AL, AH, BL, BH, CL, CH, DL, or DH) and **register 16** refers to one of the 16-bit registers AX, BX, CX, DX, SP, BP, SI, or DI (not including the segment registers, the flag register, or the instruction pointer IP). For each instruction the number of 8088 clock cycles for the operation is given. For moves where one operand is in memory this number is a minimum; a system with slow memory chips may require extra clock cycles, or **wait states**. The "number of bytes" column indicates how many bytes are used in the machine code for the instruction.

There are several things to note about the entries in Figure 4.1. First, many combinations of **mov** operands are not possible. These include

- a move with both source and destination in memory
- immediate source to segment register destination
- any move to or from the flag register
- any move to the IP register
- a move from one segment register to another segment register
- any move where the operands are not the same byte or word size

Since there is no **mov** instruction to copy from a memory source to a memory destination, two moves using an intermediate register are often employed to accomplish the same thing. For word-length data referenced by **count** and **number** the illegal instruction

```
mov   count,number      ; illegal for two memory operands
```

can be replaced by the two instructions

```
mov   ax,number         ; count := number
mov   count,ax
```

each using the accumulator AX and one direct memory operand. Some register other than AX could be used, but each of these instructions using the accumulator requires 14 clock cycles and 3 bytes, while each of the corresponding instructions using some other register requires 18 clock cycles and 4 bytes.

Figure 4.1 mov Instructions.

Destination Operand	Source Operand	Clock Cycles	Number of Bytes	Opcode
register 8	immediate byte	4	2	
AL				B0
CL				B1
DL				B2
BL				B3
AH				B4
CH				B5
DH				B6
BH				B7
register 16	immediate word	4	3	
AX				B8
CX				B9
DX				BA
BX				BB
SP				BC
BP				BD
SI				BE
DI				BF
memory byte	immediate byte			C6 *
direct		16	5	
register indirect		15	3	
based or indexed		19	4 or 5	
based & indexed (no displacement)		17 or 18	3	
based & indexed (w/ displacement)		21 or 22	4 or 5	
memory word	immediate word			C7
direct		20	6	
register indirect		19	4	
based or indexed		23	5 or 6	
based & indexed (no displacement)		21 or 22	4	
based & indexed (w/ displacement)		25 or 26	5 or 6	
register 8	register 8	2	2	88

* The C6 and C7 opcodes can also be used for moving immediate data to register 8 or register 16 destinations, respectively. They execute in 4 clock cycles, like the instructions listed above, but require an extra byte of memory.

Figure 4.1 Continued.

Destination Operand	Source Operand	Clock Cycles	Number of Bytes	Opcode
register 16	register 16	2	2	89
AL	direct	10	3	A0
AX	direct	14	3	A1
direct	AL	10	3	A2
direct	AX	14	3	A3
register 8	memory byte			8A
	direct	14	4	
	register indirect	13	2	
	based or indexed	17	3 or 4	
	based & indexed			
	(no displacement)	15 or 16	3 or 4	
	based & indexed			
	(w/ displacement)	19 or 20	3 or 4	
register 16	memory word			8B
	direct	18	4	
	register indirect	17	2	
	based or indexed	21	3 or 4	
	based & indexed			
	(no displacement)	19 or 20	3 or 4	
	based & indexed			
	(w/ displacement)	23 or 24	3 or 4	
memory byte	register 8			88
(clock cycles and number of bytes same as for register 8 ←memory byte)				
memory word	register 16			89
(clock cycles and number of bytes same as for register 16 ← memory word)				
register 16	segment register	2	2	8C
segment register	register 16	2	2	8E
memory word	segment register			8C
(clock cycles and number of bytes same as for register 16 ← memory word)				
segment register	memory word			8E
(clock cycles and number of bytes same as for register 16 ←memory word)				

The program in Figure 3.1 illustrated how to transfer immediate data to a segment register. Recall the pair of instructions

```
start:    mov   ax,SEG data     ; load data segment number
          mov   ds,ax
```

The accumulator AX is the common choice of temporary places for the data, but any other register 16 would be equally efficient in terms of the total numbers of clock cycles and bytes used by the two instructions.

Although the flag register and the instruction pointer IP cannot be set by **mov** instructions, other instructions do change their values. The instruction pointer register IP is routinely updated as new instructions are fetched and it is automatically changed by jump, call, and return instructions. Individual flags are set by a variety of instructions, and it is possible and occasionally desirable to set all bits in the flag register to desired values; some specific techniques will be covered later.

To change the size of data from a word to a byte, it is legal to transfer a word to a register, and then move out just the high-order or low-order byte to a destination. Conversely, one can piece together two bytes in a register and then copy the resulting word to some destination. These techniques are occasionally useful. It is sometimes necessary to extend a byte-length number to word-length, or a word-length number to four bytes; instructions for doing this are covered in Section 4.4.

Note that Figure 4.1 lists several instructions with the same opcode. For example, the opcode 89 is used for all of the instructions that transfer data from a register 16 source to a register 16 or any memory destination. Such instructions have a second byte that gives more information about the instruction to be executed. In the case of the opcode 89, this information is

- a *mode* field that indicates whether the destination is a register or a memory operand and additional information about a memory operand
- a *register* field that identifies the source register
- a *register/memory* field that either identifies the destination register or describes the mode of a memory operand

These fields will be described carefully in Chapter 11 (the assembly process).

Some entries in Figure 4.1 have a choice of values for the number of clock cycles and/or the number of bytes. The word "or" appears for two reasons, both related to addressing modes that barely have been mentioned. As defined in Figure 3.6, with either the based or indexed addressing modes, the data is at a memory location whose address is calculated as the sum of the contents of a register plus a number built into the instruction. The number built into the instruction is called a **displacement** and can be either a byte or a word in length. For the based and indexed addressing mode, a displacement is optional. In any of these three modes, a two-byte displacement results in an instruction one byte longer than a single-byte displacement. This explains the "or"s in the "number of bytes" column. The Microsoft Macro Assembler will normally choose a single-byte displacement, if possible, to minimize bytes of code.

The other "or"s appear in the "clock cycles" column when a based and indexed memory operand is involved. In this addressing mode, either the BP or BX registers can be used as the base register and either the DI or SI registers can be used as the index register. Instructions that use BP/DI or BX/SI combinations are one clock cycle faster than the corresponding instructions using BP/SI or BX/DI pairings. This will be covered more thoroughly in Chapter 8 (other addressing modes).

All move instructions are coded with the **mov** mnemonic. The assembler selects the correct opcode and other bytes of the machine code by looking at the operands as well as the mnemonic.

The 8088 has a very useful **xchg** instruction that exchanges data in one location with data in another location. It accomplishes in a single instruction the operation that often requires three high-level language instructions.

Suppose value1 and value2 are being exchanged. In a design or a high-level language, this might be done using

```
temp := value1;      { swap value1 and value2 }
value1 := value2;
value2 := temp
```

Assuming that value1 is stored in the BX register and value2 is stored in the CX register, the above swap can be coded as

```
xchg    bx,cx           ; swap value1 and value2
```

Instead of using the **xchg** instruction, one could code

```
mov     ax,bx           ; swap value1 and value2
mov     bx,cx
mov     cx,ax
```

However, each of these **mov** instructions takes two clock cycles and two bytes for a total of six clock cycles and six bytes of code, while the **xchg** instruction only requires four clock cycles and two bytes. In addition, it is much easier to type one line than three and the resulting code is easier to understand. Figure 4.2 lists the various forms of the **xchg** instruction. Note that when a memory reference is used, it must be the second operand of the instruction.

Many 8088 instructions affect the flags in the flag register. However neither the **mov** nor the **xchg** instructions change the flags. Just after execution of one of these instructions, the flags have the same values as just before.

Figure 4.2 xchg Instructions.

Operand 1	Operand 2	Clock Cycles	Number of Bytes	Opcode
AX	register 16	3	1	
	CX			91
	DX			92
	BX			93
	SP			94
	BP			95
	SI			96
	DI			97
register 8	register 8	4	2	86
register 16	register 16	4	2	87
register 8	memory byte			86
	direct	23	4	
	register indirect	22	2	
	based or indexed	26	3 or 4	
	based & indexed (no displacement)	24 or 25	3 or 4	
	based & indexed (w/ displacement)	28 or 29	3 or 4	
register 16	memory word			87
	direct	31	4	
	register indirect	30	2	
	based or indexed	34	3 or 4	
	based & indexed (no displacement)	32 or 33	3 or 4	
	based & indexed (w/ displacement)	36 or 37	3 or 4	

Exercises 4.1

1. For each part of this problem, assume the "before" values when the given **mov** instruction is executed. Give the requested "after" values.

	Before	Instruction	After
(a)	BX: FF 75		
	CX: 01 A2	mov bx, cx	BX, CX
(b)	AX: 01 A2	mov ax, 100	AX
(c)	DX: FF 75		
	value DW -1	mov dx, value	DX, value
(d)	AX: 01 4B	mov ah, 0	AX
(e)	AL: 64	mov al, -1	AL
(f)	BX: 3A 4C		
	value DW ?	mov value, bx	BX, value

2. For each part of this problem, assume the "before" values when the given **xchg** instruction is executed. Give the requested "after" values.

	Before	Instruction	After
(a)	BX: FF 75		
	CX: 01 A2	xchg bx, cx	BX, CX
(b)	AX: 01 A2		
	temp DW -1	xchg temp, ax	AX, temp
(c)	DX: FF 75	xchg dl, dh	DX
(d)	AX: 01 4B		
	BX: 5C D9	xchg ah, bl	AX, BX

3. How many clock cycles and how many bytes are used by each of the instructions in the following pair?

```
start:   mov   ax,SEG data; load data segment number
         mov   ds,ax
```

4. How many clock cycles and how many bytes are used by each of the **mov** instructions in the example program (Figure 3.1), except for the two in problem 3?

5. Suppose that **number** references a word in the data segment of a program, and you wish to swap the contents of that word with the contents of the DX register. Two possible methods are

```
xchg   dx,number
```

and

```
mov     ax,dx
mov     dx,number
mov     number,ax
```

(a) Compare the total number of clock cycles and the total number of bytes required by each of these methods.

(b) What difference would it make if the BX register rather than the accumulator AX were used in the "three-move" method?

6. Note that **xchg** cannot swap two words in memory. Write a sequence of **mov** and/or **xchg** instructions to swap words stored in memory at **value1** and **value2**. Assume that any register 16 you want to use is available, and make your code as time efficient and compact as possible.

7. How many clock cycles and how many bytes are required for the following instruction?

```
mov     dx,[bx]          ; copy table entry
```

4.2

2's Complement Addition and Subtraction

The Intel 8088 microprocessor has **add** and **sub** instructions to perform addition and subtraction using byte or word-length operands. The operands can be interpreted as unsigned or 2's complement signed. It also has **inc** and **dec** instructions to increment (add 1 to) and decrement (subtract 1 from) a single operand, and a **neg** instruction that negates (takes the 2's complement of) a single operand.

One difference between the instructions covered in this section and the **mov** and **xchg** instructions of Section 4.1 is that **add, sub, inc, dec,** and **neg** instructions all update flags in the flag register. The AF, OF, PF, SF, and ZF flags are set according to the value of the result of the operation. For example, if the result is negative, then the sign flag SF will be set to one; if the result is zero, then the zero flag ZF will be set to one. The carry flag CF is also given a value by each of these instructions except **inc** and **dec**.

Some new notation will help to shorten the tables showing the allowable operands for these new instructions. The number of cycles it takes an instruction to execute when a memory operand is involved is always some constant (depending on the instruction) plus a number depending on the operand type. Recall that the memory operand type is called the effective address (EA). Similarly, the number of bytes of object code is a constant plus additional bytes depending on the effective address. Figure 4.3 lists the number of extra clock cycles and extra bytes for each effective address.

Figure 4.3 Effective Address/Extra Cycles and Bytes.

Effective Address	Additional Clock Cycles	Additional Operand Bytes
direct	6	2
register indirect	5	0
based or indexed with byte displacement	9	1
based or indexed with word displacement	9	2
based and indexed BP/DI or BX/SI, no displacement	7	0
based and indexed BP/SI or BX/DI, no displacement	8	0
based and indexed BP/DI or BX/SI, with byte displacement	11	1
based and indexed BP/SI or BX/DI, with word displacement	12	2

Each **add** instruction has the form

        add   destination, source

When executed, the 2's complement value at *source* is added to the 2's complement value at *destination* and the sum replaces the old value at *destination*. The **sub** instructions all have the form

        sub   destination, source

When a **sub** instruction is executed, the 2's complement value at *source* is subtracted from the 2's complement value at *destination* and the difference replaces the old value at *destination*. For subtraction, it is important to remember that the difference calculated is

        destination - source

or "operand 1 minus operand 2." With both **add** and **sub** instructions, the *source* (second) operand is unchanged. Here are some examples showing how these instructions function at execution time.

Example

Before	*Instruction Executed*	*After*
AX: 00 75		AX: 02 17
CX 01 A2	add ax,cx	CX: 01 A2
		SF: 0
		ZF: 0
AX: 00 75		AX: FE D3
CX: 01 A2	sub ax,cx	CX: 01 A2
		SF: 1
		ZF: 0
AX: 00 75		AX: 00 75
CX: 01 A2	sub cx,ax	CX: 01 2D
		SF: 0
		ZF: 0
BL: 4B	add bl,4	BL: 4F
		SF: 0
		ZF: 0
DX: FF 20		DX: 00 00
word at value: FF 20	sub dx, value	value: FF 20
		SF: 0
		ZF: 1

For each **add** there is a corresponding **sub** instruction with exactly the same operand types, number of clock cycles, and number of bytes of object code. It is therefore redundant to make separate tables for **add** and **sub** instructions. Figure 4.4 gives this information for both addition and subtraction instructions.

Figure 4.4 makes it easy to see that addition or subtraction operands are the fastest when both operands are in registers and the slowest when the destination operand is a word in memory. It is interesting to note that it is faster to add an operand in memory to the contents of a register than to add the value in a register to a memory operand; this is true since memory must be accessed twice in the latter case—once to get the first addend and once to store the sum. Many computers do not even have instructions for 2's complement arithmetic when the destination is a memory operand. Even with the 8088, it is not possible to have both of the operands in memory.

With **add** and **sub** instructions, the accumulator AX and its low-order half AL again have special instructions, this time when AX or AL is the destination and the source is immediate. These instructions are not any faster than the other immediate-to-register instructions but do take one less byte of object code.

The total number of clock cycles or object code bytes for instructions with "+" entries in Figure 4.4 can be calculated using the information in Figure 4.3.

Figure 4.4   add and sub Instructions.

Destination Operand	Source Operand	Clock Cycles	Number of Bytes	Opcode add	sub
register 8	immediate byte	4	3	80	80
register 16	immediate byte	4	3	83	83
register 16	immediate word	4	4	81	81
AL	immediate byte	4	2	04	2C
AX	immediate word	4	3	05	2D
memory byte	immediate byte	17 +	2 +	80	80
memory word	immediate byte	25 +	2 +	83	83
memory word	immediate word	25 +	3 +	81	81
register 8	register 8	3	2	02	2A
register 16	register 16	3	2	03	2B
register 8	memory byte	9 +	2 +	02	2A
register 16	memory word	13 +	2 +	03	2B
memory byte	register 8	16 +	2 +	00	28
memory word	register 16	24 +	2 +	01	29

For example, if **total** is a direct reference to a word in memory, then the operands of the instruction

```
    sub    total,cx
```

are described by the last line of Figure 4.4. Since the destination is a direct memory operand, Figure 4.3 says to add 6 to the number of clock cycles shown in Figure 4.4 and 2 to the number of bytes. Therefore this particular **sub** instruction requires 30 (24 + 6) clock cycles and 4 (2 + 2) bytes of object code.

Notice that an immediate source can be a single byte even when the destination is a word. Such an operand is extended to word size at run time for the addition or subtraction operation. A negative operand is extended with an FF byte to get the word-length value that corresponds to the original byte-length 2's complement number. A nonnegative operand is simply extended with a zero byte.

It may be a little surprising that some **add** and **sub** instructions have the same opcode. In such cases, one of the fields in the second byte of the instruction distinguishes between addition and subtraction.

The **inc** and **dec** instructions are special-purpose addition and subtraction instructions, always using 1 as an implied source. They have the forms

```
    inc    destination
```

and

```
    dec    destination
```

Like the **add** and **sub** instructions, these instructions are paired with respect to allowable operand types, clock cycles and bytes of object code. They are summarized together in Figure 4.5.

Figure 4.5 `inc` and `dec` Instructions.

Operand	Clock Cycles	Number of Bytes	Opcode inc	dec
register 8	3	2	FE	FE
register 16	2	1		
AX			40	48
CX			41	49
DX			42	4A
BX			43	4B
SP			44	4C
BP			45	4D
SI			46	4E
DI			47	4F
memory byte	15+	2+	FE	FE
memory word	23+	2+	FF	FF

The `inc` and `dec` instructions treat the value of the destination operand as an unsigned number. They affect the OF, SF, and ZF flags just like addition or subtraction of the value one, but they do not change the carry flag CF. Here are examples showing the functions of a few increment and decrement instructions.

Example

Before	Instruction Executed	After
CX: 01 A2	inc cx	CX: 01 A3 SF: 0 ZF: 0
AL: F5	dec al	AL: F4 SF: 1 ZF: 0
word at count: 00 09	inc count	count: 00 0A SF: 0 ZF: 0
BX: 00 01	dec bx	BX: 00 00 SF: 0 ZF: 1

The `inc` and `dec` instructions are especially useful for incrementing and decrementing counters. They are more efficient than the corresponding addition or subtraction instructions.

For example, the instructions

```
add     bx,1            ; increment loop counter
```

and

```
inc     bx              ; increment loop counter
```

are functionally equivalent, but the **add** instruction requires four clock cycles and three bytes (three bytes instead of four since the immediate operand will fit in one byte), while the **inc** instruction requires two clock cycles and one byte.

Similarly, for a byte-size **counter** stored in memory, the instructions

```
sub     counter,1       ; decrement loop counter
```

and

```
dec     counter         ; decrement loop counter
```

do the same job, but the **sub** instruction requires 23 clock cycles (17 + 6 for the direct operand) and four bytes (2 + 2), while the **dec** instruction requires 21 clock cycles (15 + 6) and four bytes (2 + 2).

In Figure 4.5, note the fast, single-byte **inc** instructions for word-size operands stored in registers. A register is the best place to keep a counter, if one can be reserved for this purpose.

A **neg** instruction negates, or finds the 2's complement of, its single operand. When a positive value is negated the result is negative; a negative value will become positive. Zero remains zero. Each **neg** instruction has the form

```
neg     destination
```

Figure 4.6 shows allowable operands for **neg** instructions.

Figure 4.6   **neg** Instruction.

Operand	Clock Cycles	Number of Bytes	Opcode
register 8	3	2	F6
register 16	3	2	F7
memory byte	16 +	2 +	F6
memory word	24 +	2 +	F7

Example

Here are four examples illustrating how the **neg** instruction operates. In each case the "after" value is the 2's complement of the "before" value.

Before	*Instruction Executed*	*After*
BX: 01 A2	**neg bx**	BX: FE 5E SF: 1 ZF: 0
DH: F5	**neg dh**	DH: 0B SF: 0 ZF: 0
word at flag: 00 01	**neg flag**	flag: FF FF SF: 1 ZF: 0
AX: 00 00	**neg ax**	AX: 00 00 SF: 0 ZF: 1

This section ends with an example of a complete, if unexciting, program which uses these new instructions. The program inputs values for three numbers, x, y and z, evaluates the expression

$$- (x + y - 2z + 1)$$

and displays the result. The design implemented is

> prompt for and input value for x;
> convert x from ASCII to 2's complement form;
> expression := x;
> prompt for and input value for y;
> convert y from ASCII to 2's complement form;
> add y to expression, giving $x + y$;
> prompt for and input value for z;
> convert z from ASCII to 2's complement form;
> calculate $2z$ (as $z + z$);
> subtract $2z$ from expression, giving $x + y - 2z$;
> add 1 to expression, giving $x + y - 2z + 1$;
> negate expression, giving $-(x + y - 2z + 1)$;
> convert the result from 2's complement to ASCII;
> display the result;

To write an assembly language program, one needs to plan how registers and memory will be used. In this program the values of *x*, *y*, and *z* are not needed after they are incorporated into the expression. Therefore they will not be stored in memory. A logical place to keep the expression value would be the accumulator AX since some operations are faster with it, but this choice is impossible since the **atoi** macro always uses AX as its destination. Similarly, the **inputs** macro puts the count of characters it gets into the CX register, eliminating this register as a choice for the partial expression values. That leaves the general registers BX and DX; this program will use DX. It is very easy to run out of registers when designing assembly language programs. Memory must often be used for values even though operations are much slower. Frequently values must be moved back and forth between registers and memory. Figure 4.7 shows the source program listing.

This program follows the same general pattern of the example in Figure 3.1. In the prompts, note the use of **cr,Lf,Lf** to skip to a new line and to leave an extra blank line; it is not necessary to put in a second **cr** since the cursor will already be at the beginning of the new line after one carriage return character is displayed. The value of 2*z* is found by adding *z* to itself; multiplication will be covered in the next section, but it is far easier and more efficient to compute 2*z* by addition. Finally, note that the comments in this program do not simply repeat the instruction mnemonics; they help the human reader figure out what is really going on.

Figure 4.8 illustrates a sample run of this program. As in previous examples, user input is underlined.

Figure 4.7 Program to Evaluate $-(x + y - 2z + 1)$.

```
; program to input values for x, y and z
; and evaluate the expression - (x + y - 2z + 1)

INCLUDE io.h

cr          EQU     0dh    ; carriage return character
Lf          EQU     0ah    ; linefeed character

stack       SEGMENT stack
            DW      100h DUP (?)
stack       ENDS

data        SEGMENT
prompt1     DB      'This program will evaluate the expression',cr,Lf,Lf
            DB      '    - (x + y - 2z + 1)',cr,Lf,Lf
            DB      'for your choice of integer values.',cr,Lf,Lf
            DB      'Enter value for x:  ',0
prompt2     DB      cr,Lf,'Enter value for y:  ',0
```

Figure 4.7 Continued.

```
prompt3      DB      cr,Lf,'Enter value for z:   ',0
value        DB      16 DUP (?)
answer       DB      cr,Lf,Lf,'The result is '
result       DB      6 DUP (?)
             DB      cr,Lf,0
data         ENDS

code         SEGMENT
             ASSUME cs:code,ds:data

start:       mov     ax,SEG data         ; load data segment number
             mov     ds,ax

prompt:      output prompt1              ; prompt for x
             inputs value,16             ; read ASCII characters
             atoi    value               ; convert to integer
             mov     dx,ax               ; x

             output prompt2              ; prompt for y
             inputs value,16             ; read ASCII characters
             atoi    value               ; convert to integer
             add     dx,ax               ; x + y

             output prompt3              ; prompt for z
             inputs value,16             ; read ASCII characters
             atoi    value               ; convert to integer
             add     ax,ax               ; 2z
             sub     dx,ax               ; x + y - 2z

             inc     dx                  ; x + y - 2z + 1
             neg     dx                  ; - (x + y - 2z + 1)

             itoa    result,dx           ; convert to ASCII characters

             output answer               ; output label and result

quit:        mov     al,0                ; return code 0
             mov     ah,4ch              ; DOS function to return
             int     21h                 ; interrupt for DOS services

code         ENDS
             END     start
```

Figure 4.8 Sample Run of Program.

```
This program will evaluate the expression

   - (x + y - 2z + 1)

for your choice of integer values.

Enter value for x:   6

Enter value for y:   -5

Enter value for z:   8


The result is      14
```

──────── **Exercises 4.2** ──

1. Assume that **value** references a word in memory. How many clock cycles for execution and how many bytes of object code are required for each of the following instructions?

(a)	add	ax,value	(b)	sub	value,ax
(c)	sub	ax,10	(d)	add	value,10
(e)	add	ax,[bx]	(f)	sub	[bx],ax
(g)	sub	dl,ch	(h)	add	bl,5
(i)	inc	bx	(j)	dec	al
(k)	dec	value	(l)	inc	BYTE PTR [si]
(m)	neg	ax	(n)	neg	bh
(o)	neg	value	(p)	neg	WORD PTR [bx]

2. For each part of this problem, assume the "before" values when the given instruction is executed. Give the requested "after" values.

	Before	Instruction	After
(a)	BX: FF 75 CX: 01 A2	add bx,cx	BX, CX, SF, ZF
(b)	BX: FF 75 CX: 01 A2	sub bx,cx	BX, CX, SF, ZF
(c)	BX: FF 75 CX: 01 A2	sub cx,bx	BX, CX, SF, ZF
(d)	DX: 01 4B	add dx,40h	DX, SF, ZF

	Before	*Instruction*	*After*
(e)	AH: 64	sub ah,100	AH, SF, ZF
(f)	AX: 0A 20 word at value: FF 20	add ax,value	word at value, AX, SF, ZF
(g)	AX: 0A 20 word at value: FF 20	sub value,ax	word at value, AX, SF, ZF
(h)	CX: 03 1A	inc cx	CX, SF, ZF
(i)	AH: 01	dec ah	AH, SF, ZF
(j)	word at count: 00 99	inc count	word at count, SF, ZF
(k)	word at count: 00 99	dec count	word at count, SF, ZF
(l)	BX: FF FF	neg bx	BX, SF, ZF
(m)	CL: 5F	neg cl	CL, SF, ZF
(n)	word at value: FB 3C	neg value	word at value, SF, ZF

Programming Exercises 4.2

For complete programs, prompts for input should make it clear what is to be entered, and output should be appropriately labeled.

1. Write a complete 8088 assembly language program to prompt for values of x, y and z and display the value of the expression

   $$x - 2y + 4z$$

2. Write a complete 8088 assembly language program to prompt for values of x, y and z and display the value of the expression

   $$2(-x + y - 1) + z$$

3. Write a complete 8088 assembly language program to prompt for the length and width of a rectangle and to display its perimeter

   $$(2 * \text{length} + 2 * \text{width})$$

4.3

Multiplication Instructions

The 8088 has two multiplication instructions. The `imul` instruction treats its operands as signed numbers; the sign of the product is determined by the usual rules for multiplying signed numbers. The `mul` instruction treats its operands as unsigned binary numbers; the product is also unsigned. Although each of these instructions is much slower than addition and subtraction instructions, the `mul` instruction is slightly faster than the `imul` instruction. If only nonnegative numbers are to be multiplied, `mul` should be chosen instead of `imul`.

The `imul` and `mul` instructions are very similar. Each has a single operand; the forms are

        imul   *source*

and

        mul   *source*

The *source* operand may be either a word or a byte in length; it is unchanged by the multiplication. The location of the other number to be multiplied is always the AL register half or the AX register, depending on the size of the *source* operand. If *source* has byte length, then it is multiplied by the byte in the AL register; the product is 16 bits long, taking the entire AX register. If *source* has word length, then it is multiplied by the word in the AX register; the product is 32 bits long, with its low-order 16 bits in the AX register and its high-order 16 bits in the DX register. In the case of byte multiplication, the original contents of AH and AL are replaced; for word multiplication, the original values in AX and DX are both wiped out.

At first glance, it may seem strange that the product is twice the length of its two factors. However, this also occurs in ordinary decimal multiplication; for example, when two four-digit numbers are multiplied, the product will be seven or eight digits long. Computers that have multiplication operations often put the product in double-length locations so that there is no danger that the destination location will be too small.

Much of the time arithmetic is done with word-size operands. When the word in AX is multiplied by some other word, the product is in DX and AX. Assuming that the product is a relatively small number, then the high-order part in DX can be ignored. The `mul` and `imul` instructions set the CF and OF flags to 1 if DX contains significant bits of the product; otherwise, they are cleared to 0. (After byte multiplication, these flags are set if AH contains significant bits.) These are the only meaningful flag values following multiplication operations; previously set values of AF, PF, SF, and ZF flags may be destroyed. In Chapter 5 (branching and looping), instructions that check flag values will be covered; it is possible to check that the DX register contents can be safely ignored. In general this book will only be concerned with multiplication for small numbers.

Figure 4.9 Multiplication Instructions.

Operand	Clock Cycles		Number of Bytes	Opcode
	imul	mul		
register 8	80–98	70–77	2	F6
register 16	128–154	118–133	2	F7
memory byte	86–104 +	76–83 +	2 +	F6
memory word	138–164 +	128–143 +	2 +	F7

Figure 4.9 summarizes the allowable operand types for `imul` and `mul` instructions. The only difference between the two instructions is the number of clock cycles required. Even the opcodes are the same; the second byte of the object code distinguishes between the two types of multiplication (and between other instructions, like `neg`, which share the same F6 and F7 opcodes).

Earlier, the discussion of the example program in Figure 4.7 stated that it was faster to calculate $2z$ by adding z to itself than by using a multiplication instruction. In that situation, z was in the AX register, so

```
add     ax,ax           ; compute 2z
```

did the job. This instruction requires three clock cycles and two bytes. To do the same task using multiplication, it seems natural to code

```
imul    2               ; illegal--immediate operand not allowed
```

However, this is not acceptable since no 8088 multiplication instruction allows an immediate source operand. Instead, one could code

```
mov     bx,2            ; multiplier
imul    bx              ; 2z
```

These instructions require four clock cycles and three bytes for the `mov` and 128–154 clock cycles and two bytes for the `imul`. The number of clock cycles for multiplication instructions is variable; the actual number depends on the operand values. In any case, the pair of instructions using multiplication requires at least 132 (4 + 128) clock cycles, 44 times the three clock cycles needed by the addition.

Example

Some examples will help show how the `mul` and `imul` instructions work.

Before	Instruction Executed	After
AX: 00 05		DX: 00 00
BX: 00 02	`mul    bx`	AX: 00 0A
		CF,OF: 0

Before	*Instruction Executed*	*After*
AL: 05		AX: 00 0A
byte at factor: 02	`imul factor`	CF,OF: 0

In these examples, the numbers 5 and 2 are multiplied to give 10 (A in hex). The CF and OF flags are zero since the DX register in the first example and the AH register half in the second example contain just leading zeros. The source operands, BX, and the byte at `factor` are unchanged in both cases.

Example

Now suppose that AX contains FF 15, which is -235_{10} when viewed as a 2's complement word, or 65,301 when viewed as an unsigned number. This number is multiplied by 3.

Before	*Instruction Executed*	*After*
AX: FF 15		DX: FF FF
word at value: 00 03	`imul   value`	AX: FD 3F
		CF,OF: 0
AX: FF 15		DX: 00 02
DX: 00 03	`mul   dx`	AX: FD 3F
		CF,OF: 1

With signed multiplication (`imul`), the result is the negative number FF FF FD 3F (-705_{10}); CF and OF are 0 since the DX register is full of 1 bits, which simply extend the sign bit in the AX register. With unsigned multiplication (`mul`), the result is the unsigned number 00 02 FD 3F ($195,903_{10}$); CF and OF are set to 1 since the 2 in the DX register is significant.

Example

One more example may help to clarify the difference between significant and insignificant high-order bits.

Before	*Instruction Executed*	*After*
AL: 6E		AX: 04 4C
CH: 0A	`imul   ch`	CF,OF: 1

Before	Instruction Executed	After
AX: 00 6E		DX: 00 00
CX: 00 0A	imul cx	AX: 04 4C
		CF,OF: 0

In both examples 6E (110_{10}) and A (10_{10}) are multiplied. When the factors are bytes, the product will not fit in a single byte, but has significant bits in AH, causing CF and OF to be set to 1. When the factors are words, the significant bits of the product still fit into a word, so CF and OF are set to 0.

This section concludes with an example of a program that will input the length and width of a rectangle, and calculate its area (length * width). (Admittedly, this is a job much better suited for a hand calculator than for a computer program in assembly language or any other language.) Figure 4.10 shows the source code for the program. Note that the program uses `mul` rather than `imul` for finding the product—lengths and widths are positive numbers. Interesting errors occur in this program if a negative length or width is entered, or if a large width and length (say 200 and 300) are entered. (Why?) Such errors are unfortunately common in software.

Figure 4.10 Program to Find the Area of a Rectangle.

```
; program to find the area of a rectangle

INCLUDE io.h

cr              EQU     0dh    ; carriage return character
Lf              EQU     0ah    ; linefeed character

stack           SEGMENT stack
                DW      100h DUP (?)
stack           ENDS

data            SEGMENT
prompt1         DB      'This program will find the area of a rectangle',cr,Lf,Lf
                DB      'Width of rectangle?     ',0
prompt2         DB      cr,Lf,'Length of rectangle?   ',0
value           DB      16 DUP (?)
answer          DB      cr,Lf,Lf,'The area of the rectangle is '
area            DB      6 DUP (?)
                DB      cr,Lf,0
data            ENDS

code            SEGMENT
                ASSUME cs:code,ds:data

start:          mov     ax,SEG data       ; load data segment number
                mov     ds,ax
```

Figure 4.10 Continued.

```
prompt:      output prompt1          ; prompt for width
             inputs value,16         ; read ASCII characters
             atoi   value            ; convert to integer
             mov    bx,ax            ; width

             output prompt2          ; prompt for length
             inputs value,16         ; read ASCII characters
             atoi   value            ; convert to integer
             mul    bx               ; length * width

             itoa   area,ax          ; convert to ASCII characters

             output answer           ; output label and result

quit:        mov    al,0             ; return code 0
             mov    ah,4ch           ; DOS function to return
             int    21h              ; interrupt for DOS services

code         ENDS
             END    start
```

Exercises 4.3

1. For each part of this problem, assume the "before" values when the given instruction is executed. Give the requested "after" values.

	Before	Instruction	After
(a)	AX: 00 17		
	CX: 00 B2	imul cx	AX, DX, CF, OF
(b)	AX: FF E4		
	BX: 04 C2	imul bx	AX, DX, CF, OF
(c)	AX: FF E4		
	BX: 04 C2	mul bx	AX, DX, CF, OF
(d)	AX: FF E4		
	word at value: FF 3A	imul value	AX, DX, CF, OF
(e)	AX: FF E4		
	word at value: FF 3A	mul value	AX, DX, CF, OF
(f)	AX: FF FF	imul ax	AX, DX, CF, OF

	Before		*Instruction*	*After*
(g)	AX:	FF FF	mul ax	AX, DX, CF, OF
(h)	AL:	0F		
	BH:	4C	imul bh	AX, CF, OF
(i)	AL:	0F		
	BH:	4C	mul bh	AX, CF, OF
(j)	AL:	F0		
	BH:	C4	imul bh	AX, CF, OF
(k)	AL:	F0		
	BH:	C4	mul bh	AX, CF, OF

2. Suppose that the value for x is in the AX register and you need the value of $5x$. Compare the number of clock cycles for execution and the number of bytes of object code for each of the following schemes.

```
mov    bx,ax          ; copy value of x
add    ax,ax          ; x + x gives 2x
add    ax,ax          ; 2x + 2x gives 4x
add    ax,bx          ; 4x + x gives 5x
```

and

```
mov    bx,5           ; multiplier
imul   bx             ; 5x
```

3. Suppose you need to evaluate the polynomial

$$p(x) = 5x^3 - 7x^2 + 3x - 10$$

for some value of x. If this is done in the obvious way, as

$$5 * x* x * x - 7 * x * x + 3 * x - 10$$

there are six multiplications and three additions/subtractions. An equivalent form, based on Horner's scheme for evaluation of polynomials, is

$$(((5 * x - 7) * x + 3) * x - 10$$

This has only three multiplications.

Suppose that the value of x is in the AX register.

(a) Write 8088 assembly language statements that will evaluate $p(x)$ the "obvious" way, putting the result in AX.

(b) Write 8088 assembly language statements that will evaluate $p(x)$ using Horner's scheme, again putting the result in AX.

(c) Compare the number of clock cycles for execution and the number of bytes of object code required for the code fragments in (a) and in (b) above.

4. The 8088 has distinct instructions for multiplication of signed and unsigned numbers. It does not have separate instructions for addition of signed and unsigned numbers. Why are different instructions needed for multiplication but not for addition?

Programming Exercises 4.3

1. Write a complete 8088 assembly language program to prompt for the length, width, and height of a box and to display its volume (length * width * height).

2. Write a complete 8088 assembly language program to prompt for the length, width and height of a box and to display its surface area 2 * (length * width + length * height + width * height).

4.4

Division Instructions

The Intel 8088 instructions for division parallel those for multiplication; idiv is for division of signed 2's-complement integers and div is for division of unsigned integers. Recall that the multiplication instructions start with a multiplier and multiplicand and produce a double-length product. Division instructions start with a double-length dividend and a single-length divisor, and produce a single-length quotient and a single-length remainder. The 8088 has instructions cwd and cbw, which do the task of producing a double-length dividend prior to signed division.

The division instructions have formats

        idiv   source

and

        div   source

The *source* operand identifies the divisor. If *source* is byte length, then the double-length dividend is word size and is assumed to be in the AX register. If *source* is word length, then the dividend is a doubleword and is assumed to have its low-order 16 bits in the AX register and its high-order 16 bits in the DX register.

The source operand (divisor) is not changed by a division instruction. After a doubleword in AX and DX is divided by a word-length divisor, the quotient will be in the AX register and the remainder will be in the DX register. After a word in AX is divided by a byte-length divisor, the quotient will be in the AL register half and the remainder will be in the AH register half. For all division operations,

Figure 4.11 Operands and Results for 8088 Division Instructions.

Word length dividend divided by byte-length divisor

Doubleword length dividend divided by word-length divisor

the dividend, divisor, quotient and remainder must satisfy the equation

$$\text{dividend} = \text{quotient} * \text{divisor} + \text{remainder}$$

For unsigned **div** operations, the dividend, divisor, quotient and remainder are all treated as nonnegative numbers. For signed **idiv** operations, the sign of the quotient is determined by the signs of the dividend and divisor using the ordinary rules of signs; the sign of the remainder is always the same as the sign of the dividend.

The diagrams in Figure 4.11 summarize the locations of the dividend, divisor, quotient, and remainder for 8088 division instructions.

The division instructions do not set flags to any useful values. They may destroy previously set values of AF, CF, OF, PF, SF, and ZF flags.

Example

Some examples show how the division instructions work.

Before	*Instruction Executed*	*After*
DX: 00 00		
AX: 00 64		DX: 00 09
CX: 00 0D	idiv cx	AX: 00 07

Before	Instruction Executed	After
AX: 00 64		
byte at divisor: 0D	`div    divisor`	AX: 09 07

In these examples, the decimal number 100 is divided by 13. Since

$$100 = 7 * 13 + 9$$

the quotient is 7 and the remainder is 9. For the word-length divisor, the quotient is in AX and the remainder is in DX. For the byte-length divisor, the quotient is in AL and the remainder is in AH.

For operations where the dividend or divisor is negative, equations analogous to the one above are

$$100 = (-7) * (-13) + 9$$

$$-100 = (-7) * 13 + (-9)$$

$$-100 = 7 * (-13) + (-9)$$

Examples with word-size divisors that reflect these equations are

Before	Instruction Executed	After
DX: 00 00		
AX: 00 64		DX: 00 09
CX: FF F3	`idiv   cx`	AX: FF F9
DX: FF FF		
AX: FF 9C		DX: FF F7
CX: 00 0D	`idiv   cx`	AX: FF F9
DX: FF FF		
AX: FF 9C		DX: FF F7
CX: FF F3	`idiv   cx`	AX: 00 07

Notice that when the dividend is –100, it is represented as the 32-bit number FF FF FF 9C in the DX and AX registers.

Finally, here are two examples to help illustrate the difference between signed and unsigned division.

Before	Instruction Executed	After
AX: FE 01		
BL: E0	`idiv   bl`	AX: E1 0F
AX: FE 01		
BL: FF	`div    bl`	AX: 00 FF

Figure 4.12 Division Instructions.

Operand	Clock Cycles		Number of Bytes	Opcode
	`idiv`	`div`		
register 8	101–112	80–90	2	F6
register 16	165–184	144–162	2	F7
memory byte	107–118 +	86–96 +	2 +	F6
memory word	175–194 +	154–172 +	2 +	F7

With the signed division, –511 is divided by –32, giving a quotient of 15 and a remainder of –31. With the unsigned division, 65025 is divided by 255, giving a quotient of 255 and a remainder of 0.

With multiplication, the double-length destination guarantees that the product will fit in the destination location—nothing can go wrong during a multiplication operation. There can be errors during division. One obvious cause is an attempt to divide by zero. A less obvious reason is a quotient that is too large to fit in the single-length destination; if, say, 00 02 22 22 is divided by 2; the quotient 1 11 11 is too large to fit in the AX register. If an error occurs during the division operation, the 8088 generates a hardware interrupt, a type of subroutine call.[*] The subroutine, or interrupt handler, that services this interrupt differs from system to system and can even be altered by the user. The standard procedure on the author's 8088 system causes the letter D to be displayed and program execution to be aborted; the DOS prompt appears on the monitor below the D. The 8088 leaves the AX and DX registers undefined following a division error.

Figure 4.12 lists the allowable operand types for `idiv` and `div` instructions. Notice that `div` operations are faster than `idiv` operations, but both kinds of division operations are even slower than multiplication instructions.

When arithmetic is being done with operands of a certain length, the dividend must be converted to double length before a division operation is executed. For unsigned division, a word-size dividend must be converted to doubleword size with leading zero bits in the DX register. This can be accomplished many ways, two of which are

```
mov    dx, 0
```

and

```
sub    dx, dx
```

Similarly a byte-size dividend must be converted to word-size with leading zeros in the AH register. The instructions

```
mov    ah, 0
```

and

```
sub    ah, ah
```

---

[*] The words *trap* and *exception* are sometimes used to describe this situation. Intel uses the word *interrupt*.

Figure 4.13   cbw and cwd Instructions.

Instruction	Clock Cycles	Bytes	Opcode
cbw	2	1	98
cwd	5	1	99

can be used for this purpose.

The situation is more complicated for signed division. A positive dividend must be extended with leading 0 bits, but a negative dividend must be extended with leading 1 bits. The 8088 has two instructions for this task. The **cbw** and **cwd** instructions are different from the instructions covered before in that these instructions have no operands. The **cbw** instruction always has AL as its source and AX as its destination, whereas **cwd** always has AX as its source and DX and AX as its destination. The AX register is not changed, but conceptually the **cwd** starts with a 16-bit number in AX and produces a 32-bit number in DX and AX. These instructions are summarized together in Figure 4.13.

The **cbw** (convert byte to word) instruction extends the 2's complement number in the AL register half to word length in AX. The **cwd** (convert word to double) instruction extends the word in AX to a doubleword in DX and AX. Each instruction copies the sign bit of the original number to each bit of the high-order half of the result. Some examples are

Example

Before	Instruction Executed	After
AX: 07 0D	cwd	DX: 00 00 AX: 07 0D
AX: FA 13	cwd	DX: FF FF AX: FA 13
AL: 53	cbw	AX: 00 53
AL: C6	cbw	AX: FF C6

This section concludes with another simple program, this one to convert Celsius (centigrade) temperatures to Fahrenheit. Figure 4.14 gives the source code. The formula implemented is

$$F = (9/5) * C + 32$$

where F is the Fahrenheit temperature and C is the Celsius temperature. Since the arithmetic instructions covered so far perform only integer arithmetic, the program gives the integer to which the fractional answer would round. It is important to multiply 9 and C before dividing by 5: the integer quotient 9/5 would be simply 1. Dividing C by 5 before multiplying by 9 produces larger

Figure 4.14 Convert Celsius Temperature to Fahrenheit.

```
; program to convert Celsius temperature to Fahrenheit
; uses formula  F = (9/5)*C + 32

INCLUDE io.h

cr            EQU    0dh    ; carriage return character
Lf            EQU    0ah    ; linefeed character

stack         SEGMENT stack
              DW     100h DUP (?)
stack         ENDS

data          SEGMENT
prompt1       DB     cr,Lf,'This program will convert a Celsius '
              DB     'temperature to the Fahrenheit scale',cr,Lf,Lf
              DB     'Enter Celsius temperature:  ',0
value         DB     10 DUP (?)
answer        DB     cr,Lf,Lf,'The temperature is'
temperature   DB     6 DUP (?)
              DB     '   Fahrenheit',cr,Lf,0
data          ENDS

code          SEGMENT
              ASSUME cs:code,ds:data

start:        mov    ax,SEG data     ; load data segment number
              mov    ds,ax

prompt:       output prompt1         ; prompt for Celsius temperature
              inputs value,10        ; read ASCII characters
              atoi   value           ; convert to integer

              mov    bx,9            ; multiplier
              imul   bx              ; C*9
              add    ax,2            ; rounding factor for division
              mov    bx,5            ; divisor
              cwd                    ; prepare for division
              idiv   bx              ; C*9/5
              add    ax,32           ; C*9/5 + 32

              itoa   temperature,ax  ; convert to ASCII characters

              output answer          ; output label and result

quit:         mov    al,0            ; return code 0
              mov    ah,4ch          ; DOS function to return
              int    21h             ; interrupt for DOS services

code          ENDS
              END    start
```

errors than if the multiplication is done first. (Why?) To get a rounded answer, half the divisor is added to the dividend before dividing. Since the divisor in this formula is 5, the number 2 is added for rounding. Notice that the cwd instruction comes after the rounding factor is added. Sometimes following a multiplication, the cwd can be omitted since the product gives a double-word number in DX and AX. However, in this program the rounding factor is added only to AX; the number in AX may change sign when this addition is done, requiring a new sign extension.

Exercises 4.4

1. For each part of this problem, assume the "before" values when the given instruction is executed. Give the requested "after" values. Some of these instructions will cause division errors; identify such instructions.

Before	Instruction	After
(a) DX: 00 00		
AX: 00 9A		
BX: 00 0F	idiv bx	DX, AX
(b) AX: FF 75		
byte at count: FC	idiv count	AX
(c) AX: FF 75		
byte at count: FC	div count	AX
(d) DX: FF FF		
AX: FF 9A		
CX: 00 00	idiv cx	DX, AX
(e) DX: FF FF		
AX: FF 9A		
CX: FF C7	idiv cx	DX, AX
(f) DX: 00 00		
AX: 05 9A		
CX: FF C7	idiv cx	DX, AX
(g) DX: 00 00		
AX: 05 9A		
CX: 00 00	idiv cx	DX, AX

2. This section mentioned two methods of zeroing DX prior to unsigned division, using

```
mov dx, 0
```

or

```
sub dx, dx
```

Which instruction would give more compact code? Which instruction would execute in fewer clock cycles?

3. The Celsius-to-Fahrenheit temperature conversion program (Figure 4.14) works for Celsius temperatures that have fairly large magnitude and are either positive or negative. Suppose that you limit the Celsius temperature to the range 0 degrees to 100 degrees, yielding Fahrenheit temperatures from 32 degrees to 212 degrees. How can the program be modified to take advantage of these limited numeric ranges?

Programming Exercises 4.4

---

1. The formula for converting a Fahrenheit to a Celsius temperature is

   $$C = (5/9) * (F - 32)$$

   Write a complete 8088 assembly language program to prompt for a Fahrenheit temperature and display the corresponding Celsius temperature.

2. Write a complete 8088 assembly language program to prompt for four grades, and then display the sum and the average (sum/4) of the grades.

3. Write a complete 8088 assembly language program to prompt for four grades. Suppose that the last grade is a final exam grade, which counts twice as much as any of the other three. Display the sum (including the last grade twice) and the average (sum/5).

4. Write a complete 8088 assembly language program to prompt for four pairs of grades and weighting factors. Each weighting factor indicates how many times the corresponding grade is to be counted in the sum. The weighted sum is

   weighted_sum = grade_1 * weight_1
   + grade_2 * weight_2
   + grade_3 * weight_3
   + grade_4 * weight_4

   and the sum of the weights is

   sum_of_weights = weight_1 + weight_2 + weight_3 + weight_4

   Display the weighted sum, the sum of the weights, and the weighted average (weighted_sum/sum_of_weights).

A sample run might look like

```
grade 1? 88
weight 1? 1

grade 2? 77
weight 2? 2

grade 3? 94
weight 3? 1

grade 4? 85
weight 4? 3

weighted sum: 591
sum of weights: 7
weighted average:  84
```

5. Write a complete 8088 assembly language program to prompt for four grades, and then display the sum and the average (sum/4) of the grades in ddd.dd format.

6. Write a short program that causes a division by zero, to discover how the interrupt handler in your 8088 system responds.

4.5

2's Complement Addition and Subtraction with Larger Numbers

The **add** and **sub** instructions covered in Section 4.2 work with byte-length or word-length operands. The range of values that can be stored in a word is −32,768 to 32,767, but it is sometimes necessary to do arithmetic with larger numbers. More powerful microprocessors have instructions to do arithmetic with 2's complement numbers that are 32-bits long or even longer. With the 8088 such large numbers can be added or subtracted 16 bits at a time.

The idea behind adding large numbers is to start with the low-order 16 bits from each number and add them using an ordinary **add** instruction. This operation sets the carry flag CF, to 1 if there is a carry out of the high-order bit and to 0 otherwise. Now the next 16 bits are added using a special addition instruction **adc** (add with carry). The two 16-bit numbers are added as usual, but if CF is set to 1, then 1 is added to their sum before it is sent to the destination location. The **adc** instruction also sets CF, so this process can be continued for as many groups of 16 bits as are needed.

The **adc** instructions are identical to corresponding **add** instructions except that the extra 1 is added if CF is set to 1. For subtraction, **sbb** (subtract with

Figure 4.15 adc and sbb Instructions.

Destination Operand	Source Operand	Clock Cycles	Number of Bytes	Opcode adc	Opcode sbb
register 8	immediate byte	4	3	80	80
register 16	immediate word	4	3 or 4	81	81
AL	immediate byte	4	2	14	2C
AX	immediate word	4	3	15	2D
memory byte	immediate byte	17 +	2 +	80	80
memory word	immediate byte	25 +	2 +	83	83
memory word	immediate word	25 +	3 +	81	81
register 8	register 8	3	21	2	2A
register 16	register 16	3	21	3	2B
register 8	memory byte	9 +	2 +	12	2A
register 16	memory word	13 +	2 +	13	2B
memory byte	register 8	16 +	2 +	10	28
memory word	register 16	24 +	2 +	11	29

borrow) instructions function like **sub** instructions except that if CF is set to 1 an extra 1 is subtracted from the difference. Large numbers can be subtracted 16 bits at a time, working right to left. Figure 4.15 lists the allowable operand types for **adc** and **sbb** instructions. This table is identical to Figure 4.4 except for a few opcodes.

Suppose two 32-bit numbers are to be added or subtracted. The data segment could contain

```
nbr1_hi    DW    ?    ; high-order 16 bits of nbr1
nbr1_lo    DW    ?    ; low-order 16 bits of nbr1
nbr2_hi    DW    ?    ; high-order 16 bits of nbr2
nbr2_lo    DW    ?    ; low-order 16 bits of nbr2
```

reserving two words for each number. The following code fragment adds **nbr2** to **nbr1**, storing the sum at the words reserved for **nbr1**.

```
mov  ax,nbr1_lo      ; low-order 16 bits of nbr1
add  ax,nbr2_lo      ; add low-order 16 bits of nbr2
mov  nbr1_lo,ax      ; sum to destination
mov  ax,nbr1_hi      ; high-order 16 bits of nbr1
adc  ax,nbr2_hi      ; add high-order 16 bits of nbr2
mov  nbr1_hi,ax      ; sum to destination
```

One thing which makes this code work is that the **mov** instructions that come between the **add** and **adc** instructions do not alter the carry flag. If an intervening instruction did change CF, then the sum would be incorrect.

To apply similar techniques to longer numbers, often a loop of identical instructions is used. Even the first addition can be done using **adc** if CF is known

Figure 4.16 Control of Carry Flag CF.

Instruction	Operation	Clock Cycles	Number of Bytes	Opcode
clc	clear carry flag (CF := 0)	2	1	F8
stc	set carry flag (CF := 1)	2	1	F9
cmc	complement carry flag if CF = 0 then CF := 1 else CF := 0)	2	1	F5

to be 0 before the loop begins. The 8088 has three instructions that let the programmer manipulate the carry flag. They are summarized in Figure 4.16.

Multiplication and division with longer 2's complement numbers are even more involved than addition and subtraction. Often techniques for adding and subtracting longer numbers are used to implement algorithms that are similar to grade-school multiplication and division procedures for decimal numbers.

If one really needs to use longer 2's complement numbers, it takes more than a set of arithmetic procedures. Also needed are procedures like itoa and atoi in order to convert long numbers both to and from ASCII character format.

Exercises 4.5

1. Suppose that two 64-bit 2's complement numbers are to be added.

   (a) Show how storage for three such numbers can be reserved in the data segment of a program.

   (b) Give a fragment of 8088 code that will add the second number to the first, storing the sum at the locations reserved for the first number.

   (c) Give a fragment of 8088 code that will add the second number to the first, storing the sum at the locations reserved for the third number.

2. Suppose that two 32-bit 2's complement numbers are stored as shown in the example in this section. Give a fragment of 8088 code that will subtract nbr2 from nbr1, storing the difference at the locations reserved for nbr1.

3. For each part of this problem, assume the "before" values when the given instruction is executed. Give the requested "after" values.

	Before	Instruction	After
(a)	AX: 03 7D CX: 01 A2 CF: 0	adc ax,cx	AX, CF
(b)	AX: 03 7D CX: 01 A2 CF: 1	adc ax,cx	AX, CF
(c)	AX: FF 49 CX: 03 68 CF: 0	adc ax,cx	AX, CF
(d)	AX: FF 49 CX: 03 68 CF: 1	adc ax,cx	AX, CF
(e)	AX: 03 7D CX: 01 A2 CF: 0	sbb ax,cx	AX, CF
(f)	AX: 01 A2 CX: 03 7D CF: 1	sbb ax,cx	AX, CF

4.6

Chapter Summary

The Intel 8088 mov instruction is used to copy data from one location to another. All but a few combinations of source and destination locations are allowed. The xchg instruction swaps the data stored at two locations.

The 8088 has a full set of instructions for arithmetic with byte-length and word-length integers. The add and sub instructions perform addition and subtraction; inc and dec add and subtract 1, respectively. The neg instruction negates its operand.

There are two multiplication and two division instructions. The imul and idiv instructions assume that their operands are signed 2's complement numbers; mul and div assume that their operands are unsigned. A multiplication instruction starts with single-length operands and produces a double-length product. A division instruction starts with a double-length dividend and single-length divisor; the outcome is a single-length quotient and a single-length remainder. The cbw and cwd instructions aid in producing a double-length dividend before signed division. No error can occur during multiplication; an error during division produces a hardware interrupt, which invokes a procedure to handle the error.

Instructions that have operands in registers are faster than those that reference memory locations. Multiplication and division instructions are much slower than addition and subtraction instructions.

For operands that are not byte length or word length, the **adc** and **sbb** instructions make it possible to add longer numbers a portion at a time, incorporating a carry or borrow from one portion into the addition or subtraction of the next part to the left. The carry or borrow is recorded in the carry flag CF; the 8088 has **clc**, **stc,** and **cmc** instructions to enable the programmer to clear, set, and complement the carry flag when necessary.

CHAPTER 5

Branching and Looping

Computers derive much of their power from their ability to selectively execute code and from the speed at which they execute repetitive algorithms. Programs in high-level languages like Pascal use **if-then**, **if-then-else,** and **case** structures to selectively execute code and, to repetitively execute code, loop structures such as **while** loops, **repeat-until** loops, and **for** loops. A **goto** statement is available in Pascal but is rarely used. Somewhat more primitive languages (like older versions of BASIC) depend on fairly simple **if** statements and an abundance of **goto** statements for both selective execution and to write program loops. The BASIC language does have a **for** loop structure to make the programmer's job a little easier.

The 8088 assembly language programmer's job is similar to the BASIC programmer's job. The 8088 microprocessor can execute some instructions that are roughly comparable to **for** statements, but most branching and looping is done with 8088 statements, which are similar to, but even more primitive than, simple **if** and **goto** statements. It takes multiple 8088 statements to do the job of a single BASIC **if** statement or an **if-then-else** structure in BASIC or some other language. This chapter tells how to implement **if** and **goto** statements in 8088 assembly language, as well as how to realize loop structures such as **while**, **until**, and **for** loops.

——— 5.1 ———————————————————————————————

Unconditional Jumps

The 8088 `jmp` (jump) instruction corresponds to `goto` in Pascal or BASIC. As coded in assembly language, it usually has the form

```
jmp statement_label
```

where *statement_label* corresponds to the name field of some other assembly language statement. Recall that the name field is followed by a colon (`:`) when used to label an executable statement. The colon is *not* used in the `jmp` statement itself. For example, if there were alternative conditions under which a program should be terminated, the code might contain a jump to the executable statement indicated by `quit:`.

```
            jmp     quit        ; exit from program
             .
             .
             .
quit:       mov     al,0        ; return code 0
             .
             .
```

Figure 5.1 shows a complete example, a program that will repeatedly accept input numbers, and after each number is entered, display the count of the numbers so far, the cumulative sum, and the average. The program implements the following pseudocode design.

```
display instructions;
sum := 0;
count := 0;
forever loop
     prompt for number;
     input ASCII characters for number;
     convert number to 2's complement form;
     add number to sum;
     add 1 to count;
     convert count to ASCII;
     display label and count;
     convert sum to ASCII;
     display label and sum;
     average := sum / count;
     display label and average;
end loop;
```

Figure 5.1 Program with **forever** Loop.

```
; program to input numbers and display running average and sum

INCLUDE io.h

cr              EQU     0dh     ; carriage return character
Lf              EQU     0ah     ; linefeed character

stack           SEGMENT stack
                DW      100h DUP (?)
stack           ENDS

data            SEGMENT
sum             DW      ?
explain         DB      cr,Lf,'As you input numbers one at a time, this',cr,Lf
                DB      'program will report the count of numbers so far,',cr,Lf
                DB      'the sum so far, and the average.',cr,Lf,Lf,0
prompt          DB      'number?  ',0
number          DB      16 DUP (?)
count_lbl       DB      cr,Lf,'count',0
sum_lbl         DB      '        sum',0
avg_lbl         DB      '        average',0
value           DB      6 DUP (?)
                DB      0
next_prompt     DB      cr,Lf,Lf,Lf,'next ',0
data            ENDS

code            SEGMENT
                ASSUME cs:code,ds:data

start:          mov     ax,SEG data     ; load data segment number
                mov     ds,ax
                output  explain         ; initial instructions
                mov     sum,0           ; sum := 0
                mov     bx,0            ; count := 0

forever:        output  prompt          ; prompt for number
                inputs  number,16       ; read ASCII characters
                atoi    number          ; convert to integer

                add     sum,ax          ; add number to sum
                inc     bx              ; add 1 to count

                itoa    value,bx        ; convert count to ASCII
                output  count_lbl       ; display label for count
                output  value           ; display count
```

Figure 5.1 Continued.

```
            itoa    value,sum          ; convert sum to ASCII
            output  sum_lbl            ; display label for sum
            output  value              ; display sum

            mov     ax,sum             ; get sum
            cwd                        ; extend sum to 32 bits
            idiv    bx                 ; sum / count
            itoa    value,ax           ; convert average to ASCII
            output  avg_lbl            ; display label for average
            output  value              ; output average

            output  next_prompt        ; skip down, start next prompt
            jmp     forever            ; repeat

; the following code cannot be reached for execution

quit:       mov     al,0               ; return code 0
            mov     ah,4ch             ; DOS function to return
            int     21h                ; interrupt for DOS services

code        ENDS
            END     start
```

This program must store values for count and sum, and all registers except BX are used by the input/output macros and/or the division instruction. The value of count is kept in BX, and sum is stored in a word reserved in the data segment. Note that **sum** could have been initialized to zero by the **DW** directive instead of by the **mov** statement; as implemented, the code is more consistent with the design, but is slightly wasteful of time and space since **sum** only needs to be initialized once.

This program has several faults. One slight shortcoming is that it does not round the average. The major fault, however, is that it contains a **forever** loop, one with no way to get out. In fact, the usual termination code at the end cannot be reached since the **jmp** immediately before **quit:** transfers control away from it, and no other instruction transfers control to it. Fortunately there is a way to stop this program without turning off or resetting the computer. If either Control-C or Control-Break is pressed when the prompt for a number appears, ^C will be displayed, the program will be aborted, and the DOS prompt will appear. This works because the **inputs** macro uses a DOS service for input, and this DOS function gives special treatment to Control-C or Control-Break. Figure 5.2 shows a sample run of this program.

The one **jmp** in the program in Figure 5.1 transfers control to a point that precedes the **jmp** statement itself. This is called a **backward reference**. On

Figure 5.2 Sample Run of Program with **forever** Loop.

```
As you input numbers one at a time, this
program will report the count of numbers so far,
the sum so far, and the average.

number?  10

count    1        sum    10        average    10


next number?  20

count    2        sum    30        average    15


next number?  30

count    3        sum    60        average    20


next number?  40

count    4        sum    100       average    25


next number?  ^C

A>
```

the other hand, the example

```
            jmp     quit              ; exit from program
                     .
                     .
    quit:   mov     al,0              ; return code 0
                     .
                     .
```

illustrates a **forward reference**. Backward references cause no difficulty when the programmer is using the Microsoft Macro Assembler MASM, but forward references can sometimes benefit from the programmer's special attention, for reasons that will be explained shortly.

There are actually several 8088 **jmp** instructions. All the formats are summarized in Figure 5.3; the first two are the most commonly used.

The intra-segment forms are generated when the destination is a statement within the current code segment, the most common situation. An inter-segment jump to a statement in another code segment is rarely required. The indirect

Figure 5.3 jmp Instructions.

Type	Clock Cycles	Bytes	Opcode
intra-segment relative	15	3	E9
intra-segment relative short	15	2	EB
intra-segment indirect	11 to 18+	2–4	FF
inter-segment direct	15	5	EA
inter-segment indirect	24+	2–4	FF

forms obtain the displacement of the target statement from either a register or from a word in memory. Inter-segment and indirect jumps will not be used in this book.

The intra-segment relative forms are by far the most common. Each of these jump instructions contains the displacement of the target from the jump statement itself. This displacement is added to the offset of the next instruction to find the offset of the target. For the **short jump**, the short version of the intra-segment relative jump instruction, only a single byte of displacement is stored; this is changed to a word by extending the sign bit before the addition. In either case, the resulting 16-bit sum represents an offset within the current code segment.

The 8-bit displacement in an intra-segment relative short jump can serve for a target statement up to 128 bytes before or 127 bytes after the jmp instruction. This displacement is measured from the byte following the object code of the jmp itself. With a backward reference, MASM can tell how far away the target is, and it uses a short displacement if possible. With a forward reference, MASM does not know the displacement of the target instruction when a decision must be made about how much space to allow for the jmp so it leaves room for a 16-bit displacement. If it only needs a single byte, it replaces the extra byte by a nop (no operation) instruction. The nop instruction has opcode 90, uses one byte and does nothing, but it takes three clock cycles to execute. Since it follows a jmp instruction in this situation, it is not executed.

One often codes a forward reference to a target that is clearly going to be within just a few statements. In such a case, MASM can be told to use a short displacement by using the operand **SHORT** with the statement label. This saves one byte of object code. An example is

```
jmp     SHORT quit
```

There are other MASM operands that can be used with statement labels in jump statements, but they are not used in this book.

1. Below are two very short programs that will actually assemble, link (the linker will give a warning message), and run, but do nothing useful. Assemble both programs, and compare their listing files.

```
; very short program 1

code        SEGMENT
            ASSUME cs:code

start:      jmp     quit              ; quit
            mov     ax,bx             ; does nothing useful

quit:       mov     al,0              ; return code 0
            mov     ah,4ch            ; DOS function to return
            int     21h               ; interrupt for DOS services

code        ENDS
            END     start


; very short program 2

code        SEGMENT
            ASSUME cs:code

start:      jmp     SHORT quit        ; quit
            mov     ax,bx             ; does nothing useful

quit:       mov     al,0              ; return code 0
            mov     ah,4ch            ; DOS function to return
            int     21h               ; interrupt for DOS services

code        ENDS
            END     start
```

2. If the statement

   hard_loop: jmp   hard_loop

   is executed, it continues to execute forever. What is the object code for this statement?

Programming Exercise 5.1
---

1. Modify the program in Figure 5.1 so that the prompt rather than the response to it counts the numbers being entered. That is, the sample run in Figure 5.2 would be changed to

```
As you input numbers one at a time, this
program will report the count of numbers so far,
the sum so far, and the average.

number      1 ?  10

sum    10          average    10


number      2 ?  50

sum    60          average    30
```
and so forth.

5.2

Conditional Jumps, compare Instructions and if Structures

Conditional jump instructions give the 8088 assembly language programmer the ability to code **if**s and other control structures. There are many of these instructions. Each has the format

```
j---      target_statement
```

where the last part of the mnemonic identifies the condition under which the jump is to be executed. If the condition holds, then the jump takes place; otherwise, the next instruction (the one following the conditional jump) is executed.

With one exception (the **jcxz** instruction, covered in Section 5.4), the "conditions" considered by the conditional jump instructions are settings of various flags in the flag registers. For example, the instruction

```
jz     end_while
```

means "jump to the statement with label **end_while** if the zero flag ZF is set to 1; otherwise fall through to the next statement."

The conditional jump instructions do not modify the flags; they only react to previously set flag values. Recall how the flags in the flag register get values in the first place. Some instructions (like **mov**) leave some or all flags unchanged, some (like **add**) explicitly set some flags according to the value of a result, and still others (like **div**) unpredictably alter some or all flags, leaving them with unknown values.

Suppose, for example, that the value in the AX register is added to a sum representing an account balance, and three distinct treatments are needed, depending on whether the new balance is negative, zero, or positive. A pseudocode design for this could be

add value to balance;

if balance < 0
then
      ...{ design for negative balance }
elseif balance = 0
then
      ...{ design for zero balance }
else
      ...{ design for positive balance }
end if;

The following sequence of 8088 code implements this design.

```
                add    balance,ax    ;add value to balance
                jns    elseif        ;check for negative balance
then_1:         .                    ;code for negative balance
                .
                .
                jmp    end_if
elseif:         jnz    else_2        ;check for zero balance
then_2:         .                    ;code for zero balance
                .
                .
                jmp    end_if
else_2:         .                    ;code for positive balance
                .
                .

end_if:
```

Appropriate flags are set or cleared by the **add** instruction. The design checks first for balance < 0. The code does this with the **jns elseif** instruction, which says to jump to **elseif** if the sign flag is not set, that is, if balance < 0 is not true. Thus the code at **then_1** corresponds to statements following the first then in the design. The **jmp end_if** at the end of the then statements is necessary so that the CPU skips the statements for other cases. If control transfers to **elseif**, then the balance must be nonnegative. The design checks to see if the balance is zero; the instruction **jnz else_2** jumps to **else_2** if the zero flag ZF=0, that is, the last instruction that set flags had a nonzero result.

Again, this makes the order of the 8088 instructions correspond to the order of the design statements. The code for the balance = 0 case must again end with **jmp end_if**. Finally, the code that corresponds to the "else" in the design is at **else_2**. This last block of code does not need a jump to **end_if**, since execution will fall through to the code following that label. In this code, the labels **then_1** and **then_2** are not really needed, but they provide documentation and make it easier to relate the code to the design.

Here is an alternative sequence of 8088 code which implements an equivalent design.

```
              add   balance, ax     ;add value to balance
              js    neg_balance     ;check for negative balance
              jz    zero_balance    ;check for zero balance
pos_balance:  .                     ;code for positive balance
              .
              .
              jmp   end_if
neg_balance:  .                     ;code for negative balance
              .
              .
              jmp   end_if
zero_balance: .                     ;code for zero balance
              .
end_if:
```

Here the **js** instruction means "jump if the sign flag SF is 1" as it would be if the result of the addition were negative. The two sections of code starting with **pos_balance:** and **neg_balance:** each end with an unconditional jump to **end_if**. The order of this 8088 code does not correspond to the original design; this may be undesirable. Especially for complicated designs, it is usually better to write code parallel to the design. In all cases, it is extremely important to avoid "spaghetti code" with jumps to strange locations; code should normally flow downward except for jumps that are necessary to go to the top of a loop structure.

It is time to correct a small misstatement that appeared in Chapter 3. There it was stated that an assembly language statement always required a mnemonic. In fact, just a statement label can appear on a line by itself. This is very useful for coding a structure like the above **if**. The **end_if** statement label can be coded and references can be made to it without worrying about what comes after the **if** structure. Even if what comes afterwards is changed, it does not affect the **if** structure. The next statement can have another statement label, so that several labels actually reference the statement following the **if** structure. Because labels are not part of object code, extra labels do not add to the length of object code or to execution time.

When writing code to mirror a design, one often wants to use labels like **if**, **then, else**, and **endif**. Unfortunately, **IF**, **ELSE**, and **ENDIF** are MASM directives, so that they cannot be used as labels. In addition, **IF1**, **IF2**, and several other desirable labels are also reserved for use as directives. No reserved word contains an underscore, so labels like `if_1` and **`endif_2`** both avoid problems with reserved words and distinguish between different structures in the original design.

When referring to giving flags new values, *set* means "give the value 1" and *reset* or *clear* means "give the value 0." There are numerous ways that the flags can be set or reset. The **`atoi`** macro affects some flags, including CF, OF, SF, and ZF, according to the value of its 2's complement result. However, the **cmp** (compare) instructions are probably the ones most commonly used to establish flag values.

The **cmp** instructions compare two operands, and then set or reset AF, CF, OF, PF, SF, and ZF. The *only* job of a **cmp** instruction is to fix flag values; this is its primary function, not just a side-effect of some other action. Each has the form

     `cmp`   *`operand_1, operand_2`*

A **cmp** executes by calculating *`operand_1`* minus *`operand_2`*, just like a **sub** instruction; the value of the difference and what happens in doing the subtraction (borrow, overflow) determines the flag settings. The **cmp** instruction is unlike **sub** in that the value at the *`operand_1`* location is not changed. The flags that are of most interest in this book are CF, OF, SF, and ZF. The carry flag CF is set if there is a borrow for the subtraction and reset if no borrow is required. The overflow flag OF is set if there is an overflow and reset otherwise. The sign flag SF is set if the difference represents a negative 2's complement number (the leading bit is one) and is reset if the number is zero or positive. Finally, the zero flag ZF is set if the difference is zero and is reset if it is nonzero.

Here are a few examples showing how the flags are fixed when some representative byte-length 2's complement (signed) numbers are compared. The "sign/relation" column below gives the sign of each of the operands in order, as well as their relative sizes ($<$, $=$, $>$) as signed numbers.

Operand_1	*Operand_2*	*Difference*	*Sign/Relation*	CF	OF	SF	ZF
3B	3B	00	+ = +	0	0	0	1
3B	15	26	+ > +	0	0	0	0
15	3B	DA	+ < +	1	0	1	0
F9	F6	03	− > −	0	0	0	0
F6	F9	FD	− < −	1	0	1	0
15	F6	1F	+ > −	1	0	0	0
F6	15	E1	− < +	0	0	1	0
68	A5	C3	+ > −	1	1	1	0
A5	68	3D	− < +	0	1	0	0

What flag values characterize the relations equal to, less than, and greater than? Equality is easy; the ZF flag is set if and only if *`operand_1`* has the same value as *`operand_2`*. When one first thinks about less than, it seems as if the carry flag should be set for a borrow whenever *`operand_1`* is less than *`operand_2`*. This logic is correct if one thinks of the operands as unsigned numbers, but not if they are 2's complement representations for signed numbers. For example, A5 $<$ 68 since a negative number is always less than a positive number, but no borrow is needed to subtract 68 from A5.

Figure 5.4 cmp Instructions.

Operand 1	Operand 2	Clock Cycles	Number of Bytes	Opcode
register 8	immediate byte	4	3	80
register 16	immediate byte	4	3	83
register 16	immediate word	4	4	81
AL	immediate byte	4	2	3C
AX	immediate word	4	3	3D
memory byte	immediate byte	10+	2+	80
memory word	immediate byte	14+	2+	83
memory word	immediate word	14+	3+	81
register 8	register 8	3	2	38
register 16	register 16	3	2	39
register 8	memory byte	9+	2+	38
register 16	memory word	13+	2+	39
memory byte	register 8	9+	2+	3A
memory word	register 16	13+	2+	3B

There is another way to determine order for signed operands. The way to detect if one operand is less than another is by comparing the sign flag SF and the overflow flag OF; these are different when *operand_1* is less than *operand_2* and are always the same when *operand_1* is greater than or equal to *operand_2*. Therefore "SF not equal OF" is true if and only if *operand_1* < *operand_2*. Similarly, *operand_1* > *operand_2* if and only if SF = OF and ZF = 0. Fortunately the 8088 conditional jump instructions do not require that all of these facts be remembered; many of them reference relationships between operands in a preceding cmp instruction rather than flag settings.

The cmp instructions are listed in Figure 5.4. Notice that in Figure 4.4, the entries in the various columns for **sub** instructions are almost all the same as for cmp instructions. When the first operand is in memory, the cmp instructions require fewer clock cycles than the corresponding **sub** instructions since the result need not be stored.

A few words are in order about immediate operands. These can be coded in your choice of bases or as characters. Assuming that **pattern** references a word in the data segment, each of the following is allowable.

```
cmp    ax, 356
cmp    pattern, 0d3a6h
cmp    bh, '$'
```

Note that an immediate operand must be the second operand, not the first. The instruction

```
cmp    100,total      ; illegal
```

is not acceptable since the first operand is immediate.

Finally it is time to list the conditional jump instructions; they are shown in Figure 5.5. Many of these have alternative mnemonics that generate exactly the same machine code; and describe the same set of conditions but in a different way. Often one mnemonic is more natural than the other for implementation of a given design.

There are two sets of mnemonics for determining inequalities, and these generate different machine code. One set basically looks at the carry flag CF and therefore is appropriate when dealing with unsigned numbers. The other set of conditional jumps looks at the sign flag and overflow flag to determine order.

Figure 5.5 Conditional Jump Instructions.

Appropriate After Comparison of Unsigned Operands

Mnemonic	Meaning	Flags to Jump	Opcode
ja	jump on above	CF = 0 and ZF = 0	77
jnbe	jump on not below or equal		
jae	jump on above or equal	CF = 0	73
jnb	jump on not below		
jb	jump on below	CF = 1	72
jnae	jump on not above or equal		
jbe	jump on below or equal	CF = 1 or ZF = 1	76
jna	jump on not above		

Appropriate After Comparison of Signed Operands

Mnemonic	Meaning	Flags to Jump	Opcode
jg	jump on greater	SF = OF and ZF = 0	7F
jnle	jump on not less or equal		
jge	jump on greater or equal	SF = OF	7D
jnl	jump on not less		
jl	jump on less	SF ≠ OF	7C
jnge	jump on not greater or equal		
jle	jump on less or equal	SF ≠ OF or ZF = 1	7E
jng	jump on not greater		

Other Conditional Jumps

Mnemonic	Meaning	Flags to Jump	Opcode
je	jump on equal	ZF = 1	74
jz	jump on zero		

Figure 5.5 Continued.

Mnemonic	Meaning	Flags to Jump	Opcode
jne	jump on not equal	ZF = 0	75
jnz	jump on not zero		
js	jump on sign	SF = 1	78
jns	jump on not sign	SF = 0	79
jc	jump on carry	CF = 1	72
jnc	jump on not carry	CF = 0	73
jp	jump on parity	PF = 1	7A
jpe	jump on parity even		
jnp	jump on not parity	PF = 0	7B
jpo	jump on parity odd		
jo	jump on overflow	OF = 1	70
jno	jump on not overflow	OF = 0	71

If the value in AX were unsigned, and some action needed to be taken for a value larger than 100, then one might code

```
cmp     ax,100
ja      bigger
```

The jump would be made for any value greater than 0064_{16}, including values between 8000_{16} and $FFFF_{16}$, that represent both large unsigned numbers and negative 2's complement numbers.

If the value in AX were interpreted as signed, then the statements

```
cmp     ax,100
jg      bigger
```

would be appropriate. The jump will only be taken for values between 0064 and 7FFF, not for those bit patterns that represent negative 2's complement numbers.

Each of the conditional jump instructions requires two bytes of object code. The second byte is a short displacement, so that the destination statement can be at most 128 bytes before or 127 bytes after the conditional jump itself. There are no alternative forms of the conditional jump instructions to allow for longer jumps. Sometimes conditional jumps must be combined with unconditional jumps to reach more distant targets; examples are given below.

A conditional jump instruction takes 16 clock cycles to execute if the conditions are met and the jump is made. Only four cycles are needed to fall through to the next instruction when the conditions are not met.

Here are three examples showing implementation of **if** structures. First consider the design

> if value < 10
> then
>   add 1 to small_count;
> else
>   add 1 to large_count;
> end if;

Suppose that value is stored in the BX register and that **small_count** and **large_count** reference words in memory. The following 8088 code implements this design.

```
if_1:       cmp   bx, 10              ; value < 10 ?
            jnl   else_1
then_1:     inc   small_count;        ; add 1 to small_count
            jmp   SHORT endif_1
else_1:     inc   large_count;        ; add 1 to large_count
endif_1:
```

the labels **if_1** and **then_1** are not really needed in this code, but they make the code clearer and cost nothing at execution time. Note that this code is completely self-contained; you do not need to know what comes before or after in the overall design to implement this portion.

Now consider the design

> if (total ≥ 100) or (count = 10)
> then
>   add value to total;
> end if;

Assume that **total** and **value** reference words in memory, and that count is stored in the CX register. Here is assembly language code to implement this design.

```
if_2:       cmp   total, 100          ; total >= 100 ?
            jge   then_2
            cmp   cx, 10              ; count = 10 ?
            jne   endif_2
then_2:     mov   bx, value           ; copy value
            add   total, bx           ; add value to total
endif_2:
```

Notice that the design's **or** requires two **cmp** instructions. If either of the corresponding tests is passed, then the **add** is executed. (Why was the addition done with two statements? Why not use **add total,value** ?)

Finally consider the design

> if (count > 0) and (ch = backspace)
> then
> > subtract 1 from count;
> end if;

For this third example, assume that **count** references a word in memory, ch is in the AL register half and that **backspace** has been equated to 08h, the ASCII backspace character. This design can be implemented as follows.

```
if_3:     cmp   count, 0          ; count > 0 ?
          jng   endif_3
          cmp   al, backspace     ; ch a backspace?
          jne   endif_3
then_3:   dec   count             ; subtract 1 from count
endif_3:
```

This compound condition uses **and**, so both parts must be true in order to execute the action.

This section ends with an example implementing a simple game program. The computer asks one player to enter a number. After it is typed in, the screen is cleared, and the other player tries to guess the number. After each guess the computer reports "too low," "too high," or "you got it." After the number is finally guessed, the number of attempts is reported, and the players are asked if they want to play another game. The pseudocode design in Figure 5.6 gives a more precise description.

The assembly language source code for the game program of Figure 5.6 is shown in Figure 5.7. It contains several features which need comment. The screen is cleared by writing 24 linefeed characters; the number of characters displayed is controlled by the second parameter in **output clear, 24** rather than by a terminating null character. This is the first example to use this form of the **output** macro. The "high" and "low" sections of the **if** structure are terminated by **jmp SHORT end_if** statements. As discussed before, the **SHORT** operand saves a byte of object code in this forward reference.

The loop structure starting with **until_2** and ending with **end_until_2** faithfully follows the design of the inside until loop in the pseudocode. In particular, it checks the terminating condition at the bottom of the loop body. This

Figure 5.6 Design for Game Program.

```
until response='N' or response='n' loop

    prompt first player for target;
    input target and convert to 2's complement form;
    clear screen;
    count := 0;

    until guess=target loop

        add 1 to count;
        prompt second player for guess;
        input guess and convert to 2's complement;

        if guess=target
        then
            display "you got it" ;
        elseif guess < target
        then
            display "too low" ;
        else
            display "too high" ;
        end if;

    end until; { guess=target }

    convert count to ASCII;
    display count;
    display "Do you want to play again?" ;
    input response;

end until; { response='N' or response='n' }
```

Figure 5.7 Assembly Language Code for Game Program.

```
; program to implement number guessing game

INCLUDE io.h

cr              EQU     0dh    ; carriage return character
Lf              EQU     0ah    ; linefeed character

stack           SEGMENT stack
                DW      100h DUP (?)
stack           ENDS

data            SEGMENT
prompt_1        DB      cr,Lf,Lf,'Player 1, please enter a number:   ',0
target          DW      ?
clear           DB      24 DUP (Lf)
count           DW      ?
prompt_2        DB      cr,Lf,'Player 2, your guess?    ',0
number          DB      8 DUP (?)
low_lbl         DB      'too low',cr,Lf,0
high_lbl        DB      'too high',cr,Lf,0
got_it_lbl      DB      'you got it',cr,Lf,0
count_lbl       DB      Lf,'Number of guesses: '
count_val       DB      6 DUP (?)
                DB      cr,Lf,Lf,Lf,'Do you want to play again?   ',0
data            ENDS

code            SEGMENT
                ASSUME cs:code,ds:data

start:          mov     ax,SEG data     ; load data segment number
                mov     ds,ax

until_1:        output prompt_1         ; ask player 1 for target
                inputs number,8         ; get number
                atoi    number          ; convert to integer
                mov     target,ax       ; store target
                output clear,24         ; clear screen
                mov     count,0         ; zero count

until_2:        inc     count           ; increment count of guesses
                output prompt_2         ; ask player 2 for guess
                inputs number,8         ; get number
                atoi    number          ; convert to integer

if_1:           cmp     ax,target       ; compare guess and target
                je      equal           ; guess = target ?
                jl      low             ; guess < target ?
high:           output high_lbl         ; display "too high"
```

Figure 5.7 Continued.

```
                jmp     SHORT end_if_1
low:            output  low_lbl         ; display "too low"
                jmp     SHORT end_if_1
equal:          output  got_it_lbl      ; display "you got it"
end_if_1:
                cmp     ax,target       ; compare guess and target
                jne     until_2         ; ask again if guess not = target
end_until_2:

                itoa    count_val,count ; convert count to ASCII
                output  count_lbl       ; display label, count and prompt
                inputc                  ; get response
                cmp     al,'n'          ; response = 'n' ?
                je      end_until_1     ; exit if so
                cmp     al,'N'          ; response = 'N' ?
                je      end_until_1     ; exit if so
                jmp     until_1         ; repeat
end_until_1:

quit:           mov     al,0            ; return code 0
                mov     ah,4ch          ; DOS function to return
                int     21h             ; interrupt for DOS services

code            ENDS
                END     start
```

is somewhat inefficient, since the same condition has already been checked as part of the **if** structure. Here is alternative code for this loop.

```
until_2:        inc     count           ; increment count of guesses
                output  prompt_2        ; ask player 2 for guess
                inputs  number,8        ; get number
                atoi    number          ; convert to integer

if_1:           cmp     ax,target       ; compare guess and target
                je      equal           ; guess = target ?
                jl      low             ; guess < target ?
high:           output  high_lbl        ; display "too high"
                jmp     until_2         ; continue since not equal
low:            output  low_lbl         ; display "too low"
                jmp     until_2         ; continue since not equal
equal:          output  got_it_lbl      ; display "you got it"
end_until_2:
```

This code is more efficient, but not as easy to understand. This program does not profit from increased efficiency; in other situations, changes like this could be important.

The outside **until** loop in the game program is terminated by either an "N" or "n" response to a query to the players. The **inputc** macro is used to get the response as a single character in the AL register half without requiring that the user press the Return key. This is the first example to illustrate the **inputc** macro. One **cmp** and **je** pair of instructions checks for "N" and another checks for "n." At first glance, it appears that the following alternative sequence could be used.

```
        inputc                     ; get response
        cmp     al,'n'             ; response = 'n' ?
        je      end_until_1        ; exit if so
        cmp     al,'N'             ; response = 'N' ?
        jne     until_1            ; repeat if not 'N'
end_until_1:
```

This code will not work since the target of the last **jne** is more than 127 bytes away. The assembler will detect this problem and report "Relative jump out of range."

───────── *Exercises 5.2* ─────────────────────────────────

1. Assume for each part of this problem that the AX register contains 00 4F and the word referenced by **value** contains FF 38. Determine whether or not each of the conditional jump statements causes a jump to **dest** (assumed to be within 127 bytes).

    (a) cmp   ax,value   (b) cmp   ax,value
         jl   dest   jb   dest
    (c) cmp   ax,004fh   (d) cmp   ax,79
         je   dest   jne   dest
    (e) cmp   value,0   (f) cmp   value,-200
         jbe   dest   jge   dest
    (g) add   ax,200   (h) add   value,200
         js   dest   jz   dest

2. Each part of this problem gives a design with an **if** structure and some assumptions about how the variables are stored in an assembly language program. Give a fragment of assembly language code that implements the design.

    (a) if count = 0
         then
                 count := value;
         end if;

Assume that count is in CX; **value** references a word in memory.

(b) if a + b = c
    then
        check := "Y" ;
    else
        check := "N" ;
    end if;

Assume that **a**, **b** and **c** each reference a word in memory; store the character check in the AL register half.

(c) if (value ≤ –1000) or (value ≥ 1000)
    then
        value := 0;
    end if;

Assume that value is in DX.

(d) if (ch ≥ "a") and (ch ≤ "z")
    then
        add 1 to lower_count;
    else
        if (ch ≥ "A") and (ch ≤ "Z")
        then
            add 1 to upper_count;
        else
            add 1 to other_count;
        end if;
    end if;

Assume that ch is in AL; each of **lower_count**, **upper_count**, and **other_count** references a word in memory.

Programming Exercises 5.2

1. Modify the game program to accept only numbers between 0 and 1000 from either player. A design for this is

until (value > 0) and (value < 1000) loop
    input value and convert to 2's complement;
    if (value < 0) or (value > 1000)
    then
        display "enter value 0 to 1000";
    end if;
end until;

2. Modify the game program so that it only allows Player 2 five attempts at guessing the number entered by Player 1. If the fifth attempt is incorrect, display `Sorry, the number is` *value of* `target` and proceed to asking the players if they want another game.

5.3

Implementing while loops, until loops, and for loops

Most programs contain loops. Commonly used loop structures include `while`, `until`, and `for` loops. This section describes how to implement all three of these structures in 8088 assembly language. The next section describes additional instructions that can be used to implement `for` loops.

A `while` loop can be indicated by the following pseudocode design.

> while *continuation condition* loop
> ... { body of loop }
> end while;

The continuation condition, a Boolean expression, is checked first; if it is true, then the body of the loop is executed. The continuation condition is then checked again. Whenever the value of the Boolean expression is false, execution continues with the statement following end while.

An 8088 implementation of a `while` loop follows a pattern much like this one.

```
while:          .          ; code to check Boolean expression
                .
                .

body:           .          ; loop body
                .
                .

        jmp  while  ; go check condition again
end_while:
```

It often takes several statements to check the value of the Boolean expression. If it is determined that the value is false, then there will be a jump to `end_while`. If it is determined that the continuation condition is true, then the code will either fall through to `body` or there will be a jump to that label. Notice that the body of the loop ends with `jmp while` to go check the condition again. Two common mistakes are to omit `jmp while` or to code `jmp body` instead.

For an example, suppose that the design

```
while (sum < 1000) loop
    ... { body of loop }
end while;
```

is to be coded in 8088 assembly language. Assuming that **sum** references a word in memory, one possible implementation is

```
while:      cmp    sum,1000       ; sum < 1000?
            jnl    end_while       ; exit loop if not
body:        .                     ; body of loop

             .

             .

            jmp    while           ; go check condition again
end_while:
```

The statement

```
jnl    end_while
```

directly implements the design. An alternative would be to use

```
jge    end_while
```

which transfers control to the end of the loop if sum ≥ 1000. This works since the inequality (sum ≥ 1000) will be true exactly when the inequality (sum < 1000) is false, but the **jnl** mnemonic makes it easier to implement the design without having to reverse the inequality. Neither of these would work if the body of the loop used more than 127 bytes of code—the relative jump would be out of range. If the loop had a large body, one could use the following alternative code.

```
while:      cmp    sum,1000       ; sum < 1000?
            jl     body            ; execute body if so
            jmp    end_while       ; otherwise exit from loop
body:        .                     ; body of loop

             .

             .

            jmp    while           ; go check condition again
end_while:
```

For a short example showing a complete loop body, suppose that the integer base 2 logarithm of a positive number needs to be determined. The integer base 2 logarithm of a number is the largest integer x such that

$$2^x \leq \text{number}$$

The following design does the job.

```
x := 0;
two_to_x := 1;

while two_to_x ≤ number
     multiply two_to_x by 2;
     add 1 to x
end while;

subtract 1 from x;
```

Assuming that **number** references a word in memory, the following 8088 code implements the design, using the AX register for "two_to_x" and the CX register for "x."

```
              mov    cx,0          ; log := 0
              mov    ax,1          ; two_to_x := 1

while:        cmp    ax,number     ; two_to_x <= number?
              jnle   end_while     ; exit if not
body:         add    ax,ax         ; multiply two_to_x by 2
              inc    cx            ; add 1 to x
              jmp    while         ; go check condition again
end_while:
              dec    cx            ; subtract 1 from x
```

Often the continuation condition in a **while** is compound, having two parts connected by Boolean operators **and** or **or**. Both operands of an **and** must be true for a true conjunction. With an **or**, the only way the disjunction can be false is if both operands are false.

Changing a previous example to include a compound condition, suppose that the following design is to be coded.

```
while (sum < 1000) and (count ≤ 24) loop
     ... { body of loop }
end while;
```

Assuming that **sum** references a word in memory, the value of count is in CX, and the body of the loop is short enough to be skipped by conditional jumps, an implementation is

```
while:          cmp     sum,1000        ; sum < 1000?
                jnl     end_while       ; exit if not
                cmp     cx,24           ; count <= 24
                jnle    end_while       ; exit if not
body:           .                       ; body of loop
                .
                .
                jmp     while           ; go check condition again
end_while:
```

Modifying the example another time, here is a design with an **or** instead of an **and**.

```
while (sum < 1000) or (flag = 1) loop
    ... { body of loop }
end while;
```

This time, assume that sum is in the AX register, that flag is a single byte in the DH register half, and that the body of the loop is too long to be skipped by a short relative jump. Here is 8088 code that implements the design.

```
while:          cmp     ax,1000         ; sum < 1000?
                jl      body            ; execute body if so
                cmp     dh,1            ; flag = 1?
                je      body            ; execute body if so
                jmp     end_while       ; exit since neither true
body:           .                       ; body of loop
                .
                .
                jmp     while           ; go check condition again
end_while:
```

Notice the difference in the previous two examples. For an **and** the loop is *exited* if either part of the compound condition is *false*. For an **or** the loop body is *executed* if either part of the compound condition is *true*.

Sometimes processing in a loop is to continue while normal values are encountered, and terminated when some sentinel value is encountered. If data are being entered from the keyboard, this design can be written

```
get value from keyboard;
while (value is not sentinel) loop
    ... { body of loop }
    get value from keyboard;
end while;
```

In some high-level languages, implementation code must exactly parallel this design. One of the advantages of assembly language is that one has more flexibility in the programming. An equivalent design is

> while (value entered from keyboard is not sentinel) loop
>   ... { body of loop }
> end while;

This design does not have two separate instructions to input data. It can be coded in some high-level languages, and also in 8088 assembly language.

For a concrete example illustrating implementation of such a design, suppose that nonnegative numbers entered at the keyboard are to be added, with any negative entry serving as a sentinel value. A design looks like

> sum := 0;
> while (number keyed in is not negative) loop
>   add number to sum;
> end while;

In 8088 assembly language, assuming appropriate definitions have been made in the data segment, the code could be

```
            mov     bx,0            ; sum := 0
while:      output  prompt          ; prompt for input
            inputs  number,10       ; get number from keyboard
            atoi    number          ; convert to 2's complement
            js      end_while       ; exit if negative
body:       add     bx,ax           ; add number to sum
            jmp     while           ; go get next number
end_while:
```

Recall that the `atoi` macro affects the sign flag SF, setting it if the ASCII characters are converted to a negative number in the AX register and clearing it otherwise.

The body of a `for` loop, a counter-controlled loop, is executed once for each value of a loop index (or counter) in a given range. In Pascal and some other high-level languages, the indices can be some type other than integer; in assembly language the indices are usually integers. A `for` loop can be described by the following pseudocode.

> for index := initial_value to final_value loop
>   ... { body of loop }
> end for;

A `for` loop can easily be translated into a `while` structure.

> index := initial_value;
> while index ≤ final_value loop
>   ... { body of loop }
>   add 1 to index;
> end while;

Such a `while` structure is readily coded in 8088 assembly language.

Suppose that a collection of numbers needs to be added and no value is convenient as a sentinel. Then one might want to ask a user how many numbers are to be entered and loop for that many entries. The design looks like

```
prompt for tally of numbers;
input tally;
sum := 0
for count := 1 to tally loop
        prompt for number;
        input number;
        add number to sum;
end for;
```

Making straightforward assumptions about definitions in the data segment, here is an 8088 implementation of the design.

```
              output  prompt1          ; prompt for tally
              inputs  value,10         ; get tally (ASCII)
              atoi    value            ; convert to 2's complement
              mov     tally,ax         ; store tally

              mov     dx,0             ; sum := 0
              mov     bx,1             ; index := 1

for:          cmp     bx,tally         ; index <= tally?
              jnle    end_for          ; exit if not
              output  prompt2          ; prompt for number
              inputs  value,10         ; get number (ASCII)
              atoi    value            ; convert to 2's complement
              add     dx,ax            ; add number to sum
              inc     bx               ; add 1 to index
              jmp     for              ; repeat
end_for:
```

In a `for` loop implementation where one is sure that the body of the loop will be executed at least once (that is, the initial value is less than or equal to the final value), one can check the index against the final value at the end of the loop body rather than prior to the body. Other variations are also possible. Other instructions for implementing `for` loops will be covered in Section 5.4.

An `until` loop can be expressed as follows in pseudocode.

```
until termination condition  loop
        ... { body of loop }
end until;
```

The body of the loop is executed at least once, then the termination condition is checked. If it is false, then the body of the loop is executed again; if true, execution continues with the statement following end until.

An 8088 implementation of an `until` loop usually looks like the following code fragment.

```
until:          .              ; start of loop body
                .
                .
                .              ; code to check termination condition
                .
                .
end_until:
```

If the code to check the termination condition determines that the value is false, then there will be a jump to `until`. If it is determined that the value is true, then the code will either fall through to `end_until` or there will be a jump to that label.

The game program implemented in Figure 5.7 contained two simple `until` loops. Here is an example with a compound terminating condition. Given the design

```
count := 0;
until (sum > 1000) or (count = 100) loop
    ... { body of loop }
    add 1 to count;
end until;
```

the following 8088 code provides an implementation. Assume that **sum** references a word in the data segment.

```
            mov   cx,0          ; count := 0
until:          .              ; body of loop
                .
                .
            inc   cx            ; add 1 to count
            cmp   sum,1000      ; sum > 1000 ?
            jg    end_until     ; exit if sum > 1000
            cmp   cx,100        ; count = 100 ?
            jne   until         ; continue if count not = 100
end_until:
```

If the body of the loop were too long for the relative jump `jne  until` then the last part of the code could be

```
            cmp   cx,100        ; count = 100 ?
            je    end_until     ; exit if count = 100
            jmp   until         ; continue loop execution
end_until:
```

Other loop structures can also be coded in assembly language. The **forever** loop is frequently useful. As it appears in designs, it almost always has an exit loop statement to transfer control to the end of the loop; this is often conditional, that is, in an **if** statement. Here is a fragment of a typical design.

```
forever loop
    .
    .
    .
    if (response = 's') or (response = 'S')
    then
        exit loop;
    end if;
    .
    .
    .
end loop;
```

Assuming that the value of response is in the AL register half, this can be implemented as follows in 8088 assembly language.

```
forever:        .
                .
                .
                cmp     al,'s'          ; response = 's'?
                je      end_loop        ; exit loop if so
                cmp     al,'S'          ; response = 'S'?
                je      end_loop        ; exit loop if so
                .
                .
                .
                jmp     forever         ; repeat loop body
end_loop:
```

--- **Exercises 5.3** ---

1. Each part of this problem contains a design with a **while** loop. Assume that **sum** references a word in the data segment and that the value of count is in the CX register. Give a fragment of 8088 code that implements the design.

   (a) sum := 0;
        count := 1;
        while (sum < 1000) loop
            add count to sum;
            add 1 to count;
        end while;

(b) sum := 0;
    count := 1;
    while (sum < 1000) and (count < 50) loop
        add count to sum;
        add 1 to count;
    end while;

(c) sum := 0;
    count := 100;
    while (sum < 1000) or (count > 0) loop
        add count to sum;
        subtract 1 from count;
    end while;

2. Each part of this problem contains a design with a `until` loop. Assume that **sum** references a word in the data segment and that the value of count is in the CX register. Give a fragment of 8088 code which implements the design.

(a) sum := 0;
    count := 1;
    until (sum > 5000) loop
        add count to sum;
        add 1 to count;
    end until;

(b) sum := 0;
    count := 1;
    until (sum > 5000) or (count = 40) loop
        add count to sum;
        add 1 to count;
    end until;

(c) sum := 0;
    count := 1;
    until (sum > 5000) and (count > 40) loop
        add count to sum;
        add 1 to count;
    end until;

3. Each part of this problem contains a design with a `for` loop. Assume that **sum** references a word in the data segment and that the value of count is in the CX register. Give a fragment of 8088 code that implements the design.

(a) sum := 0;
　　for count := 1 to 100 loop
　　　　add count to sum;
　　end for;

(b) sum := 0;
　　for count := –10 to 50 loop
　　　　add count to sum;
　　end for;

(c) sum := 1000;
　　for count := 100 downto 50 loop
　　　　subtract 2*count from sum;
　　end for;

Programming Exercises 5.3

1. Write a complete 8088 assembly language program that will accept numbers from the keyboard and report the minimum and maximum of the numbers. Implement the following design, adding appropriate labels to output.

display "First number?　　" ;
input number;
minimum := number;
maximum := number;
while (response to "Another number? " is 'Y' or 'y') loop

　　input number;

　　if (number < minimum)
　　then
　　　　minimum := number;
　　end if;

　　if (number > maximum)
　　then
　　　　maximum := number;
　　end if;

end while;

display the minimum value;
display the maximum value;

2. Write a complete 8088 assembly language program that will accept numbers from the keyboard and report the sum and average of the numbers. The count of numbers is not known in advance; use the value –9999 as a sentinel to terminate input. Implement the following design, adding appropriate prompts for input and labels for output.

```
sum := 0;
count := 0;
while (number entered from keyboard ≠ –9999) loop
        add number to sum;
        add 1 to count;
end while;
if (count = 0)
then
        display "No numbers entered" ;
else
        average := sum/count;
        display sum and average;
end if;
```

3. Write a complete 8088 assembly language program to help your overworked instructor analyze examination grades. The program should input an unknown number of examination grades, using any negative grade as a sentinel, and then report the number of A's (90–100), B's (80–89), C's (70–79), D's (60–69) and F's (under 60). Implement the following design. Prompt for input as appropriate.

```
A_count := 0;
B_count := 0;
C_count := 0;
D_count := 0;
F_count := 0;

while (grade entered at keyboard ≥ 0) loop

if (grade ≥ 90)
        then
                add 1 to A_count;
        elseif (grade ≥ 80)
        then
                add 1 to B_count;
        elseif (grade ≥ 70)
        then
                add 1 to C_count;
```

```
        elseif (grade ≥ 60)
        then
                add 1 to D_count;
        else
                add 1 to F_count;
        end if;

end while;

display "Number of A's" , A_count;
display "Number of B's" , B_count;
display "Number of C's" , C_count;
display "Number of D's" , D_count;
display "Number of F's" , F_count;
```

4. The greatest common divisor of two positive integers is the largest integer that evenly divides both numbers. The following algorithm will find the greatest common divisor of number1 and number2.

```
gcd := number2;
dividend := number1;
remainder := number1 mod number2;

while (remainder ≠ 0) loop
    dividend := gcd;
    gcd := remainder;
    remainder := dividend mod gcd;
end while;
```

Write a complete 8088 assembly language program that implements the following design, with appropriate prompts for input and labels for output.

```
until (number1 > 0) loop
    input number1;
end until;

until (number2 > 0) loop
    input number2;
end until;

find gcd of number1 and number2;

display gcd;
```

5. Write a complete 8088 assembly language program to simulate a simple calculator. The calculator can do addition and subtraction operations, and also accepts commands to clear the accumulated value or to quit. Implement the following design.

total := 0;

forever loop

    display "number? " ;
    input number;

    display "action (+, – , c or q) ? " ;
    input action;

    if (action = "+")
    then
        add number to total;
    elseif (action = "–")
    then
        subtract number from total;
    elseif (action = "c") or (action = "C")
    then
        total := 0;
    elseif (action = "q") or (action = "Q")
    then
        exit loop;
    else
        display "Unknown action" ;
    end if;

    display "total", total;

end loop;

5.4

for loops in Assembly Language

Often the number of times the body of a loop must be executed is known in advance, either as a constant that can be coded when a program is written, or as the value of a variable that is known before the loop is executed. The **for** loop structure is ideal for coding such a loop.

The previous section showed how to translate a `for` loop into a `while` loop. This always works and is frequently the best way to code a `for` loop. However, the 8088 microprocessor has instructions that make coding certain for loops very easy.

Consider the following two `for` loops, the first of which counts forward and the second of which counts backward.

```
for index := 1 to count loop
    ... { body of loop }
end for;
```

and

```
for index := count downto 1 loop
    ... { body of loop }
end for;
```

The body of each loop executes count times. If the value of index is not needed for display or for calculations within the body of the loop, then the loop that counts down is equivalent to the loop that counts up, although the design may not be as natural. Backward `for` loops are very easy to implement in 8088 assembly language using the `loop` instruction.

The `loop` instruction has the format

```
loop    statement_label
```

where *statement_label* is the label of a statement that is a short displacement (128 bytes backward or 127 bytes forward) from the `loop` instruction. The `loop` causes the following actions to take place:

- the value in CX is decremented
- if the new value in CX is zero, then execution continues with the statement following the `loop` instruction
- if the new value in CX is nonzero, then a jump to the instruction at *statement_label* takes place

The `loop` instruction requires two bytes of object code; the first byte is the opcode E2; the second byte is the displacement to the destination statement. It takes 17 clock cycles to execute if the jump is executed (the new value of CX is not zero) and five clock cycles if the jump is not executed (the new value of CX is zero). No flags are changed when a `loop` is executed.

Although the CX register is a general register, it has a special place as a counter in the `loop` instruction and in several other instructions. No other register can be substituted for CX in these instructions. In practice this often means that when a `loop` is coded, either CX is not used for other purposes or a counter value is put in CX before a `loop` instruction is executed but is saved elsewhere to free CX for other uses for most of the body of the loop.

The backward **for** loop structure

```
for count := 20 downto 1 loop
    ... { body of loop }
end for;
```

can be coded as follows in 8088 assembly language.

```
            mov    cx,20      ; number of iterations
    for:    .                 ; body of loop
            .
            .
            loop   for        ; repeat body 20 times
```

The counter in the CX register will be 20 the first time the body of the loop is executed and will be decremented to 19 by the **loop** instruction. The value 19 is not zero, so control transfers to the start of the loop body at label **for**. The second time the body of the loop is executed, the CX register will contain 19. The last time the value in CX will be one; it will be decremented to zero by the **loop** instruction.

Now suppose that the word in memory referenced by **number** contains the number of times a loop is to be executed. The 8088 code to implement a backward **for** loop could be

```
            mov    cx,number  ; number of iterations
    for:    .                 ; body of loop
            .
            .
            loop   for        ; repeat body number times
```

This is safe code only if the value stored at **number** is not zero. If it is zero, then the loop body is executed, the zero value is decremented to FFFF (a borrow is required to do the subtraction), the loop body is executed again, the value FFFF is decremented to FFFE, and so forth. The body of the loop is executed 65,536 times before the value in CX gets back down to zero! To avoid this problem, one could code

```
            mov    cx,number  ; number of iterations
            cmp    cx,0       ; cx = 0 ?
            je     end_for    ; skip loop if number = 0
    for:    .                 ; body of loop
            .
            .
            loop   for        ; repeat body "number" times
    end_for:
```

If **number** is a signed value and might be negative, then

```
    jle    end_for       ; skip loop if number <= 0
```

is a more appropriate test.

There is another way to guard a **for** loop so that it is not executed when the value in CX is zero. The 8088 instruction set has a **jcxz** conditional jump instruction that jumps to its destination if the value in the CX register is zero. Using the **jcxz** instruction, the example above can be coded as

```
              mov    cx,number       ; number of iterations
              jcxz   end_for         ; skip loop if number = 0
      for:     .                     ; body of loop
               .
               .
              loop   for             ; repeat body "number" times
      end_for:
```

The **jcxz** instruction has opcode E3. Like the other conditional jump instructions, it takes two bytes of object code, and it affects no flag value. It does take slightly longer to execute, 18 clock cycles if the jump takes place (if the value in CX is zero), and six clock cycles to fall through to the next statement.

The **jcxz** instruction can be used to code a backward **for** loop when the body of the instruction is longer than 127 bytes, and when the **loop** instruction cannot be used. For example, the structure

```
      for counter := 50 downto 1 loop
          ... { body of loop }
      end for;
```

can be coded as

```
              mov    cx,50           ; number of iterations
      for:     .                     ; body of loop
               .
               .
              dec    cx              ; decrement loop counter
              jcxz   end_for         ; exit if counter = 0
              jmp    for             ; otherwise repeat body
      end_for:
```

However, since the **dec** instruction sets or resets the zero flag ZF, the slightly faster conditional jump

```
      jz   end_for
```

can be used instead of the **jcxz** instruction.

It is often convenient to use a **loop** statement to implement a **for** loop, even when the loop index increases and must be used within the body of the loop. The **loop** statement uses CX to control the number of iterations, while a separate counter serves as the loop index.

For example, to implement the **for** loop

```
      for index := 1 to 50 loop
          ...{ loop body using index }
      end for;
```

the BX register might be used to store index counting from 1 to 50 while the CX register counts down from 50 to 1.

```
          mov   bx, 1        ; index := 1
          mov   cx, 50       ; number of iterations for loop
     for:   .
                .            ; use value in BX for index
                .
          inc   bx           ; add 1 to index
          loop  for          ; repeat
```

There are two variants of the `loop` instruction. Each of these work like `loop`, decrementing the counter in CX. However, each also examines the value of the zero flag ZF as well as the new value in the CX register to decide whether or not to jump to the destination location. The `loopz` instruction (which also uses the mnemonic `loope`) has the form

> `loopz   statement_label`

The `loopz` instruction jumps to the instruction at **statement_label** (a short displacement away) if the new value in CX is nonzero *and* the zero flag ZF is one. The `loopnz` instruction (also known as `loopne`) has the format

> `loopnz   statement_label`

The `loopnz` instruction jumps to the instruction at **statement_label** if the new value in CX is nonzero and the zero flag ZF is zero. As with the `loop` instruction, the `loopz` and `loopnz` instructions do not affect any flag value. Each instruction takes two bytes of object code. The `loopz` instruction has opcode E1 and takes 18 clock cycles to execute if the jump is made, and six clock cycles otherwise. The `loopnz` instruction has opcode E0; it takes 19 clock cycles to execute if the jump is made, and five clock cycles otherwise.

The `loopz` and `loopnz` instructions are useful in special circumstances. Some programming languages allow loop structures such as

> for year := 10 downto 1 until balance = 0 loop
>   ... { body of loop }
> end for;

This confusing structure means to terminate loop execution using whichever loop control is satisfied first. That is, the body of the loop is executed 10 times (for year = 10, 9,...,1) unless the condition balance = 0 is true at the bottom of some execution of the loop body, in which case the loop terminates with fewer than 10 iterations. If the value of balance is in BX register, the following 8088 code could be used.

```
                    mov    cx,10    ; maximum number of iterations
         for:        .               ; body of loop
                     .
                     .
                    cmp    bx,0     ; balance = 0 ?
                    loopne for      ; repeat 10 times if balance not 0
```

Exercises 5.4

1. Each part of this problem has a **for** loop implemented with a **loop** statement. How many times is the body each loop executed?

   (a)
   ```
              mov  cx,  10
      for:     .
               .                    ; body of loop
               .
              loop for
   ```

   (b)
   ```
              mov  cx,  1
      for:     .
               .                    ; body of loop
               .
              loop for
   ```

   (c)
   ```
              mov  cx,  0
      for:     .
               .                    ; body of loop
               .
              loop for
   ```

   (d)
   ```
              mov  cx,  -1
      for:     .
               .                    ; body of loop
               .
              loop for
   ```

2. Each part of this problem contains a design with a for loop. Give a fragment of 8088 code that uses a **loop** statement to implement the design. Assume that **sum** references a word in the data segment. Use the **itoa** and **output** macros for display, assuming that the data segment contains

   ```
   ASCII_count   DB    6 DUP (?)
   ASCII_sum     DB    6 DUP (?)
                 DB    13, 10, 0    ; carriage return, linefeed
   ```

(a) sum := 0;
     for count := 50 downto 1 loop
        add count to sum;
        display count, sum;
     end for;

(b) sum := 0;
     for count := 1 to 50 loop
        add count to sum;
        display count, sum;
     end for;

(c) sum := 0;
     for count := 1 to 50 loop
        add (2*count – 1) to sum;
        display count, sum;
     end for;

Programming Exercises 5.4

1. Write a complete 8088 program to input a positive integer value N and to display a table of integers from 1 to N and their squares. Use a two-column format such as

number	square
1	1
2	4
3	9
4	16
5	25

2. A Pythagorean triple consists of three positive integers A, B and C such that $A^2 + B^2 = C^2$. For example, the numbers 3, 4, and 5 form a Pythagorean triple since $9 + 16 = 25$. Write a complete 8088 program to input a value for C and then display all possible Pythagorean triples, if any with this value for C. For example, if 5 is entered for the value of C, then the output might be

A	B	C
3	4	5
4	3	5

5.5

Arrays

Programs frequently use arrays to store collections of data values. Loops are commonly used to manipulate the data in arrays. This section shows one way to access one-dimensional arrays in 8088 assembly language; other techniques will appear in Chapter 8 (other addressing modes).

This section contains a complete program to implement the design below. The program first accepts a collection of positive numbers from the keyboard, counting them and storing them in an array. It then calculates the average of the numbers by going back through the numbers stored in the array, accumulating the total in sum. Finally the numbers in the array are scanned again, and this time the numbers larger than the average are displayed. The first two loops could be combined, of course, with the sum being accumulated as the numbers are keyed in. As a general programming philosophy, clearer code results from separating tasks; tasks should be combined only if there is a real need to save execution time or bytes of object code.

```
nbr_elts := 0;                              { input numbers into array }
get address of first word of array;

while (number from keyboard > 0) loop
    convert number to 2's complement;
    store number at address in array;
    add 1 to nbr_elts;
    get address of next word of array;
end while;

sum := 0;                                   { find sum and average }
get address of first word of array;

for count := nbr_elts downto 1 loop
    add word at address in array to sum;
    get address of next word of array;
end for;

average := sum/nbr_elts;
display average;

get address of first word of array;        { list "big" numbers }
```

```
    for count := nbr_elts downto 1 loop
        if word of array > average
        then
                convert word to ASCII;
                display word;
        end if;
        get address of next word of array;
    end for;
```

This design contains the curious instructions "get address of first word of array" and "get address of next word of array." These reflect the particular assembly language implementation, one that works well if the task at hand involves moving sequentially through an array. The 8088 feature that makes this possible is register indirect addressing, first discussed in Section 3.5. The example will use the BX register to contain the address of the word currently being accessed; then [bx] references the word at the address in the BX register rather than the word in the register itself. Recall that the other register choices are BP, DI, and SI. The BP register is not appropriate here since it references data in the stack segment. The DI and SI registers are often reserved for use with strings, which are usually arrays of characters. String operations are covered in Chapter 7. The program listing appears in Figure 5.8.

The design statement "get address of first word of array" is implemented by the 8088 statement

```
    lea    bx, nbr_array
```

The mnemonic lea stands for "load effective address." The lea instruction has the format

```
    lea    destination,source
```

The destination must be a 16-bit general register, and the source is any reference to memory. The *address* of the source is loaded into the register. (Contrast this with mov *destination,source* where the *value* at the source address is copied to the destination.) The lea instruction takes 2+ clock cycles and requires 2+ bytes (both depending on the effective address).

In this program "get address of first word of array" could be accomplished using

```
    mov bx, OFFSET nbr_array
```

The lea instruction offers more flexibility with regard to the type of source operand and is often used for this sort of application.

The design statement "get address of next word of array" is implemented using the 8088 statement

```
    add   bx, 2
```

Since each word occupies two bytes of storage, adding 2 to the address of the current element of an array gives the address of the next element of the array.

Figure 5.8 Program Using Array.

```
; input a collection of numbers
; report their average and the numbers which are above average

INCLUDE io.h

cr              EQU     0dh   ; carriage return character
Lf              EQU     0ah   ; linefeed character
max_nbrs        EQU     100   ; size of number array

stack           SEGMENT stack
                DW      100h DUP (?)
stack           ENDS

data            SEGMENT
directions      DB      cr,Lf,'You may enter up to 100 numbers'
                DB      ' one at a time.',cr,Lf
                DB      'Use any negative number to terminate input.',cr,Lf,Lf
                DB      'This program will then report the average and list',cr,Lf
                DB      'those numbers which are above the average.',cr,Lf,Lf,Lf,0
prompt          DB      'Number?  ',0
number          DB      8 DUP (?)
nbr_array       DW      max_nbrs DUP (?)
nbr_elts        DW      ?
avg_lbl         DB      cr,Lf,Lf,'The average is'
out_value       DB      6 DUP (?), cr,Lf,0
above_lbl       DB      cr,Lf,'Above average:',cr,Lf,Lf,0
data            ENDS

code            SEGMENT
                ASSUME cs:code,ds:data

start:          mov     ax,SEG data     ; load data segment number
                mov     ds,ax

; input numbers into array

                output directions       ; display directions
                mov     nbr_elts,0       ; nbr_elts := 0
                lea     bx,nbr_array     ; get address of number array

while:          output prompt            ; prompt for number
                inputs number,8          ; get number
                atoi    number           ; convert to integer
                jng     end_while        ; exit if not positive
                mov     [bx],ax          ; store number in array
                inc     nbr_elts         ; add 1 to nbr_elts
                add     bx,2             ; get address of next word of array
                jmp     while            ; repeat
end_while:
```

Figure 5.8 Continued.

```
; find sum and average

                mov     ax,0                ; sum := 0
                lea     bx,nbr_array        ; get address of number array
                mov     cx,nbr_elts         ; count := nbr_elts

                jcxz    quit                ; quit if no numbers

for_1:          add     ax,[bx]             ; add number to sum
                add     bx,2                ; get address of next word of array
                loop    for_1               ; repeat nbr_elts times

                cwd                         ; extend sum to doubleword
                idiv    nbr_elts            ; calculate average
                itoa    out_value,ax        ; convert average to ASCII
                output  avg_lbl             ; print label and average
                output  above_lbl           ; print label for big numbers

; display numbers above average

                lea     bx,nbr_array        ; get address of number array
                mov     cx,nbr_elts         ; count := nbr_elts

for_2:          cmp     ax,[bx]             ; average < word
                jnl     end_if              ; continue if not
                itoa    out_value,[bx]      ; convert word of array to ASCII
                output  out_value           ; display word
end_if:
                add     bx,2                ; get address of next word of array
                loop    for_2               ; repeat

quit:           mov     al,0                ; return code 0
                mov     ah,4ch              ; DOS function to return
                int     21h                 ; interrupt for DOS services

code            ENDS
                END     start
```

If one were planning to code this program in a high-level language, then the design of the first two loops might be

```
nbr_elts := 0;                              { input numbers into array }

while number from keyboard > 0 loop
        add 1 to nbr_elts;
        store number in nbr_array[nbr_elts];
end while;

sum := 0;                                   { find sum and average }

for count := 1 to nbr_elts loop
        add nbr_array[count] to sum;
end for;
```

This design exploits one of the principal features of arrays, namely that any element can be accessed at any time by simply giving its index; the elements do not have to be accessed sequentially. Such random access can be accomplished using register indirect addressing. For example, the design statement "add array[count] to sum" can be implemented as follows, assuming that the CX register still is used for count and that the AX register is used for sum.

```
mov   dx,cx            ; count
dec   dx               ; count-1
add   dx,dx            ; 2*(count-1)
lea   bx,nbr_array     ; starting address of array
add   bx,dx            ; address of nbr_array[count]
add   ax,[bx]          ; add array[count] to sum
```

The technique here is to calculate the number of bytes in the array prior to the desired element, and add this number to the starting address. There are somewhat more efficient ways to directly access an array element; these will be covered in Chapter 8.

Exercises 5.5

1. Modify the program in Figure 5.8, adding a loop that will display those elements of the array that are smaller than the average. (The numbers that are equal to the average should not be displayed by either loop.)

2. Modify the program in Figure 5.8, replacing the last loop by one that displays all numbers which are within five of the average. Include values equal to the average −5 or to the average +5.

3. Modify the program in Figure 5.8, adding a loop that will display the list of numbers backwards.

   (Hint: Find the address of `nbr_array[nbr_elts]`, display the element at this address first, and subtract 2 repeatedly until all elements are displayed.)

4. Modify the program in Figure 5.8 to ensure that the user gives at most `max_nbrs` values.

Programming Exercises 5.5

1. It is often necessary to search an array for a given value. Write a complete program that accepts as input a collection of integers and then searches for values stored in the array. Implement the following design.

   ```
   nbr_elts := 0;
   get address of first word of array;

   while (number from keyboard > 0) loop
           convert number to 2's complement;
           store number at address in array;
           add 1 to nbr_elts;
           get address of next word of array;
   end while;

   until (response = "N" ) or (response = "n" )
           display "Search for?  " ;
           input key_value;
           convert key_value to 2's complement;
           get address of first word of array;
           count := 1;

           forever loop
                   if count > nbr_elts
                   then
                           display key_value, "not in array" ;
                           exit loop;
                   end if;
                   if key_value = current element of array
                   then
                           display key_value, "is element" , count;
                           exit loop;
                   end if;
   ```

```
        add 1 to count;
            get address of next word of array;
    end loop;

        display "Search for another number?    " ;
        input response;
    end until;
```

2. The previous program given in Programming Exercise 1 shows one way to search an array. An alternative way is to put the value you are searching for at the end of the array. A search then always finds the value, and success or failure depends on whether the value was found before or after position nbr_elts. Write a complete program that uses this technique. The design is the same as in Exercise 1 except for the body of the **until** loop which is replaced by the following.

```
until (response = "N" ) or (response = "n" )
        display "Search for? " ;
        input key_value;
        convert key_value to 2's complement;
        store key_value at position (nbr_elts+1) in array;
        get address of first word of array;
        count := 1;

        while key_value not equal to current array element loop
            add 1 to count;
            get address of next word of array;
        end while;

        if count > nbr_elts
        then
            display key_value, "not in array" ;
            exit loop;
        else
            display key_value, "is element" , count;
            exit loop;
        end if;

        display "Search for another number? " ;
        input response;
    end until;
```

—— 5.6 ————————————————————————————

Chapter Summary

This chapter has introduced 8088 instructions that can be used to implement such high-level design and language features as **if** statements, loop structures, and arrays.

The **jmp** instruction unconditionally transfers control to a destination statement. It has several versions, including a form that jumps to a short destination 128 bytes before or 127 bytes after the **jmp**, and other forms capable of jumping anywhere in a segment or even between segments. The **jmp** instruction is used in implementing various loop structures, typically transferring control back to the beginning of the loop, and in the **if-then-else** structure at the end of the **then** code to transfer control to "end_if" so that the **else** code is not also executed. A **jmp** statement corresponds directly to the **goto** statement, available in most high-level languages.

Conditional jump instructions examine the settings of one or more flags in the flag register and jump to a destination statement or fall through to the next instruction depending on the flag values. The destination must always be a short displacement away. There is a large collection of conditional jump instructions. They are used in **if** statements and loops, often in combination with compare instructions, to check Boolean conditions.

The **cmp** (compare) instructions have the sole purpose of setting or resetting flags in the flag register. Each compares two operands and assigns flag values. The comparison is done by subtracting the second operand from the first. The difference is not retained as it is with a **sub** instruction. Compare instructions often precede conditional jump instructions.

Loop structures like **while**, **until** and **for** loops can be implemented using compare, jump, and conditional jump instructions. The **loop** instruction provides another way to implement many **for** loops. To use the **loop** instruction, a counter is placed in the CX register prior to the start of the loop. The **loop** instruction itself is at the bottom of the loop body; it decrements the value in CX and transfers control to a destination (normally the first statement of the body) if the new value in CX is not zero. This results in the body of the loop being executed the number of times originally placed in the CX register. The conditional jump **jcxz** instruction can be used to guard against executing such a loop when the initial counter value is zero.

Storage for an array can be reserved using the **DUP** operator in a **DW** directive in the data segment of a program. The elements of an array can be sequentially accessed by putting the address of the first element of the array in the BX register, and adding the size of an array element repeatedly to get to the next element. The current element can be referenced as **[bx]**. The **lea** (load effective address) instruction is commonly used to load the address of the array into the BX register.

CHAPTER 6

Procedures

The word *procedure* is used in the Pascal and other high-level languages to describe a subprogram that is almost a self-contained unit. The main program or another subprogram can call a procedure by including a statement that consists of the procedure name followed by a parenthesized list of "arguments" to be associated with the procedure's "formal parameters."

Pascal allows another type of subprogram known as a *function*. A Pascal function is similar to a procedure except that it is called by using its name and argument list in an expression. It returns a value associated with its name; this value is then used in the expression.

This chapter describes how to write procedures for PCs using MASM to assemble the 8088 code and LINK to combine separate modules. Information is included on how to define a procedure, and how to transfer execution control to a procedure and back to the calling program. Important concepts that are covered are how to pass arguments to a procedure and how to make the procedure as independent as possible from the calling program. The 8088 stack plays an important role with procedures. It saves the return address to get back to the calling program, it can be used to store register values so that they are the same upon return to the caller as they were when the procedure was called, it can be used to pass arguments to or from a procedure, and it can even be used to allocate space for local variables. The last section of the chapter covers recursive procedure calls.

In assembly languages and with some high-level languages such as Modula-2, the term **procedure** is often used to describe both of the types of subprograms that are implemented as procedures and functions in Pascal. The term procedure will be used in both senses in this book.

Procedures are valuable in assembly language for the same reasons as in high-level languages. They help divide programs into manageable tasks and they isolate code that can be used many times within a single program, or that can be saved and reused in several programs.

6.1

Procedure Body; `call` and `return`

The code for a procedure is always enclosed within some code segment. The body of a procedure is bracketed by two directives, **PROC** and **ENDP**; each of these directives has a label which gives the name of the procedure. In addition, the **PROC** directive usually includes one of the operands **NEAR** or **FAR**. A **NEAR** procedure is defined in the same code segment from which it is called, and a **FAR** procedure is ordinarily defined in a separate code segment. Figure 6.1 shows essential parts of a program that incorporates a procedure `initialize`. The job of the procedure is to initialize several variables; the calling program is sketched, but the code for the procedure itself is complete.

The procedure `initialize` is defined in the same code segment as the main program. Although this example shows the procedure prior to the main code, it could also have been placed afterwards, just before `code` **ENDS**. Recall that execution of a program does not necessarily begin at the first statement of the code segment; it begins at the statement identified by the operand of the **END** directive, which terminates assembly. In this case the label `start` marks the first instruction to be executed.

Most of the statements of procedure `initialize` are ordinary **mov** instructions. These could have been used in the main program at both of the places that the `call` statements are coded, but in this case using the procedure makes the main code both shorter and clearer. The procedure affects words defined in the usual data segment and the BX register; it has no local variables.

Figure 6.1 Program with a NEAR Procedure.

```
stack           SEGMENT stack
                DW      100h DUP (?)
stack           ENDS

data            SEGMENT
count1          DW      ?
count2          DW      ?
total1          DW      ?
total2          DW      ?
                ...
data            ENDS

code            SEGMENT
                ASSUME cs:code,ds:data

initialize PROC     NEAR
                mov     count1,0        ; zero first count
                mov     count2,0        ; zero second count
                mov     total1,0        ; zero first total
                mov     total2,0        ; zero second total
                mov     bx,0            ; zero balance
                ret
initialize ENDP

; -- main (calling) program

start:          mov     ax,SEG data     ; load data segment number
                mov     ds,ax

                call    initialize      ; initialize variables

                ...

                call    initialize      ; reinitialize variables

                ...

quit:           mov     al,0            ; return code 0
                mov     ah,4ch          ; DOS function to return
                int     21h             ; interrupt for DOS services

code            ENDS
                END     start
```

When the main program executes, the instruction

```
call   initialize
```

transfers control from the main code to the procedure. The main program calls the procedure twice; in general, a procedure may be called any number of times. The return instruction

```
ret
```

transfers control from the procedure back to the caller; there is normally at least one **ret** instruction in a procedure and there can be more than one. If there is only one **ret,** it is ordinarily last since subsequent instructions of the procedure would be unreachable without "spaghetti code" including **jmp** instructions. Although a **call** instruction must identify its destination, the **ret** instruction does not—control will transfer to the instruction following the most recent **call**. The 8088 uses memory reserved in the stack segment to store the return address.

The 8088 stack was introduced in Chapter 2; it is now time to have a closer look at it. When a program including the code

```
stack          SEGMENT stack
               DW      100h DUP (?)
stack          ENDS
```

is processed with the usual assembly, link, and load steps, the operating system puts the segment number of the beginning of this 256-word (512-byte) block in the stack segment register SS. In addition, DOS initializes the stack pointer SP to the offset 0200; that is, SP points at the byte that is 512 bytes above the beginning of the area that has been reserved, at the first byte following the stack area. Figure 6.2(a) diagrams this starting situation.

When the stack is used to save values, one or more words is saved, never a single byte.[*] To save a word, first SP is decremented by 2 (bytes). For the initial use of the stack sketched in Figure 6.2(b), SP would then contain the offset of byte 510. A word being saved is then stored at SS:SP, that is, at the new offset in the stack segment. In this example, the first word is stored in the bytes at offsets 510 and 511. Note that the stack is used from top to bottom; the first words stored are at higher addresses than subsequent words. Note also that the stack segment register SS does not change as words are stored, only SP changes.

When a word is retrieved from the stack, the value is first copied from the word at address SS:SP and then SP is incremented by 2. The value stored in the stack area is not actually changed, but it normally is no longer of interest and is replaced when some subsequent word is stored on the stack.

For the example program in Figure 6.1, the **call** instruction saves a word on the stack and the **ret** instruction retrieves it. Specifically, when the 8088 executes either **call**, it saves the offset of the instruction following the call on

---

[*] Some other computer architectures do allow single bytes to be pushed onto the stack.

Figure 6.2 The 8088 Stack.

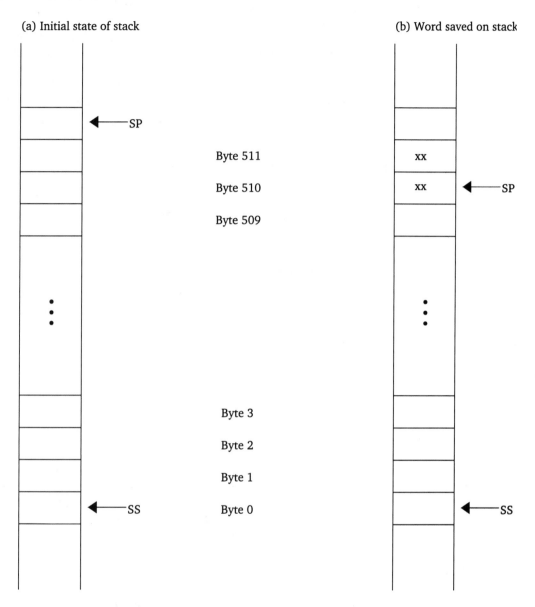

(a) Initial state of stack

(b) Word saved on stack

the stack. The instruction pointer register IP is then changed to contain the offset of **initialize** and execution proceeds with the instruction at CS:IP, that is, at the first instruction of the procedure. Since the main program and the procedure are in the same code segment, the segment number in the code segment register CS does not need to be changed. When the **ret** instruction is executed, the top word in the stack is retrieved and is stored in IP. Execution then proceeds with the instruction located at CS:IP, back in the calling program since the offset of the instruction following the `call` was restored. This intra-segment, call or return is known as a **near**, or **intra-segment**.

When a procedure is located in a different code segment from the call, both the offset of the next instruction and the segment number in the code segment register CS must be saved on the stack. The source code forms of the call and return instructions themselves do not change; directives (covered below) tell the assembler to use machine code for **far**, or **inter-segment**, calls and returns. The far version of a `call` instruction first saves the contents of CS on the stack and loads the segment number of the code segment containing the procedure. Then it saves the offset of the next instruction on the stack and loads the offset of the procedure (in the new code segment) into IP. A total of four bytes of the stack area are used. The far version of a `ret` instruction reverses these steps, first restoring IP to the offset of the instruction following the original call, and then restoring CS to contain the segment number of the caller; both of these words are copied from the stack.

Each `call` instruction has the format

    call   procedure

The operand *procedure* is usually direct, actually naming the procedure, but it can be indirect, using an address contained in a register or in memory. Figure 6.3 lists the various formats of the `call` instruction.

There are two formats for the `ret` instruction. The more common form has no operand, and is simply coded

    ret

A less common version has a single operand, and is coded

    ret   pop_value

The operand pop_value is added to the contents of SP after completion of the other steps of the return process (restoring IP and, for a FAR procedure, CS). This can be useful if other words (sometimes parameter values) have been saved on the stack just for the procedure call, and can be logically discarded when the procedure is exited. Figure 6.4 lists the various formats of `ret` instructions.

Figure 6.3 `call` Instructions.

Procedure Operand	Location of Address	Clock Cycles	Number of Bytes	Opcode
near direct	immediate word	23	3	E8
near indirect	register 16	24	2	FF
near indirect	memory word	29+	2+	FF
far direct	immediate doubleword	36	5	9A
far indirect	memory doubleword	53+	2+	FF

Figure 6.4 `ret` Instructions.

Type	Operand?	Clock Cycles	Number of Bytes	Opcode
near	no	20	1	C3
near	yes	24	3	C2
far	no	34	1	CB
far	yes	33	3	CA

If a procedure's **PROC** directive has the operand **FAR**, then the assembler generates far calls to the procedure and far returns to exit from it. This is true even if the procedure is located in the same code segment from which it is called.

To construct building blocks for large programs, it is often desirable to assemble a procedure or group of procedures separately from the code that calls them. This can be accomplished as outlined in Figure 6.5. Here the procedures are enclosed in a segment named **procedures**. (The name **code** could be used again, but **procedures** is more descriptive.) The **PROC** directive for each procedure contains the operand **FAR**. In addition, the directive

```
PUBLIC        procedure1, procedure2
```

tells the assembler and linker that the labels **procedure1** and **procedure2** may be referenced by other, separately assembled code. As outlined here, the procedures in this segment have no access to any data segment. Mechanisms for storing local data will be covered in Section 6.2. Figure 6.5 shows an **END** directive on the assumption that this is a separate file. This **END** directive has no operand since execution will not begin with a statement in this file. It is possible to include **FAR** directives in the same file as the calling program. In such a combination, there is only one **END**, since this directive terminates assembly.

Figure 6.5 Code for External Procedures.

```
PUBLIC        procedure1, procedure2

procedures    SEGMENT
              ASSUME cs:procedures

procedure1    PROC   FAR
              . . .
procedure1    ENDP

procedure2    PROC   FAR
              . . .
procedure2    ENDP

procedures    ENDS
              END
```

Code that calls these separately assembled procedures must include one or more **EXTRN** directives to tell the assembler that the labels `procedure1` and `procedure2` are **external**, that is, not locally defined. Using one directive, the **EXTRN** statement has the form

```
EXTRN  procedure1:FAR, procedure2:FAR
```

Alternatively, one uses separate **EXTRN** directives to identify the external procedures. Normally **EXTRN** directives are placed near the beginning of the code that includes them.

Suppose that the files used for the main program and the procedures are MAIN.ASM and PROCS.ASM, respectively. The following steps serve to make an executable program:

- Use MASM to assemble MAIN and PROCS (either one first). This produces two .OBJ files, MAIN.OBJ and PROCS.OBJ.
- Link the package, specifying "main+procs+io" as the object modules. (In general one specifies all the .OBJ units to be linked, separated by plus (+) signs. The unit io is needed only if the macros in IO.H have been used.) LINK will normally use the name of the first unit as the name of the .EXE program; the units can be listed in any order.

Following these steps, the .EXE file can be executed by giving its name to DOS.

Techniques for passing values to and from procedures will be discussed in Section 6.3. In the meantime, one method will be used, namely, passing values in the general registers AX, BX, CX, and DX. These registers are not affected by call or return instructions, nor do they have many other assigned duties, so they are well suited to transmit word-size values to or from procedures. Figure 6.6 shows a simple **FAR** procedure `add3` that adds the three integers passed in the BX, CX, and DX registers, returning the sum in the AX register. The code is written for separate compilation.

Figure 6.6 Procedure to Add Three Integers.

```
PUBLIC      add3
code        SEGMENT
            ASSUME cs:code
; procedure to add three integers in BX, CX and DX
; sum is returned in AX

add3        PROC  FAR
            mov   ax,bx      ; copy first value
            add   ax,cx      ; add second value
            add   ax,dx      ; add third value
            ret              ; return to caller
add3        ENDP
code        ENDS
            END
```

——— **Exercises 6.1** ———

1. Suppose that SP contains the offset 0200 and that the statement

   ```
   call   procedure1
   ```

   is a **near** direct procedure `call` at offset 013C in the data segment. What word will be stored on the stack by the call? At what offset will it be stored? What will be the value of SP following the call?

2. Suppose that CS contains the segment number 5A07, that SP contains the offset 0200 and that the statement

   ```
   call   procedure1
   ```

   is a **far** direct procedure `call` at offset 013C in the data segment. What words will be stored on the stack by the call? At what offset will each be stored? What will be the value of SP following the call?

——— **Programming Exercises 6.1** ——————————————————————————————————

1. Write a **NEAR** procedure named **max** that determines which of the 2's complement numbers in the AX and BX registers is larger and copies the larger value into the CX register. Test your procedure by writing a main program that inputs two values, calls **max**, and displays the value that is returned in CX. Recall that code for **max** must be contained in the same code segment as the main program.

2. Repeat Exercise 1, but make **max** a **FAR** procedure by changing the operand on the **PROC** directive. (Still use only one code segment for **max** and the main program.) Find and explain the differences in the listing files for the **NEAR** and **FAR** versions of this program.

3. Write a **FAR** procedure named **max** that determines which of the 2's complement numbers in the AX and BX registers is larger and copies the larger value into the CX register. Include **max** and appropriate directives in file MAX.ASM so that this file can be independently assembled. Write a main program that inputs two values, calls **max**, and displays the value that is returned in CX. Include your main program, data segment, stack segment, and appropriate directives in file MAIN.ASM so that this file can also be independently assembled. Assemble both MAIN.ASM and MAX.ASM to get MAIN.OBJ and MAX.OBJ, link these two files and IO.OBJ to get MAIN.EXE, and run the resulting program.

6.2

push and pop Instructions; Local Data

Breaking a large program into procedures makes it possible to concentrate on one task at a time. For this to be most effective, each procedure should be written in such a way that it does not destroy data in registers or memory that may be needed by the caller. This is usually done using **push** instructions to save data on the stack and **pop** instructions to retrieve them. Sometimes a procedure needs to store local variables in memory; in order to make a logical package, DW and DB directives for such variables may be included with the procedure rather than in the caller's data segment. This section describes how these tasks are accomplished in 8088 assembly language. Section 6.3 examines additional uses for the stack, including another way to reserve space for local variables.

In order to save the contents of a register or word of memory, the value is usually stored on the stack just after execution of a procedure begins, and removed from the stack just before a return instruction is executed. The 8088 instructions used for these jobs are named **push** and **pop**, respectively. Source code for the **push** instruction has the format

Figure 6.7 push Instructions.

Operand	Clock Cycles	Number of Bytes	Opcode
register 16	15	1	
AX			50
CX			51
DX			52
BX			53
SP			54
BP			55
SI			56
DI			57
segment register	14	1	
ES			06
CS			0E
SS			16
DS			1E
memory word	24 +	2 +	FF

push *source*

The operand *source* can be any register except for the flag register and the instruction pointer register IP, or it can reference a word in memory. An immediate operand is not allowed. Neither **push** nor **pop** instructions affect flag settings. Figure 6.7 shows the forms of the **push** instruction.

The **push** instruction uses the 8088 stack in exactly the same way as the **call** instruction. The stack pointer SP is decremented by two bytes and then the word referenced by the source operand is stored in the two bytes with address given by SS:SP. Execution continues with the next instruction, of course, rather than with the first instruction of a procedure as it would with a **call**.

Each **pop** instruction has the format

pop *destination*

where *destination* can reference a word in memory, or any register except the flag register, the instruction pointer IP and the code segment register CS. (The **push** instruction does not exclude CS.) The **pop** instruction restores a value from the stack by copying the word at SS:SP to the destination, and then incrementing SP by 2. Figure 6.8 gives information about **pop** instructions for different destination operands.

Normally **push** and **pop** instructions are used in pairs. Suppose that procedure **proc1** needs to use the AX, CX, and DX registers, and that it is important

Figure 6.8 pop Instructions.

Destination	Clock Cycles	Number of Bytes	Opcode
register 16	12	1	
AX			58
CX			59
DX			5A
BX			5B
SP			5C
BP			5D
SI			5E
DI			5F
segment register	12	1	
ES			07
SS			17
DS			1F
memory word	25 +	2+	8F

to return to the caller with the original values in these registers. Then **proc1** might be structured as follows.

```
proc1 PROC    NEAR
      push    ax        ; save AX
      push    cx        ; save CX
      push    dx        ; save DX

      . . .

      pop     dx        ; restore DX
      pop     cx        ; restore CX
      pop     ax        ; restore AX
      ret
proc1 ENDP
```

Notice that the first register saved (AX) is the last one restored, and that the last register saved (DX) is the first one restored. This is because the value at the address SS:SP (the top of the stack) is always the last one stored on the stack.

Using the stack to preserve variables within a procedure does not interfere with using the stack to store a return address. The **call** instruction pushes the return address on the stack before the procedure is called and other values are pushed on the stack; the **ret** instruction pops the return address off after other values are popped off the stack. If, however, an extra value is popped off the stack before the return instruction, then the return address will be missing when the **ret** is executed and the program will almost certainly crash. Similarly, if an extra value is pushed onto the stack and not popped off, then the **ret** instruction will not retrieve the correct return address; this also would cause a program to fail at execution time. It is very important to match **push** and **pop** instructions!

Occasionally one needs to write a procedure in such a way that it does not alter the flags. (Most of the procedures called by macros in IO.H are written this way.) The ordinary **push** and **pop** instructions cannot be used with the flag register, but a pair of special push and pop instructions serves just for these tasks. The **pushf** (push flags) instruction pushes all 16 bits of the flag register (even those that have no meaning as flags) onto the stack, and the **popf** (pop flags) instruction pops them off the stack. Figure 6.9 summarizes these two instructions. The **popf** instruction also provides the means to load the flag register with any desired values. For instance, a word can be loaded into a general purpose register, pushed onto the stack, and then be retrieved into the flag register with a **popf** instruction.

Figure 6.9 **pushf** and **popf** Instructions.

Instruction	Clock Cycles	Number of Bytes	Opcode
pushf	14	1	9C
popf	12	1	9D

The above discussion concentrated on saving register contents for a calling program. The stack can be used in exactly the same way to save register contents for a procedure itself. This might be needed, for instance, when some complicated expression is being coded and there are not enough registers to hold various partial results. Then the contents of one or more registers can be pushed on the stack only to be popped off a few instructions later.

As an example, suppose that the AX register contains value1, the DX register contains value2 and that the expression (value1 * value2 – value2) must be calculated using only AX and DX, but without changing DX. Multiplication of two word-size operands does use DX, of course. One possible code sequence is

```
push   dx          ; save value2
imul   dx          ; calculate value1*value2
pop    dx          ; retrieve value2
sub    ax,dx        ; value1*value2 - value2
```

Note again that **push** and **pop** instructions are paired.

Simple procedures can be written using only registers to store local variables, or the stack to briefly hold values. Complex procedures often require access to data stored in memory. Sometimes a procedure may use the same data area as the main program, but it is often easier to have data for the procedure in a separate area. There are a variety of ways to do this, and two methods are outlined below. One uses a separate data segment for the procedure, and the other stores data in the same segment as the code for the procedure.

Suppose that the procedure **proc2** needs to reserve space in a data segment, and that this segment is to be assembled with **proc2** but separately from the code that calls **proc2**. Figure 6.10 shows how the code might look. The file contains two segments, **proc_data** for the procedure's data and **proc_code** for the code. These are identified with **SEGMENT** directives in the same way as has been seen for entire programs. The **ASSUME** directive

```
ASSUME cs:proc_code,ds:proc_data
```

tells the assembler to assume that the code segment register CS will point to the segment **proc_code** when the subsequent code executes, and that the data segment register DS will point to the segment **proc_data**. With this directive, the assembler will calculate offsets for references to variables in **proc_data** from the first of that segment, and offsets to instructions in **proc_code** from the beginning of that segment.

Because **proc2** is a **FAR** procedure, the original value in CS will be saved on the stack and CS will be loaded with the segment number of **proc_code** by the **call** instruction. The **ret** instruction will restore CS and transfer control back to the caller. The data segment register DS is not automatically loaded with a new value as a result of a **call** instruction. It is the job of the programmer to save data segment information for the caller, load a new data segment number, and restore DS to the original value before returning. This is accomplished by the code

Figure 6.10 Procedure with Separate Data Segment.

```
proc_data    SEGMENT
             ...
proc_data    ENDS

proc_code    SEGMENT
             ASSUME cs:proc_code,ds:proc_data

proc2        PROC FAR
             push  ds                 ;save old data segment number
             mov   ax,SEG proc_data   ;load new data segment number
             mov   ds,ax
             ...

             pop   ds                 ;restore original data segment
             ret                       ;return
proc2        ENDP

proc_code    ENDS
```

```
             push  ds                 ; save old data segment number
             mov   ax,SEG proc_data   ; load new data segment number
             mov   ds,ax
             ...

             pop   ds                 ; restore original data segment
```

The new segment number is loaded into DS using a pair of instructions similar to those used in main programs. The difference for a procedure is that DS must be saved; **push** and **pop** instructions are used to save and restore DS exactly as one would do with any registers whose contents need to be saved. Notice that the value in AX is destroyed by this sequence. If it were important that the value in AX not be changed, it could also be saved on the stack with a **push** and restored with a **pop**.

```
             push  ax                 ; save AX
             push  ds                 ; save old data segment number
             mov   ax,SEG proc_data   ; load new data segment number
             mov   ds,ax
             ...

             pop   ds                 ; restore original data segment
             pop   ax                 ; restore AX
```

Another option is illustrated in Figure 6.11. It is appropriate when a procedure

Figure 6.11 Data and Procedure in One Segment.

```
proc_seg       SEGMENT
               ASSUME cs:proc_seg,ds:proc_seg

                                     ; local data
index          DW ?
stars          DB '******'

                                     ; procedure
proc3          PROC FAR
               push  ds              ;save old data segment number
               mov   ax,SEG proc_seg ;load new data segment number
               mov   ds,ax
               ...

               pop   ds              ;restore original data segment
               ret                   ;return
proc3          ENDP

proc_seg       ENDS
```

needs a small amount of local data space in memory. The procedure **proc3** uses a word **index** and a string **stars**, spaces for which are reserved in the same segment as the code. Both data and code are contained in the segment **proc_seg**, so the **ASSUME** directive tells the assembler to assume that both CS and DS registers will point to this segment. As in the previous example, CS will be automatically changed by call and return instructions. It is again the programmer's job to put the correct value in DS; the same instructions as before will work. There are many places in the segment where the definitions for **index** and **stars** can be placed. Normally a good practice is to group all data definitions together, and place them either at the beginning or end of the segment.

The reader may wonder at this point, "Why bother with separate code and data segments at all?" It is true that the structure shown in Figure 6.11 is the simplest shown so far, and that it will even work for a main program. A separate data segment is not required. The main reason for keeping separate code and data segments is to allow for programs with more code and/or data than would be possible with a single segment. Recall that a segment contains 64K bytes. Using separate code and data segments allows for a main program that uses up to 128K bytes total. When additional segments are used for procedures, the total program can be even longer. It is also conceptually easier to view code and data as separate, although they actually share the same memory.

Another possibility needs to be mentioned here although it will not be used in this book. The sections of code that are designated by **SEGMENT** directives do not actually have to correspond to memory segments. If certain operands are used with **SEGMENT** directives, then the Microsoft linker will combine all program segments having the same name into a single memory segment. This allows, for example, a data area to be defined in pieces along with distinct procedures, but to be combined into one memory segment for execution. Offsets are adjusted by the linker to be from the beginning of this combined segment. Since there is only one data segment, the data segment register DS does not need to be saved and loaded every time a procedure is called. If an assembly language procedure is to be linked with code written in a high-level language, it is sometimes required that the procedure share a data segment with the main program. In such a case, the documentation for the high-level language normally specifies the name that must be given to the data segment.

One of the most important techniques for reserving local variable space uses stack space. This method will be covered in the next section.

Exercises 6.2

---

1. Many microprocessors do not have an instruction equivalent to **xchg**. With such systems, a sequence of instructions like the following can be used to exchange the contents of two registers:

   ```
   push   ax
   push   bx
   pop    ax
   pop    bx
   ```

   Explain why this sequence works to exchange the contents of the AX and BX registers. Compare the number of bytes of code and clock cycles required to execute this sequence with those required for the instruction

   ```
   xchg ax,bx
   ```

2. Another alternative to the **xchg** instruction is to use

   ```
   push   ax
   mov    ax, bx
   pop    bx
   ```

   Explain why this sequence works to exchange the contents of the AX and BX registers. Compare the number of bytes of code and clock cycles required to execute this sequence with those required for the instruction

   ```
   xchg ax,bx
   ```

—————— **Programming Exercises 6.2** ———

Each of these exercises asks for a procedure **exprn** to evaluate the expression

$$x^2 + y^2 + z^2 + xy + xz + yz$$

for given values of x, y, and z. In each procedure, pass the values as follows:

x in AX
y in BX
z in CX

Return the value of the expression in DX.

The values in AX, BX, and CX and the flag register should be the same upon return to the caller as they were when the procedure was called (use the stack). To code these procedures, it is almost certainly going to be necessary to store intermediate results somewhere. The problems below restrict where these intermediate results may be stored. The procedures should all be tested using the same main program that inputs appropriate values for x, y and z, calls procedure **exprn**, and outputs the value returned by the procedure.

1. Write a **FAR** procedure **exprn** that evaluates the above expression. Use the stack only to store intermediate results; this procedure should have no local data definition.

2. Write a **FAR** procedure **exprn** that evaluates the above expression. Intermediate results should be stored in a separate data segment that is defined just for this procedure.

3. Write a **FAR** procedure **exprn** that evaluates the above expression. Intermediate results should be stored in the same segment as the code for the procedure.

—————— 6.3 ———

Passing Values to or from a Procedure

Using a high-level language, a procedure definition often includes parameters that are associated with arguments when the procedure is called. For the procedure's **value parameters**, when the procedure is called, values of the argu-

Figure 6.12 Using Arguments from the Stack.

```
proc_code    SEGMENT
             ASSUME cs:proc_code

add2         PROC FAR      ; add two parameters passed on the stack
                           ; return the sum in the AX register
             mov    bp,sp              ; copy stack pointer
             mov    ax,[bp+4]          ; copy second parameter
             add    ax,[bp+6]          ; add first parameter
             ret                       ; return
add2         ENDP

proc_code    ENDS
```

ments (which may be expressions) are copied to the parameters, and these values may then be used in the procedure using their local names (the identifiers used to define the parameters). **Variable parameters** associate a parameter identifier with an argument that is a single variable, and can be used to pass a value either to the procedure from the caller or from the procedure back to the caller. Values can be passed to or from assembly language procedures in an even greater variety of ways. Some techniques will be discussed in this section.

Here are two of the possibilities for passing a word-size value to a procedure:

- put the value in a register
- push the value on the stack

Using a register to pass word-size values to a procedure (or from a procedure back to the caller) is straightforward; previous examples and exercises in this chapter have used this technique. The first examples in this section show how to use the stack to pass values of arguments to a procedure.

Suppose that a procedure **add2** is to add two values for two word-size integers and that a calling program pushes these values on the stack before calling **add2**. Code in the calling program might look like

```
      push    value1       ; first argument value
      push    cx           ; second argument value
      call    add2         ; call procedure to find sum
```

Figure 6.12 shows one way the procedure can retrieve these values from the stack. This example uses the **based addressing** mode. In this mode, the offset of a memory location is calculated as the sum of the contents of a base register (one of BP or BX) and a number built into the instruction. The MASM assembler accepts several alternative notations for a based address; this book will use

```
[bp + number]
```

for BP and

```
[bx + number]
```

for BX. If the base register used is BP, then the offset is in the stack segment; that is, the actual address is SS:(BP+*number*). On the other hand, if BX is used, then the offset is in the data segment; the actual address is DS:(BX+*number*).

This method of passing argument values works as follows. The instruction

```
mov     bp,sp                    ; copy stack pointer
```

copies the current value of the stack pointer SP to the base pointer BP. The doubleword at address SS:SP (now the same as SS:BP) will contain the return address for the subroutine call. (The return address will consist of both the code segment and instruction pointer values since this is a **FAR** procedure.) Assuming that the arguments were pushed on the stack immediately before the call to **add2**, they will be at the addresses immediately above the return address. (Remember that SP is decremented when values are pushed on the stack.) The second argument (the last one pushed on the stack) is four bytes above the current SS:BP (or SS:SP) address, the four bytes of the return address. Therefore it is at SS:(BP+4) and is copied by the instruction

```
mov     ax,[bp+4]                ; copy second parameter
```

The first argument is an additional two bytes above the current SS:BP address, since the second argument and the return address were pushed onto the stack after the first argument. It is at SS:(BP+6) and can be added using the instruction

```
add     ax,[bp+6]                ; add first parameter
```

The diagram in Figure 6.13 shows the locations of the return address and the arguments on the stack after SP has been copied to BP.

There are many variations on this basic theme. If **add2** were a **NEAR** procedure but were otherwise unchanged from Figure 6.12, then only the offset of the return address, not the code segment, would be pushed on the stack. In this case, the second parameter would be at offset (BP+2) and the first would be at offset (BP+4).

It is often important to return to the caller with the base pointer BP unchanged. In this case, the value in BP must be pushed on the stack at the beginning of the procedure, before copying the stack pointer SP value to BP. This makes each of the arguments an additional two bytes further up on the stack, relative to SS:BP. Assuming that the procedure has been declared FAR, the second parameter is at offset (BP+6) and the first is at offset (BP+8). If other registers need to be saved, this may be done after SP is copied to BP.

The real strength of this system is that once BP is fixed, the stack can be freely used for any purpose, with SP changing, while it is still possible to locate parameter values from the reference point provided by BP. Figure 6.14 shows typical procedure entry code and exit code assuming that AX, BX, CX, and the flag register need to be saved.

Figure 6.13 Arguments on the Stack.

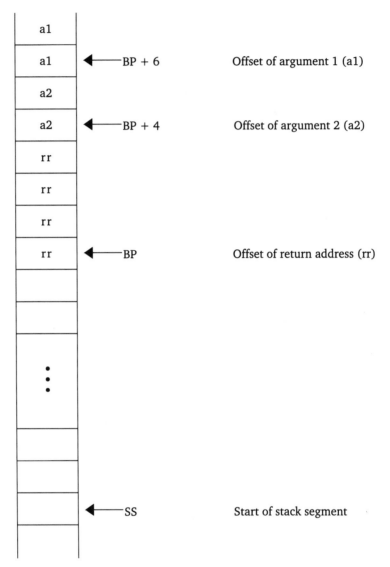

BP + 6	Offset of argument 1 (a1)
BP + 4	Offset of argument 2 (a2)
BP	Offset of return address (rr)
SS	Start of stack segment

The previous section discussed various ways that a procedure could store local variables. An additional very important method is to use the stack segment and based addresses below the base pointer. The technique is to use a **sub** instruction to move SP down in the stack, so that subsequent **push** instructions will not store data in the space directly below the BP location. An **add** instruction as part of the exit code restores SP. (Exercise 2 gives an alternative to the **add** instruction.)

Figure 6.14 Typical Procedure Entry and Exit Code.

```
push  bp              ; save base pointer
mov   bp, sp          ; new base pointer value
push  ax              ; save other registers
push  bx
push  cx
pushf                 ; save flags
  .
  .
  .
popf                  ; restore flags
pop   cx              ; restore registers
pop   bx
pop   ax
pop   bp
ret                   ; return to caller
```

Figure 6.15 Local Variable Space Using the Stack.

```
push  bp              ; save base pointer
mov   bp, sp          ; new base pointer value
sub   sp, 6           ; three words on the stack for local data
push  ax              ; save registers
push  bx
push  cx
pushf                 ; save flags
  .
  .
  .
popf                  ; restore flags
pop   cx              ; restore registers
pop   bx
pop   ax
add   sp, 6           ; move stack pointer above local data area
pop   bp              ; restore base pointer
ret                   ; return to caller
```

Figure 6.15 expands on the entry code and exit code in Figure 6.14, reserving three words of local storage on the stack. The word directly below where BP is saved can be referenced by [bp-2], the next word down by [bp-4] and the bottom word by [bp-6]. Parameter values can still be referenced by addresses like [bp+8]. Assuming that this is a **FAR** procedure with two parameters, Figure 6.16 sketches how the stack is used.

Figure 6.16 Use of the Stack.

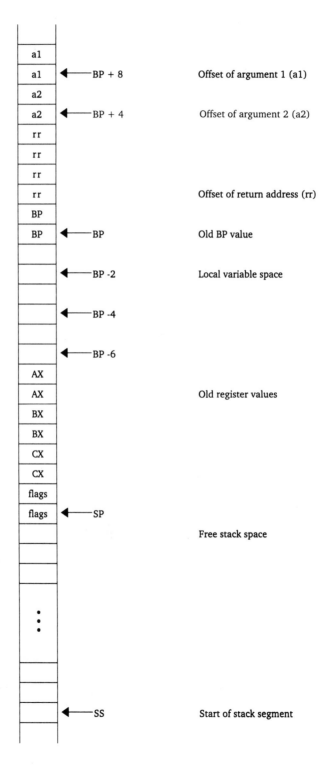

a1		
a1	◄── BP + 8	Offset of argument 1 (a1)
a2		
a2	◄── BP + 4	Offset of argument 2 (a2)
rr		
rr		
rr		
rr		Offset of return address (rr)
BP		
BP	◄── BP	Old BP value
	◄── BP -2	Local variable space
	◄── BP -4	
	◄── BP -6	
AX		
AX		Old register values
BX		
BX		
CX		
CX		
flags		
flags	◄── SP	
		Free stack space
	◄── SS	Start of stack segment

Figure 6.17 Addresses of Arguments Passed to Procedure.

```
proc_code    SEGMENT
             ASSUME cs:proc_code


add2         PROC FAR
; add two numbers whose offsets are passed in BX and CX, respectively
; return sum in AX
             mov     ax,[bx]       ; copy first argument
             mov     bx,cx         ; copy offset of second argument
             add     ax,[bx]       ; add second argument
             ret                   ; return
add2         ENDP

proc_code    ENDS


             END
```

Coding with operands like [bp+8] or [bp-4] is sometimes confusing. The EQU directive can be used to establish meaningful labels that can be used instead. For example, if [bp+8] is used to transmit an argument length and [bp-4] is used for a local variable area, one could code

```
length  EQU   [bp+8]
area    EQU   [bp-4]
```

Using these directives, length and area can be coded instead of [bp+8] and [bp-4].

How can a high-level language implement variable parameters? The basic scheme is to pass the address of an argument rather than the value of the argument to the procedure. The procedure can then either use the value at the address or store a new value at the address. Figure 6.17 shows a version of add2 that adds two 2's complement numbers, the offsets of which are passed in the BX and CX registers. This procedure does not use a local data segment; since DS is not changed, the offsets that are passed to the procedure will still give the effective addresses of the arguments. The first argument is copied into the AX register from the word whose offset is stored in the BX register. (Recall that the notation [bx] indicates register indirect addressing.) Since the CX register cannot be used for register indirect addressing, the offset of the second argument is copied to BX in order to access the value of second argument.

Figure 6.18 shows portions of a program that calls this version of add2. The arguments to be added are stored in memory at the words value1 and value2. The offsets of these words (in the data segment) are loaded into BX and CX respectively before add2 is called.

Suppose that a procedure does need to change the segment number in DS. Then the address [bx] would reference the wrong value since the offset would be calculated from the beginning of a different segment. One possible fix for

Figure 6.18 Passing Addresses of Arguments.

```
EXTRN add2:FAR
    ...

data        SEGMENT
    ...

value1      DW      ?
value2      DW      ?
data        ENDS

code        SEGMENT
            ASSUME cs:code,ds:data

start:      mov     ax,SEG data     ; load data segment address
            mov     ds,ax
    ...

            mov     bx,OFFSET value1 ; offset of value1
            mov     cx,OFFSET value2 ; offset of value2
            call    add2             ; get sum in cx
            itoa    out_value,ax     ; convert sum to ASCII
    ...

code        ENDS

            END     start
```

this problem is to pass the original segment number in the extra segment register ES. This could be done in the calling program using

```
        mov     ax,ds       ; copy segment number
        mov     es,ax
```

(The instruction mov es,ds is illegal.) Procedure add2 in Figure 6.17 can then be modified by changing the lines which calculate the sum to

```
        mov     ax,es:[bx]  ; copy second parameter
        mov     bx,cx       ; copy offset of first parameter
        add     ax,es:[bx]  ; add first parameter
```

The new notation es: indicates a **segment override**. When the instructions are executed, the offset is calculated in the extra segment ES rather than in the data segment DS. That is, the memory operand used is ES:BX rather than the default DS:BX. Since ES contains the segment number of the data segment in the calling program, this results in the addresses of the original arguments. A segment override adds one byte to the object code of each instruction in which it is included and increases an instruction's execution time by two clock cycles.

To pass an argument that is longer than a word or two in length, usually the address (offset, or segment number and offset) is sent to a procedure. This is typically used when character strings, arrays, or records are used as arguments in procedure calls.

Most of the discussion in this section has concentrated on sending values to a procedure. Word-size results have been returned in a register. Another possibility is to return a result on the stack. If a **FAR** procedure has two parameters and is coded as outlined in Figure 6.15, then the first parameter could be replaced by a result using, for example

```
mov    [bp+8], ax      ; store result
```

The calling program can then pop the result off the stack.

This raises another issue. If a program continues to push arguments on the stack and to call procedures, then either the calling program or the procedures must remove these values from the stack or risk it eventually overflowing. The calling program can do this by adding the number of bytes to be freed to SP. A complete calling sequence might look like

```
push   value1          ; first value
push   value2          ; second value
call   add2            ; add values
add    sp,4            ; discard parameters from stack
itoa   result,ax       ; use sum placed in AX by add2
```

Another possibility is to use the version of the **ret** instruction that adds a value to SP. When this is done, the instruction **add sp,4** in the calling program is not used, but **ret 4** is used instead of **ret** with no operand in **add2**.

Notice that neither of these techniques will work without modification if the stack is used to return one or more results to the calling program. This book will normally assign the job of discarding parameters to the calling program, not the procedure.

This section has illustrated some of the ways that values can be passed to or from procedures. Many options are available. However, when writing assembly language procedures to interface with code written in high-level languages, a programmer must be careful to follow the parameter passing conventions required by the implementation of that language.

───────── Exercises 6.3 ───

1. Suppose that a FAR procedure begins with

```
push   bp              ; save BP
mov    bp,sp           ; new base pointer
push   cx              ; save registers
push   si
. . .
```

Assuming this procedure has three parameters passed on the stack, how can each be addressed?

2. In Figure 6.15, the statement add sp, 6 is used to delete local variable space from the stack. An alternative is to code mov sp, bp. Why will this mov statement do the same job? Which choice takes fewer clock cycles? Which choice takes fewer bytes of object code?

3. Some assembly languages pass parameters by using a register to point at a block of parameter addresses. This could be done with an 8088 computer using

```
value1      DW      ?
...
value2      DW      ?
...
addr_list DW      OFFSET value1
          DW      OFFSET value2
```

Note that value1 and value2 do not need to be in consecutive words, but their addresses are in consecutive words at addr_list. The address of the address list can be loaded into AX using

```
mov ax, OFFSET addr_list
```

or lea ax, addr_list. Assuming this has been done just prior to calling a procedure, how can the procedure access the two parameter values?

--------- **Programming Exercises 6.3** ---------

Write a **FAR** procedure to accomplish each task specified below. For each procedure, use the stack to pass arguments to the procedure. Except for those problems that explicitly say to return a result in a register, register contents should be unchanged by the procedures; that is, registers (including the flag register) that are used in the procedure should be saved at the beginning of the procedure and restored before returning. Use the ret instruction with no operand. In each case, write a separately assembled main program that will input appropriate values and display results. The main program should remove arguments from the stack. Link and run the complete package.

1. Write a procedure min to find the minimum of two word-size integer parameters. Return the minimum in the AX register.

2. Write a procedure min to find the minimum of two word-size integer parameters. Return the minimum on the stack, replacing the first parameter.

3. Write a procedure **max** to find the maximum of two word-size integer parameters. The main program will pass two additional values to the procedure, the segment number of the main program's data segment and the offset of a word in this data segment; these values will also be passed on the stack. Return the maximum to the main program by storing it at the address determined by the segment number and offset.

4. Write a procedure **write_value** to display the value of the expression

    ```
    3 * parameter_1  +  5 * parameter_2
    ```

    Output the six-character format produced by the **itoa** macro. The procedure should not display anything other than the six characters of the sum.

6.4

Recursion

A **recursive** procedure or function is one that calls itself, either directly or indirectly. The best algorithms for manipulating many data structures are recursive. It can be very difficult to code certain algorithms in a programming language that does not support recursion.

It is almost as easy to code a recursive procedure in 8088 assembly language as it is to code a nonrecursive procedure. If parameters are passed on the stack, then each call of the procedure gets new storage allocated for its parameters so that there is no danger of the arguments passed to one call of a procedure being confused with those for another call. Similarly, if critical values are stored on the stack to avoid their being wiped out by a procedure call, then the same registers or even memory locations can be used by each recursive call of a procedure.

This section gives one example of a recursive procedure in 8088 assembly language. It solves the Towers of Hanoi puzzle, pictured in Figure 6.19 with four

Figure 6.19 Towers of Hanoi Puzzle.

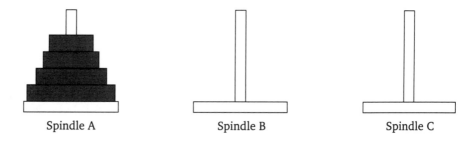

Spindle A   Spindle B   Spindle C

Figure 6.20 Program Design for Towers of Hanoi Solution.

```
procedure move(number_of_disks, source, destination, spare);
begin
    if number_of_disks = 1
    then
        display " Move disk from ", source, " to ", destination
    else
        move(number_of_disks – 1, source, spare, destination);
        move(1, source, destination, spare);
        move(number_of_disks – 1, spare, destination, source);
    end if;
end procedure move;
begin {main program}
    prompt for and input number_of_disks;
    move(number_of_disks, 'A', 'B', 'C');
end;
```

disks. The object of the puzzle is to move all disks from source spindle A to destination spindle B, one at a time, never placing a larger disk on top of a smaller disk. Disks can be moved to spindle C, a spare spindle. For instance, if there are only two disks, the small disk can be moved from spindle A to C, the large one can be moved from A to B, and finally the small one can be moved from C to B.

In general, the Towers of Hanoi puzzle is solved by looking at two cases. If the number of disks to be moved is 1, then the single disk is simply moved from the source spindle to the destination. If the number of disks is greater than one, then the top (number – 1) disks are moved to the spare spindle, the largest one is moved to the destination, and finally the (number – 1) smaller disks are moved from the spare spindle to the destination. Each time (number – 1) disks are moved, exactly the same procedure is followed, except that different spindles have the roles of source, destination, and spare. Figure 6.20 expresses the algorithm in pseudocode.

Figure 6.21 shows 8088 code that implements the design. The stack is used to pass parameters. Because procedure **move** needs to use the base pointer BP after a recursive call to itself, BP must be saved on the stack before the stack pointer is copied. Even though **move** uses other registers, it is not important that their contents be saved and restored. The code is a fairly straightforward translation of the pseudocode design. The operator **WORD PTR** is required in the statement

```
cmp WORD PTR [bp+10],1
```

so that the assembler knows whether to compare words or byte-size operands. Notice that each character that labels a spindle is stored with an extra space in a word rather than as a single byte. This is because single bytes cannot be pushed on the 8088's stack.

Figure 6.21 Towers of Hanoi Solution.

```
; program to print instructions for "Towers of Hanoi" puzzle

INCLUDE io.h

cr          EQU     0dh    ; carriage return character
Lf          EQU     0ah    ; linefeed character


stack       SEGMENT stack
            DW      200h DUP (?)
stack       ENDS


data        SEGMENT
prompt      DB      cr,Lf,'How many disks?  ',0
number      DB      16 DUP (?)
message     DB      cr,Lf,'Move disk from spindle '
source      DB      ?
            DB      ' to spindle '
dest        DB      ?
            DB      '.',0
data        ENDS


code        SEGMENT
            ASSUME cs:code,ds:data


move        PROC NEAR

; procedure move(number : integer; { number of disks to move }
;                source, dest, spare : character { spindles to use } )
; parameters are passed in words on the stack

            push    bp              ; save base pointer
            mov     bp,sp           ; copy stack pointer

            cmp     WORD PTR [bp+10],1  ; number of disks = 1?
            jne     move_stack      ; if not, more work to do
just_one:   mov     bx,[bp+8]       ; source
            mov     source,bl       ; copy character to output
            mov     bx,[bp+6]       ; destination
            mov     dest,bl         ; copy character to output
            output message          ; print line
            jmp     return          ; return
move_stack: mov     ax,[bp+10]      ; get number
            dec     ax              ; number - 1
            push    ax              ; parameter 1
            push    [bp+8]          ; parameter 2: source does not change
            push    [bp+4]          ; parameter 3: old spare is new destination
            push    [bp+6]          ; parameter 4: old destination is new spare
            call    move            ; move(number-1,source,spare,destination)
            add     sp,8            ; pop parameters off stack
```

Figure 6.21 Continued

```
            mov    ax,1          ; for one disk
            push   ax            ; parameter 1
            push   [bp+8]        ; parameter 2: source does not change
            push   [bp+6]        ; parameter 3: destination unchanged
            push   [bp+4]        ; parameter 4: spare unchanged
            call   move          ; move(1,source,destination,spare)
            add    sp,8          ; pop parameters off stack

            mov    ax,[bp+10]    ; original number
            dec    ax            ; number - 1
            push   ax            ; parameter 1
            push   [bp+4]        ; parameter 2: source is original spare
            push   [bp+6]        ; parameter 3: original destination
            push   [bp+8]        ; parameter 4: original source is spare
            call   move          ; move(number-1,spare,destination,source)
            add    sp,8          ; pop parameters off stack
return:     pop    bp            ; restore base pointer
            ret                  ; return

move        ENDP

start:      mov    ax,SEG data   ; load data segment number
            mov    ds,ax

            output prompt        ; ask for number of disks
            inputs number,16     ; read ASCII characters
            atoi   number        ; convert to integer
            push   ax            ; argument 1 (number)
            mov    ax,' A'       ; source spindle
            push   ax            ; argument 2
            mov    ax,' B'       ; destination spindle
            push   ax            ; argument 3
            mov    ax,' C'       ; spare spindle
            push   ax            ; argument 4
            call   move          ; move(number,source,dest,spare)
            add    sp,8          ; pop parameters off stack

quit:       mov    al,0          ; return code 0
            mov    ah,4ch        ; DOS function to return
            int    21h           ; interrupt for DOS services

code        ENDS
            END    start
```

Exercises 6.4

1. What would go wrong in the Towers of Hanoi program if BP were not saved at the beginning of procedure **move** and restored at the end?

2. Suppose that the Towers of Hanoi program is executed and 2 is entered for the number of disks. Trace the stack contents from the first **push** in the main program through the instruction **add sp, 8** in the main program.

Programming Exercises 6.4

1. The factorial function is defined for a nonnegative integer argument n by

$$\text{factorial}(n) = \begin{cases} 1 & \text{if } n = 0 \\ n * \text{factorial}(n-1) & \text{if } n > 0 \end{cases}$$

Write a recursive assembly language procedure named **factorial** that implements this recursive definition. The stack should be used to pass the single integer argument; the value of the function should be returned in the AX register. Test your function by calling it from a main program that inputs an integer, calls the factorial function, and displays the value returned by the function. (Your program will only give correct answers for a few small argument values. Why?)

2. The greatest common divisor (gcd) of two positive integers m and n can be calculated recursively by the function described below in pseudocode.

function gcd(m, n : integer) : integer;

remainder := n mod m;

if remainder = 0
then
      return m;
else
      return gcd(remainder, m);
end if;

Implement this recursive definition in assembly language. Use the stack to pass the two argument values. Return the value of the function in the AX register. Test your function using a main program that accepts as input two integers, calls the greatest common divisor function **gcd,** and displays the value returned.

───── 6.5 ──

Chapter Summary

This chapter has discussed techniques for implementing procedures in 8088 assembly language. The code for a procedure is bracketed between **PROC** and **ENDP** directives. This code is contained in a code segment; a **FAR** procedure is usually in a different segment from the calling program and a **NEAR** procedure must be in the same segment as the calling program.

The 8088 stack serves many functions. When a procedure is called, the offset of the next instruction (and, for a **FAR** procedure, the segment number) is stored on the stack before control transfers to the first instruction of the procedure. A return instruction removes these from the stack in order to transfer control back to the correct point in the calling program. Argument values can be pushed onto the stack to pass them to a procedure; when this is done, the base pointer BP and based addressing provide a convenient mechanism for accessing the values in the procedure. The stack is also used to "preserve the environment"; for example, the contents of a register can be pushed onto the stack when a procedure begins and popped off before returning to the calling program, so that the calling program will have the register unchanged, even though it is used by the procedure.

In addition to using the stack to pass argument values, it is possible to pass some values in registers. In order to transmit arguments larger than words or to pass values from the procedure to the calling program via parameters, the addresses of arguments rather than their values can be sent to a procedure.

A procedure may store data in memory several ways. An important method uses stack space below the base pointer. Another method is to include DW, DB, and similar directives in the code segment for the procedure itself; this is suitable for small procedures that need a small amount of data area. A procedure can use the same data area as the calling program, or a completely separate data area can be established. It is the programmer's job to ensure that the data segment register DS contains the segment number of the correct segment.

Recursive algorithms arise naturally in many computing applications. Recursive procedures are no more difficult than nonrecursive procedures to implement in 8088 assembly language.

CHAPTER 7

String
Operations

This chapter covers 8088 instructions that are used to handle strings. Computers are frequently used to manipulate strings of characters as well as numeric data. For example, in business data processing applications names, street addresses, and other information must be stored and sometimes rearranged. Text editor and word processor programs must be capable of searching for and moving strings of characters like words or phrases. Even when computation is primarily numerical, it is often necessary to convert a character string to an internal numerical format when a number is entered at the keyboard, or to convert an internal format to a character string for display purposes. As shown in previous examples, the `atoi` and the `itoa` macros can perform these conversion tasks.

The 8088 microprocessor can manipulate strings of words as well as strings of single bytes. Many applications are given, including procedures that are similar to those in some high-level languages and the procedure that is called by the `itoa` macro.

—— 7.1 ————————————————————————————————

Using String Instructions

There are five 8088 instructions designed for string manipulation, **movs** (move string), **cmps** (compare string), **scas** (scan string), **stos** (store string), and **lods** (load string). The **movs** instruction is used to copy a string from one memory location to another. The **cmps** instruction is designed to compare the contents of two strings. The **scas** instruction can be used to search a string for one particular value. The **stos** instruction can store a new value in some position of a string. Finally, the **lods** instruction copies a value out of some position of a string.

A **string** in the 8088 environment refers to a contiguous collection of bytes or words in memory. Strings are commonly defined in a program's data segment using such directives as

```
response      DB    20 DUP (?)
label_1       DB    'The results are ', 0
word_string   DW    50 DUP (?)
```

Each string instruction applies to a source string, a destination string, or both. The bytes or words of these strings are processed one at a time by an instruction. Register indirect addressing is used to locate the individual byte or word elements. The 8088 instructions access elements of the source string using the offset in the source index register SI. Elements in the destination string are accessed using the offset in the destination index register DI. The source element is where one would expect in the data segment; that is, its actual address is DS:SI. However, for string instructions the destination element is in the extra segment; its actual address is ES:DI.

One consequence of using offsets in the extra segment is that the programmer has the job of ensuring that ES contains the correct segment number. The extra segment can be the same as the data segment. If source and destination strings are both in the usual data segment, then the familiar instructions for initialization of the data segment register DS can be extended to

```
start:   mov    ax,SEG data    ; load data segment number
         mov    ds,ax
         mov    es,ax
```

also initializing ES. Following these instructions, each of DS and ES point at (contain the segment number of) the segment **data**. The sample program in Figure 7.3 shows another way that ES can be made to point to the right segment.

Since the source and destination addresses of string elements are always given by SI and DI, respectively, no operands are needed to identify these locations. Without any operand, however, the assembler cannot tell the size of the string element to be used. For example, writing **movs** by itself without any operand could mean to move either a byte or a word. The Microsoft Macro Assembler offers two ways around this dilemma. The first option is to use destination and source operands; these are ignored except that MASM notes their byte or word type (both operands must be the same type) and uses that element size. The second option is to use special versions of the mnemonics that define the element size—instructions that operate on bytes use a "b" suffix; word string instructions use a "w" suffix. For example, **movsb** is used to move byte strings and **movsw** is used to move word strings. Both of these instructions assemble as a **movs** and neither uses an operand since the assembler knows the element size from the mnemonic. This book will use the mnemonics with "b" and "w" suffixes rather than operands for string instructions.

Although a string instruction operates on only one string element at a time, it gets ready to operate on the next element. It does this by changing the source index register SI and/or the destination index register DI to contain the offset of the next element of the string(s). When byte-size elements are being used, the index registers are changed by one; for words, SI and DI are changed by two. The 8088 can move either forward through a string (from lower to higher addresses) or backward (from higher to lower addresses). The movement direction is determined by the value of the **direction flag** DF, which is bit 10 of the flag register. If DF is set to 1, then the values in SI and DI are decremented by string instructions, causing right to left string operations. If DF is clear (0), then the values in SI and DI are incremented by string instructions, so that strings are processed left to right.

The 8088 has two instructions whose sole purpose is to reset or set the direction flag DF. The **cld** instruction clears DF so that strings are processed left to right. The **std** sets DF to 1 so that SI and DI are decremented by string instructions and strings are processed backward. Information about these instructions appears in Figure 7.1.

Finally it is time to present a string instruction in detail. The move string instruction **movs** transfers one string element (byte or word) from a source string to a destination string. The source element at address DS:SI is copied to address ES:DI. After the string element is copied, both index registers are changed by the element size, incremented if the direction flag DF is 0 or decremented if DF is 1. The **movs** instruction does not affect any flag. It comes in **movsb** and **movsw** versions; Figure 7.2 gives information about both forms.

Figure 7.1 **cld** and **std** Instructions.

Instruction	Clock Cycles	Number of Bytes	Opcode
cld	2	1	FC
std	2	1	FD

Figure 7.2 movs Instructions.

Mnemonic	Element Size	Clock Cycles	Number of Bytes	Opcode
movsb	byte	18	1	A4
movsw	word	26	1	A5

Figure 7.3 gives an example of a program that uses the movs instruction. The important part of the example is the procedure strcopy. This procedure has two parameters (passed on the stack) that give the destination and source offsets of byte (character) strings in the segment whose segment number is in the data segment register DS. The source string is assumed to be null-terminated, and the procedure strcopy produces an exact copy of the source string at the destination location. The procedure terminates the destination string by a null byte.

The procedure strcopy has no local data segment. It uses some of the 8088 registers for local data; each of these (and the flag register) is saved on the stack so that the procedure will return with them unchanged.

Because a movs instruction will be used, several preliminary steps must be done:

- The extra segment register ES must contain the segment number for the destination string.
- The index registers SI and DI must be initialized to the offsets of the first string bytes to be processed.
- The direction flag must be assigned the appropriate value.

The values for SI and DI are the arguments that were pushed on the stack. Since DS is assumed to contain the segment number of the segment where both source and destination strings are located, its value is copied to ES. Finally, cld clears the direction flag, ensuring left to right processing.

The main part of the procedure executes the following pseudocode design:

```
while next source byte is not null
      copy source byte to destination;
      increment source index;
      increment destination index;
end while;

put null byte at end of destination string;
```

To check whether the next source byte is null, the statement

```
while:       cmp      BYTE PTR [si],0   ;null source byte?
```

is used. The notation [si] indicates register indirect addressing, so that the element at the offset in SI is used, that is, the current byte of the source string.

Figure 7.3 String Copy Program.

```
; implementation of "strcopy" procedure

proc_code    SEGMENT
             ASSUME cs:proc_code
strcopy      PROC FAR

; Procedure to copy string until null byte in source is copied.
; It is assumed that destination location is long enough for copy.

; Parameters are passed on the stack:
;    (1)  offset of destination
;    (2)  offset of source

; DS contains the segment number for both destination and source.
; No register is modified.

             push    bp               ;save base pointer
             mov     bp,sp            ;copy stack pointer

             push    ax               ;save registers and flags
             push    di
             push    si
             push    es
             pushf

             mov     si,[bp+6]        ;initial source offset
             mov     di,[bp+8]        ;destination
             mov     ax,ds            ;copy DS to ES
             mov     es,ax
             cld                      ;clear direction flag

while:       cmp     BYTE PTR [si],0  ;null source byte?
             je      endwhile         ;stop copying if null
             movsb                    ;copy  one byte
             jmp     while            ;go check next byte
endwhile:
             mov     BYTE PTR [di],0  ;terminate destination string

             popf                     ;restore flags and registers
             pop     es
             pop     si
             pop     di
             pop     ax
             pop     bp
```

Figure 7.3 Continued

```
            ret                         ;exit procedure

strcopy     ENDP
proc_code   ENDS

; program to test "strcopy"

INCLUDE io.h

cr          EQU     0dh                 ;carriage return character
Lf          EQU     0ah                 ;linefeed character

stack       SEGMENT stack
            DW      200h DUP (?)
stack       ENDS

data        SEGMENT
prompt      DB      cr,Lf,'Original string?  ',0
string_in   DB      80 DUP (?)
display     DB      cr,Lf,Lf,'Your string was',cr,Lf
string_out  DB      80 DUP (?)
data        ENDS

code        SEGMENT
            ASSUME cs:code,ds:data


start:      mov     ax,SEG data         ;load data segment number
            mov     ds,ax

            output prompt               ;ask for string
            inputs string_in,80         ;read source string
            mov     ax,OFFSET string_out    ; destination
            push    ax                  ;first parameter
            mov     ax,OFFSET string_in     ; source
            push    ax                  ;second parameter
            call    strcopy             ;call string copy procedure
            add     sp,4                ;remove arguments from stack
            output display              ;print result

quit:       mov     al,0                ;return code 0
            mov     ah,4ch              ;DOS function to return
            int     21h                 ;interrupt for DOS services

code        ENDS
            END     start
```

The operator **BYTE PTR** is necessary since MASM cannot tell from the operands [si] and 0 whether byte or word comparison is needed. Copying the source byte and incrementing both index registers is accomplished by the **movsb** instruction. Finally,

```
mov     BYTE PTR [di],0   ;terminate destination string
```

serves to move a null byte to the end of the destination string, since DI was incremented after the last byte of the source was copied to the destination. Again, the operator **BYTE PTR** tells MASM that the destination is a byte rather than a word.

Recall that when the destination index register DI is used for the register indirect addressing mode, the actual address of the operand is DS:DI, that is, in the data segment. In the string instructions only, the address of the destination element is ES:DI, in the extra segment. The **mov** instruction is not a string instruction, but **movsb** is a string instruction. In this procedure ES has been given the same value as DS, so that the data segment and extra segment are the same.

The program to test **strcopy** simply inputs a string from the keyboard, calls **strcopy** to copy it somewhere else, and finally displays the string copy. The most interesting part of the code is the collection of instructions needed to call the procedure, pushing arguments on the stack, doing the actual call, and removing the arguments from the stack.

Exercises 7.1

---

1. What will be the output of the following program?

```
INCLUDE io.h
cr          EQU    0dh    ; carriage return character
Lf          EQU    0ah    ; linefeed character

stack       SEGMENT stack
            DW     100h DUP (?)
stack       ENDS

program     SEGMENT
            ASSUME cs:program, ds:program

string      DB     'ABCDEFGHIJ'     ; data is in the program segment
            DB     cr,Lf,0
```

```
setup1      PROC NEAR
            mov     si, OFFSET string        ; beginning of string
            mov     di, OFFSET string + 5    ; offset of "F
            cld                              ; forward movement
            ret
setup1      ENDP

start:      mov     ax,SEG program           ; load segment number
            mov     ds,ax                    ;    into DS
            mov     es,ax                     ;    and ES
            call    setup1                   ; set source, destination, direction
            movsb                            ; move 4 characters
            movsb
            movsb
            movsb
            output  string                   ; display modified string

quit:       mov     al,0                     ; return code 0
            mov     ah,4ch                   ; DOS function to return
            int     21h                      ; interrupt for DOS services

program     ENDS
            END     start
```

2. Repeat Exercise 1, replacing the procedure **setup1** by

```
setup2      PROC NEAR
            mov     si, OFFSET string        ; beginning of string
            mov     di, OFFSET string + 2    ; offset of "C"
            cld                              ; forward movement
            ret
setup2      ENDP
```

3. Repeat Exercise 1, replacing the procedure **setup1** by

```
setup3      PROC NEAR
            mov     si, OFFSET string + 9    ; end of string
            mov     di, OFFSET string + 4    ; offset of "E"
            std                              ; backward movement
            ret
setup3      ENDP
```

4. Repeat Exercise 1, replacing the procedure **setup1** by

```
setup4      PROC NEAR
            mov     si, OFFSET string + 9   ; end of string
            mov     di, OFFSET string + 7   ; offset of "H"
            std                             ; backward movement
            ret
setup4      ENDP
```

―――――― *Programming Exercise 7.1* ―――――――――――――――――――――――――

1. Write a program that copies strings read in one at a time from the keyboard into a large storage area for later processing. Specifically, use the **inputs** macro to input a string; then copy the string to the first of a 1024 byte block of storage that has been reserved in the data segment. (Recall that the **inputs** macro produces a null-terminated string.) Follow the string by a carriage return and a linefeed character in this storage area. Repeat the process with additional strings, copying each subsequent string to the storage area so that it immediately follows the linefeed after the last string. Exit the loop when the first character of the source string is $ and do not copy this last string to the storage area. Do, however, place a null byte after the linefeed of the last string in the storage area. Finally, use the **output** macro to display all the characters in the data area. The resulting display should show the strings that were entered, one per line.

――――― 7.2 ――

Repeat Prefixes and More String Instructions

Each 8088 string instruction operates on one string element at a time. However, the 8088 instruction set includes three **repeat prefixes** that change the string instructions into versions that repeat automatically either for a fixed number of iterations or until some condition is satisfied. The three repeat prefixes actually correspond to two different single-byte opcodes; these are not themselves instructions, but supplement machine codes for the primitive string instructions, making new instructions.

Figure 7.4 Copying a Fixed Number of Characters of a String.

(a) **movsb** Iterated in a Loop.

```
                mov     si, OFFSET source_str   ; source string
                mov     di, OFFSET dest_str     ; destination
                cld                             ; forward movement
                mov     cx,count                ; count of characters to copy
                jcxz    endcopy                 ; skip loop if count is zero
        copy:   movsb                           ; move 1 character
                loop    copy                    ; decrement count and continue
        endcopy:
```

(b) Repeat Prefix with **movsb**.

```
                mov     si, OFFSET source_str   ; source string
                mov     di, OFFSET dest_str     ; destination
                cld                             ; forward movement
                mov     cx,count        ; count of characters to copy
                rep movsb               ; move characters
```

Figure 7.4 shows two program fragments, each of which copies a fixed number of characters from **source_str** to **dest_str**. The number of characters is loaded into the CX register from **count**. The code in part (a) uses a loop. Since the count of characters might be zero, the loop is guarded by a **jcxz** instruction. The body of the loop uses **movsb** to copy one character at a time. The **loop** instruction takes care of counting loop iterations. The program fragment in part (b) is functionally equivalent to the one in part (a). After the count is copied into CX, it uses the repeat prefix **rep** with a **movsb** instruction; the **rep movsb** instruction does the same thing as the last four lines in part (a).

The **rep** prefix is normally used with the **movs** instructions and with the **stos** instruction (discussed below). It causes the following design to be executed.

> while count in CX ≠ 0 loop
>   perform primitive instruction;
>   decrement CX by 1;
> end while;

Note that this is a **while** loop. The primitive instruction is not executed at all if CX contains zero. It is not necessary to guard a repeated string instruction as is often the case with an ordinary **for** loop implemented with the **loop** instruction.

The other two repeat prefixes are **repe** (with equivalent mnemonic **repz**) and **repne** (which is the same as **repnz**). The mnemonic **repe** stands for

Figure 7.5 Repeat Prefixes.

Mnemonic	Loop While	Number of Bytes	Opcode
rep	CX ≠ 0	1	F3
repz/repe	CX ≠ 0 and ZF = 1	1	F3
repnz/repne	CX ≠ 0 and ZF = 0	1	F2

Figure 7.6 `rep movs` Instructions.

Mnemonic	Element Size	Clock Cycles	Number of Bytes	Opcode
rep movsb	byte	9 + 17/repetition	2	F3 A4
rep movsw	word	9 + 25/repetition	2	F3 A5

"repeat while equal" and **repx** stands for "repeat while zero." Similarly, **repne** and **repnz** mean "repeat while not equal" and "repeat while not zero," respectively. Each of these repeat prefixes is appropriate for use with the two string instructions **cmps** and **scas**, which affect the zero flag ZF.

The names of these mnemonics partially describe their actions. Each instruction works the same as does **rep**, iterating a primitive instruction while CX is not zero. However, each also examines ZF after the string instruction is executed. The **repe** and **repz** continue iterating while ZF = 1, as it would be following a comparison where two operands were equal. The **repne** and **repnz** continue iterating while ZF = 0, as it would be following a comparison where two operands were different. Repeat prefixes themselves do not affect any flag. The three repeat prefixes are summarized in Figure 7.5. Note that **rep** and **repz** (**repe**) generate exactly the same byte of object code.

The **repz** and **repnz** prefixes do not quite produce true **while** loops. The value in CX is checked prior to the first iteration of the primitive instruction, as it should be with a **while** loop. However, ZF is not checked until after the primitive instruction is executed. In practice, this is very convenient since the instruction is skipped for a zero count, but the programmer does not have to do anything special to initialize ZF prior to repeated instructions.

Figure 7.6 shows how the repeat prefix **rep** combines with the **movs** instructions. Looking back at Figure 7.2, one sees that each instruction iteration takes one clock cycle less than the nonrepeated version, but that there is a "set up" time of 9 clock cycles.

The **cmps** instructions, summarized in Figure 7.7, compare elements of source and destination strings. Chapter 5 explained how a **cmp** instruction sub-

Figure 7.7 cmps Instructions.

Mnemonic	Element Size	Clock Cycles (rep)	Number of Bytes	Opcode
cmpsb	byte	22 (+9)	1	A6
cmpsw	word	30 (+9)	1	A7

tracts two operands and sets flags based on the difference. Similarly, cmps subtracts two string elements and sets flags based on the difference; neither operand is changed. If a cmps instruction were used in a loop written by the programmer, it would be appropriate to follow cmps by almost any of the conditional jump instructions, depending on the design being implemented. For the particular task of finding if two strings are identical, the **repe** prefix is a perfect companion for cmps. The entries in the clock cycles column of Figure 7.7 give the number of cycles needed for each iteration of a cmps instruction (22 for cmpsb and 30 for cmpsw); the notation "+9" denotes the nine extra clock cycles required one time when a repeat prefix is used.

It is often necessary to search for one string embedded in another. Suppose that the task at hand is to find the position (if any) at which the string at key appears in the string at target. One simple algorithm to do this is

```
position := 1;
while position ≤ (target_length – key_length + 1) loop
        if key matches substring of target starting at position
        then
                report success;
                exit program;
        end if;
        add 1 to position;
end while;
report failure;
```

This algorithm checks to see if the key string matches the portion of the target string starting at each possible position. Using 8088 registers, checking for one match can be done as follows:

```
SI := address of key;
DI := address of target + position – 1;
CX := length of key;

forever loop
        if CX = 0 then exit loop; end if;
```

compare [SI] and [DI] setting ZF;
increment SI;
increment DI;
decrement CX;
if ZF = 0 then exit loop; end if;
end loop;

if ZF = 1
then
match was found;
end if;

The **forever** loop is exactly what is done by the repeated string instruction **repe cmpsb**. Since the loop is terminated when either CX = 0 or when ZF = 0, it is necessary to be sure that the last pair of characters compared were the same; this is the reason for the extra **if** statement at the end of the design. Figure 7.8 shows a complete program that implements this design.

Figure 7.8   String Search Program.

```
; program to search for one string embedded in another

INCLUDE io.h

cr              EQU     0dh     ; carriage return character
Lf              EQU     0ah     ; linefeed character

stack           SEGMENT stack
                DW      100h DUP (?)
stack           ENDS

data            SEGMENT
prompt_1        DB      'String to search?  ', 0
prompt_2        DB      cr, Lf, 'Key to search for?  ', 0
target          DB      80 DUP (?)
key             DB      80 DUP (?)
trgt_length DW  ?
key_length  DW  ?
last_posn   DW  ?
failure         DB      cr,Lf,Lf,'The key does not appear in the string.',cr,Lf,0
success         DB      cr,Lf,Lf,'The key appears at position'
position        DB      6 DUP (?)
                DB      ' in the string.', cr, Lf, 0
data            ENDS
```

Figure 7.8 Continued.

```
code        SEGMENT
            ASSUME cs:code, ds:data

start:      mov     ax,SEG data       ; load data segment number
            mov     ds,ax             ;    into DS
            mov     es,ax             ;    and ES

            output prompt_1           ; ask for
            inputs target,80          ;    and input target string
            mov    trgt_length,cx     ; save length of target
            output prompt_2           ; ask for
            inputs key,80             ;    and input key string
            mov    key_length,cx      ; save length of key

; calculate last position of target to check
            mov     ax,trgt_length
            sub     ax,key_length
            inc     ax                ; trgt_length - key_length + 1
            mov     last_posn,ax

            mov     ax,1              ; starting position
while:      cmp     ax,last_posn      ; position : last_posn
            jnle    end_while         ; exit if past last position

            lea     si,target         ; address of string
            add     si,ax             ; add position
            dec     si                ; address of position to check
            lea     di,key            ; address of key
            mov     cx,key_length     ; number of positions to check
            repe cmpsb                ; check
            jz      found             ; exit on success
            inc     ax                ; increment position
            jmp     while             ; repeat
end_while:

            output failure            ; the search failed
            jmp     SHORT quit         ; exit

found:      itoa    position,ax       ; convert position to ASCII
            output success            ; search succeeded

quit:       mov     al,0              ; return code 0
            mov     ah,4ch            ; DOS function to return
            int     21h               ; interrupt for DOS services

code        ENDS
            END     start
```

Figure 7.9 scas Instructions.

Mnemonic	Element Size	Clock Cycles (Rep)	Number of Bytes	Opcode
scasb	byte	15 (+9)	1	AE
scasw	word	19 (+9)	1	AF

The scan string instruction **scas** is used to scan a string for the presence or absence of a particular string element. The string that is examined is a destination string; that is, the offset of the element being examined is in the destination index register DI. With a **scasb** instruction the element searched for is the byte in the AL register half; with a **scasw** it is the word in the AX register. The **scasb** and **scasw** forms use no operand since the mnemonics tell the element size. Figure 7.9 summarizes the **scas** instructions; as with the other string instructions so far, the notation "15 (+9)" means that 15 clock cycles are used for each repetition of the instruction plus an additional 9 cycles one time if the instruction is repeated.

The program shown in Figure 7.10 inputs a string and a character and uses **repne scasb** to locate the position of the first occurrence of the character in the string. It then displays the part of the string from the character to the end. Note that the data segment number is loaded into both DS and ES segment registers; ES must be initialized since the destination index register DI is used in the **scas** instructions. Recall that the **inputs** macro puts the length of the string that it reads from the keyboard in the CX register; this length is incremented so that the null character will also be searched. The **inputc** macro puts the character to scan for in the AL register half. The **lea** instruction is used to load the offset of the string to be searched and **cld** ensures a forward search.

After the search, the destination index DI will be one greater than desired since a string instruction always increments index registers whether or not flags were set. If the search succeeded, DI will contain the offset of the character following the one which matched with AL, or the offset of the character after the end of the string if CX was decremented to zero. The **dec di** instruction takes care of both cases, backing up to the position of the matching character if there was one, or to the null byte at the end of the string otherwise. The **output** macro, used with register indirect addressing, displays the last portion of the string.

Figure 7.10 Program to Find Character in String.

```
; Program to locate a character within a string.
; The string is displayed from the character to the end.

INCLUDE io.h

cr          EQU     0dh     ; carriage return character
Lf          EQU     0ah     ; linefeed character

stack       SEGMENT stack
            DW      100h DUP (?)
stack       ENDS

data        SEGMENT
prompt1     DB      'String? ',0
prompt2     DB      cr, Lf, Lf, 'Character? ',0
string      DB      50 DUP (?)
label1      DB      cr, Lf, Lf, 'The rest of the string is--',0
crlf        DB      cr,Lf,0
data        ENDS

program     SEGMENT
            ASSUME cs:program, ds:data

start:      mov     ax,SEG data    ; load data segment number
            mov     ds,ax          ;    into DS
            mov     es,ax          ;    and ES

            output prompt1         ; prompt for string
            inputs string,50       ; get string
            output prompt2         ; prompt for character
            inputc                 ; get character

            inc   cx               ; include null in string length
            lea   di, string       ; offset of string
            cld                    ; forward movement
            repne scasb            ; scan while character not found
            dec   di               ; back up to null or matching character

            output label1          ; print label
            output [di]            ; output string
            output crlf            ; skip to new line

quit:       mov     al,0           ; return code 0
            mov     ah,4ch         ; DOS function to return
            int     21h            ; interrupt for DOS services

program     ENDS
            END     start
```

Figure 7.11   stos Instructions.

Mnemonic	Element Size	Clock Cycles	Number of Bytes	Opcode
stosb	byte	11	1	AA
stosw	word	15	1	AB
rep stosb	byte	9 + 10/repetition	2	F3 AA
rep stosw	word	9 + 14/repetition	2	F3 AB

The store string instruction **stos** copies a byte or a word from the AL register half or the AX register to an element of a destination string. A **stos** instruction affects no flag, so that when it is repeated with **rep**, it copies the same value into consecutive positions of a string. For example, the following code will store spaces in the first 30 bytes of **string**.

```
mov    cx,30              ; 30 bytes
mov    al, ' '            ; character to store
mov    di, OFFSET string  ; address of string
cld                       ; forward direction
rep stosb                 ; store spaces
```

Information about the **stos** instructions is in Figure 7.11. The instruction is shown separately with the repeat prefix **rep**, since repeated executions take less time per iteration than a single execution of the instruction.

The load string instruction **lods** is the final string instruction. This instruction copies a source string element to the AL register half or to the AX register. A **lods** instruction sets no flag. It is possible to use a **rep** prefix with **lods** but it is not helpful, because all values except for the last string element would be replaced as successive values were copied to the destination register. A **lods** instruction is useful in a loop set up with other instructions, making it possible to easily process string elements one at a time. The **lods** instructions are summarized in Figure 7.12. Repeated versions are not included in the figure since they will not be used.

Figure 7.12   lods Instructions.

Mnemonic	Element Size	Clock Cycles	Number of Bytes	Opcode
lodsb	byte	12	1	AC
lodsw	word	16	1	AD

Exercises 7.2

For each exercise below, assume that the data segment contains

```
source    DB    "brown"
dest      DB    "brine"
```

Suppose that both DS and ES contain the segment number of the data segment.

1. Suppose that the following instructions are executed:

```
lea    si, source
lea    di, dest
cld
mov    cx, 5
repne  cmpsb
```

Assuming that SI starts at 0000 and DI starts at 0005, what will be the values stored in SI and DI following the **repne cmpsb** instruction? What will be stored in CX?

2. Suppose that the following instructions are executed:

```
lea    si, source
lea    di, dest
cld
mov    cx, 5
repe   cmpsb
```

Assuming that SI starts at 0000 and DI starts at 0005, what will be the values stored in SI and DI following the **repe cmpsb** instruction? What will be stored in CX?

3. Suppose that the following instructions are executed:

```
mov    al, "w"
lea    di, dest
cld
mov    cx, 5
repe   scasb
```

Assuming that DI starts at 0005, what will be the value stored in DI following the **repe scasb** instruction? What will be stored in CX?

4. Suppose that the following instructions are executed:

```
mov    al, "n"
lea    di, dest
cld
mov    cx, 5
repne  scasb
```

Assuming that DI starts at 0005, what will be the value stored in DI following the **repne scasb** instruction? What will be stored in CX?

5. Suppose that the following instructions are executed:

```
mov    al,  '*'
lea    di,  dest
cld
mov    cx,  5
rep    stosb
```

Assuming that DI starts at 0005, what will be the value stored in DI following the **rep stosb** instruction? What will be stored in CX? What will be stored in the destination string?

6. Suppose that the following instructions are executed:

```
        lea    si,  source
        lea    di,  dest
        cld
        mov    cx,  5
for:    lodsb
        inc    al
        stosb
        loop   for
endfor:
```

Assuming that SI starts at 0000 and DI starts at 0005, what will be the values stored in SI and DI following the **for** loop? What will be stored in CX? What will be stored in the destination string?

Programming Exercises

1. Write a **FAR** procedure **strlen** to find the length of a null-terminated string. Specifically, the procedure must have one parameter, the offset of a string in the data segment. Use the stack to pass the value for this parameter. Assume that the data segment number is stored in DS. Use the AX register to return the number of characters of the string prior to the null byte that marks its logical end. No other register should be altered.

2. Write a **FAR** procedure **index** to find the position of the first occurrence of a character in a null-terminated string. Specifically, the procedure must have two parameters

   (1) a character
   (2) the offset of a string in the data segment

Use the stack to pass values for the parameters; for the character, use an entire word with the character in the low-order byte. Assume that the data segment number is stored in DS. Use the AX register to return the position of the character within the string; return zero if the character is not found. No other register should be altered.

3. Write a **FAR** procedure **append** that will append one null-terminated string to the end of another. Specifically, the procedure must have two parameters

   (1) the offset of string_1 in the data segment
   (2) the offset of string_2 in the data segment

   Use the stack to pass values for the parameters. Assume that the data segment number is stored in DS. The procedure should copy the characters of string_2 to the end of string_1 with the first character of string_2 replacing the null byte at the end of string_1, etc. (Warning: In the data section, there must be enough space reserved after the null byte of the first string to hold the characters from the second string.) All registers used by the procedure should be saved and restored.

4. Write a complete program that prompts for and accepts as input a person's name in the format last_name, first_name and builds a new string with the name in the format first_name ␣ last_name. A comma and a space separate the names originally and there is no character (except the null) following first_name; only a space separates the names in the new string. Display the new string.

5. Write a complete program that prompts for and accepts as input a person's name in the format last_name ␣␣ first_name ␣␣ and builds a new string with the name in the format first_name ␣ last_name. One or more spaces separate the names originally and there may be spaces following first_name. Only a single space separates first_name and last_name in the result. Display the new string.

6. Write a complete program that prompts for and accepts as input a string and a single character. Construct a new string that is identical to the old one except that it is shortened by removing each occurrence of the character. Display the new string.

7. Write a complete program that prompts for and accepts as input a sentence and a single word. Construct a new sentence that is identical to the old one except that it is shortened by removing each occurrence of the word. Display the new sentence.

8. Write a complete program that prompts for and inputs a sentence and two words. Construct a new sentence that is identical to the old one except that each occurrence of the first word is replaced by the second word. Display the new sentence.

—— 7.3 ——

Character Translation

Sometimes character data are available in one format but need to be in another format for processing, for example, when ASCII characters are transmitted to another computer system that normally uses EBCDIC character codes. Or if codes need to be transmitted to a device that cannot process all possible codes, it is sometimes easier to replace the unsuitable codes by acceptable codes than to delete them entirely.

The 8088 instruction set includes the **xlat** instruction to translate one character to another character. In combination with other string-processing instructions, it can easily translate all the characters in a string.

The **xlat** instruction requires only one byte of object code, the opcode D7. It takes 11 clock cycles to execute. Prior to execution, the character to be translated is in the AL register half. The instruction works by using a **translation table** in the data segment to look up the translation of the byte in AL. This translation table normally contains 256 bytes of data, one for each possible 8-bit value in AL. The byte at offset zero in the table (the first byte) is the character to which 00 is translated. The byte at offset one is the character to which 01 is translated. In general **xlat** uses the character being translated as an offset into the table, and the byte at that offset replaces the character in AL.

The BX register must contain the address (offset) of the translation table. There are two forms of the **xlat** instruction,

```
xlat
```

and

```
xlat table_name
```

In the second format, the operand *table_name* should reference the translation table. However, use of this operand does not automatically initialize the BX register. It can be omitted except for the rare cases when a segment-override prefix is needed.

Figure 7.13 presents a short program that translates each character of **string** in place; that is, it replaces each character by its translation using the original location in memory. The heart of the program is the translation table and the sequence of instructions

```
mov    cx, str_len   ; string length
lea    bx, table     ; offset of translation table
lea    si, string    ; offset of string
lea    di, string    ; destination also string
```

```
for:    lodsb              ; copy next character to AL
        xlat               ; translate character
        stosb              ; copy character back into string
        loop    for        ; repeat for all characters
```

These instructions implement a **for** loop with the design

```
for index := 1 to string_length loop
        load source character into AL;
        translate character in AL;
        copy character in AL to destination;
    end for;
```

Each ASCII code is translated to another ASCII code by this program. Uppercase letters are translated to lowercase, lowercase letters and digits are unchanged, and all other characters are translated to spaces. Construction of such a table involves looking at a table of ASCII codes (see front inside cover). For this program the translation table is defined by

```
table   DB      48 DUP (' '), '0123456789', 7 DUP (' ')
        DB      'abcdefghijklmnopqrstuvwxyz', 6 DUP (' ')
        DB      'abcdefghijklmnopqrstuvwxyz', 133 DUP (' ')
```

Figure 7.13 Translation Program.

```
; Translate upper case letters to lower case; don't change lower
; case letters and digits.  Translate other characters to spaces.
INCLUDE io.h
cr          EQU     0dh     ; carriage return character
Lf          EQU     0ah     ; linefeed character


stack       SEGMENT stack
            DW      200h DUP (?)
stack       ENDS


data        SEGMENT
string      DB      'This is a #!$& STRING',0
str_len     EQU     $-string-1
label1      DB      'Original string--',0
label2      DB      cr, Lf, 'Translated string--',0
crlf        DB      cr, Lf, 0
table       DB      48 DUP (' '), '0123456789', 7 DUP (' ')
            DB      'abcdefghijklmnopqrstuvwxyz', 6 DUP (' ')
            DB      'abcdefghijklmnopqrstuvwxyz', 133 DUP (' ')
data        ENDS
```

Figure 7.13 Continued

```
code        SEGMENT
            ASSUME cs:code,ds:data
start:      mov     ax,SEG data  ; load data segment address
            mov     ds,ax
            mov     es,ax

            output label1         ; display original string
            output string
            output crlf

            mov     cx, str_len   ; string length
            lea     bx, table     ; offset of translation table
            lea     si, string    ; offset of string
            lea     di, string    ; destination also string
for:        lodsb                 ; copy next character to AL
            xlat                  ; translate character
            stosb                 ; copy character back into string
            loop    for           ; repeat for all characters

            output label2         ; display altered string
            output string
            output crlf

quit:       mov     al,0          ; return code 0
            mov     ah,4ch        ; DOS function to return
            int     21h           ; interrupt for DOS services

code        ENDS
            END     start
```

Careful counting will show that exactly 256 bytes are defined. Recall that a DB stores the ASCII code of each character operand. Each of the first 48 bytes of the table will contain the ASCII code for a space (blank), 20_{16}. Therefore if the code in the AL register represents any of the first 48 ASCII characters—a control character, or one of the printable characters from 20_{16} (space) to $2F_{16}$ (/)—it will be translated to a space.

Note that it is legal to translate a character to itself. Indeed, this is what will happen for digits; the ASCII codes 30_{16} to 39_{16} for digits 0 through 9 appear at offsets 30_{16} to 39_{16}. The codes for the seven characters : through @ are next in an ASCII chart; each of these will be translated to a space. The next ASCII characters are the uppercase letters and the next entries in the table are codes for the lowercase letters. For example, the table contains 61_{16} at offset 41_{16}, so an uppercase A (ASCII code 41_{16}) will be translated to a lowercase a (ASCII

Figure 7.14 Output from Translation Program.

```
Original string--This is a #!$& STRING
Translated string--this is a     string
```

code 61_{16}). The next six blanks are at the offsets 91_{16} ([) through 96_{16} (`), so that each of these characters is translated to a blank. The ASCII code for each lowercase letter is assembled at an offset equal to its value, so each lowercase letter is translated to itself. Finally, the translation table contains 133 ASCII codes for blanks; these are the destinations for { , | , } , ~ , DEL and each of the 128 bit patterns starting with a 1, none of them codes for ASCII characters.

Figure 7.14 shows the output of the program in Figure 7.13. Notice that "strange" characters are not deleted, they are replaced by blanks.

Exercises 7.3

1. Here is a partial hexadecimal/EBCDIC conversion table:

81 a	99 r	C9 I	E9 Z
82 b	A2 s	D1 J	40 space
83 c	A3 t	D2 K	4B .
84 d	A4 u	D3 L	6B ,
85 e	A5 v	D4 M	F0 0
86 f	A6 w	D5 N	F1 1
87 g	A7 x	D6 O	F2 2
88 h	A8 y	D7 P	F3 3
89 i	A9 z	D8 Q	F4 4
91 j	C1 A	D9 R	F5 5
92 k	C2 B	E2 S	F6 6
93 l	C3 C	E3 T	F7 7
94 m	C4 D	E4 U	F8 8
95 n	C5 E	E5 V	F9 9
96 o	C6 F	E6 W	
97 p	C7 G	E7 X	
98 q	C8 H	E8 Y	

Give a translation table that would be suitable for **xlat** translation of EBCDIC codes for letters, digits, space, period, and comma to the corresponding ASCII codes, translating every other EBCDIC code to a null character (00).

2. Give a translation table that would be suitable for **xlat** translation of ASCII codes for lowercase letters to the corresponding uppercase letters, leaving all other characters unchanged.

3. Here is an alternative to the **xlat** instruction.

```
mov    ah, 0         ; clear high order bits in AX
mov    si, ax        ; copy character to be translated
mov    al, [bx+si]   ; copy new character from table to AL
```

The third instruction uses based and indexed addressing—it fetches a byte at the address whose offset is the sum of the values in BX and SI. Explain why this sequence of three instructions is equivalent to a single **xlat** instruction.

Programming Exercise 7.3

---

1. In the United States, decimal numbers are written with a decimal point separating the integral part from the fractional part and with commas every three positions to the left of the decimal point. In many European countries, decimal numbers are written with the roles of commas and decimal points reversed. For example, the number 1,234,567.89 written in U.S. notation would be written in Europe as 1.234.567,89. Write a program that will interchange commas and periods, translating a string of characters representing either format of number to the other format. Use the **xlat** instruction with a translation table that translates a period to a comma, a comma to a period, each digit to itself, and any other character to a space. Prompt for and accept as input the number to be translated. Translate the string. (Recall that the **inputs** macro puts the number of characters read from the keyboard in the CX register.) Display the new number format with an appropriate label.

7.4

Converting a 2's Complement Integer to an ASCII String

The **itoa** macro has been used to convert a 2's complement integer to a string of six ASCII characters for output. This macro expands into the following sequence of instructions.

```
push    ax            ; save AX
push    di            ; save DI
mov     ax,source     ; copy source to AX
lea     di,dest       ; destination address to DI
```

```
          call    itoa_proc              ; call procedure
          pop     di                     ; restore DI
          pop     ax                     ; restore AX
```

These instructions use AX and DI to pass parameters to a procedure `itoa_proc`. So that the user does not need to worry about any register contents being altered, AX and DI are initially saved on the stack and are restored at the end of the sequence. The 2's complement number at **source** is placed in AX and the destination address for the string is placed in DI. (The actual source and destination are used in the expanded macro, not the names **source** and **dest**.)

The real work of 2's complement integer-to-ASCII conversion is done by the procedure `itoa_proc`. The assembled version of this procedure is contained in the file IO.OBJ. The source code for `itoa_proc` is shown in Figure 7.15. The procedure begins by saving all of the registers that it alters on the stack; the flag register is also saved so that the procedure call to `itoa_proc` will not change flag settings. The flag register and other registers are restored immediately before returning from the procedure.

Figure 7.15   Integer-to-ASCII Conversion Procedure.

```
; Convert integer in AX to string of 6 characters at (DI)

itoa_proc   PROC    FAR
            push    ax                     ; Save registers
            push    bx                     ;    used by
            push    cx                     ;    procedure
            push    dx
            push    di
            push    es
            pushf                          ; save flags

            cmp     ax,8000h               ; special case -32,768?
            jne     normal                 ; if not, then normal case
            mov     BYTE PTR [di],'-'      ; manually put in ASCII codes
            mov     BYTE PTR [di+1],'3' ;    for -32,768
            mov     BYTE PTR [di+2],'2'
            mov     BYTE PTR [di+3],'7'
            mov     BYTE PTR [di+4],'6'
            mov     BYTE PTR [di+5],'8'
            jmp     SHORT finish           ; done with special case

normal:     mov     dx,ax                  ; save number
            mov     ax,ds                  ; copy data segment
            mov     es,ax                  ;    number to extra segment
```

Figure 7.15 Continued.

```
                mov     al,' '              ; put blanks in
                mov     cx,5                ;    first five
                cld                         ;    bytes of
                rep stosb                   ;    destination field

                mov     ax,dx               ; restore number
                mov     cl,' '              ; default sign (blank)
                cmp     ax,0                ; check sign of number
                jge     setup               ; skip if not negative
                mov     cl,'-'              ; sign for negative number
                neg     ax                  ; number in AX now >= 0

setup:          mov     bx,10               ; divisor

divloop:        mov     dx,0                ; extend number to doubleword
                div     bx                  ; divide by 10
                add     dl,30h              ; convert remainder to character
                mov     [di],dl             ; put character in string
                dec     di                  ; move forward to next position
                cmp     ax,0                ; check quotient
                jne     divloop             ; continue if quotient not zero

                mov     [di],cl             ; insert blank or "-" for sign

finish:         popf                        ; restore flags
                pop     es                  ; restore registers
                pop     di
                pop     dx
                pop     cx
                pop     bx
                pop     ax
                ret                         ;exit
itoa_proc       ENDP
```

The basic approach of the procedure is to build a string of characters right to left by repeatedly dividing the number by 10, using the remainder to determine the rightmost character. For instance, dividing the number 2895 ($0B4F_{16}$) by 10 gives a remainder of 5 and a quotient of 289 (0121_{16}), the last digit of the number and a new number with which to repeat the process. This method works nicely for positive numbers, but a negative number must be changed to its absolute value before starting the division loop. To complicate things further, the bit pattern 8000_{16} represents the negative number $-32{,}768_{10}$, but $+32{,}768$ cannot be represented in 2's-complement form in a 16-bit word.

The procedure first checks for the special case 8000_{16}; if AX contains this value, the ASCII codes for −32768 are moved one at a time to the destination offset in the DI register. The location for the minus sign is in the DI register, so register indirect addressing can be used to put this character in the correct memory byte. The operand **BYTE PTR** in the instruction

```
mov BYTE PTR [di],'-'
```

tells MASM that the destination location is a byte; it is also legal to move a single character to a word. The location for the character 3 is one byte beyond the offset contained in DI. The instruction

```
mov BYTE PTR [di+1],'3'
```

uses indexed addressing. The notation [di+1] describes exactly what is needed: a destination location one byte beyond the offset contained in DI. The displacement 1 is stored as immediate data within the instruction; this **mov** takes more object code and also executes more slowly than the prior **mov** using register indirect addressing. The remaining four characters are similarly put in place, and the procedure is exited.

Note that when either register indirect or indexed addressing modes are used, addresses in the DI register are interpreted as offsets in the data segment. The next step of the procedure is to put five leading blanks in the six-byte destination field. The procedure does this with a **rep stosb**, which uses DI to point to successive bytes in the extra segment. This necessitates copying the segment number from DS into ES. The **stosb** instruction is repeated five times, so that DI is left pointing at the last byte of the destination field.

The procedure next stores the correct sign symbol in the CL register half. A blank is used for a number greater than or equal to zero, and the dash character (-) is used for a negative number. A negative number is also negated, giving its absolute value for subsequent processing.

Finally the main part of the procedure is executed. The divisor 10 is placed in the BX register. The nonnegative number is extended to a doubleword by moving zeros to DX. Division by the 10 in BX gives a remainder from 0 to 9 in DX, the last decimal digit of the number. This is converted to the corresponding ASCII code by adding 30_{16}. (Recall that the ASCII codes for digits 0 through 9 are 30_{16} through 39_{16}.) A **mov** using register indirect addressing puts the character in place in the destination string, and DI is decremented to point at the next position to the left.

This process is repeated until the quotient is zero. Finally the sign symbol stored in CL (blank or -) is copied to the immediate left of the last code for a digit.

Exercises 7.4

1. Why does **itoa_proc** use a destination string six bytes long?

2. Suppose that negative numbers are not changed before the division loop of **itoa_proc** begins, and that an **idiv** instruction is used rather than a **div** instruction in this loop. Recall that when a negative number is divided by a positive number, both quotient and remainder will be negative. For instance,

   $$-1273 = 10 * (-127) + (-3)$$

   How could the rest of the division loop be modified to produce the correct ASCII code for both positive and negative numbers?

Programming Exercises 7.4

1. Rewrite **itoa_proc**, using the stack to pass parameters and adding a length parameter. Specifically, the new **itoa_proc** will be a **FAR** procedure with three parameters, each a word long:

   (1) the 2's complement number to convert to ASCII characters
   (2) the offset in the data segment of the ASCII string
   (3) the desired length of the ASCII string

   The number should be converted to a string of ASCII characters starting at the offset in the data segment. If the length is less than or equal to the actual number of characters needed to display the number, use the minimal space required. If the length is larger than needed, pad with extra spaces to the left of the number. The procedure should modify no register.

2. Write a **FAR** procedure **hex_string** that converts a 16-bit integer to a string of exactly four characters representing its value as a hexadecimal number. The procedure should have two parameters, the number, passed in the AX register, and the offset of the destination string, passed in the DI register. The procedure should modify no register. (The remainder upon division by 16 produces a decimal value corresponding to the rightmost hex digit.)

3. Write a **FAR** procedure **binary_string** that converts a 16-bit integer to a string of exactly 16 characters representing its value as a binary number. The procedure should have two parameters: (1) the number, and (2) the offset of the destination string in the data segment. Use the stack to pass the parameters to the procedure. The procedure should modify no register. (The remainder upon division by 2 gives the rightmost bit.)

7.5

Chapter Summary

The word string refers to a collection of consecutive bytes or words in memory. The 8088 instruction set includes five instructions for operating on strings: **movs** (to move or copy a string from a source to a destination location), **cmps** (to compare two strings), **scas** (to scan a string for a particular element), **stos** (to store a given value in a string) and **lods** (to copy a string element into AX or AL). Each of these has two mnemonic forms ending with "b" or "w" to give the size of the string element.

A string instruction operates on one string element at a time. When a source string is involved, the source index register SI contains the offset of the string element; this offset is assumed to be in the data segment. When a destination string is involved, the destination index register DI contains the offset of the string element; this offset is assumed to be in the extra segment. An index register is incremented or decremented after the string element is accessed, depending on whether the direction flag DF is reset to zero or set to one; the **cld** and **std** instructions are used to give the direction flag a desired value.

Repeat prefixes **rep**, **repe** (**repz**), and **repne** (**repnz**) are used with some string instructions to cause them to automatically repeat. The number of times to execute a primitive instruction is placed in the CX register. The conditional repeat forms will terminate instruction execution if the zero flag gets a certain value; these are appropriate for use with the **cmps** and **scas** instructions that set or reset ZF.

The **xlat** instruction is used to translate the characters of a string. It is used with a 256 byte long translation table that starts with the destination byte to which the source byte 00 is translated and ends with the destination byte to which the source byte FF is translated. The **xlat** instruction can be used for such applications as changing ASCII codes to EBCDIC codes, or for changing letters from uppercase to lowercase (or the reverse) within a given character coding system.

The **itoa** macro expands to code that calls a procedure **itoa_proc**. This procedure works by repeatedly dividing a nonnegative number by 10, and using the remainder to get the rightmost character of the destination string.

CHAPTER 8

Other Addressing Modes

This chapter takes a more detailed look at addressing modes, reviewing those that have already been presented and introducing the others. Intel 8088 instructions use several types of operands. These addressing modes were listed in Figure 3.6. Section 3.5 discussed immediate, register, and some memory modes for operands. Beginning with the program in Figure 3.1, almost all of the example programs in this book have used immediate, register, and direct memory operands. Register indirect memory operands were used to sequentially access elements of arrays in Section 5.5. Based memory operands were used in Chapter 6 to access procedure parameters passed on the stack. Indexed memory operands were used in procedure `itoa_proc` discussed in Chapter 7. Random access to array elements is discussed in this chapter and the Microsoft assembler's facility for defining structures is also presented.

8.1

Addressing Modes

There are three major categories of operands for 8088 instructions: immediate, register, and memory. **Immediate** operands are source values which are embedded in the instruction. **Register** mode operands involve source values that are taken from a register or results with a register destination. **Memory** operands fall into two groups, direct and indirect. The offset for a **direct** mode operand is encoded in the instruction. The offset for an operand using one of the **indirect** modes is calculated from the contents of one or two registers and (sometimes) a **displacement** contained in the instruction. Loosely speaking, an instruction using a direct memory operand contains the address of the data to use and an instruction using an indirect memory operand contains a specification for a register which at run time will contain the address of the data to use. Figure 8.1 shows the categories of addressing modes, including the four indirect modes.

In each of these two examples, the first operand is register mode and the second operand is immediate mode.

```
mov   ax, 1000
cmp   dh, 'y'
```

Register operands are embedded in machine language as a three-bit code. For the above examples, 000 is used for AX and 110 is used for DH. When the mov instruction is executed, the code 000 says that the destination is the AX register. When the cmp instruction is executed, the 110 code says to use the contents of DH as one of the operands to compare. Notice that three bits allow for only eight distinct values. Separate opcodes distinguish between word-size and byte-size operands, so that the same three-bit register code represents a 16-bit register in one context and an 8-bit register half in the other context. Instruction encoding is considered in more detail in Chapter 11.

Immediate operands are embedded in the machine code for an instruction.

Figure 8.1   Categories of Intel 8088 Addressing Modes.

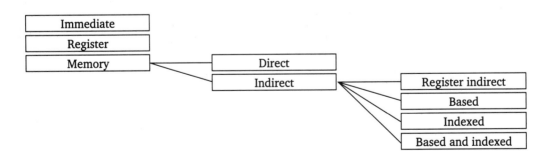

In the first example above, machine code for the **mov** instruction contains $03E8_{16}$, the word-length 2's complement version of 1000_{10}; the instruction copies this value from the instruction itself into the AX register. The machine code for the **cmp** instruction contains 79_{16}, the ASCII code for the letter *y* and this value is fetched from the instruction's object code to compare with the contents of the DH register.

Direct mode is probably the most frequently used memory addressing mode. Suppose that the first directives in the data segment **data** reserve 1000 bytes of memory, and that the next statement is

```
value    DW    4 DUP (?)
```

Under these assumptions, the symbol **value** is identified with the offset $03E8_{16}$ (1000_{10}), the offset of the first byte of the four-word block. Given source statements assembled with the directive **ASSUME ds:data**, the instruction

```
add    ax, value
```

will yield machine code containing $03E8_{16}$. In this case $03E8_{16}$ is not the value to be added to the contents of AX, but is the effective address of the value to be added. Of course $03E8_{16}$ is not the physical hardware address; it is an offset to be combined at run-time with the segment number in DS to yield the five-hex-digit physical address. However, the offset effectively gives the address since DS rarely changes during execution of a program. There is no ambiguity about the meaning of $03E8_{16}$ in the instructions used in these examples; the 8088 uses one opcode to mean that $03E8_{16}$ is an immediate operand and another opcode to mean that $03E8_{16}$ is the offset of a direct operand.

Continuing the example from the previous paragraph, suppose that the same program contains the instruction

```
add    ax, value+4
```

The machine code for this instruction will contain $03EC_{16}$. This indicates that a word at offset 1004 in the data segment (the third of the four words reserved) will be added to the contents of AX. Notice that the offset of **value** and the number 4 are not encoded separately; the assembler adds them to get a single 16-bit offset for the machine code.

The remaining addressing modes are all indirect memory addressing modes. In source code, the Microsoft assembler distinguishes an indirect operand from other types of operands by the presence of at least one register name in square brackets. For instance, **[bx]** indicates an indirect memory operand, while **bx** is a register mode operand.

Register indirect mode is the simplest indirect mode. There are only four source code formats for a register indirect mode operand, **[bx]**, **[si]**, **[di]**, and **[bp]**. That is, only the four registers BX, SI, DI, and BP can be used for register indirect addressing, and no other value can be specified along with the register. With register indirect mode, a code for the register is assembled into the instruction. At execution time, the contents of the designated register are fetched and interpreted as the offset of the memory operand to be used.

For example, suppose that the directive

```
value    DW    4 DUP (?)
```

follows 1000 bytes in the data segment, so that **value** is at offset $03E8_{16}$. If BX contains 03EA at run-time and the instruction

```
add    ax, [bx]
```

is executed, then the word at offset $03EA_{16}$ in the data segment (the second of the four words at **value**) will be added to the contents of the AX register.

With register indirect mode, the three registers BX, SI, and DI hold offsets in the data segment. For example, the operand coded [**si**] is at the address DS:SI with segment number in DS and offset in SI. The register BP is different; the operand coded [**bp**] is at the address SS:BP with segment number in SS and offset in BP. This means that in register indirect addressing, BP points to operands in the stack and the other three registers point to operands in the data segment. However, a segment override operator can be used to alter the normal choice of SS for BP or DS for BX, SI, and DI. For example, the operand **ss:**[**di**] causes the contents of DI to be interpreted as an offset in the stack segment and the operand **ds:**[**bp**] causes the contents of BP to be interpreted as an offset in the data segment. Segment override operators **cs:** and **es:** can also be used with any of the four registers.

The registers BX and BP are known as **base registers** and the registers SI and DI are known as **index registers**. An operand with a format like [**bp+6**] or [**bx-4**] is in **based** mode. An operand with a format like [**si+20**] or [**di+2**] is in **indexed** mode. These two modes are very similar to register indirect. However, the machine code for a based or indexed mode operand contains one or two bytes for a **displacement** (the values 6, –4, 20, and 2 in the preceding examples). At execution time, the displacement is added to the contents of the specified register to get the offset for the operand to be used.

A based operand using BP normally references a value in the stack segment. A based operand using BX as well as indexed operands using SI or DI usually reference values in the data segment. A segment override operator can alter the standard segment choice for any based or indexed mode.

The final memory addressing mode is **based and indexed**. For this mode one base register is used with one index register. The simplest source code operand formats are [**bx+si**], [**bx+di**], [**bp+si**], and [**bp+di**]. More complicated formats such as [**bx+si+24**] include a displacement. At execution time the contents of the base register, the contents of the index register, and the displacement (if any) are all added, and the sum is interpreted as the offset of the operand to be used. This offset is in the data segment for base register BX and in the stack segment for base register BP, barring use of a segment override operator.

Figure 8.2 Addressing Modes.

(a) Immediate

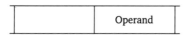

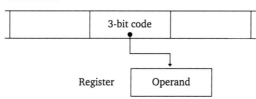

(b) Register

(c) Direct

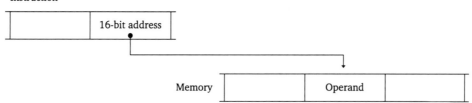

(d) Register indirect

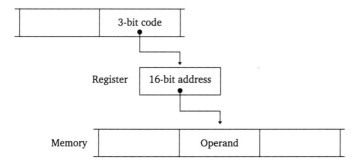

Figure 8.2 Continued

(e) Based or indexed
Instruction

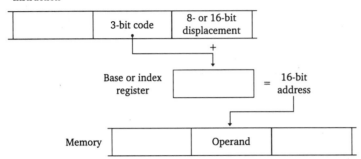

(f) Based and indexed (no displacement)
Instruction

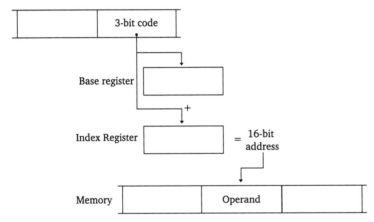

(g) Based and indexed (with displacement)
Instruction

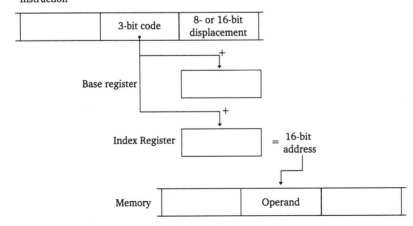

To use the previous example one more time, suppose that the data segment contains

```
value    DW    4 DUP (?)
```

at offset $03E8_{16}$, BX contains 03E8, and SI contains 0002. Then the instruction

```
mov    ax, [bx+si+4]
```

copies a word from offset 03E8 + 0002 + 4 = 03EE to AX. That is, the fourth of the four words at `value` is copied to AX.

When a base register and an index register are both used, the BX/SI combination is slightly more efficient than the BX/DI pairing—address calculations take one clock cycle less. Similarly, the BP/DI combination is slightly more efficient than the BP/SI set.

Figure 8.2 summarizes the 8088 addressing modes. For simplicity, the picture does not show the segment register whose contents are also combined with each 16-bit address to give the actual five-hex-digit address. The 8088 addressing modes, especially the memory indirect modes, give a great deal of flexibility to the way that operands can be accessed. The next sections will show some specific ways they can be used.

8.1 Exercises

1. Identify the addressing mode of each operand in each of the following addition instructions.

   (a) `add  ax, bx`   (b) `add  ax, [bx]`
   (c) `add  si, 100`   (d) `add  [di], bx`
   (e) `add  cx, [bp+8]`   (f) `add  bx, es:[si-4]`
   (g) `add  [bp+di+6], 10`   (h) `add  ax, [bx+si]`

2. Suppose that the directive

   ```
   value    DW    10 DUP (?))
   ```

   is at offset $04F8_{16}$ in the data segment whose segment number is in DS. Suppose that BX contains $04F8_{16}$, SI contains $04FA_{16}$ and DI contains 0006_{16}. Numbering the reserved words 1, 2, ... , 10, identify the word referenced by the memory operand in each of the following `mov` statements.

   (a) `mov  ax, value`   (b) `mov  ax, value+2`
   (c) `mov  ax, value+10`   (d) `mov  ax, [bx]`
   (e) `mov  ax, [si]`   (f) `mov  ax, [si-2]`
   (g) `mov  ax, [bx+6]`   (h) `mov  ax, [bx+di]`
   (i) `mov  ax, [bx+di+4]`   (j) `mov  ax, [bx+di-2]`

—— **8.2** ——————————————————————————

Nonsequential Array Access

In high-level languages, an array is a collection of elements of the same type that share one name; individual elements are identified by the name of the entire array and the position (index or subscript) of the particular element. In assembly language, memory space for an array can be allocated by reserving a contiguous block of memory. Computer programs frequently use arrays. It is often necessary to sort the elements of an array into increasing or decreasing order; many algorithms have been devised to do this task. Another common programming job is to search the elements stored in an array for a particular value. This section shows assembly language implementations for the insertion sort algorithm and for the binary search algorithm. These procedures illustrate the use of many 8088 addressing modes.

The insertion sort is one of the best simple sort algorithms. Figure 8.3 describes the insertion sort in pseudocode form. The basic idea of the method is to view the first (position – 1) elements of the array as already sorted, and then insert the next element of the array into its correct spot. When this is repeated for all positions (from 2 through the end of the array), a sorted array results.

Figure 8.4 shows code that implements the insertion sort algorithm as a **FAR** procedure. This procedure assumes that two parameters are passed on the stack, (1) the array, that is, the address of the array in the caller's data segment and (2) the number of elements in the array. The procedure begins with entry code that saves registers to be used and loads BP so that parameters can be accessed. The offset of the start of the array is copied from the first parameter into the

Figure 8.3 Insertion Sort Algorithm.

```
{ sort array a[1..nbr_elts] into increasing order }

for position := 2 to nbr_elts loop
        spot := position;
        value := a[position];

        while (spot > 1) and (a[spot-1] > value) loop
                a[spot] := a[spot-1];
                subtract 1 from spot;
        end while;

        a[spot] := value;
end for;
```

Figure 8.4 Insertion Sort Procedure.

```
sort    PROC    FAR
; Procedure to sort array of 2's complement integers into increasing order.
; Parameters passed on stack:
;       (1)   offset in caller's data segment of array to be sorted
;       (2)   number of elements in array
; This procedure implements the insertion sort algorithm.

            push    bp              ; save base pointer
            mov     bp, sp          ; reload base pointer
            push    ax              ; save other registers
            push    bx
            push    cx
            push    dx
            push    si
            push    di

            mov     bx, [bp+8]      ; offset of start of array
            mov     cx, 2           ; CX holds position
for:        cmp     cx, [bp+6]      ; position <= nbr_elts ?
            jnle    end_for
            mov     dx, cx          ; DX holds spot
            mov     si, cx          ; SI holds displacement in
            dec     si              ;   array corresponding to position
            add     si, si          ;   (position - 1 ) * 2
            mov     ax, [bx+si]     ; value := a[position]

while:      cmp     dx, 1           ; spot > 1 ?
            jng     end_while
            cmp     [bx+si-2], ax   ; a[spot-1] > value ?
            jng     end_while
            mov     di, [bx+si-2]   ; a[spot] := a[spot-1]
            mov     [bx+si], di
            dec     dx              ; subtract 1 from spot
            dec     si              ; adjust displacement to
            dec     si              ;   correspond to new value of spot
            jmp     while
end_while:
            mov     [bx+si], ax     ; a[spot] := value
            inc     cx              ; add 1 to position
            jmp     for
end_for:
```

Figure 8.4 Continued.

```
        pop     di              ; restore registers
        pop     si
        pop     dx
        pop     cx
        pop     bx
        pop     ax
        pop     bp
        ret
sort    ENDP
```

base register BX. The CX register is used to hold the value of position and DX is used for spot.

The **for** loop of the design is implemented with **cmp** and **jnle** instructions at the beginning of the loop body and **inc** and **jmp** instructions at the end of the loop body; this facilitates using position in the body of the loop. To access the value of a[position] the index position must be converted into the byte displacement from the beginning of the array to this element. This displacement is computed in SI; the value of position is copied from CX to SI, subtracting 1 gives the word displacement and adding SI to itself (multiplying the value by 2) gives the byte displacement. Since the offset of the start of the array is in BX, **[bx+si]** now references a[position] and this value is copied to AX.

The **while** loop makes three references to a[spot] or a[spot – 1]. Since the value of spot is the same as the value of position before the **while** loop begins, SI already contains the initial displacement required for a[spot]. No additional calculation is required for a[spot – 1]—if **[bx+si]** references a[spot], then **[bx+si-2]** references a[spot – 1] in the adjacent memory word. Each time spot is decremented in the body of the **while** loop, the displacement in SI is decremented twice so that the values correspond.

In this implementation it is not necessary to calculate a new displacement in the array every time an array element is accessed. This is true since the array elements are examined in order as the **while** loop is executed. Less efficient high-level language compilers might insert code to convert an array index to a displacement every time an array element is used. When using such a compiler, if the same array element is examined many times, a programmer can produce more efficient code by assigning an array element to a simple variable.

Searching an array for a given value is another common programming task. If the elements in the array are not in any particular order, then a sequential search must be utilized; starting with the first, the elements are examined one at a time (see Programming Exercise 2 in this section). If the elements of the array are sorted, then a much more efficient procedure, the binary search algorithm, can be employed. Pseudocode for this algorithm appears in Figure 8.5.

The binary search algorithm calculates the middle position of the array and

Figure 8.5 Binary Search Algorithm.

```
{ search for search_key in a[1..nbr_elts] }
{ assume array values are in increasing order }
{ return position of search_key if found in array, 0 otherwise }

left := 1;
right := nbr_elts;

while left ≤ right loop
      middle := (left + right) / 2;

      if search_key < a[middle]
      then
            right := middle - 1;
      else
            if search_key > a[middle]
            then
                  left := middle+1;
            else
                  return middle;
            end if;
      end if;
end while;
return 0;
```

compares the value at that position to the search key. If the search key is equal to the value at the middle position of the array, then the search succeeds. If the search key is less than the value at the middle position, then the search key must be in the left half of the array if it is in the array at all. If the search key is greater than the value at the middle position, then the search key must be in the right half of the array if it is in the array at all. The algorithm repeatedly checks the half of the array that potentially contains the search key; this part has bounds given by the variables left and right. If left becomes greater than right, then the array half is empty and cannot possibly contain the search key.

The program design in Figure 8.5 differs slightly from the informal description above. It checks first to see if the search key is less than the middle value, then if it is greater. If both of these conditions fail, then the only remaining possibility is that the search key equals the middle value. Since the search key is more likely to differ from the middle value than to be the same, it is more efficient to check the inequalities first. This version of the binary search algorithm communicates failure or success by returning an integer value: 0, if the search fails, and the position of the search key in the array, if the search succeeds.

Figure 8.6 Binary Search Procedure.

```
search  PROC    FAR
; Procedure to search a sorted array of 2's complement integers.
; Parameters passed on stack:
;       (1)  offset in caller's data segment of array to be searched
;       (2)  number of elements in array
;       (3)  search key
; This procedure implements the binary search algorithm.

          push    bp              ; save base pointer
          mov     bp, sp          ; reload base pointer
          sub     sp, 4           ; local stack space for left and right
          push    bx              ; save other registers
          push    cx
          push    dx
          push    si

          mov     bx, [bp+10]     ; offset of start of array
          mov     WORD PTR [bp-2], 1    ; left := 1
          mov     dx, [bp+8]      ; nbr_elts
          mov     [bp-4], dx      ; right := nbr_elts
          mov     cx, [bp+6]      ; search_key

while:    mov     ax, [bp-2]      ; left
          cmp     ax, [bp-4]      ; left <= right ?
          jnle    end_while
          add     ax, [bp-4]      ; left + right
          shr     ax, 1           ; middle := (left + right) / 2

if_1:     mov     si, ax          ; calculate displacement for a[middle]
          dec     si
          add     si, si          ; 2*(middle-1)
          cmp     cx, [bx+si]     ; search_key < a[middle] ?
          jnl     else_1
then_1:   dec     ax              ; middle-1
          mov     [bp-4], ax      ; right := middle-1
          jmp SHORT endif_1
else_1:   jng     else_2          ; search_key > a[middle] ?
then_2:   inc     ax              ; middle+1
          mov     [bp-2], ax      ; left := middle+1
          jmp SHORT endif_2
else_2:   jmp SHORT return        ; return with middle in AX
endif_2:
endif_1:
          jmp     while           ; continue while loop
end_while:
```

Figure 8.6 Continued.

```
        mov     ax, 0           ; search failed, return 0

return: pop     si              ; restore registers
        pop     dx
        pop     cx
        pop     bx
        add     sp, 4           ; discard local variables
        pop     bp

        ret

search  ENDP
```

Figure 8.6 gives 8088 code that implements the binary search algorithm as a **FAR** procedure. There are three parameters passed on the stack: (1) the offset in the caller's data segment of the array to be searched, (2) the number of elements in the array, and (3) the search key value. There are not enough registers to store local variables, so the entry code includes **sub sp,4** to reserve stackspace for the design variables left and right. As the procedure is implemented, the offset of the start of the array is stored in BX, search_key is stored in CX and middle is stored in AX.

In the **while** loop, middle is calculated by adding left and right and dividing by two. The division is done using the instruction **shr ax,1** which shifts the bits in the AX register one position to the right. Shift instructions will be covered in Chapter 9. A **div** or **idiv** instruction could be used in this procedure, but the **shr** instruction is much more efficient. After middle is computed, the corresponding byte displacement in the array to middle is calculated in SI. Then a[middle] can be referenced by **[bx+si]**.

Notice that only one **cmp** instruction is required for both **if**s appearing in the design. The second **if** compares the same two values and the **jnl** instruction, which transfers control to **else_1**, does not change flag settings. Many high-level language compilers would calculate the byte displacement of middle for both **if** statements; a programmer can produce more efficient code in such a case by inserting the statement

```
        middle_value := a[middle];
```

prior to the **if**s and then substituting middle_value for a[middle]. The 8088 code here could also be made slightly more efficient by substituting **jng SHORT return** for the statement at **else_1**.

Only arrays of word-length 2's complement integers have been used in this section. Obviously, other types of values can be stored in arrays. In addition, each array has had 1 as the index of its first element. Modern high-level languages allow integer indexes to start at any value (positive, negative, or zero), and also permit noninteger indexes. The displacement of an array element in these nontraditional situations can be easily found. For example, suppose that the array a contains elements that are 10 bytes long, and that the subscripts of a range from a smallest index of 5 to a largest index of 25. Then the displacement of a[9] from the beginning of the array is 40 bytes, 10 bytes for each of the four elements (a[5],a[6],a[7] and a[8]) prior to a[9] in the array. In general, for arrays with integer indexes the displacement of an element is

$$\text{displacement} = (\text{length of each element})$$
$$* (\text{index of element} - \text{index of first element})$$

If array indexes are of some type other than integer, then they must be translated into some integer value. For instance, ASCII codes can be used for indexes of type character.

8.2 Exercises

1. Suppose that the array **a** contains elements of length 8 and has integer indexes from 4 to 20.

   (a) Find the byte displacement of **a[12]** from the beginning of the array.
   (b) Suppose that the array index **i** is stored in the CX register. Assuming that $4 \le i \le 20$, give 8088 code that will compute in the SI register the byte displacement of **a[i]**.

2. Suppose that the array **a** contains elements of length 4 and has integer indexes from 0 to 63.

   (a) Find the byte displacement of **a[20]** from the beginning of the array.
   (b) Suppose that the array index **i** is stored in the CX register. Assuming that $0 \le i \le 63$, give 8088 code that will compute in the SI register the byte displacement of **a[i]**.

3. Suppose that the array **a** contains elements of length 6 and has integer indexes from –10 to 10.

   (a) Find the byte displacement of **a[5]** from the beginning of the array.
   (b) Suppose that the array index **i** is stored in the CX register. Assuming that $-10 \le i \le 10$, give 8088 code that will compute in the SI register the byte displacement of **a[i]**.

4. Suppose that the array **a** contains elements of length 4 and has character indexes from '**A**' to '**Z**'.

   (a) Find the byte displacement of **a['G']** from the beginning of the array.
   (b) Suppose that the array index **char** is in the CL register. Assuming that 'A' $\le$ char $\le$ 'Z', give 8088 code that will compute in the SI register the byte displacement of **a[char]**.

1. The first nbr_elts values in an array a can be sorted into increasing order using the selection sort algorithm:

```
for position := 1 to nbr_elts-1 loop
      small_spot := position;
      small_value := a[position];

      for i := position+1 to nbr_elts loop
          if a[i] < small_value
          then
                  small_spot := i;
                  small_value := a[i];
          end if;
      end for;

      a[small_spot] := a[position];
      a[position] := small_value;
end for;
```

Implement this algorithm in a **FAR** procedure **sort** like that of the insertion sort algorithm of Figure 8.3. Specifically, the procedure must sort an array of 2's complement integers into increasing order, with two parameters passed to the procedure on the stack: (1) the offset in caller's data segment of array to be sorted and (2) the number of elements in array.

2. If the elements of an array a[1..nbr_elts] are not in increasing or decreasing order, a sequential search must be used to determine if search_key is in the array. The following design returns the position at which search_key is in a or zero if it is not in the array.

```
for i := 1 to nbr_elts loop
      if a[i] = search[key]
      then
              return i;
      end if;
end for;
return 0;
```

Implement this sequential search algorithm as a **FAR** procedure with three parameters passed on the stack: (1) the offset in the caller's data segment of the array to be searched, (2) the number of elements in the array, and (3) the search key value.

3. The quick sort algorithm sorts an array a[1..nbr_elts] into increasing order by identifying a middle value in the array and moving elements of the array

so that all elements on the left are smaller than the middle value and all on the right are larger than the middle value. Then the procedure is recursively called to sort the left and right sides. The recursion terminates when the portion to be sorted has one or fewer elements. Here is a design to quick sort the portion of a from index left_end to index right_end.

```
if left_end < right_end
then
        left := left_end;
        right := right_end;

        while left < right loop
            while (left < right) and (a[left] < a[right]) loop
                add 1 to left;
            end while;
            swap a[left] and a[right];

            while (left < right) and (a[left] < a[right]) loop
                subtract 1 from right;
            end while;
            swap a[left] and a[right];
        end while;

            quick_sort(a, left_end, left-1);
            quick_sort(a, right+1, right_end);
    end if;
```

Implement the quick sort algorithm in a **FAR** procedure **qsort**, with three parameters passed to the procedure on the stack: (1) the offset in caller's data segment of entire array, (2) the index left_end, and (3) the index right_end. Notice that a main program would sort an entire array by using 1 for the second parameter and the number of elements in the array for the third parameter. (Warning: In testing this program, you should probably allocate more stack space than usual.)

8.3

Structures

In high-level languages, an array is a collection of elements of the same type that share one name; individual elements are identified by the name of the entire array and the position of the particular element. A **structure** is a collection of elements of possibly different types that share one name; individual elements are distinguished by the identifier of the entire structure and the field name of a particular element. Many high-level languages provide for structures, sometimes using a different designation for the concept. For example, COBOL identifies an entire structure by an 01 level in the data division and fields in a structure by higher level numbers. Pascal and Modula-2 use the reserved word **RECORD** to define a structure.[*]

For example, consider the structure type defined in the Modula-2 language by

```
PartType = RECORD
            PartNbr : CARDINAL;
            Description : ARRAY [0..19] OF CHAR;
            Quantity : CARDINAL
        END; (* RECORD *)
```

If a variable **SparePart** is of type **PartType**, then each of

SparePart.PartNbr and **SparePart.Quantity**

are of type **CARDINAL** (nonnegative integer) and a string of 20 characters can be stored in **SparePart.Description**. One option for defining the variable **SparePart** in 8088 assembly language is

```
SparePart  DW  ?              ; part number
           DB  20 DUP (?)     ; description
           DW  ?              ; quantity
```

Using direct addressing, **SparePart** references the part number field and **SparePart+22** references the quantity field. Since the identifier **SparePart** is associated with a DW directive, normally **BYTE PTR SparePart+2** is used to reference the first byte of the string.

The Microsoft Macro Assembler provides a better way to implement structures in assembly language. As in the Modula-2 example, a type definition for **PartType** can be coded:

```
PartType     STRUC
PartNbr      DW  ?
Description  DB  20 DUP (?)
Quantity     DW  ?
PartType     ENDS
```

A structure-type definition always begins with a **STRUC** directive and ends with an **ENDS** directive. As in a high-level language, this type definition by itself does not set aside any memory; memory is reserved when a variable of type **PartType** is defined in a data segment. The variable **SparePart** can be defined for MASM by

```
SparePart     PartType     < >
```

---

[*] The word *record* is used by the Microsoft Macro Assembler to describe a collection of bit fields in a variable eight or sixteen bits long; MASM's record facility is not covered in this book.

This statement reserves 24 bytes of memory associated with the identifier `SparePart`. In addition, MASM recognizes `SparePart.PartNbr` and `SparePart.Quantity` as word variables and `SparePart.Description` as a byte variable. The angle brackets `<` `>` are used to enclose initial values for the fields of the structure; they are required even if initial values are not used. Initial values for structures will not be used in this book.

An array of elements of type `PartType` can also be defined. The directive

```
parts    PartType    100 DUP (< >)
```

reserves memory space for 100 parts structures, a total of 2400 bytes.

Given the above definitions, a code segment might include instructions such as

```
mov    cx, SparePart.Quantity
mov    ax, [bx].Quantity
mov    [bx+si].Description, '*'
```

The operand `SparePart.Quantity` is direct mode, and is equivalent to `SparePart+22`. The operand `[bx].Quantity` is based mode, equivalent to `[bx+22]`. The operand `[bx+si].Description` is based and indexed mode, equivalent to `[bx+si+2]`. What the assembler does is translate the field name into the appropriate number of bytes from the start of the structure. MASM also uses the type of the field identifier, usually eliminating the need for BYTE PTR and WORD PRTR operators. Since field names can be used independently of the structure identifier, all field names must be unique; that is, different structure definitions cannot use the same field name. This is different from most high-level languages where the same field name can be used in several structures.

Suppose that `parts` is an array of elements of structure type `PartType`, and that the first NbrElts positions in this array are to be searched for the array element containing a particular part number KeyPart. The design below shows a sequential search of the array `parts`, returning the position of the first element for which the PartNbr field matches the value of KeyPart, or 0 if there is no such element.

```
position := 1;

while position ≤ NbrElts loop
    if parts[position].PartNbr = KeyPart
    then
        return position;
    end if;
    add 1 to position;
end loop;

return 0;
```

Figure 8.7 implements this sequential search design as a **FAR** procedure with three parameters passed on the stack: (1) the offset of the array (in the caller's data segment), (2) the value of NbrElts, and (3) the value of KeyPart. The code is straightforward. The structure type definition for **PartType** is included on the assumption that this procedure will be part of a file that is assembled separately; in general, a structure type definition must be included in each file where it is referenced. (One option is to put structure definitions in a separate file and incorporate them into every file that needs them with an **INCLUDE** directive.) Notice the use of based and indexed addressing to access the elements of the array. Based addressing could have been used by dropping SI and adding 24 bytes to the address in BX rather than to the displacement in SI.

Figure 8.7 Sequential Search of Array of Structures.

```
PartType    STRUC
PartNbr     DW   ?
Description DB   20 DUP (?)
Quantity    DW   ?
PartType    ENDS

search  PROC    FAR
; Procedure to sequentially search the first part of array of structures
;    of type PartType for an element with a specified PartNbr value.
; Parameters passed on stack:
;       (1)   offset in caller's data segment of array to be searched
;       (2)   number of elements to examine
;       (3)   part number of target element
; If a matching element is found, its position is returned in AX;
;    otherwise 0 is returned in AX.

        push    bp              ; save base pointer
        mov     bp, sp          ; reload base pointer
        pushf                   ; save other registers
        push    bx
        push    dx
        push    si

        mov     bx, [bp+10]     ; offset of start of array
        mov     ax, 1           ; AX holds position
        mov     dx, [bp+6]      ; KeyPart
        mov     si, 0           ; offset of first element in array
```

Figure 8.7 Continued.

```
while:  cmp     ax, [bp+8]      ; position <= NbrElts ?
        jnle    endwhile
        cmp     dx, [bx+si].PartNbr  ; KeyPart = PartNbr in this element?
        je      return          ; exit if so
        add     si, 24          ; offset of next element in array
        inc     ax              ; increment position counter
        jmp     while
endwhile:
        mov     ax, 0           ; search failed

return: pop     si              ; restore registers
        pop     dx
        pop     bx
        popf
        pop     bp
        ret                     ; return to caller

search  ENDP
```

--------- **8.3 Exercises** ---

1. Give an MASM **STRUC** definition that would implement the following Modula-2 **TYPE** definition.

   StudentType = RECORD
                    ID : CARDINAL;
                    FirstName : ARRAY [0..9] OF CHAR;
                    MI : CHAR;
                    LastName : ARRAY [0..14] OF CHAR;
                    Class : [1..4]
                 END; (* RECORD *)

2. The instruction

   mov   ax, [bx].Quantity

   was used in this section to show how register indirect addressing can be used with structure definitions. This example assumed that BX would point to the beginning of a record in an array of **PartType** records. What would happen if BX did not point at one of the records in the array, but instead BX contained the address of a byte in the middle of a description field?

1. Write a complete program to maintain parts inventory for up to 100 parts. The program should define an array of **PartType** structures and implement the following design

```
NbrElts := 0;
forever loop
    display "Choose A[dd], D[elete], R[eport], L[ist], Q[uit]: " ;
    input choice;
    case choice of
        'a' or 'A':
                prompt for and input part number;
                if part number in list
                then
                        display Duplicate part number;
                else
                        prompt for and input description;
                        prompt for and input quantity;
                        add 1 to NbrElts;
                        put new parts data in parts[NbrElts];
                end if;
        'd' or 'D':
                prompt for part number;
                if part number in list
                then
                        delete entry from parts;
                        subtract 1 from NbrElts;
                else
                        display No such part number;
                end if;
        'r' or 'R':
                prompt for part number;
                if part number in list
                then
                        display description and quantity;
                else
                        display No such part number;
                end if;
        'l' or 'L':
                for i := 1 to NbrElts loop
                        display parts[i].PartNbr,
                            parts[i].Description,
                            parts[i].Quantity;
                end for;
        'q' or 'Q':    terminate program;
    end case;
end loop;
```

Notice that this design maintains inventory records in the order they are originally added. Use a sequential search procedure to implement "if part number in list."

2. Repeat Exercise 1, but maintain inventory records in order by part number rather than in chronological order. Use a binary search procedure to implement "if part number in list".

8.4

Chapter Summary

This chapter has taken a closer look at addressing modes used by the Intel 8088 processor. These modes are immediate, register, direct, register indirect, based, indexed, and based and indexed. All of these modes except immediate and register are used to reference operands in memory. Direct mode operands encode the offset of the data in the instruction's object code. Register indirect, based, indexed, and based and indexed modes are all indirect; that is, they use the contents of a base register and/or an index register to calculate the offset of the operand.

Indirect addressing modes are often used to implement algorithms involving arrays. The binary search algorithm and the insertion sort algorithm can be implemented using these modes.

The Microsoft Macro Assembler includes a facility for defining and using structures. MASM translates a field name into an appropriate displacement. The 8088 addressing modes and the MASM structure facility make it relatively easy to sequentially search an array of structures for an element with a particular value in one of its fields.

CHAPTER 9

Bit Manipulation

Previous chapters have examined the 8088 microprocessor's instructions for moving data, performing arithmetic operations, handling strings, branching, and utilizing subroutines. The 8088 (and most other CPUs) can also execute instructions that perform Boolean operations on several pairs of bits at one time. This chapter defines the Boolean operations and describes the 8088 instructions that implement them. It also covers the instructions that cause bit patterns to shift or rotate in a byte or word. Although bit manipulation instructions are very primitive, they are widely used in assembly language programming, often because they provide the sort of control that is rarely available in a high-level language. This chapter contains several application examples, including the procedure called by the `atoi` macro. This procedure uses bit manipulation instructions in several places.

—— 9.1 ————————————————————————

Logical Operations

A computer contains many integrated circuits that enable it to perform its functions. Each chip incorporates from a few to many thousand logic gates, each an elementary circuit that performs Boolean "and," "or," "exclusive or" or "not" operations on bits that are represented by electronic states. The CPU is usually the most complex integrated circuit in a PC.

Many high-level languages allow variables of Boolean type, that is, variables that are capable of storing **true** or **false** values. Virtually all high-level languages allow expressions with Boolean values to be used in conditional (**if**) statements. In assembly language the Boolean value **true** is identified with the bit value 1 and the Boolean value **false** is identified with the bit value 0. Figure 9.1 gives the definitions of the Boolean operations using bit values as the operands. The **or** operation is sometimes called "inclusive or" to distinguish it from "exclusive or" (**xor**). The only difference between **or** and **xor** is for two 1 bits; 1 **or** 1 is 1, but 1 **xor** 1 is 0; that is, "exclusive or" corresponds to the condition "one operand or the other true, but not both."

The 8088 has **and**, **or**, **xor** and **not** instructions implementing the logical operations. The formats of these instructions are

```
and    destination, source
or     destination, source
xor    destination, source
not    destination
```

The first three instructions act on pairs of words or bytes, performing the logical operations on the bits in corresponding positions from the two operands. For example, when the instruction **and bx,cx** is executed, bit 0 from the BX register is "anded" (that is, combined by operation **and**) with bit 0 from the CX register, bit 1 from BX is "anded" with bit 1 from CX, and so forth to bit 15 from BX and bit 15 from CX; the results of these 16 **and** operations are put in the corresponding positions in the destination.

The **not** instruction has only a single operand. It changes each 0 bit in that operand to 1 and each 1 bit to 0. For example, if the AH register half contains 10110110 and the instruction **not ah** is executed, then the result in AH will be 01001001. This is sometimes called "taking the one's complement" of the operand.

The **not** instruction does not affect any flag. However, each of the other three Boolean instructions affects CF, OF, PF, SF, ZF, and AF. The carry flag CF and overflow flag OF flags are both reset to 0; the value of the auxiliary carry flag AF may be changed but is undefined. The parity flag PF, the sign flag SF, and the zero flag ZF are set or reset according to the value of the result of the operation. For instance, if the result is a pattern of all 0 bits, then ZF will be set to 1; if any bit of the result is not 0, then ZF will be reset to 0.

Figure 9.1 Definitions of Logical Operations.

(a) **and** Operation

bit_1	bit_2	bit_1 **and** bit_2
0	0	0
0	1	0
1	0	0
1	1	1

(b) **or** Operation

bit_1	bit_2	bit_1 **or** bit_2
0	0	0
0	1	1
1	0	1
1	1	1

(c) **xor** Operation

bit_1	bit_2	bit_1 **xor** bit_2
0	0	0
0	1	1
1	0	1
1	1	0

(d) **not** Operation

bit	**not** bit
0	1
1	0

The **and**, **or**, and **xor** instructions all accept the same types of operands, use the same number of clock cycles for execution, and require the same number of bytes of object code. They are summarized together in Figure 9.2. Information about the **not** instruction is given in Figure 9.3.

Figure 9.2 and, or, and xor Instructions.

Destination Operand	Source Operand	Clock Cycles	Number of Bytes	Opcode and	or	xor
register 8	immediate byte	4	3	80	80	80
register 16	immediate byte	4	3	83	83	83
register 16	immediate word	4	4	81	81	81
AL	immediate byte	4	2	24	0C	34
AX	immediate word	4	3	25	0D	35
memory byte	immediate byte	17 +	2 +	80	80	80
memory word	immediate byte	25 +	2 +	83	83	83
memory word	immediate word	25 +	3 +	81	81	81
register 8	register 8	3	2	22	0A	32
register 16	register 16	3	2	23	0B	33
register 8	memory byte	9 +	2 +	22	0A	32
register 16	memory word	13 +	2 +	23	0B	33
memory byte	register 8	16 +	2 +	20	08	30
memory word	register 16	24 +	2 +	21	09	31

Figure 9.3 not Instruction.

Operand	Clock Cycles	Number of Bytes	Opcode
register 8	3	2	F6
register 16	3	2	F7
memory byte	16 +	2 +	F6
memory word	24 +	2 +	F7

Here are some examples showing how the logical instructions work. To compute the results by hand, it is necessary to expand each hex value to binary, do the logical operations on corresponding pairs of bits, and convert the result back to hex. Many hex calculators can perform the logical operations.

Example

Before	Instruction Executed	Operation in Binary	After
AX: E2 75		1110 0010 0111 0101	AX: A0 55
CX: A9 D7	and ax,cx	1010 1001 1101 0111	SF: 1
		1010 0000 0101 0101	ZF: 0

| | *Instruction* | | |
| *Before* | *Executed* | *Operation in Binary* | *After* |

DX: E2 75		1110 0010 0111 0101	DX: EB F7
value: A9 D7	`or dx,value`	1010 1001 1101 0111	SF: 1
		1110 1011 1111 0111	ZF: 0
BX: E2 75	`xor bx,0a9d7h`	1110 0010 0111 0101	BX: 4B A2
		1010 1001 1101 0111	SF: 0
		0100 1011 1010 0010	ZF: 0
AX: E2 75	`not ax`	1110 0010 0111 0101	AX: 1D 8A
		0001 1101 1000 1010	

Each of the logical instructions has a variety of uses. One such use of the **and** instruction is to clear selected bits in a destination. Note that if any bit value is "anded" with 1, the result is the original bit. On the other hand, if any bit value is "anded" with 0, the result is 0. Because of this, selected bits in a byte or word can be cleared by "anding" the destination with a bit pattern that has 1's in positions that are not to be changed and 0's in positions that are to be cleared.

For example, to clear all but the last four bits in the AX register, the following instruction can be used.

```
and    ax, 000fh      ; clear first 12 bits of AX
```

If AX originally contained 1D7B, this **and** operation would yield 000B:

0001 1101 0111 1011	1D7B
0000 0000 0000 1111	000F
0000 0000 0000 1011	000B

Only one of the leading zeros is needed in the operand `000fh`, but coding three zeros helps clarify the purpose of the operand. The trailing hex digit "f" corresponds to 1111 in binary, providing the four 1's that will leave the last four bits in AX unchanged.

A value that is used with a logical instruction to alter bit values is often called a **mask**. The Microsoft assembler MASM accepts numeric values in decimal, hexadecimal, binary, and octal formats. Hex and binary are preferable to be used as constants for masks since the bit pattern is obvious for binary values or easy to figure out for hex values.

As seen above, the **and** instruction is useful when selected bits of a byte or word need to be cleared. The **or** instruction is useful when selected bits of a byte or word need to be set to 1 without changing other bits. Observe that if the value 1 is combined with either a 0 or 1 using the **or** operation, then the result is 1. However, if the value 0 is used as one operand, then the result of an **or** operation is the other operand.

The "exclusive or" instruction will complement selected bits of a byte or word without changing other bits. This works since 0 **xor** 1 is 1 and 1 **xor** 1 is 0; that is, combining any operand with 1 using an **xor** operation results in the opposite of the operand value.

Clearing, setting or complimenting bit values is one use of logical instructions. A second use of these instructions is to implement high-level language Boolean operations. One byte in memory could be used to store eight Boolean values. If such a byte is at **flags**, then the statement

```
and     flags,11011101b     ; flag5 := false;  flag1 := false
```

assigns value **false** to bits 1 and 5, leaving the other values unchanged. (Recall that bits are numbered from right to left, starting with zero for the right most bit.)

If the byte in memory at **flags** is being used to store eight Boolean values, then an **or** instruction can assign true values to any selected bits. For instance, the instruction

```
or     flags,00001100b     ; flag3 := true;    flag2 := true
```

assigns **true** values to bits 2 and 3 without changing the other bits.

If the byte in memory at **flags** is being used to store eight Boolean values, then an **xor** instruction can negate selected values. For instance, the design statement

```
flag6 := NOT flag6;
```

can be implemented as

```
xor  flags, 01000000b     ; flag6 := not flag6
```

A third use of logical instructions is to perform certain arithmetic operations instead of arithmetic instructions. Suppose that the value in the AX register is interpreted as an unsigned integer. The expression (value mod 32) could be computed using the following sequence of instructions.

```
mov   dx,0        ; extend value to doubleword
mov   bx,32       ; divisor
div   bx          ; divide value by 32
```

Following these instructions, the remainder (value mod 32) will be in the DX register. The following alternative sequence leaves the same result in the DX register.

```
mov   dx,ax       ; copy value to DX
and   dx,001fh    ; compute value mod 32
```

This choice is much more efficient than the first one (see Exercise 2). It works because the value in DX is a binary number; as a sum it is

$$\text{bit\_15} * 2^{15} + \text{bit\_14} * 2^{14} + \cdots + \text{bit\_2} * 2^{2} + \text{bit\_1} * 2 + \text{bit\_0}$$

Each of these terms from $\text{bit\_15} * 2^{15}$ down to $\text{bit\_5} * 2^{5}$ is divisible by 32 (2^{5});

the remainder upon division by 32 is the bit pattern represented by the trailing 5 bits, those left after masking by 001F. Similar instructions will work whenever the second operand of **mod** is a power of 2.

A fourth use of logical instructions is to manipulate ASCII codes. Recall that the ASCII codes for digits are 30_{16} for 0, 31_{16} for 1, and so forth, to 39_{16} for 9. Suppose that the AL register contains the ASCII code for a digit, and that the corresponding integer value is needed in AX. If the value in AH were known to be zero, then the instruction

```
sub    ax, 0030h     ; convert ASCII code to integer
```

would do the job. If the value in AH is unknown, then the instruction

```
and    ax, 000fh     ; convert ASCII code to integer
```

is a much safer choice. It ensures that all but the last four bits of AX are cleared. For example, if the AX register contains F036, "junk" in AH and the ASCII code for the character 6 in AL, then **and ax,000fh** produces the integer 0006 in AX.

The **or** instruction can be used to convert an integer value between 0 and 9 in a register to the corresponding ASCII character code. For example, if the integer is in BL, then the following instruction changes the contents of BL to the ASCII code.

```
or    bl,30h        ; convert digit to ASCII code
```

If BL contains 04, then the **or** instruction will yield 34:

0000 0100	04
0011 0000	30
0011 0100	34

With an 8088 processor, the instruction **add bl,30h** accomplishes the same result using the same number of clock cycles and object code bytes; however, addition is less efficient with some other microprocessors.

An **xor** instruction can be used to change the case of the ASCII code for a letter. Suppose that the CL register contains the ASCII code for some uppercase or lowercase letter. The ASCII code for an uppercase letter and the ASCII code for the corresponding lowercase letter differ only in the value of bit 5. For example, the code for the letter S is 53_{16} (01010011_2) and the code for s is 73_{16} (01110011_2). The instruction

```
xor    cl, 00100000b     ; change case of letter in CL
```

"flips" the value of bit 5 in the CL register, changing the value to the ASCII code for the other case of the letter.

The 8088 instruction set includes **test** instructions, which function the same as **and** instructions except that destination operands are not changed. This means that the only job of a **test** instruction is to set flags. (Remember that a **cmp** instruction is essentially a **sub** instruction that sets flags but does not

Figure 9.4 test Instructions.

Destination Operand	Source Operand	Clock Cycles	Number of Bytes	Opcode
register 8	immediate byte	5	3	F6
register 16	immediate word	5	4	F7
AL	immediate byte	4	2	A8
AX	immediate word	4	3	A9
memory byte	immediate byte	11+	2+	F6
memory word	immediate word	15+	3+	F7
register 8	register 8	3	2	84
register 16	register 16	3	2	85
register 8	memory byte	9+	2+	84
register 16	memory word	13+	2+	85

change the destination operand.) One application of a **test** instruction is in examining a particular bit of a byte or word. The following instruction "tests" bit 13 of the DX register.

```
test    dx, 2000h    ; check bit 13
```

Note that 2000 in hex is the same as 0010 0000 0000 0000 in binary, with bit 13 equal to 1. Often this **test** instruction would be followed by a **jz** or **jnz** instruction, and the effect would be to jump to the destination if bit 13 were 0 or 1, respectively.

The **test** instruction can also be used to get information about a value in a register. For example,

```
test    cx, cx    ; set flags for value in CX
```

"ands" the value in the CX register with itself, resulting in the original value. (Combining any bit with itself using the **and** operation gives the common value.) The flags are set according to the value in CX. The instruction

```
and    cx, cx    ; set flags for value in CX
```

will accomplish the same goal and is equally efficient. However, using **test** makes it clear that the only purpose of the instruction is testing.

The various forms of the **test** instruction are listed in Figure 9.4. They are almost the same as for **and**, **or**, and **xor** instructions, but there are no forms where the destination operand is in memory and the source operand is in a register.

-------- Exercises 9.1 --------

1. For each part of this problem, assume the "before" values when the given instruction is executed. Give the requested "after" values.

	Before		Instruction		After
(a)	BX:	FA 75			
	CX:	31 02	and	bx,cx	BX, SF, ZF
(b)	BX:	FA 75			
	CX:	31 02	or	bx,cx	BX, SF, ZF
(c)	BX:	FA 75			
	CX:	31 02	xor	bx,cx	BX, SF, ZF
(d)	BX:	FA 75	not	bx	BX
(e)	AX:	FA 75	and	ax,000fh	AX, SF, ZF
(f)	AX:	FA 75	or	ax,0fff0h	AX, SF, ZF
(g)	AX:	FA 75	xor	ax,0ffffh	AX, SF, ZF
(h)	AX:	FA 75	test	ax,0004h	AX, SF, ZF

2. Recall the two methods given in this section for computing (value mod 32), where value is an unsigned integer in the AX register:

```
mov     dx,0      ; extend value to doubleword
mov     bx,32     ; divisor
div     bx        ; divide value by 32
```

and

```
mov     dx,ax     ; copy value to DX
and     dx,001fh  ; compute value mod 32
```

Find the total number of clock cycles required for execution and the number of bytes of object code necessary for each of these methods.

3. Suppose that value is an unsigned integer in the AX register. Give appropriate instructions to compute (value mod 8), putting the result in the BX register.

4. Suppose that each bit of the word at flags represents a Boolean value, with bit 0 for flag0, and so forth, up to bit 15 for flag15. Give a single 8088 instruction to implement each of the following design statements.

   (a) flag2 := true;
   (b) flag5 := false; flag6 := false; flag9 := false;
   (c) flag12 := NOT flag12

5. (a) Suppose that the AL register half contains the ASCII code for an upper-case letter. Give a logical instruction that will change its contents to the code for the corresponding lowercase letter.

(b) Suppose that the AL register half contains the ASCII code for a lower-case letter. Give a logical instruction that will change its contents to the code for the corresponding uppercase letter.

Programming Exercises 9.1

1. The Pascal programming language includes the predefined function odd, which has a single integer parameter and returns **true** for an odd integer and **false** for an even integer. Write a **NEAR** procedure that implements this function in assembly language, passing the parameter to the procedure in the AX register and returning 1 in AX for **true** and 0 in AX for **false**. The procedure should not change any register other than AX. Use an appropriate logical instruction to generate the return value.

2. In two-dimensional graphics programming, a rectangular region of the plane is mapped to the display; points outside this region are "clipped" (not displayed). The region, bounded by four lines $x = x_{min}$, $x = x_{max}$, $y = y_{min}$ and $y = y_{max}$, can be pictured

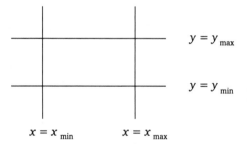

$y = y_{max}$

$y = y_{min}$

$x = x_{min}$ $x = x_{max}$

An **outcode** is associated with each point (x, y) of the plane. This 4-bit code is assigned according to the following rules:

- Bit 0 (rightmost) is 1 if the point is to the right of the rightmost vertical line, that is, if $x > x_{max}$; it is 0 otherwise.
- Bit 1 is 1 if the point is left of the leftmost vertical line (if $x < x_{min}$).
- Bit 2 is 1 if the point is above the upper horizontal line (if $y > y_{max}$).
- Bit 3 is 1 if the point is below the lower horizontal line (if $y < y_{min}$).

(a) Suppose that the outcode for point (x_1, y_1) is in the low-order four bits of AL, that the outcode for point (x_2, y_2) is in the low-order four bits of BL, and that other bits of these registers are reset to 0. Give a single 8088 statement that will set ZF to 1 if the two points are both inside the rectangular region and to 0 otherwise. The value in AL or BL may be changed.

(b) Suppose that the outcode for point (x_1, y_1) is in the low-order four bits of AL, that the outcode for point (x_2, y_2) is in the low-order four bits of BL, and that other bits of these registers are reset to 0. Give a single 8088 statement that will set ZF to 0 if the two points are both on the same side of the rectangular region. ("Both on the same side" means both right of $x = x_{max}$, both left of $x = x_{min}$, both above $y = y_{max}$ or both below $y = y_{min}$.) The value in AL or BL may be changed.

(c) Write a **FAR** procedure **setcode** that returns the outcode for a point (x, y). Specifically, **setcode** has six integer parameters: $x, y, x_{min,} x_{max,}$ $y_{min,}$ and y_{max} that are to be passed on the stack in order given. Return the outcode in the low-order four bits of the AL register half, assigning 0 to each of the high-order four bits.

9.2

Shift and Rotate Instructions

The logical instructions introduced in the previous section enable the assembly language programmer to set or clear bits in a word or byte stored in a register or memory. Shift and rotate instructions enable the programmer to change the position of bits within a word or byte. This section describes the shift and rotate instructions and gives examples of some ways that they are used.

Shift instructions slide the bits in a location given by the destination operand to the left or to the right. The direction of the shift can be determined from the last character of the mnemonic—**sal** and **shl** are left shifts; **sar** and **shr** are right shifts. Shifts are also categorized as **logical** or **arithmetic**—**shl** and **shr** are logical shifts; **sal** and **sar** are arithmetic shifts. The mnemonics are summarized in a two-by-two matrix:

	Left	Right
Logical	shl	shr
Arithmetic	sal	sar

The source code format of any shift instruction is

```
s--     destination, count
```

There are two versions of the *count* operand. The single-bit variation codes the number 1.

```
s--    destination, 1     ; shift 1 bit
```

This version causes a shift of exactly one position within the destination location. The multiple-bit source code format is

```
s--    destination, cl    ; shift number of bits given by CL
```

In this format the value in the CL register half is interpreted as an unsigned number telling how many times to shift the value in the destination. It is legal for CL to contain any value from 0 to 255_{10} even though a shift of more than 16 positions makes no sense because the longest destination operand is a word. It is not possible with 8088 instructions to indicate a multiple-bit shift by coding a number that gives the number of positions to be shifted.

Arithmetic and logical left shifts are identical; the mnemonics **sal** and **shl** are synonyms that generate the same object code. When a left shift is executed, the bits in the destination slide to the left and 0 bits fill in on the right. The bits that fall off the left are lost except for the very last one shifted off; it is saved in the carry flag CF. (The last bit shifted off is the only one when the count operand is 1.) The sign flag SF, zero flag ZF, and parity flag PF are assigned values corresponding to the final value in the destination location. The overflow flag OF is undefined for a multiple-bit shift; for a single-bit shift it is reset to 0 if the sign bit of the result is the same as the sign bit of the original operand value, and set to 1 if they are different. The auxiliary carry flag AF is undefined.

Arithmetic and logical right shifts are not the same. With both, the bits in the destination slide to the right and the bits that fall off the right are lost except for the very last one shifted off; it is saved in CF. For a logical right shift (**shr**) 0 bits fill in on the left. However, with an arithmetic right shift (**sar**) the original sign bit is used to fill in on the left. Therefore, for an arithmetic right shift, if the original operand represents a negative 2's complement number, then the new operand will have leading 1 bits for each position shifted and will also be negative. As with left shifts, the values of SF, ZF, and PF depend on the result of the operation, and AF is undefined. The overflow flag OF is undefined for a multiple-bit shift. For a single-bit logical right shift **shr**, OF is reset to 0 if the sign bit in the result is the same as the sign bit in the original operand value, and set to 1 if they are different. (Notice that this is equivalent to assigning OF the sign bit of the original operand.) With a single-bit arithmetic right shift **sar**, OF is always cleared—the sign bits of the original and new value are always the same.

Some hex calculators can directly do shift operations. Hand evaluation requires writing the operand in binary, shifting or regrouping the bits (filling in with 0's or 1's as appropriate), and then translating the new bit pattern back to hex. The process is a little simpler for a multiple-bit shift, which shifts four positions, or some multiple of four positions. Each group of four bits corresponds to one hex digit, so one can think of shifting hex digits instead of bits. Here are a few examples that illustrate execution of shift instructions; each example begins with a word containing the hex value A9 D7 (1010 1001 1101 0111 in binary).

Before	Instruction Executed	Operation in Binary	After
CX: A9 D7	sal cx, 1	1010 1001 1101 0111 /// ///// ///// /// 0101 0011 1010 1110	CX: 53 AE SF: 0 ZF: 0 CF: 1 OF: 1
AX: A9 D7	shr ax, 1	1010 1001 1101 0111 \\\\ \\\\ \\\\ \\\\ 0101 0100 1110 1011	AX: 54 EB SF: 0 ZF: 0 CF: 1 OF: 1
BX: A9 D7	sar bx, 1	1010 1001 1101 0111 \\\\ \\\\ \\\\ \\\\ 1101 0100 1110 1011	BX: D4 EB SF: 1 ZF: 0 CF: 1 OF: 0
ace: A9 D7 CL: 04	sal ace, cl	1010 1001 1101 0111 1001 1101 0111 0000	ace: 9D 70 SF: 1 ZF: 0 CF: 0
DX: A9 D7 CL: 04	shr dx, cl	1010 1001 1101 0111 0000 1010 1001 1101	DX: 0A 9D SF: 0 ZF: 0 CF: 0
AX: A9 D7 CL: 04	sar ax, cl	1010 1001 1101 0111 1111 1010 1001 1101	AX: FA 9D SF: 1 ZF: 0 CF: 0

Figure 9.5 gives the number of clock cycles and number of bytes required using various operand types in shift instructions. The same data, including opcodes, apply to all shift instructions and rotate instructions. The size of the destination and the type of the count operand are implied by the opcode. As with some other instructions, the second byte of the object code is used to choose among the different types of shifts and rotates, as well as between register and memory destinations. Notice that for registers the single-bit shifts are much faster than the multiple-bit shifts. When the number of positions to shift is known in advance, it is better to use several single-bit shifts than one multiple-bit shift unless it is necessary to conserve bytes of object code.

The shift instructions are quite primitive, but they have many applications. Recall that multiplication and division instructions take many more clock cycles than most 8088 instructions, and that some microprocessors do not even have multiplication and division instructions. When the multiplier is 2, a single-bit left shift of the multiplicand results in the correct product. It is easy to see why

Figure 9.5 Shift and Rotate Instructions.

Destination Operand	Count Operand	Clock Cycles	Number of Bytes	Opcode
register 8	1	2	2	D0
register 16	1	2	2	D1
memory byte	1	15 +	2 +	D0
memory word	1	23 +	2 +	D1
register 8	CL	4/bit + 8	2	D2
register 16	CL	4/bit + 8	2	D3
memory byte	CL	4/bit + 20 +	2 +	D2
memory word	CL	4/bit + 28 +	2 +	D3

this works for unsigned numbers: shifting each bit to the left one position makes it the coefficient of the next higher power of two in the binary representation of the number. A single-bit left shift also correctly doubles a signed operand. In fact, one can use multiplication by 2 on a hex calculator to find the result of any single-bit left shift.

With the 8088, a left shift instruction can be more convenient than a multiplication instruction since it does not require use of the AX and DX registers. After a shift the product is word length, of course, not a doubleword in the AX and DX registers. The word-length product will be the correct multiple of 2 if the overflow flag OF has value 0 after a single-bit left shift. Using a shift to double an operand in a register requires two clock cycles; this is even faster than the three clock cycles required to add the operand to itself.

A single-bit right shift can be used to efficiently divide an unsigned operand by 2. Suppose, for example, that the BX register contains an unsigned operand. Then the logical right shift **shr bx,1** shifts each bit in BX to the position corresponding to the next lower power of two, resulting in half the original value. The original units bit is copied into the carry flag CF, and is the remainder for the division.

If BX contains a signed operand, then the arithmetic right shift **sar bx,1** does almost the same job as an **idiv** instruction with a divisor of 2. The difference is that if the dividend is an odd, negative number, then the quotient is rounded down; that is, it is one smaller than it would be using an **idiv** instruction. As an example, suppose that the AX register contains FF F7, the 2's complement representation for –9, and the BL register half contains 02. Then **idiv bl** gives a result of FF FC in AX, that is, a remainder of –1 (FF in AH) and quotient of –4 (FC in AL). However, **sar ax,1** gives a result of FF FB in AX and 1 in CF, a quotient of –5 and a remainder of +1. Both quotient-remainder pairs satisfy the equation

$$dividend = quotient * divisor + remainder$$

but with the –5 and +1 combination, the sign of the remainder differs from the sign of the dividend, contrary to the rule followed by `idiv`.

Instead of multiplying an operand by 2, it can be doubled either by adding it to itself or by using a left shift. A shift is slightly more efficient than addition and either method is much more efficient than multiplication. To divide an operand by 2, a right shift is the only alternative to division, and is much faster; however, the right shift is not quite the same as division by 2 for a negative dividend. To multiply or divide an operand by 4, 8, or some other small power of two, either repeated single-bit shifts or one multiple-bit shift can be used.

Shifts can be used in combination with other logical instructions to combine distinct groups of bits into a byte or a word, or to separate the bits in a byte or word into different groups. The program shown in Figure 9.6 prompts for an integer, uses the `atoi` macro to convert it to 2's complement form in the AX register, and then displays the word in the AX register as four hexadecimal digits. To accomplish this display, four groups of four bits must be extracted from the value in AX. Each group of four bits represents a decimal value from 0 to 15, and each group must be converted to a character for display. This character is a digit 0 through 9 for integer value 0 (0000_2) through 9 (1001_2) or a letter A through F for integer value 10 (1010_2) through 15 (1111_2). The four characters are stored right to left in contiguous bytes of memory as they are generated; the BX register is used to point at the destination byte for each character. The design for the middle of the program is

```
for count := 4 down to 1 loop
    copy AX to DX;
    mask off all but last 4 bits in DX;

    if value in DX ≤ 9
    then
        convert value in DX to a digit 0 through 9;
    else
        convert value in DX to a letter A through F;
    end if;

    store character in memory at address in BX;
    decrement BX to point at next position to the left;
    shift value in AX right four bits;
end for;
```

To implement this design, the instruction

```
and     dx,000fh          ; zero all but last hex digit
```

masks off all but the last four bits in DX. The `if` is implemented by

Figure 9.6 Program to Display an Integer in Hex.

```
; program to display integer in word-length 2's complement form
INCLUDE io.h
cr          EQU     0dh    ; carriage return character
Lf          EQU     0ah    ; linefeed character

stack       SEGMENT stack
            DW      100h DUP (?)
stack       ENDS

data        SEGMENT
prompt      DB      'Enter a number:  ',0
number      DB      10 DUP (?)
result      DB      cr,Lf,"The 2's complement representation is "
char        DB      4 DUP (?),cr,Lf,0
data        ENDS

code        SEGMENT
            ASSUME cs:code,ds:data
start:      mov     ax,SEG data     ; load data segment number
            mov     ds,ax

            output prompt           ; prompt for number
            inputs number,10        ; read ASCII characters
            atoi   number           ; convert to integer

            lea     bx,char+3       ; address for last character
            mov     cx,4            ; number of characters
for:        mov     dx,ax           ; copy pattern
            and     dx,000fh        ; zero all but last hex digit
if_1:       cmp     dx,9            ; digit?
            jnle    else_1          ; letter if not
then_1:     or      dx,30h          ; convert to character
            jmp     SHORT endif_1
else_1:     add     dx,'A'-10       ; convert to letter
endif_1:
            mov     BYTE PTR [bx],dl ; copy character to memory
            dec     bx              ; point at next character
            shr     ax,1            ; shift AX 4 bits right
            shr     ax,1
            shr     ax,1
            shr     ax,1
            loop    for             ; repeat

            output result           ; output label and sum

quit:       mov     al,0            ; return code 0
            mov     ah,4ch          ; DOS function to return
            int     21h             ; interrupt for DOS services
code        ENDS
            END     start
```

```
if_1:      cmp      dx,9            ; digit?
           jnle     else_1          ; letter if not
then_1:    or       dx,30h          ; convert to character
           jmp      SHORT endif_1
else_1:    add      dx,'A'-10       ; convert to letter
endif_1:
```

A value from 0 to 9 is converted to the ASCII code for a digit using the **or** instruction; **add dx,30h** would work just as well here. The operand **'A'-10** in the **add** instruction actually adds the decimal number 55, but the code used is clearer than **add dx,55**. Four **shr** instructions shift the value in AX right four bits, discarding the four bits that were just converted to a character.

Programming Exercise 2 of Section 7.4 asked for a procedure to do a job similar to that done by the program in Figure 9.6. That procedure was to use the remainder upon division by 16 to produce a value corresponding to the right-most hex digit. Notice that the **shr** and **and** instructions used in the present program are both easier to code and more efficient.

Rotate instructions are very similar to shift instructions. With shift instructions, the bits that are shifted off one end are discarded while vacated space at the other end is filled by 0's (or 1's for a right arithmetic shift of a negative number). However, with rotate instructions, the bits that are shifted off one end of the destination are used to fill in the vacated space at the other end.

A single-bit rotate instruction has the format

```
r--     destination, 1       ; rotate 1 bit
```

whereas a multiple-bit version looks like

```
r--     destination, cl      ; rotate number of bits given by CL
```

The instructions **rol** (rotate left) and **ror** (rotate right) can be used for byte or word length operands in a register or in memory. As each bit "falls off" one end, it is copied to the other end of the destination. In addition, the last bit copied to the other end is also copied to the carry flag CF; this "last bit" is the only bit for a single-bit rotate. The overflow flag OF is the only other flag affected by rotate instructions; OF is undefined for multiple-bit rotates; familiarity with its definition for single-bit rotate instructions is not needed for discussions in this book.

As an example, suppose that the DX register contains D25E and the instruction

```
    rol dx, 1
```

is executed. In binary, the operation looks like

and the result in the DX register is A4BD. The carry flag CF is set to 1 since a 1 bit was rotated from the left end to the right.

A rotate instruction can be used to make a cleaner version of the program in Figure 9.6. The hex characters are generated in left-to-right order by the following code.

```
            lea    bx,char          ; address for last character
            mov    cx,4             ; number of characters
for:        rol    ax,1             ; rotate high-order 4 bits
            rol    ax,1             ;    into rightmost position
            rol    ax,1
            rol    ax,1
            mov    dx,ax            ; copy pattern
            and    dx,000fh         ; zero all but last hex digit
if_1:       cmp    dx,9             ; digit?
            jnle   else_1           ; letter if not
then_1:     or     dx,30h           ; convert to character
            jmp    SHORT endif_1
else_1:     add    dx,'A'-10        ; convert to letter
endif_1:
            mov    BYTE PTR [bx],dl ; copy character to memory
            inc    bx               ; point at next character
            loop   for              ; repeat
```

An additional minor advantage of this version of the program is that the original value in the AX register is unchanged by the process. The 16 rotations bring each bit back to its original position.

There is an additional pair of rotate instructions, **rcl** (rotate through carry left) and **rcr** (rotate through carry right). Each of these instructions treats the carry flag CF as if it were part of the destination. This means that **rcl ax,1** shifts bits 0 through 14 of AX left one position, copies the old value of bit 15 into CF, and copies the old value of CF into bit 0 of AX. The rotate through carry instructions obviously alter CF; they also affect OF but no other flag.

Exercises 9.2

---

1. For each part of this problem, assume the "before" values when the given instruction is executed. Give the requested "after" values.

	Before			Instruction	After
(a)	AX:	A8	B5	shl ax, 1	AX, CF, OF
(b)	AX:	A8	B5	shr ax, 1	AX, CF, OF
(c)	AX:	A8	B5	sar ax, 1	AX, CF, OF
(d)	AX:	A8	B5	rol ax, 1	AX, CF

	Before		*Instruction*	*After*
(e)	AX:	A8 B5	ror ax, 1	AX, CF
(f)	AX:	A8 B5		
	CL:	04	sal ax, cl	AX, CF
(g)	AX:	A8 B5		
	CL:	04	shr ax, cl	AX, CF
(h)	AX:	A8 B5		
	CL:	04	sar ax, cl	AX, CF
(i)	AX:	A8 B5		
	CL:	04	rol ax, cl	AX, CF
(j)	AX:	A8 B5		
	CL:	04	ror ax, cl	AX, CF

2. Compare the total number of clock cycles and bytes of object code for each of these alternative ways of dividing the unsigned integer in the AX register by 32:

   (a)
   ```
   mov    dx,0   ; extend value to doubleword
   mov    bx,32  ; divisor
   div    bx     ; value div 32
   ```
   (b)
   ```
   shr    ax,1   ; divide by 2
   shr    ax,1   ; divide by 2
   shr    ax,1   ; divide by 2
   shr    ax,1   ; divide by 2
   shr    ax,1   ; divide by 2
   ```

3. Compare the total number of clock cycles and bytes of object code for each of these alternative ways of multiplying the value in the AX register by 32:

   (a)
   ```
   mov    bx,32  ; multiplier
   mul    bx     ; value * 32
   ```
   (b)
   ```
   shl    ax,1   ; multiply by 2
   shl    ax,1   ; multiply by 2
   shl    ax,1   ; multiply by 2
   shl    ax,1   ; multiply by 2
   shl    ax,1   ; multiply by 2
   ```

4. Suppose that **value1**, **value2**, and **value3** each reference a byte in memory and that an unsigned integer is stored in each byte. Assume that the first value is no larger than 31 so that it has at most 5 significant bits and at least 3 leading 0 bits. Similarly assume that the second value is no larger than 15 (4 significant bits) and the third value is no larger than 127 (7 bits).

   (a) Give code to pack all three of these numbers into a 16-bit word in the AX register, copying the low-order 5 bits from **value1** to bits 11–15 of AX, the low-order 4 bits from **value2** to bits 7–10 of AX, and the low-order 7 bits from **value3** into bits 0–6 of AX.

(b) Give code to unpack the 16-bit number in the AX register into 5-bit, 4-bit ,and 7-bit numbers, padding each value with zeros on the left to make 8 bits, and storing the resulting bytes at **value1**, **value2**, and **value3**, respectively.

5. The instructions

```
mov   bx, ax     ; value
shl   ax, 1      ; 2 * value
add   ax, bx     ; 3 * value
```

multiplies the value in AX by 3. Write similar code sequences that efficiently multiply by 5, 7, 9, and 10.

Programming Exercises 9.2

1. Write a **FAR** procedure **binary_string** that converts a 16-bit integer to a string of exactly 16 characters representing its value as a binary number. The procedure should have two parameters: (1) the number, and (2) the offset of the destination string in the data segment. Use the stack to pass the parameters to the procedure. The procedure should modify no register. Use a rotate instruction to extract the bits one at a time, left-to-right; recall that jc or jnc instructions look at the carry bit. (This exercise is the same as Programming Exercise 3 in section 7.4 except for the method of producing the bits.)

2. An 8-bit number can be represented using three octal digits. Bits 7 and 6 determine the left octal digit, bits 5, 4, and 3 the middle digit, and bits 2, 1 and 0 the right digit. For instance, 11010110_2 is 11 010 110$_2$ or 326$_8$. The value of a 16-bit number is represented in **split octal** by applying the 2-3-3 system to the high-order and low-order bytes separately. Write a **FAR** procedure **split_octal** that converts an 16-bit integer to a string of exactly six characters representing the value of the number in split octal. The procedure should have two parameters: (1) the number, and (2) the offset of the destination string in the data segment. Use the stack to pass the parameters to the procedure. The procedure should modify no register.

9.3

Converting an ASCII String to a 2's Complement Integer

The **atoi** macro has been used to scan an area of memory containing an ASCII representation of an integer, producing the corresponding word-length 2's complement integer in the AX register. This macro expands into the following sequence of instructions.

```
push    si              ;; save SI
lea     si,source       ;; source address to SI
call    atoi_proc       ;; call procedure
pop     si              ;; restore SI
```

These instructions use the SI register to pass the offset of the ASCII string to a procedure `atoi_proc`. The original value in SI is saved on the stack to preserve its value in case the programmer is using this register for other purposes. The user's source identifier is used in the expanded macro, not the name `source`.

The actual ASCII to 2's complement integer conversion is done by the procedure `atoi_proc`. The assembled version of this procedure is contained in the file IO.OBJ. Source code for `atoi_proc` is shown in Figure 9.7. The procedure begins by saving all of the registers that it alters (except for AX and SI) on the stack. The flag register is also saved so that flag values that are not explicitly set or reset as promised in the comments can be returned unchanged. The `popf` and `pop` instructions at `atoi_exit:` restore these values; however, the word on the stack that is popped by `popf` will have been altered by the body of the procedure, as discussed below.

The first job of `atoi_proc` is to skip leading spaces, if any. This is implemented with a straightforward `while` loop. Note that `BYTE PTR [si]` uses register indirect addressing to reference a byte of the source string in the data segment. Following the `while` loop, SI points at some nonblank character.

The main idea of the procedure is to compute the value of the integer by implementing the following left-to-right scanning algorithm.

```
value := 0;
while pointing at code for a digit loop
      multiply value by 10;
      convert ASCII character code to integer;
      add integer to value;
      point at next byte in memory;
end while;
```

This design works for an unsigned number; a separate multiplier is used to give the correct sign to the final signed result. The second job of the procedure, after skipping blanks, is to store this multiplier, 1 for a positive number or –1 for a negative number. The multiplier is given the default value 1 and changed to –1 if the first nonblank character is a minus (–). If the first nonblank character is either + or – the offset in SI is incremented to skip over the sign character.

Now the main design is executed. The value is accumulated in the AX register. If multiplication by 10 produces an overflow, then DX contains significant bits of the product, so the result is too large to represent in AX. The `jo overflow` instruction transfers control to the code at `overflow:`, which takes care of all error situations.

Figure 9.7 ASCII to Integer Conversion.

```
; Procedure to scan data segment starting at offset in SI, interpreting
; ASCII characters as an integer value which is returned in AX.

; Leading blanks are skipped.  A leading - or + sign is acceptable.
; Digit(s) must immediately follow the sign (if any).
; Memory scan is terminated by any nondigit, and the address of
; the terminating character is in SI.

; The following flags are affected:
;   PF, SF and ZF reflect sign of number returned in AX.
;   CF reset to 0
;   AF is undefined
;   OF set to indicate error.  Possible error conditions are:
;     - no digits in input
;     - more than 5 digits in input
;     - value outside range -32,768 to 32,767
;   (AX) will be 0 if OF is set.

atoi_proc    PROC   FAR
             push   bx                ; Save registers
             push   cx
             push   dx
             pushf                    ; save flags

while_blank:cmp      BYTE PTR [si],' '  ; space?
             jne    end_while_blank   ; exit if not
             inc    si                ; increment character pointer
             jmp    while_blank       ; and try again
end_while_blank:

             mov    ax,1              ; default sign multiplier
if_plus:     cmp    BYTE PTR [si],'+' ; leading + ?
             je     skip_sign         ; if so, skip over
if_minus:    cmp    BYTE PTR [si],'-' ; leading - ?
             jne    save_sign         ; if not, save default +
             mov    ax,-1             ; -1 for minus sign
skip_sign:   inc    si                ; move past sign

save_sign:   push   ax                ; push sign multiplier on stack
             mov    ax,0              ; number being accumulated
             mov    cx,0              ; count of digits so far

while_digit:cmp      BYTE PTR [si],'0'  ; compare next character to '0'
             jl     end_while_digit   ; not a digit if smaller than '0'
             cmp    BYTE PTR [si],'9' ; compare to '9'
             jg     end_while_digit   ; not a digit if bigger than '9'
```

Figure 9.7 Continued.

```
                mov     bx,10                     ; multiplier
                mul     bx                        ; multiply old number by 10
                jo      overflow                  ; exit if product too large
                mov     bl,[si]                   ; ASCII character to BL
                and     bx,000fh                  ; convert to single-digit integer
                add     ax,bx                     ; add to sum
                jc      overflow                  ; exit if sum too large
                inc     cx                        ; increment digit count
                inc     si                        ; increment character pointer
                jmp     while_digit               ; go try next character
end_while_digit:

                cmp     cx,0                      ; no digits?
                jz      overflow                  ; if so, set overflow error flag

; if value is 8000h and sign is '-', want to return 8000h (-32768)

                cmp     ax,8000h                  ; 8000h ?
                jne     too_big?
                pop     bx                        ; retrieve multiplier
                cmp     bx,-1                     ; -1 ?
                je      ok1                       ; return 8000h
                push    bx                        ; save multiplier again

too_big?:       test    ax,ax                     ; check sign flag
                jns     ok                        ; will be set if number > 32,767

overflow:       pop     bx                        ; discard multiplier
                pop     ax                        ; get flags
                or      ax,0000100001000100b  ; set overflow, zero & parity flags
                and     ax,1111111101111110b  ; reset sign and carry flags
                push    ax                        ; push new flag values
                mov     ax,0                      ; return value of zero
                jmp     atoi_exit                 ; quit
ok:             pop     bx                        ; sign
                imul    bx                        ; make signed number
ok1:            popf                              ; get original flags
                test    ax,ax                     ; set flags for new number
                pushf                             ; save flags

atoi_exit:      popf                              ; get flags
                pop     dx                        ; restore registers
                pop     cx
                pop     bx
                ret                               ;exit
atoi_proc       ENDP
```

To convert a character to a digit, the character is loaded into the BL register half and the instruction **and bx,000fh** is used to clear all bits except the low-order four in the entire BX register. Thus, for example, the ASCII code 37_{16} for 7 becomes 0007 in the BX register. If adding the digit to the accumulated value produces a carry, the sum is too large for AX; the **jc** instruction transfers control to **overflow:**.

The main loop terminates as soon as SI points at any character code other than one for a digit. Thus an integer is terminated by a space, comma, letter, null, or *any* nondigit. In order to determine if a valid integer has been entered, the main loop keeps a count of decimal digits in the CX register. When the loop terminates, this count is checked. If it is zero, there was no digit and the **jz** instruction jumps to **overflow:** for error handling. There is no need to check for too many digits; this would already have been caught in the main loop.

If the accumulated value in the AX register is larger than 8000_{16} (32,768 as an unsigned number), then the magnitude of the number is too great to be represented in word-length 2's complement form. If it is equal to 8000_{16}, then the multiplier must be -1 since $-32,768$ can be represented (as 8000_{16}), but $+32,768$ is too large. The next section of code checks for 8000_{16} in AX and a multiplier of -1; in this case the work is almost done. Otherwise, the instruction **test ax,ax** is used to see if the accumulated value is larger than 8000_{16}; the sign bit will be 1 for a value of this magnitude.

If any of the error conditions occur, the instructions starting at **overflow:** are executed. The multiplier from the stack is discarded using **pop bx** and then the original flags are popped into the AX register by **pop ax** instead of using **popf**. The overflow flag is set to 1 to indicate an error, and a value of 0000 will be returned in AX; other flags are set or reset to correspond to the zero value. The instruction

```
or  ax,0000100001000100b  ; set overflow, zero & parity flags
```

sets bit 11 (the position of overflow flag), bit 6 (zero flag), and bit 2 (parity flag). The zero flag is set since the result returned will be zero; the parity flag is set since 0000_{16} has even parity (an even number of 1 bits). The instruction

```
and     ax,1111111101111110b  ; reset sign and carry flags
```

clears bit 7 (sign flag) since 0000 is not negative and bit 0 (carry), which is always cleared. The bit pattern resulting from these **or** and **and** instructions is pushed back on the stack to be popped by **popf** before exiting the procedure.

When no exceptional condition exists, an **imul** instruction finds the product of the unsigned value and the multiplier (1 or -1) giving the correct signed result. Flag values are set in this normal situation by using **popf** to recover the original flag values; **test ax,ax** clears CF and OF and assigns appropriate values to PF, SF, and ZF. The new flag values are then pushed back on the stack with another **pushf** to be recovered by the normal **popf** in the exit code. The **test** instruction leaves AF undefined; this is why the comments at the beginning of the procedure mention AF.

Exercises 9.3

---

1. The code for `atoi_proc` includes

```
too_big?:   test    ax,ax       ; check sign flag
            jns     ok          ; will be set if number > 32,767
```

An alternative sequence would be

```
too_big?:   cmp     ax,8000h    ; AX < 32,768 ?
            jb      ok          ; ok if so
```

Compare the number of clock cycles and number of bytes of object code for the `test` and the `cmp` instructions.

2. The `atoi_proc` procedure checks for zero digits in the number it is converting, but not for too many digits. Show why this is unnecessary by tracing the code for 100000, the smallest possible six-digit number.

Programming Exercise 9.3

---

1. Write a **FAR** procedure `hex_to_int` that has one parameter passed in SI, the offset of a string in the data segment. This procedure will be similar to `atoi_proc` except that it will convert a string of characters representing an unsigned hexadecimal number to a word-length 2's complement integer in AX. The procedure should skip leading blanks, and then accumulate a value until a character that does not represent a hex digit is encountered. (Valid characters are 0 through 9, A through F, and a through f.) If there are no hex digits or more than four digits, then return 0 and set OF; these are the only possible errors. Clear OF if no error occurs. In all cases set SF, ZF, and PF according to the value returned in AX and clear CF.

9.4

Chapter Summary

This chapter has explored the various 8088 instructions that allow bits in a byte or word destination to be manipulated. The logical instructions **and**, **or**, and **xor** perform Boolean operations using pairs of bits from a source and destination. Applications of these instructions include setting or clearing selected bits in a destination. The **not** instruction takes the one's complement of each bit in its destination operand, changing each 0 to a 1 and each 1 to a 0. The **test** instruction is the same as the **and** instruction except that it only affects flags; the destination operand is unchanged.

Shift instructions move bits left or right within a destination operand. These instructions come in single-bit and multiple-bit versions. Single-bit shifts use **1** for the second operand; multiple-bit versions use **cl** for the second operand and shift the destination the number of positions given in the CL register. Vacated positions are filled by 0 bits in all shift operations except for the arithmetic right shift of a negative number for which 1 bits are used. Shift instructions can be used for efficient, convenient multiplication or division by 2, 4, 8, or some higher power of 2.

Rotate instructions are similar to shift instructions. However, the bit that falls off one end of the destination fills the void on the other end. Shift or rotate instructions can be used in combination with logical instructions to extract groups of bits from a location or to pack multiple values into a single byte or word.

The **atoi** macro generates code that calls the procedure **atoi_proc**. This procedure scans a string in the data segment to which SI points, skipping leading blanks, noting a sign (if any), and accumulating an integer value as ASCII codes for digits are encountered. Logical instructions are used in several places in the procedure.

CHAPTER 10

Interrupts
and Input/Output

Programs in previous chapters have used the **inputs** and **inputc** macros to accept input data from the PC keyboard and the **output** macro to send output data to the monitor. Input and output from an assembly language program have been limited to the keyboard and the monitor. DOS commands and utilities have made it possible to do other input and output with a PC; for example, the **print** command may have been used to accept input data from a disk file and send it as output to a printer.

This chapter describes how the DOS operating system uses 8088 hardware to provide services. Typical operating systems provide a variety of services that an assembly language programmer can invoke. Some of these are for input and output; some are for other purposes. This chapter examines how to use DOS for input and output for different devices. There is also a discussion of input and output without DOS, instead using instructions that directly access the I/O ports of a PC.

10.1

The int Instruction and the Interrupt Vector Table

To use operating system services, the programmer may code a procedure call or a macro (typically expanded by the assembler into a sequence of instructions that include a procedure call.) Sometimes ordinary procedure calls are used, but DOS and many other operating systems use a special type of procedure call: a software **interrupt**, sometimes called a **trap** or an **exception**.

Any interrupt can be invoked by using the 8088 int instruction. In addition, some interrupts can be generated by PC hardware itself. This section explains the interrupt structure used in an 8088 system.

An 8088 system is designed to accommodate up to 256 distinct interrupts. Each interrupt actually used has an **interrupt handler**, a block of code that is almost the same as an ordinary procedure. An interrupt handler is called by an int instruction rather than a call instruction. To return from an interrupt handler, an iret (interrupt return) is used instead of the ret for an ordinary procedure.

The int instruction has the format

        int interrupt_type

where *interrupt_type* is an integer from 0 to 255. An int instruction requires two bytes of object code.* The first byte is the opcode CD and the second byte is the interrupt type. The instruction requires 71 clock cycles to execute. When it executes, it first pushes the contents of the flag register on the stack. Then the interrupt-enable flag IF and the trap flag TF are both cleared to 0. (When IF is 0 the 8088 ignores hardware interrupts except for a **nonmaskable interrupt**. When TF is 1 the 8088 operates in **single-step mode**; clearing TF disables this debugging mode.) The last steps in the execution of an int instruction are the same as a far procedure call—the segment number in the code segment register CS is pushed on the stack and a new code segment number is loaded into CS, and the instruction offset in the instruction pointer register IP is pushed on the stack and a new instruction offset is loaded into IP. No flags other than IF and TF are changed by an int instruction.

Where do the new code segment number and the new instruction offset come from? They are *not* built into the object code as they are with the far procedure calls used in this book. Instead the first 1024 bytes of the computer's memory, addresses 00000 to 003FF, are always used for an **interrupt vector table**, which contains a new instruction offset and code segment number for

---

* The instruction int 3 (interrupt type 3) generates a special interrupt called a "breakpoint interrupt," which has an object code format and a method of execution different from that of the other 255 interrupt types. This book will not consider the breakpoint interrupt; the discussion applies to interrupt types 0–2 and 4–255.

each of the 256 interrupts. For interrupt type 0 the new instruction offset is stored in the word at address 00000, and the new code segment number is stored in the word at address 00002. For interrupt type 1 the new instruction offset is stored in the word at address 00004, and the new code segment number is stored in the word at address 00006. In general, for interrupt type t the new instruction offset is stored in the word at address $4 * t$, and the new code segment number is stored in the word at address $4 * t+2$.

The interrupt return instruction **iret** has no operand. It uses a single byte of object code for opcode CF and takes 44 clock cycles to execute. It first carries out the same steps as a far return instruction, popping IP and CS from the stack. Then it pops flag values from the stack. Consequently all flags are affected as they are restored to the values that were pushed on the stack by an **int** instruction.

Interrupts are used for a variety of purposes. Interrupt type 0 is automatically called by the 8088 CPU when division by zero is attempted. A simple program containing the instruction

```
int 0
```

also calls the divide-by-zero interrupt handler, showing how a particular 8088 system is set up to handle division errors without actually doing a division. The **vector** of instruction offset and segment number at words 00000 and 00002 respectively normally points to the division-by-zero interrupt handler provided for a particular PC. An assembly language program can be written to change this vector to point to a procedure written by the user, thus changing the way a system handles division errors.

The handler for interrupt type 4 also has an assigned purpose, namely to handle overflow conditions that result from instructions. This interrupt handler is *not* called automatically by the 8088. It can be called using **int 4** but is more commonly invoked by the **into** (interrupt on overflow) instruction. This is a conditional call—the overflow interrupt handler is called if the overflow flag OF is set, but otherwise execution continues with the next instruction. Typically an **into** instruction would follow an instruction that might cause overflow to occur. An **into** instruction takes one byte of object code for opcode CE, and takes 73 clock cycles to execute if OF = 1 or 4 clock cycles if OF = 0.

Other low-numbered interrupt types are also reserved for specific uses in 8088-based PCs. Some are used to handle hardware interrupts; for example, on many PC systems an interrupt of type 9 is generated when a key on the keyboard is pressed, making it possible for an interrupt handler to snatch a character and store it for later processing. Others are used by DOS itself to carry out its tasks; one of these, interrupt type 21_{16} (33_{10}) is often used by assembly language programmers to request DOS functions. The next two sections will describe several uses of **int 21h**. Most interrupt types greater than 128 are not used by 8088 hardware or by DOS; these can be used by an applications program.

1. Write and execute a very short assembly language program that includes the instruction **int 0**. Write and execute another very short program that divides by zero. Compare the output from the two programs.

2. What are the 5-hex-digit addresses in the interrupt vector table for the instruction offset and code segment number of the interrupt handler for a type 21_{16} interrupt?

10.2

DOS Function Requests

The DOS operating system uses interrupt type 21_{16} to make many functions available to the user.[*] Most of these functions provide for input and/or output to devices. Many are for various operations with disk files. A few have special purposes (such as to set the system date.) This section contains a general explanation of how to use DOS functions and describes some of the simpler ones. Section 10.3 examines a few of the functions for handling disk files. It is the intent of this book to illustrate how interrupts are used in DOS for requesting operating system services, not to provide a comprehensive manual on DOS functions.

All functions called with **int 21h** invoke the same interrupt handler. The desired function is selected by placing its function number in the AH register half. Many functions either require additional data to be sent to the interrupt handler procedure and/or they return information. Such parameters are normally passed using registers. The only registers altered by this interrupt handler are those used to return information to the user. Flags are not changed, of course, since they are preserved by the **int** and **iret** instructions. Figure 10.1 summarizes the functions covered in this section, indicating how values are passed to and from the interrupt handler for each function number.

Each complete program example in this book has used DOS function $4C_{16}$ to terminate program execution. The following set of statements should be quite familiar.

```
quit:   mov   al,0        ; return code 0
        mov   ah,4ch      ; DOS function to return
        int   21h         ; interrupt for DOS services
```

Function $4C_{16}$ terminates a **process** (one example of which is a program). It closes all files that the process has open (files will be discussed in Section 10.3),

[*] Version 3.1 of MS-DOS provides over ninety functions with **int 21h**.

Figure 10.1 Simple DOS Functions.

Function Number	Action	Parameter(s) for DOS	Parameter(s) Returned by DOS
1	input character (with echo)	none	character in AL
2	display character	character in DL	none
5	print character	character in DL	none
8	input character (no echo)	none	character in AL
9	display string	DS:DX string address	none
$0A_{16}$	input string	DS:DX buffer address, maximum character count first byte of buffer	string in buffer, actual character count second byte of buffer
$4C_{16}$	terminate process	return code in AL	none

transfers control to the parent process (DOS when the process is a program), and returns an **exit code** or **return code** to the parent process. The value for the return code is placed in the AL register half. Zero is used to convey no error; positive values indicate errors, with larger numbers for more severe errors.[*] Notice that normal program termination could be accomplished by a slightly more efficient sequence of instructions:

```
quit:   mov    ax,4c00h   ; return with error code 0
int     21h               ; interrupt for DOS services
```

Function $4C_{16}$ is unusual in that control does not return to the user program after the interrupt is executed.

Function 1 is one of the simplest DOS functions. It waits for the user to press a key on the keyboard, then echoes the character to the display and returns its ASCII code in the AL register half. The following two statements are typical of those used to invoke function 1:

```
mov    ah, 01h           ; function to input character
int    21h               ; call DOS
```

The procedure called by the `inputc` macro does nothing except request DOS function 1, clear AH, and return.

Function 2 is used to output a single character to the monitor display. The character code is sent to the interrupt handler in the DL register half. As an illustration, the following instructions display a carriage return and a linefeed character.

---

[*] The reader may wish to investigate how exit codes can be used in the DOS **IF** command.

```
newline:    mov    ah, 02h    ; display single character
            mov    dl, 0dh    ; carriage return
            int    21h        ; request DOS function
            mov    dl, 0ah    ; linefeed
            int    21h
```

Notice that it is not necessary to put the function number in AH for the second call—since function 2 does not return any value, it does not modify any user register.

Function 8 is like function 1 in that it waits for the user to type a character at the keyboard and returns the ASCII code for the character in AL. Function 8, however, does not echo the character to the display.

Figure 10.2 shows a fragment of code that uses function 8 to input characters until y, Y, n or N is entered. When one of these four characters is entered, it is then displayed in uppercase using function 2. The following design is implemented:

> until character is one of 'y', 'Y', 'n' or 'N' loop
> > input character;
>
> end loop;
>
> convert character to upper case;
>
> output character;

Function $0A_{16}$ inputs a string of characters from the keyboard. It waits for characters to be typed and stores them in a buffer (a block of memory); pressing

Figure 10.2 Use DOS to Get and Echo 'Y' or 'N'.

```
            mov    ah,08h        ; input character without echo
until:      int    21h           ; call DOS
            cmp    al,'y'        ; character = 'y'?
            je     end_until     ; quit if so
            cmp    al,'Y'        ; 'Y'?
            je     end_until
            cmp    al,'n'        ; 'n'?
            je     end_until
            cmp    al,'N'        ; 'N'?
            jne    until         ; continue trying if not 'N'
end_until:
            and    al,11011111b  ; convert character to upper case

            mov    ah,02h        ; display character function
            mov    dl,al         ; copy character
            int    21h           ; call DOS
```

the return key terminates input. The user must send the interrupt handler the location of the buffer where characters are to be stored. This address is passed in segment:offset form in DS:DX. For a buffer in the data segment, only the offset must be loaded into DX. The user must also tell DOS the maximum number of characters (excluding the carriage return); this is stored as a single-byte unsigned number in the first byte of the buffer (at address DS:DX). The function sets the second byte of the buffer to the number of characters actually read in (not count-ing the carriage return), and places ASCII codes for the characters themselves in the rest of the buffer (starting at the third byte). The ASCII code for a carriage return ($0D_{16}$) is the last byte stored, and any remaining bytes in the buffer will not be assigned values. Since the first two bytes of the buffer are used for coun-ters and the carriage return character is stored, the maximum character count sent to DOS should be three smaller than the size of the buffer. If this count is larger, then data stored in memory following the buffer may be destroyed.

One of the advantages of using function $0A_{16}$ is that this input routine allows corrections to be made before the Return key is pressed. In particular, the Backspace key deletes the last character typed, both on the monitor display and from the buffer. It takes a fairly complex procedure to accomplish the same task using only character input and output functions (see Programming Exercise 1 at the end of this section).

The procedure called by the **inputs** macro uses DOS function $0A_{16}$ to input a string. The code for this procedure is shown in Figure 10.3. Instead of reading characters directly into the user's destination string, the procedure uses a local

Figure 10.3 Procedure Called by the **inputs** Macro.

```
; Procedure to input string from keyboard.

; CX contains the length of the user's buffer.  It is assumed that this
; length is between 1 and 81.

; DI contains the offset in DS of the user's buffer where the string will
; be stored.

; The string will be terminated by a null character (00h).

; The actual number of characters (not counting the null) is returned in CX.
; This number will be between 0 and 80.

; Flags are unchanged.

buffer      DB      83 DUP (?)              ; local buffer for string

ins_proc    PROC    FAR
            push    ax                      ; Save registers
            push    dx
            push    di
```

Figure 10.3 Continued.

```
            push   si
            push   ds
            push   es
            pushf                        ; save flags

            mov    ax,ds                 ; copy data segment number to ES
            mov    es,ax

            mov    ax,cs                 ; copy code segment number to DS
            mov    ds,ax

            dec    cx                    ; maximum number of characters
            mov    buffer,cl
            mov    dx,OFFSET buffer      ; local buffer address
            mov    ah,0ah                ; DOS function 10 does the input
            int    21h

            mov    cl,buffer+1           ; actual number of characters
            mov    ch,0                  ; convert to word
            jcxz   end_in                ; skip if no characters

            push   cx                    ; save count to return
            mov    si,OFFSET buffer+2    ; start in local buffer
            cld                          ; ensure forward copy
            rep movsb                    ; copy string from local to user buffer
            pop    cx                    ; restore count

end_in:     mov    BYTE PTR es:[di],0    ; null character terminator
            mov    dl,10                 ; output linefeed
            mov    ah,2                  ;    using DOS function 2
            int    21h

            popf                         ; restore flags
            pop    es                    ; restore registers
            pop    ds
            pop    si
            pop    di
            pop    dx
            pop    ax
            ret                          ; exit

ins_proc    ENDP
```

buffer. This ensures adequate room for the two counts required by function $0A_{16}$, the number of characters that the user wants to input and a carriage-return character. (If the user's buffer were utilized, the maximum number of characters would be three less than the length of the buffer.) Function $0A_{16}$ puts a carriage-return character at the end of the string and the **inputs** macro promises a null character as a string terminator, so the string without the carriage return is copied from the local buffer to the user's buffer and a null byte is appended.

After saving registers, the **ins_proc** procedure copies DS to ES so that when **movs** is later used to copy the string, the extra segment that contains the destination will be the user's data segment. Then the data segment is changed to be the same as the code segment since the local buffer is contained in the same segment as the code for the procedure.

The user passes the length of the buffer in the CX register. This value must be decremented to correspond to the maximum number of characters that can be keyed in, allowing for the null byte at the end of the user's buffer. The maximum number of characters is stored in the first byte of the local buffer before calling function $0A_{16}$. After the call, the actual character count is retrieved from the second byte of the local buffer and is converted to a word. If this count is nonzero, it is necessary to copy the string from the local buffer to the user's buffer. The **rep movsb** instruction does this job.

Notice that the segment override prefix in the statement

```
end_in:     mov     BYTE PTR es:[di],0  ; null character terminator
```

puts the trailing null byte in the user's buffer. This is not a string instruction, and without the segment override prefix, the null byte would end up somewhere in the current data segment (actually the segment containing all the code for the input/output routines as well as the local buffer) rather than the user's data segment.

Function $0A_{16}$ echoes the carriage return, which terminates input. The **ins_proc** procedure displays a linefeed character to ensure that the cursor ends up at the beginning of the next line. The procedure finishes by restoring all registers that have been used, except for CX, which returns the length of the string.

The DOS operating system also provides a function to display a string. Function 9 works very much like the **output** macro. The address of the string is sent to the interrupt handler in DS:DX. It is the user's task to ensure that DS:DX points at the string; that is, the DX register contains the offset of the string in the segment whose segment number is in DS. The source string must be terminated by a dollar sign ($) instead of the null character used by the **output** macro; the dollar sign is not displayed. The following statements might be used to display instructions.

```
instruct  DB    'Enter three values',cr,Lf
          DB    'when requested.',cr,Lf,'$'
          ...
          mov   dx, OFFSET instruct    ; offset of instructions
          mov   ah, 09h                ; display string function
          int   21h                    ; call DOS
```

The DOS functions discussed up to this point input data from the keyboard and output data to the display. Function 5 is used to output a character to a printer. It is used like function 2—the character to be printed is sent to the interrupt handler in the DL register half. The following instructions print the character that is at the offset stored in the SI register.

```
mov   dl, [si]        ; copy character to DL
mov   ah, 05h         ; print character function
int   21h             ; call DOS
```

Such a sequence of instructions could be included in a loop to print an entire string. If the length of the string were known, a **for** loop could be used; otherwise a **while** loop could be used to stop printing when the next character is a known terminator like a null or a dollar sign.

Function 5 points out one of the strengths of an operating system. A PC system often has two or more connectors for printers or other peripheral devices. These are wired to interface circuits that have distinct sets of I/O port addresses. Function 5 normally sends a character to a parallel printer port. However, DOS can be configured so that a character sent to the usual parallel printer port is redirected to another parallel printer port or even to a serial communications port. Therefore a program that prints information by using DOS function 5 will work correctly on a variety of PC systems with different printer setups. This would not be possible if the assembly language programmer directly coded the I/O port addresses for a particular printer.

Figure 10.3 summarizes the DOS functions covered in this section. The table indicates the action of each function as well as how information is sent to and from the interrupt handler.

Exercises 10.2

1. Write a program fragment to implement the design

   until character is a digit '0' through '9' loop
       input character;
   end loop;
   output character;

   Use only DOS functions for input and output.

2. Write a program fragment to implement the design

   display "Enter your name: ";
   input name;

   Allow for a name up to 20 characters long. Use only DOS functions for input and output.

3. Assume that memory in the data segment at **buffer** contains a collection of ASCII codes terminated by a null character. Write a program fragment to output to a printer all characters prior to the null byte. Use DOS function 5.

---

1. Write a procedure **getstring** that uses DOS functions 2 and 8 to do almost the same job as DOS function $0A_{16}$. Specifically, use the CX register to pass **getstring** the maximum number of characters to be keyed in, and DX to pass the offset of a destination string in the data segment (segment number in DS). Input should be terminated by pressing the Return key. The carriage-return character should be stored in the destination string but does not count as one of the "maximum number." If the Backspace key is pressed, erase the last character on the screen (by displaying a backspace-space-backspace sequence) and delete the previous character from the destination string. Sound the bell if the user attempts to enter more than the maximum number of characters. (Allow Return and Backspace keypresses even if the maximum has been reached.)

2. Using only DOS functions for input and output, write a program that will input lines up to 80 characters long from the keyboard, echo each to the display, and print each on the printer. Be sure to display and print carriage return and linefeed characters as needed.

10.3

Sequential File I/O Using DOS

Most of the DOS functions invoked via **int 21h** provide for disk file operations. Included are functions to

- create a new file
- open a file (prepare an existing file for reading or writing)
- close a file (write memory buffers to disk and update the file directory)
- read data from a file
- write data to a file
- delete a file

Figure 10.4 DOS File Functions.

Function Number	Action	Parameter(s) for DOS	Parameter(s) Returned by DOS

$3C_{16}$	create file	DS:DX file name
		CX file attributes
			if CF = 1 then
			    AX error code
			else
			    AX file handle

$3D_{16}$	open file	DS:DX file name
		AL access/mode request
			if CF = 1 then
			    AX error code
			else
			    AX file handle

$3E_{16}$	close file	BX file handle	if CF = 1 then AX error code

$3F_{16}$	read from file	BX file handle
		CX bytes to read
		DS:DX destination
			if CF = 1 then
			    AX error code
			else
			    AX bytes read

40_{16}	write to file	BX file handle
		CX bytes to write
		DS:DX source
			if CF = 1 then
			    AX error code
			else
			    AX bytes written

41_{16}	delete file	DS:DX file name	if CF = 1 then AX error code

In fact, DOS has two distinct functions available for many possible operations. For example, either function 13_{16} or function 41_{16} can be used to delete a file. In such cases, the higher-numbered function was included with version 2 and later versions of DOS. In fact, most users have version 2 or 3 of DOS.[*] The lower-numbered functions are considered nearly obsolete, and the higher-numbered functions are easier to use. The discussion in this section will be limited to a few of the higher-numbered functions.

To identify a file, most DOS functions use a 16-bit number called its **file handle**. The name of a file is passed to DOS when the file is opened, and DOS returns the file handle to be used in subsequent operations. The file handle is passed to DOS to read from the file, write to it, or close it. Figure 10.4 summarizes the DOS file functions discussed in this section.

---

[*] The **ver** command will display the version of DOS which is running on a particular system.

When $3D_{16}$ is loaded into the AH register half for an **int 21h** call, DOS is asked to open a file. For this function call other parameters are passed to DOS in the DS, DX, and AL registers.

The DS and DX registers together provide the address of a string of ASCII characters giving the name of the file. This null-terminated string may include disk drive and/or path specifications. Such a string will usually be in the data segment whose segment number is already in DS, so all that is necessary is to put the offset of the string in DX.

The AL register half sends information on how the file is to be opened. The four low-order bits (0–3) contain an unsigned number, which should be assigned one of the following values:

- 0000 if the file is to be opened for reading only
- 0001 if the file is to be opened for writing only
- 0010 if the file is to be opened for both reading and writing

Bits 4–6 tell DOS how other processes will be able to use the file while it is opened from this call. A value of 000 is appropriate in a single-user PC environment; this value asks for **compatibility mode** where other processes could also open the file. The high-order bit (bit 7) tells DOS that if the current process creates a child process, that child process can or cannot use the file handle. In a simple setting the choice is immaterial; a value of 0 tells DOS that a child process can use the file handle. Assuming a simple PC environment, all of this reduces to moving a simple decimal number to AL for the desired file operations:

- 0 to read the file
- 1 to write the file
- 2 to read and write the file

DOS responds to function $3D_{16}$ by returning in AX either a file handle for the newly opened file or an error code. The carry flag is set or cleared to indicate whether the number in AX is an error code (CF = 1) or a file handle (CF = 0). There are several possible error codes; they include codes for invalid value in AL, file not found, and too many open files. Recall that the conditional jump instructions **jc** and **jnc** enable the 8088 programmer to check the status of the carry flag. A complete example using the file open, file read, and file close functions will be given as soon as the close and read functions are discussed.

The file close function is invoked using function number $3E_{16}$. The only parameter is the file handle, which is passed to DOS in the BX register. The only possible error condition is that the number passed in BX is not a valid file handle. In this case DOS sets the carry flag and returns a value of 6 in the AX register. If the file handle is valid, the carry flag is cleared and the file is closed.

The DOS operating system does not actually read or write to the disk every time a file read or write function is used. When reading, DOS physically reads a relatively large block of the file into a **file buffer**, a section of memory reserved for this purpose by DOS. Then when a read function is used, bytes are copied from this buffer to the specified destination. If reading is done sequentially and all the bytes in the buffer are logically used by a read function, then DOS physically reads another block from the disk to the file buffer.

The situation is similar for write operations. These functions place bytes of data into a file buffer and when this buffer is full, DOS physically writes its contents to the disk. When a file is closed, remaining bytes in the buffer are **flushed**, that is, written to the disk. In addition, the file directory that DOS maintains is updated, if necessary.

Function $4C_{16}$ for program termination automatically closes all open files. However, it is good programming practice to close any open file as soon as it is no longer being used. This guards against data being lost in a file buffer if a program has an abnormal termination (such as in a loss of power to the computer.) It may free a file for another user, depending on the mode in which the file was opened. There is also a limit on the number of open file handles in a single user's program.

Function $3F_{16}$ reads data from a file that has previously been opened. The file handle is sent to DOS in the BX register. The number of bytes to be read is placed in CX. The DS and DX registers together point to the destination in the user's data segment where the data from the file is placed. Since DS normally contains the segment number for the data segment, it is usually only necessary to put the offset of this destination in DX.

As with the other file functions, the carry flag is used to indicate errors. If CF = 1, then AX will contain an error code. If there is no error, AX will contain the number of bytes actually read. If there are not as many bytes remaining in the file as were requested, then the number in AX will be smaller than the number requested in CX; otherwise it will be the same.

Figure 10.5 gives a complete program that does much the same job as the DOS `type` command. It asks for the name of a file and then uses the monitor to display that file. The program uses DOS function calls for all input and output, even though the macros from IO.H would be more convenient. The following design is implemented by the program.

```
prompt for and input file name;
open file for reading;
if error opening file
then
      display error message;
      exit program;
end if;
forever loop
      read 1 byte from file;
      if error reading file
      then
            display error message;
            exit program;
      end if;
```

```
            if zero bytes read
            then
                    exit loop;
            else
                    display byte;
            end if;
        end loop;
        close file;
        if error closing file
        then
                display error message;
        end if;
```

The file display program begins like previous programs. The first lines of code that deserve comment are

```
mov     ah, 0ah              ; input file name
mov     dx, OFFSET filename
mov     filename,17          ; maximum length
int     21h
```

Here DOS function $0A_{16}$ is used to input the filename. Notice that there were 20 bytes reserved for **filename** in the data segment, so the maximum number of characters to be read is 17; this number is placed in the first byte of the destination buffer.

Function $0A_{16}$ will terminate the name with a carriage-return character and the file-open function needs a null-terminated string, so the next segment of code replaces the return by a null.

```
mov     bx, dx               ; offset of filename
mov     al, filename+1       ; number of characters read
sub     ah, ah               ; zero AH
add     bx, ax
mov     BYTE PTR [bx+2], 0 ; replace CR by null
```

The offset of the filename is copied to the BX register, and the number of characters actually read is added to this offset. Based addressing with the BX register and a displacement of 2 (for the two count bytes at the beginning of the **filename** field) then locates the position where the null byte is needed.

When the file is opened the two extra count bytes at the beginning of the **filename** field must again be considered; the offset of **filename+2** is copied into the DX register to point at the actual string, skipping the extra bytes. Moving

Figure 10.5 File Display Program.

```
; program to display text file

cr            EQU    0dh    ; carriage return character
Lf            EQU    0ah    ; linefeed character

stack         SEGMENT STACK
              DW     100h DUP (?)
stack         ENDS

data          SEGMENT
prompt        DB     cr,Lf,'Enter file name:  $'
filename      DB     20 DUP (?)
handle        DW     ?
error_1       DB     'Unable to open file',cr,Lf,'$'
error_2       DB     cr,Lf,'Error reading file',cr,Lf,'$'
error_3       DB     cr,Lf,'Error closing file',cr,Lf,'$'
char          DB     ?
data          ENDS

code          SEGMENT
              ASSUME cs:code, ds:data

start:        mov    ax, SEG data        ; load data segment number
              mov    ds, ax

              mov    ah, 09h             ; prompt for file name
              mov    dx, OFFSET prompt
              int    21h

              mov    ah, 0ah             ; input file name
              mov    dx, OFFSET filename
              mov    filename,17         ; maximum length
              int    21h
              mov    bx, dx              ; offset of filename
              mov    al, filename+1      ; number of characters read
              sub    ah, ah              ; zero AH
              add    bx, ax
              mov    BYTE PTR [bx+2], 0 ; replace CR by null

              mov    ah, 02h             ; display two linefeeds
              mov    dl, Lf
              int    21h
              int    21h

              mov    al, 0               ; open file for reading
              mov    ah, 3dh
              mov    dx, OFFSET filename+2
              int    21h
```

Figure 10.5 Continued.

```
                jnc     read                    ; carry indicates error
                mov     ah, 09h                 ; display string
                mov     dx, OFFSET error_1
                int     21h
                jmp     quit

read:           mov     handle, ax              ; save file handle
                mov     bx, ax                  ; copy file handle to BX
                mov     cx, 1                   ; number of bytes to read

loop1:          mov     ah, 3fh                 ; read file function
                mov     dx, OFFSET char         ; destination for data
                int     21h
                jnc     check                   ; carry indicates error
                mov     ah, 09h                 ; error message
                mov     dx, OFFSET error_2
                int     21h
                jmp     quit

check:          cmp     ax, 0                   ; zero bytes?
                jz      end_loop1               ; quit if no byte was read
                mov     ah, 02h                 ; display character function
                mov     dl, char                ; character to display
                int     21h
                jmp     loop1                   ; go get next character
end_loop1:

                mov     ah, 3eh                 ; close file
                mov     bx, handle              ; handle for file
                int     21h
                jnc     quit                    ; exit if no error
                mov     ah, 09h                 ; error message
                mov     dx, OFFSET error_3
                int     21h

quit:           mov     al,0                    ; return code 0
                mov     ah,4ch                  ; function to exit
                int     21h

code            ENDS
                END     start
```

0 to AL opens the file for reading. After `int 21h`, to ask DOS to open the file, the instruction

```
jnc     read                    ; carry indicates error
```

skips error handling code when CF = 0.

To read the file, the file handle is copied to BX, and the value 1 is placed in CX since the file will be logically read one byte at a time. Notice that both of these registers can be loaded outside the loop since DOS preserves registers that are not used to return values. On the other hand, inside the loop AX is altered by the read function and AH and DX are used by DOS function 2 to display a character, so it is necessary to repeatedly load AH with function number $3F_{16}$ for reading and DX with the offset of the destination buffer.

In this example program, the destination buffer to receive characters is only a single byte long since the file is read one byte at a time. It is more efficient to use a longer buffer. If, say, a 16-byte-long buffer were used, then the count returned in AX can be used to determine if a full 16 characters were available; if fewer characters were available, then all characters in the file have been read. A **for** loop can be used to process the characters in the buffer one at a time. (See Exercise 1 in this section.)

If one uses this program to display a file containing non-ASCII codes, then a garbled display with many unusual characters will result. Even if a text file (such as an assembly language source file) is displayed, the last character shown will look like a right arrow. This symbol is the graphic representation used in a PC system for a Control-z ($1A_{16}$) character. A Control-z character is normally used as a sentinel character for a text file. Therefore an alternative way of controlling the main read-file-and-display-character loop in the example program is to exit the loop when the next character to be displayed is a Control-z. (See Exercise 2 in this section.)

The open function will not open a file unless the file has a directory entry. However, when DOS function $3C_{16}$ is sent a file name it will open the file if it already exists or create a new file with the given name if one did not already exist. This create file function uses the DS and DX registers to point at an ASCII string with the file name, just like the open file function. The file is opened for read/write access. Any data in an existing file is discarded; that is, the file is truncated to zero bytes long. The AL register half is not used to pass access or mode data to DOS for function $3C_{16}$. Another difference from the open file function is that the create file function uses the value in the CX register to set "file attributes" for the new file. These file attributes are such things as "read only" and "system." Generally files have no special attributes and this is indicated by putting zero in the CX register. The create file function uses the AX register to return the file handle or an error code, depending on whether CF is 0 or 1.

DOS function 40_{16} is used to write data to a file that is open for write or read/write access. The BX register sends the file handle to DOS, and the CX register transmits the number of bytes to be written. The source of data bytes to be written is a buffer in the data segment; DS:DX points to this source buffer.

As with the other DOS file functions, CF = 1 indicates an error. If CF = 0, then AX contains the number of bytes actually written. If this number is less than the number in CX then there was an error even when the carry flag is clear.

Figure 10.6 gives the listing of a program that creates a text file from terminal input. It first prompts for a file name, and terminates it with a null byte. The code

```
mov     ah, 3ch                 ; create and/or open file
mov     dx,OFFSET string+2 ; file name
mov     cx, 0                   ; no special file attribute
int     21h
```

creates the file or clears an old file with the same name.

Figure 10.6 Create a File from Terminal Input.

```
; program to create a file from lines typed at the terminal

cr              EQU     0dh     ; carriage return character
Lf              EQU     0ah     ; linefeed character
control_z       EQU     1ah

stack           SEGMENT STACK
                DW      100h DUP (?)
stack           ENDS

data            SEGMENT
handle          DW      ?
prompt1         DB      cr, Lf, 'Destination file name? $'
instruct        DB      cr, Lf, Lf, 'At each "-->" prompt, type a line of text '
                DB      'to be stored in your file.', cr, Lf, 'After your last '
                DB      'line, type control-z and press return.', cr, Lf, '$'
prompt2         DB      cr, Lf, '--> $'
error_1         DB      cr, Lf, 'Error creating file', cr, Lf, '$'
error_2         DB      cr, Lf, 'Error closing file', cr, Lf, '$'
error_3         DB      cr, Lf, 'Error writing file', cr, Lf, '$'
string          DB      80 DUP (?)
data            ENDS

code            SEGMENT
                ASSUME cs:code, ds:data

start:          mov     ax, SEG data        ; load data segment number
                mov     ds, ax

                mov     ah, 09h             ; prompt for file name
                mov     dx, OFFSET prompt1
                int     21h
```

Figure 10.6 Continued.

```
            mov    ah, 0ah               ; input file name
            mov    dx, OFFSET string
            mov    string, 30            ; maximum length
            int    21h
            mov    bx, dx                ; offset of filename
            mov    al, string+1          ; number of characters read
            sub    ah, ah                ; zero AH
            add    bx, ax
            mov    BYTE PTR [bx+2], 0 ; replace CR by null

            mov    ah, 3ch               ; create and/or open file
            mov    dx,OFFSET string+2 ; file name
            mov    cx, 0                 ; no special file attribute
            int    21h
            jnc    write                 ; check for error
            mov    ah, 09h
            mov    dx, OFFSET error_1
            int    21h
            jmp    quit

  write:    mov    handle, ax            ; save file handle

            mov    ah, 09h               ; display instructions
            mov    dx, OFFSET instruct
            int    21h

  loop1:    mov    ah, 09h               ; prompt for line
            mov    dx, OFFSET prompt2
            int    21h

            mov    ah, 0ah               ; input line
            mov    dx, OFFSET string
            mov    string, 75            ; maximum length
            int    21h

            cmp    string+2, control_z  ; control-z at first of line?
            je     close

            mov    bx, dx                ; offset of string
            mov    al, string+1          ; number of characters read
            inc    al                    ; add 1 for return character
            sub    ah, ah                ; make word length
            add    bx, ax                ; string length
            mov    BYTE PTR [bx+2],Lf ; append linefeed to line
```

Figure 10.6 Continued.

```
               mov     cx, ax              ; find length
               inc     cx                  ;     including CR & LF
               mov     ah, 40h             ; write file function
               mov     bx, handle
               mov     dx,OFFSET string+2 ; source of data
               int     21h
               jc      write_error         ; carry indicates error
               jmp     loop1
end_loop1:

close:         mov     ah, 40h             ; write control-z to file
               mov     bx, handle
               mov     dx,OFFSET string+2 ; source of data
               mov     cx, 1
               int     21h
               jc      write_error         ; check for error

               mov     ah, 3eh             ; close file
               mov     bx, handle          ; handle for file
               int     21h
               jnc     quit                ; exit if no error
               mov     ah, 09h             ; error message
               mov     dx, OFFSET error_2
               int     21h
               jmp     quit


write_error:
               mov     ah, 09h             ; error message
               mov     dx, OFFSET error_3
               int     21h

quit:          mov     al,0                ; return code 0
               mov     ah,4ch              ; function to exit
               int     21h

code           ENDS
               END     start
```

After instructions are displayed, the main program loop repeatedly prompts with an arrow (--›) for a line of text to be entered. The read string function accepts a string from the keyboard and returns the number of characters read. This number of characters is incremented once to find the position for a linefeed character to be appended after the carriage-return character already in the buffer, and is incremented a second time to yield the correct count of characters to write to the disk file. The loop is exited when the user types a Control-z for the first character of a new line. The Control-z is written to the text file to provide the usual sentinel character.

DOS function 41_{16} is used to delete a file, removing its directory entry. The name of the file is sent to DOS using DS:DX to point to a string of ASCII characters, just like the open and create functions. No other parameter is used. DOS responds by giving the carry flag the value 0 if there is no error and the file is deleted; CF = 1 indicates an error.

Exercises 10.3

1. Modify the file display program shown in Figure 10.5 to read the source file 16 characters at a time. Terminate the read-display loop when a file read yields fewer than 16 characters. Be sure to process the last partially full buffer, which may contain from 0 to 15 characters.

2. Modify the file display program from Figure 10.5 to read the source file 16 characters at a time. Terminate the read-display loop when the next character to be displayed is a Control-z. (Do not display the Control-z.)

Programming Exercises 10.3

1. Write a program that will copy a source file to a destination file. Specifically, the program should prompt for the source file name, attempt to open the source file, and exit with an error message if it cannot do so. If the source file is opened successfully, then the user should be prompted for the destination file name. If the destination file exists (which can be determined by attempting to open it), the user should be asked if the old file is to be destroyed, and the program should terminate if the answer is negative. If the destination file does not exist, no warning is needed before making the file copy. Use only DOS function calls for input/output, not macros from IO.H.

2. Write a program that will copy a source file to a destination file, changing all uppercase letters to lowercase letters, but leaving other characters unchanged. The program should prompt for both file names. It is not necessary to warn the user if the destination file exists before replacing it with the copy. Use only DOS function calls for input/output, not macros from IO.H.

3. Write a program that will print a source file on the standard printer. The program should prompt for the source file name. (Note: This can be done in at least two ways. One is to use DOS function 5 to print characters read

from the file. Another is to use the code from Programming Exercise 1 above, using **prn** as the destination file; DOS provides an interface so that input/output devices can be treated like files.) Use only DOS function calls for input/output, not macros from IO.H.

4. Write a program which will process a collection of fixed format records from the file RECORDS.DAT. Each line of the file will consist of ASCII data with

   - a person's name in columns 1–20
   - an integer right-justified in columns 21–25

   Each line of the file will be terminated by a carriage-return and a linefeed character. A Control-z character will follow the last line. Such a file can be produced by a standard text editor.

   The program should echo the lines of data and then report

   - the number of records
   - the sum of the numbers
   - the person with the largest number

   Use only DOS function calls for input/output. The **atoi** and **itoa** macros from IO.H may be used.

5. (a) Write a program that accepts as input integers from the terminal, converts each to word-length 2's complement form, and writes the 2's-complement word to the file INTEGERS.DAT. Terminate input and close the output file when the user enters the number –9999. (Warning: INTEGERS.DAT is not an ASCII file. If you attempt to display the file on the monitor, expect unusual and illegible results. (See part (b) of this exercise.) Use only DOS function calls for input/output. The **atoi** macro from IO.H may be used.

   (b) Write a program that reads word-length 2's complement integers one at a time from the file INTEGERS.DAT. Terminate the read when the file runs out of data. Calculate and display the sum of the integers. Use only DOS function calls for input/output. The **itoa** macro from IO.H may be used.

10.4

I/O Without the Operating System (Using in and out)

This book has emphasized the use of procedures and DOS function calls for input/output operations. These provide for programs that are relatively transportable from one computer system to another. At the lowest level, however,

Figure 10.7 in and out Instructions.

Instruction	Destination Operand	Source Operand	Clock Cycles	Number of Bytes	Opcode
in	al	port	10	2	E4
	ax	port	14	2	E5
	al	dx	8	1	EC
	ax	dx	12	1	ED
out	port	al	10	2	E6
	port	ax	14	2	E7
	dx	ax	12	1	EF
	dx	al	8	1	EE

input and output must be done using in and out instructions. This section shows how to print a file using in and out instructions to access the ports used for parallel printer 1.

The in and out instructions, summarized in Figure 10.7, are much like **mov** instructions. No flag is changed by an in or out instruction. Each has formats to transmit a single byte or a word. The source for an out instruction must be AX (a word) or AL (for a byte). Similarly the destination for an in instruction must be AX or AL.

Each in or out instruction has one version in which the actual port address is coded in the instruction and another in which **dx** is coded to indicate that the I/O port address is in the DX register. Recall that the 8088 has 64K input/output ports with addresses from 0000_{16} to $FFFF_{16}$. The actual address format can be used only when the address is from 0 to 255 since it is stored in a single byte of object code. A larger port address must be first placed in the DX register, and the **dx** version of an in or out instruction is used. For example, the instruction

```
in    ax, 07ch
```

is functionally equivalent to the pair of instructions

```
mov   dx, 07ch
in    ax, dx
```

However, the instruction

```
out   04a5h, al     ; illegal port address for this format
```

is not acceptable, since $04A5_{16}$ is too large.

Figure 10.8 gives the source listing for a program similar to the file display program in Figure 10.5. Both use DOS functions to input a file name, open the file, and read characters from the file one at a time. This program terminates the file read loop when a Control-z is read.

Figure 10.8   Print a File Using LPT1 I/O Ports.

```
; print a file using parallel printer port LPT1

cr            EQU     0dh      ; carriage return character
Lf            EQU     0ah      ; linefeed character
control_z     EQU     1ah      ; control-z

lpt1_data     EQU     378h            ; parallel printer #1 data port address
lpt1_status   EQU     lpt1_data+1 ; printer status port
lpt1_control  EQU     lpt1_data+2 ; printer control port

stack         SEGMENT STACK
              DW      100h DUP (?)
stack         ENDS

data          SEGMENT
prompt        DB      cr,Lf,'Enter file name:  $'
filename      DB      20 DUP (?)
handle        DW      ?
error_1       DB      'Unable to open file',cr,Lf,'$'
error_2       DB      cr,Lf,'Error reading file',cr,Lf,'$'
error_3       DB      cr,Lf,'Error closing file',cr,Lf,'$'
char          DB      ?
data          ENDS

code          SEGMENT
              ASSUME cs:code, ds:data

start:        mov     ax, SEG data        ; load data segment number
              mov     ds, ax

              mov     al, 00001000b       ; bit 2 zero to initialize printer
              mov     dx, lpt1_control    ; control port
              out     dx, al

; The loop below takes 20 clock cycles per iteration for 1000 cycles.
; A 4.77 MHz machine takes at least (1000 cycles)/(4770000 cycles/sec)
; This is more than 200 microseconds.

              mov     cx, 50              ; loop counter
init_wait:    nop                         ; do nothing 50 times
              loop    init_wait

              mov     al, 00001100b       ; finish initialization pulse
              out     dx, al
```

Figure 10.8 Continued.

```
                mov     ah, 09h                 ; prompt for file name
                mov     dx, OFFSET prompt
                int     21h

                mov     ah, 0ah                 ; input file name
                mov     dx, OFFSET filename
                mov     filename,17             ; maximum length
                int     21h
                mov     bx, dx                  ; offset of filename
                mov     al, filename+1          ; number of characters read
                sub     ah, ah                  ; zero AH
                add     bx, ax
                mov     BYTE PTR [bx+2], 0      ; replace CR by null

                mov     ah, 02h                 ; display two linefeeds
                mov     dl, Lf
                int     21h
                int     21h

                mov     al, 0                   ; open file for reading
                mov     ah, 3dh
                mov     dx, OFFSET filename+2
                int     21h
                jnc     read                    ; carry indicates error
                mov     ah, 09h                 ; display string
                mov     dx, OFFSET error_1
                int     21h
                jmp     quit

read:           mov     handle, ax              ; save file handle
                mov     bx, ax                  ; copy file handle to BX
                mov     cx, 1                   ; number of bytes to read

loop1:          mov     ah, 3fh                 ; read file function
                mov     dx, OFFSET char         ; destination for data
                int     21h
                jnc     check                   ; carry indicates error
                mov     ah, 09h                 ; error message
                mov     dx, OFFSET error_2
                int     21h
                jmp     quit

check:          cmp     char, control_z         ; end of file?
                je      end_loop1               ; quit if so
```

Figure 10.8 Continued.

```
                mov     dx, lpt1_status     ; printer status port
while_busy: in      al, dx              ; get status
                and     al, 10000000b       ; mask all but busy bit
                jz      while_busy          ; 0 means busy

                mov     al, char            ; character to print
                mov     dx, lpt1_data       ; printer data port address
                out     dx, al              ; output character

                mov     dx, lpt1_control    ; printer control port
                mov     al, 00001101b       ; set strobe bit
                out     dx, al              ; start strobe pulse
                mov     al, 00001100b       ; clear strobe bit
                out     dx, al              ; finish strobe pulse

                jmp     loop1               ; go get next character
end_loop1:

                mov     ah, 3eh             ; close file
                mov     bx, handle          ; handle for file
                int     21h
                jnc     quit                ; exit if no error
                mov     ah, 09h             ; error message
                mov     dx, OFFSET error_3
                int     21h

quit:           mov     al,0                ; return code 0
                mov     ah,4ch              ; function to exit
                int     21h

code            ENDS
                END     start
```

Instead of using a DOS function to display a character, each byte from the file is sent to the input/output port at address 0378_{16}. This is the address for the parallel printer port called "LPT1" on a standard PC system. An *out* instruction is used to send the byte to the **data port**. Unfortunately things are not quite as simple as this implies. There are actually three input/output ports associated with LPT1, at addresses 0378_{16}, 0379_{16} and $037A_{16}$. The second port is called the **printer status port** and the third port is the **printer control port**.

Reading a byte from the printer status port provides six bits of meaningful information about the state of the printer, plus two inconsequential bits. Bit 7 is 0 when the printer is busy processing a previous character and is 1 if the printer is not busy and can accept another character. As will be discussed below, this status bit must be checked before each character is sent to the printer. Bit 5 is 1 if the printer is out of paper or 0 if the printer has paper. Bits 6, 5, 3, and 2 also provide status information.

The printer control port is used to direct various printer operations. Bit 0 is normally 0, but is set to 1 for a brief period to inform the printer that a byte of data has been sent to it. This process will be described more carefully below. Bit 2 is used to initialize the printer. Bit 3 must be 1 for some printers to **select** them, or enable them to print. Each of bits 0 through 5 has some control function.

The beginning of the program includes `EQU` directives to equate symbolic names with the various port addresses. This makes the program somewhat easier to adapt to a system that uses the same type of printer ports, but at other addresses. It would also be possible to change this program to print on a standard PC's second parallel printer by changing `378h` to `278h`.

A printer usually has certain default settings for such things as character size and style. These settings are in effect when the printer is first turned on and can be changed by software commands. To illustrate use of the control port, this program starts with a sequence of code that initializes the printer to the default settings even if they have been changed. To do this, bit 2 of the control port must be reset to 0 for a short period. Bit 3 is always set to 1 to ensure that the printer is enabled.

```
mov     al, 00001000b      ; bit 2 zero to initialize printer
mov     dx, lpt1_control   ; control port
out     dx, al
```

Bit 2 must be left at zero for a minimum time period; a typical printer requires 0.2 to 1.0 microseconds. The minimum interval is guaranteed by including a "do nothing" loop executing `nop` (no operation) and `loop` instruction 50 times. A `nop` takes 3 clock cycles and a `loop` takes 17 (when CX is nonzero), so 50 iterations take a total of 1000 cycles. The comments include calculations that show that this requires more than 200 microseconds. This is ample. Note that a faster clock rate would cut this total time interval.

```
            mov     cx, 50              ; loop counter
init_wait:  nop                         ; do nothing 50 times
            loop    init_wait
```

After the delay, the initialization sequence is completed by setting bit 2 to 1. Notice that the control port address is already in the DX register.

```
mov     al, 00001100b      ; finish initialization pulse
out     dx, al
```

Before each character is transmitted to the printer, the program must check to be sure that the printer is not busy. It does this by accepting a byte from the printer status port and checking bit 7, the bit that indicates status. This process is repeated while this bit is zero.

```
                 mov     dx, lpt1_status      ; printer status port
while_busy: in   al, dx                       ; get status
                 and     al, 10000000b        ; mask all but busy bit
                 jz      while_busy           ; 0 means busy
```

As soon as the printer is not busy, the character to be printed is placed in the AL register half, the data port address is put in DX, and an out instruction transmits the byte.

```
mov    al, char           ; character to print
mov    dx, lpt1_data      ; printer data port address
out    dx, al             ; output character
```

It is not enough to simply send the character to the data port. Bit 0 of the control port must be **strobed**—set to 1 for a very brief period and then reset to 0. This signals the printer that data are to be **latched** from the data port—captured by the printer. The strobe bit must be 1 for at least 0.5 microseconds. It is left as an exercise to show that the following sequence provides a sufficient time interval.

```
mov    dx, lpt1_control   ; printer control port
mov    al, 00001101b      ; set strobe bit
out    dx, al             ; start strobe pulse
mov    al, 00001100b      ; clear strobe bit
out    dx, al             ; finish strobe pulse
```

The method of waiting for the printer in this program is sometimes called **polling** or **busy-waiting**. The loop that is executed while the printer is busy uses all of the CPU's resources—no useful work is done while waiting on the printer. There are alternative techniques. A parallel printer generates an **acknowledge** pulse that starts just before and terminates right after the busy condition ends. If bit 4 of the control port is set to 1, then the PC generates a hardware interrupt from this acknowledge pulse. If external interrupts are enabled, then this interrupt is processed (as described in the beginning of this chapter). With an appropriate interrupt handler, the CPU can do other work instead of just waiting on the printer.

The methods presented in this section for communicating with a printer at LPT1 are specific to IBM compatible computers. Some other computer systems use a parallel input/output (PIO) chip to make the programmer's job easier. A PIO chip uses more than three port addresses, one for data and the others for status and control information. The main benefit in using a PIO chip is that the chip takes care of pulsing the strobe bit; the programmer does not have to do this manually.

A PC can also communicate with peripherals via serial input/output ports. The difference between parallel and serial communications is that in parallel communications eight bits are transmitted at the same time through eight wires whereas in serial communications the bits of a byte plus additional **start** and **stop bits** are transmitted one at a time over a single wire. The PC uses a serial input/output (SIO) chip. The programmer transmits a byte by sending it to the data port of the SIO chip; the chip takes care of converting the byte to the appropriate series of bits. Polling or interrupts can be used to determine when the chip is able to accept a character for transmission. An incoming series of bits is assembled into a complete byte by the SIO chip; the program can read a status port to determine when the character is available, or can depend on an interrupt signal.

Exercises 10.4

1. For how long is the strobe bit set to 1 by the following sequence of instructions? Assume a 4.77 MHz PC, and count cycles for one **mov** and one **out** instruction.

```
mov     dx, lpt1_control    ; printer control port
mov     al, 00001101b       ; set strobe bit
out     dx, al              ; start strobe pulse
mov     al, 00001100b       ; clear strobe bit
out     dx, al              ; finish strobe pulse
```

Would that time interval still be sufficient (at least 0.5 microseconds) on an 8 MHz PC? On a 20 MHz PC?

2. Modify the program in Figure 10.8, adding code to check if the printer is out of paper before transmitting each character. If it is, display an appropriate warning message for the user, and continue printing only after the user answers "Y" or "y" to the question "Ready to go on?"

10.5

Chapter Summary

An 8088 computer system reserves the first 1024 bytes of memory for an interrupt vector table. This table stores 256 segment numbers and offsets for interrupt handlers, blocks of code similar to ordinary procedures. An interrupt handler can be called by an **int** instruction in a program, or by an interrupt generated by a hardware device. The handler for interrupt type 0 is also called when an error occurs during execution of a **div** or **idiv** instruction.

Interrupt type 21_{16} is used by DOS to access a variety of functions for input and output to peripheral devices and disk files. The function number is passed to DOS in the AH register half. Other registers are used to pass additional parameters to or from the interrupt handler.

At the lowest level input and output can be accomplished by `in` and `out` instructions that access I/O ports. Programs using these instructions may be less portable than programs that use DOS procedure calls.

CHAPTER 11

The Assembly Process

The job of an assembler is to turn assembly language source code into object code. With simpler computer systems this object code is machine language, ready to be loaded into memory and executed. With more complex systems, object code produced by the assembler must be "fixed up" by a linker and/or loader before it can be executed. The first section of this chapter describes the assembly process for a typical assembler; it gives some details particular to the Microsoft Macro Assembler. Section 11.2 is very specific to the 8088 and 8086 microprocessors—it details the structure of their machine language. The third section of the chapter discusses several directives for the Microsoft assembler; these directives appear in some form in most assembly languages.

Two-Pass Assembly

The Microsoft Macro Assembler is a two-pass assembler. This means that an assembly language source program is scanned twice by MASM in order to build the corresponding object code file. It is possible to design a one-pass assembler and some assemblers use three or more passes through the source code, but most assemblers use two passes. This section describes the operation of a typical two-pass assembler.

One advantage of writing in assembly language rather than in machine language is that assemblers allow the use of identifiers or symbols to reference data in the data segment and instructions in the code segment. To code in machine language a programmer must know addresses for data and instructions. One job of an assembler is to maintain a **symbol table** that associates each identifier with various attributes. One attribute is the **type** of the symbol; possible types include labels for data or instructions, symbols equated to constants, procedure names, macro names, and segment names. Some assemblers start assembling a source program with a symbol table that includes all the mnemonics for the language, all register names, and other symbols with reserved usage.

If a symbol is a label for data, then the symbol table may include the size of the data. For example, if MASM assembles the directive

```
result    DW    ?
```

then the symbol `result` is recorded as the label of a word. This enables MASM to detect incorrect usage of a symbol. Given the above DW directive, MASM would indicate an error for the instruction

```
mov    bh, result
```

since the BH register is byte size and the symbol table would identify `result` as word size. In addition to the size, if a symbol is associated with several objects, a symbol table may contain the number of objects or the total number of bytes associated with the symbol.

If a symbol is equated to a value, then the value is usually stored in the symbol table. When the assembler encounters the symbol in subsequent code, it substitutes the value recorded in the symbol table.

If a symbol is a label for data or an instruction, then its location is entered in the symbol table. An assembler keeps a **location counter** to compute this value. With a typical assembler, the location counter is set to zero at the beginning of a program, or at the beginning of each major subdivision of the program. The Microsoft Macro Assembler sets the location counter to zero at the beginning of each segment. As an assembler scans source code, the location of each datum or instruction is the value of the location counter *before* the statement is assembled. The number of bytes required by the statement is added to the location counter to give the location of the *next* statement.

As an example of how the location counter is used, suppose that an 8088 assembly language program contains the following data segment:

```
data    SEGMENT
x       DW    ?
y       DB    10 DUP (?)
z       DW    ?
data    ENDS
```

The location counter (expressed as four hex digits) starts at 0000, so the symbol table would get 0000 as the location for **x.** The **DW** directive is then assembled and one word of storage is reserved for **x.** The two bytes required for this word are added to the location counter, making its new value 0002. Therefore when the assembler reaches the symbol **y**, the value of the location counter is 0002, and this is the location recorded for **y**. There are ten bytes associated with **y** so after the **DB** directive is assembled, the location counter will be 000C. The location counter is 000C when the symbol **z** is encountered, so 000C is the location recorded for **z**. As a result of the **DW** directive, the location counter is advanced to 000E; some assemblers record this in the symbol table as the length of the segment named **data**.

The location counter is used the same way when instructions are assembled. Suppose that the location counter has value 012E when MASM reaches the following code fragment.

```
while:  cmp   cx, 100       ; cx <= 100 ?
        jnle  end_while      ; exit if not
        add   ax, [bx]       ; add value to sum
        add   bx, 2          ; address of next value
        inc   cx             ; add 1 to counter
        jmp   while
end_while:
```

The location for the symbol **while** will be 012E. The **cmp** instruction requires three bytes of object code. (Section 11.2 tells how to determine the object code corresponding to 8088 instructions.) Therefore the location counter will have value 0131 when MASM reaches the **jnle** instruction. The **jnle** instruction requires two bytes of object code, so the location counter will increase to 0133 for the first add instruction. The first **add** instruction takes two bytes of object code, so the location counter is 0135 when MASM reaches the second **add** instruction. Three bytes are required for **add bx, 2** so the location counter is 0138 for the **inc** instruction. The **inc** instruction takes a single byte, so the location counter is 0139 for the **jmp** instruction. The **jmp** instruction requires two bytes, making the location counter 013B when the assembler reaches the label **end_while**. Therefore 013B is recorded in the symbol table as the location of **end_while**.

The location of a symbol is needed for a variety of purposes. Suppose that MASM encounters the statement

```
mov    ax, value
```

where `value` is the label on a `DW` directive in the data section. Since the addressing mode for `value` is direct, the assembler needs the offset of `value` for the object code; this offset is precisely the location of `value` recorded in the symbol table.

There is a problem with the scheme described in the previous paragraph—it is possible that the symbol `value` is not in the symbol table when the assembler first reaches the `mov` instruction. (Although examples in this book have placed the data segment prior to the code segment, this is not required by MASM. Data can also be defined in the code segment, before or after executable statements.) What an assembler does in such a case is make a reasonable assumption, in this case that `value` will sooner or later be defined as a reference to a word in memory. The assembler cannot produce the final object code without knowing the location of `value` but it can determine how many bytes will be required for the `mov` instruction, adjust the location counter, and proceed with subsequent statements. On its *second* pass, the assembler either will have a location for `value` in the symbol table from the first pass, or it will know that there is an undefined symbol error.

If an assembler enforced a rule requiring data to be defined prior to executable statements, then the symbol table would contain entries for data labels during the first pass. It might appear that with such a rule, one-pass assembly would be easy. However, there is also a problem with forward references to executable statements. Consider again the code fragment

```
while:   cmp   cx, 100        ; cx <= 100 ?
         jnle  end_while       ; exit if not
         add   ax, [bx]        ; add value to sum
         add   bx, 2           ; address of next value
         inc   cx              ; add 1 to counter
         jmp   while
end_while:
```

When the assembler gets to the `jnle` instruction during the first pass, the symbol `end_while` is not yet in the symbol table. The final object code cannot be determined since it must contain the displacement to `end_while`. However, the assembler can still determine that the `jnle` instruction takes two bytes of object code, adjust the location counter, and continue assembling instructions. During the second pass, the symbol table will contain the location for `end_while` when the `jnle` is assembled. Notice that the statement `jmp while` can be completely assembled during the pass one, since `while` will be in the symbol table.

Different assemblers do different amounts of work during the first pass. Some just use the location counter to build the symbol table. Others build the symbol table and also generate almost-complete object code. The Microsoft Macro

Assembler is in the latter category.

The primary job of an assembler is to generate object code. However, a typical assembler does many other tasks. One duty is to reserve storage. A statement like

```
DW    20 DUP(?)
```

sets aside 20 words of storage. This storage reservation is typically done one of two ways:

- the assembler may write 40 bytes with some known value (like 00) to the object file, or
- the assembler may insert a command that ultimately causes the loader to skip 40 bytes when the program is loaded into memory

In the latter case, storage at run-time will contain whatever values are left over from execution of other programs.

In addition to reserving storage, assemblers can initialize the reserved memory with specified values. The MASM statement

```
DW    10, 20, 30
```

not only reserves three words of storage, it initializes the first to 000A, the second to 0014 and the third to 001E. Initial values may be expressed in a variety of ways using MASM and most other assemblers. Numbers may be given in different number systems, often binary, octal, decimal, and hexadecimal. The assembler converts character values to corresponding ASCII or EBCDIC character codes. Assemblers usually allow expressions as initial values. The Microsoft Macro Assembler is typical in accepting expressions that are put together with addition, subtraction, negation, multiplication, division, not, and, or, exclusive or, shift, and relational operators. Such an expression is evaluated *at assembly time,* producing the value that is actually used in the object code.

Most assemblers can produce a listing file that shows the original source code and some sort of representation of the corresponding object code. Another responsibility of an assembler is to produce error messages when there are errors in the source code. Rudimentary assemblers just display a line number and an error code for each error. Slightly less primitive assemblers produce a separate page with line numbers and error messages. Most assemblers can include an error message in the listing file at the point where the error occurs. The Microsoft Macro Assembler includes messages in the (optional) listing file and also displays them on the console.

In addition to the listing that shows source and object code, an assembler often can generate a listing of symbols used in the program. Such a listing may include information about each symbol's attributes (taken from the assembler's symbol table) as well as **cross-references** that indicate both the line where the symbol is defined and each line where it is referenced.

Some assemblers begin assembling instructions with the location counter set to a particular actual memory address and thus generate object code ready to be loaded at that address. This is the only way to generate object code with some simpler systems. Generally such code is not linked; it is ready to load and run.

One file can reference objects in another. Recall that the **EXTRN** directive facilitates this for MASM. A linker combines separate object code files into a single file. If one file references objects in the other, the linker changes the references from "to be determined" to locations in the combined file.

Most assemblers produce **relocatable** object code, that is, code that can be loaded at any address. One way to do this is to put a **map** in the object code file that records each place in the program where an address must be modified. Address modifications are usually carried out by the loader. The loader finally produces true machine language, ready for execution.

Another way to get relocatable code is to write it with only relative references, that is, so that each instruction only references objects at some distance from itself, not at a fixed address. In an 8088 system, most jump instructions are relative, so if a programmer stores data in registers or on the stack, it is fairly easy to produce such a program.

In summary, the Microsoft Macro Assembler is a fairly typical two-pass assembler. It produces object code files that may contain references to symbols defined in other files, and that may contain symbols to be relocated. The MS-DOS utility LINK combines separate object code files, resolving the external references. The MS-DOS loader, which is automatically invoked by giving the name of an executable program file, does the final translation of the file as it loads it in memory just prior to initiating execution.

Exercises 11.1

1. Describe the differences between object code and machine language.

2. Use MASM to assemble a program. Select the option that produces a listing (.LST) file. Examine the symbol listing at the end of the listing file. What information is included that has come from the assembler's symbol table?

3. Use MASM to assemble a program. Select the option that produces a cross reference (.CRF) file. Use the CREF program, which comes with the Microsoft Macro Assembler, to convert the .CRF file to a printable (.REF) file. How could the assembler generate the information in the cross-reference?

─────11.2─────

8088 Instruction Coding

This section describes the structure of 8088 machine language. From this information one could almost assemble an 8088 assembly language program by hand. However, the primary purpose here is to impart a better understanding of the capabilities and limitations of the 8088 microprocessor.

Figure 11.1 lists all the 8088 instructions in order of their opcodes. The machine code for each instruction begins with its opcode, of course. For those instructions that consist of just the opcode, (none) is indicated in the "additional bytes" column of the table. The machine code for most instructions consists of several bytes; for such instructions the "additional bytes" column shows how the additional byte or bytes of machine code are structured.

Figure 11.1   8088 Instructions.

Opcode	Instruction and Operands	Additional Bytes
00	add *mem8,reg8*	mod reg r/m, (address)
01	add *mem16,reg16*	mod reg r/m, (address)
02	add *reg8,mem8*	mod reg r/m, (address)
	add *reg8,reg8*	11 dest_reg source_reg
03	add *reg16,mem16*	mod reg r/m, (address)
	add *reg16,reg16*	11 dest_reg source_reg
04	add al,*imm8*	immediate byte
05	add ax,*imm16*	immediate word
06	push es	(none)
07	pop es	(none)
08	or *mem8,reg8*	mod reg r/m, (address)
09	or *mem16,reg16*	mod reg r/m, (address)
0A	or *reg8,mem8*	mod reg r/m, (address)
	or *reg8,reg8*	11 dest_reg source_reg
0B	or *reg16,mem16*	mod reg r/m, (address)
	or *reg16,reg16*	11 dest_reg source_reg
0C	or al, *imm8*	immediate byte
0D	or ax, *imm16*	immediate word
0E	push cs	(none)
0F	(not used with 8088)	
10	adc *mem8,reg8*	mod reg r/m, (address)
11	adc *mem16,reg16*	mod reg r/m, (address)
12	adc *reg8,mem8*	mod reg r/m, (address)
	adc *reg8,reg8*	11 dest_reg source_reg
13	adc *reg16,mem16*	mod reg r/m, (address)

Figure 11.1 Continued.

Opcode	Instruction and Operands	Additional Bytes
	adc *reg16,reg16*	11 dest_reg source_reg
14	adc al, *imm8*	immediate byte
15	adc ax, *imm16*	immediate word
16	push ss	(none)
17	pop ss	(none)
18	sbb *mem8,reg8*	mod reg r/m, (address)
19	sbb *mem16,reg16*	mod reg r/m, (address)
1A	sbb *reg8,mem8*	mod reg r/m, (address)
	sbb *reg8,reg8*	11 dest_reg source_reg
1B	sbb *reg16,mem16*	mod reg r/m, (address)
	sbb *reg16,reg16*	11 dest_reg source_reg
1C	sbb al,*imm8*	immediate byte
1D	sbb ax,*imm16*	immediate word
1E	push ds	(none)
1F	pop ds	(none)
20	and *mem8,reg8*	mod reg r/m, (address)
21	and *mem16,reg16*	mod reg r/m, (address)
22	and *reg8,mem8*	mod reg r/m, (address)
	and *reg8,reg8*	11 dest_reg source_reg
23	and *reg16,mem16*	mod reg r/m, (address)
	and *reg16,reg16*	11 dest_reg source_reg
24	and al,*imm8*	immediate byte
25	and ax,*imm16*	immediate word
26	ES segment override prefix byte	
27	daa	(none)
28	sub *mem8,reg8*	mod reg r/m, (address)
29	sub *mem16,reg16*	mod reg r/m, (address)
2A	sub *reg8,mem8*	mod reg r/m, (address)
	sub *reg8,reg8*	11 dest_reg source_reg
2B	sub *reg16,mem16*	mod reg r/m, (address)
	sub *reg16,reg16*	11 dest_reg source_reg
2C	sub al,*imm8*	immediate byte
2D	sub ax,*imm16*	immediate word
2E	CS segment override prefix byte	
2F	das	(none)
30	xor *mem8,reg8*	mod reg r/m, (address)
31	xor *mem16,reg16*	mod reg r/m, (address)
32	xor *reg8,mem8*	mod reg r/m, (address)
	xor *reg8,reg8*	11 dest_reg source_reg
33	xor *reg16,mem16*	mod reg r/m, (address)

Figure 11.1 Continued.

Opcode	Instruction and Operands	Additional Bytes
	xor *reg16,reg16*	11 dest_reg source_reg
34	xor al,*imm8*	immediate byte
35	xor ax,*imm16*	immediate word
36	SS segment override prefix byte	
37	aaa	(none)
38	cmp *mem8,reg8*	mod reg r/m, (address)
39	cmp *mem16,reg16*	mod reg r/m, (address)
3A	cmp *reg8,mem8*	mod reg r/m, (address)
	cmp *reg8,reg8*	11 dest_reg source_reg
3B	cmp *reg16,mem16*	mod reg r/m, (address)
	cmp *reg16,reg16*	11 dest_reg source_reg
3C	cmp al,*imm8*	immediate byte
3D	cmp ax,*imm16*	immediate word
3E	DS segment override prefix byte	
3F	aas	(none)
40	inc ax	(none)
41	inc cx	(none)
42	inc dx	(none)
43	inc bx	(none)
44	inc sp	(none)
45	inc bp	(none)
46	inc si	(none)
47	inc di	(none)
48	dec ax	(none)
49	dec cx	(none)
4A	dec dx	(none)
4B	dec bx	(none)
4C	dec sp	(none)
4D	dec bp	(none)
4E	dec si	(none)
4F	dec di	(none)
50	push ax	(none)
51	push cx	(none)
52	push dx	(none)
53	push bx	(none)
54	push sp	(none)
55	push bp	(none)
56	push si	(none)
57	push di	(none)
58	pop ax	(none)

Figure 11.1 Continued.

Opcode	Instruction and Operands	Additional Bytes
59	pop cx	(none)
5A	pop dx	(none)
5B	pop bx	(none)
5C	pop sp	(none)
5D	pop bp	(none)
5E	pop si	(none)
5F	pop di	(none)
60-6F	(not used with 8088)	
70	jo	displacement byte
71	jno	displacement byte
72	jb/jnae/jc	displacement byte
73	jnb/jae/jnc	displacement byte
74	je/jz	displacement byte
75	jne/jnz	displacement byte
76	jbe/jna	displacement byte
77	jnbe/ja	displacement byte
78	js	displacement byte
79	jns	displacement byte
7A	jp/jpe	displacement byte
7B	jnp/jpo	displacement byte
7C	jl/jnge	displacement byte
7D	jnl/jge	displacement byte
7E	jle/jng	displacement byte
7F	jnle/jg	displacement byte
80	add *mem8,imm8*	mod 000 r/m,(address),immediate byte
	add *reg8,imm8*	11 000 reg, immediate byte
	or *mem8,imm8*	mod 001 r/m,(address),immediate byte
	or *reg8,imm8*	11 001 reg, immediate byte
	adc *mem8,imm8*	mod 010 r/m,(address),immediate byte
	adc *reg8,imm8*	11 010 reg, immediate byte
	sbb *mem8,imm8*	mod 011 r/m,(address),immediate byte
	sbb *reg8,imm8*	11 011 reg, immediate byte
	and *mem8,imm8*	mod 100 r/m,(address),immediate byte
	and *reg8,imm8*	11 100 reg, immediate byte
	sub *mem8,imm8*	mod 101 r/m,(address),immediate byte
	sub *reg8,imm8*	11 101 reg, immediate byte
	xor *mem8,imm8*	mod 110 r/m,(address),immediate byte
	xor *reg8,*imm8	11 110 reg, immediate byte
	cmp *mem8,imm8*	mod 111 r/m,(address),immediate byte
	cmp *reg8,imm8*	11 111 reg, immediate byte

Figure 11.1 Continued.

Opcode	Instruction and Operands	Additional Bytes
81	add *mem16,imm16*	mod 000 r/m,(address),immediate word
	add *reg16,imm16*	11 000 reg, immediate word
	or *mem16,imm16*	mod 001 r/m,(address),immediate word
	or *reg16,imm16*	11 001 reg, immediate word
	adc *mem16,imm16*	mod 010 r/m,(address),immediate word
	adc *reg16,imm16*	11 010 reg, immediate word
	sbb *mem16,imm16*	mod 011 r/m,(address),immediate word
	sbb *reg16,imm16*	11 011 reg, immediate word
	and *mem16,imm16*	mod 100 r/m,(address),immediate word
	and *reg16,imm16*	11 100 reg, immediate word
	sub *mem16,imm16*	mod 101 r/m,(address),immediate word
	sub *reg16,imm16*	11 101 reg, immediate word
	xor *mem16,imm16*	mod 110 r/m,(address),immediate word
	xor *reg16,imm16*	11 110 reg, immediate word
	cmp *mem16,imm16*	mod 111 r/m,(address),immediate word
	cmp *reg16,imm16*	11 111 reg, immediate word
82	(not used with 8088)	
83	add *mem16,imm8*	mod 000 r/m,(address),immediate byte
	add *reg16,imm8*	11 000 reg, immediate byte
	or *mem16,imm8*	mod 001 r/m,(address),immediate byte
	or *reg16,imm8*	11 001 reg, immediate byte
	adc *mem16,imm8*	mod 010 r/m,(address),immediate byte
	adc *reg16,imm8*	11 010 reg, immediate byte
	sbb *mem16,imm8*	mod 011 r/m,(address),immediate byte
	sbb *reg16,imm8*	11 011 reg, immediate byte
	and *mem16,imm8*	mod 100 r/m,(address),immediate byte
	and *reg16,imm8*	11 100 reg, immediate byte
	sub *mem16,imm8*	mod 101 r/m,(address),immediate byte
	sub *reg16,imm8*	11 101 reg, immediate byte
	xor *mem16,imm8*	mod 110 r/m,(address),immediate byte
	xor *reg16,imm8*	11 110 reg, immediate byte
	cmp *mem16,imm8*	mod 111 r/m,(address),immediate byte
	cmp *reg16,imm8*	11 111 reg, immediate byte
84	test *reg8,mem8*	mod reg r/m, (address)
	test *reg8,reg8*	11 dest_reg source_reg
85	test *reg16,mem16*	mod reg r/m, (address)
	test *reg16,reg16*	11 dest_reg source_reg
86	xchg *reg8,mem8*	mod reg r/m, (address)
	xchg *reg8,reg8*	11 dest_reg source_reg
87	xchg *reg16,mem16*	mod reg r/m, (address)

Figure 11.1 Continued.

Opcode	Instruction and Operands	Additional Bytes
	xchg *reg16,reg16*	11 dest_reg source_reg
88	mov *mem8,reg8*	mod reg r/m, (address)
	mov *reg8,reg8*	11 dest_reg source_reg
89	mov *mem16,reg16*	mod reg r/m, (address)
	mov *reg16,reg16*	11 dest_reg source_reg
8A	mov *reg8,mem8*	mod reg r/m, (address)
8B	mov *reg16,mem16*	11 dest_reg source_reg, (address)
8C	mov *mem16,sreg*	mod reg r/m, (address)
	mov *reg16,sreg*	11 reg r/m
8D	lea *reg16,mem*	mod reg r/m, (address)
8E	mov *sreg,mem16*	mod reg r/m, (address)
	mov *sreg,reg16*	11 reg r/m
8F	pop *mem16*	mod 000 r/m, (address)
90	nop	(none)
91	xchg ax,cx	(none)
92	xchg ax,dx	(none)
93	xchg ax,bx	(none)
94	xchg ax,sp	(none)
95	xchg ax,bp	(none)
96	xchg ax,si	(none)
97	xchg ax,di	(none)
98	cbw	(none)
99	cwd	(none)
9A	call (far direct)	offset and segment number words
9B	wait	(none)
9C	pushf	(none)
9D	popf	(none)
9E	sahf	(none)
9F	lahf	(none)
A0	mov al, *mem8*	offset word (direct addressing)
A1	mov ax, *mem16*	offset word
A2	mov *mem8*,al	offset word
A3	mov *mem16*,ax	offset word
A4	movsb	(none)
A5	movsw	(none)
A6	cmpsb	(none)
A7	cmpsw	(none)
A8	test al,*imm8*	immediate byte
A9	test ax,*imm16*	immediate word

Figure 11.1 Continued.

Opcode	Instruction and Operands	Additional Bytes
AA	stosb	(none)
AB	stosw	(none)
AC	lodsb	(none)
AD	lodsw	(none)
AE	scasb	(none)
AF	scasw	(none)
B0	mov al,*imm8*	immediate byte
B1	mov cl,*imm8*	immediate byte
B2	mov dl,*imm8*	immediate byte
B3	mov bl,*imm8*	immediate byte
B4	mov ah,*imm8*	immediate byte
B5	mov ch,*imm8*	immediate byte
B6	mov dh,*imm8*	immediate byte
B7	mov bh,*imm8*	immediate byte
B8	mov ax,*imm16*	immediate word
B9	mov cx,*imm16*	immediate word
BA	mov dx,*imm16*	immediate word
BB	mov bx,*imm16*	immediate word
BC	mov sp,*imm16*	immediate word
BD	mov bp,*imm16*	immediate word
BE	mov si,*imm16*	immediate word
BF	mov di,*imm16*	immediate word
C0,C1	(not used with 8088)	
C2	ret *imm16* (near return)	immediate word
C3	ret (near return)	(none)
C4	les *reg16*,mem	mod reg r/m, (address)
C5	lds *reg16*,mem	mod reg r/m, (address)
C6	mov *mem8*,*imm8*	mod 000 r/m,(address),immediate byte
	mov *reg8*,*imm8*	11 000 r/m, immediate byte
C7	mov *mem16*,*imm16*	mod 000 r/m,(address),immediate word
	mov *reg1*,*imm16*	11 000 r/m, immediate word
C8,C9	(not used with 8088)	
CA	ret *imm16* (far return)	immediate word
CB	ret (far return)	(none)
CC	int 3	(none)
CD	int *imm8*	immediate byte

Figure 11.1 Continued.

Opcode	Instruction and Operands	Additional Bytes
CE	`into`	(none)
CF	`iret`	(none)
DO	`rol mem8,1`	mod 000 r/m, (address)
	`rol reg8,1`	11 000 reg
	`ror mem8,1`	mod 001 r/m, (address)
	`ror reg8,1`	11 001 reg
	`rcl mem8,1`	mod 010 r/m, (address)
	`rcl reg8,1`	11 010 reg
	`rcr mem8,1`	mod 011 r/m, (address)
	`rcr reg8,1`	11 011 reg
	`shl/sal mem8,1`	mod 100 r/m, (address)
	`shl/sal reg8,1`	11 100 reg
	`shr mem8,1`	mod 101 r/m, (address)
	`shr reg8,1`	11 101 reg
	`sar mem8,1`	mod 111 r/m, (address)
	`sar reg8,1`	11 111 reg
		(110 not used with 8088)
Dl	`rol mem16,1`	mod 000 r/m, (address)
	`rol reg16,1`	11 000 reg
	`ror mem16,1`	mod 001 r/m, (address)
	`ror reg16,1`	11 001 reg
	`rcl mem16,1`	mod 010 r/m, (address)
	`rcl reg16,1`	11 010 reg
	`rcr mem16,1`	mod 011 r/m, (address)
	`rcr reg16,1`	11 011 reg
	`shl/sal mem16,1`	mod 100 r/m, (address)
	`shl/sal reg16,1`	11 100 reg
	`shr mem16,1`	mod 101 r/m, (address)
	`shr reg16,1`	11 101 reg
	`sar mem16,1`	mod 111 r/m, (address)
	`sar reg16,1`	11 111 reg
		(110 not used with 8088)
D2	`rol mem8,cl`	mod 000 r/m, (address)
	`rol reg8,cl`	11000 reg
	`ror mem6,cl`	mod 001 r/m, (address)
	`ror reg8,cl`	11 001 reg
	`rcl mem8,cl`	mod 010 r/m, (address)
	`rcl reg8,cl`	11 010 reg
	`rcr mem8,cl`	mod 011 r/m, (address)
	`rcr reg8,cl`	11 011 reg

Figure 11.1 Continued.

Opcode	Instruction and Operands	Additional Bytes
	shl/sal *mem8*,cl	mod 100 r/m, (address)
	shl/sal *reg8*,cl	11 100 reg
	shr *mem8*,cl	mod 101 r/m, (address)
	shr *reg8*,cl	11 101 reg
	sar *mem8*,cl	mod 111 r/m, (address)
	sar *reg8*,cl	11 111 reg
		(110 not used with 8088)
D3	rol *mem16*,cl	mod 000 r/m, (address)
	rol *reg16*,cl	11 000 reg
	ror *mem16*,cl	mod 001 r/m, (address)
	ror *reg16*,cl	11 001 reg
	rcl *mem16*,cl	mod 010 r/m, (address)
	rcl *reg16*,cl	11 010 reg
	rcr *mem16*,cl	mod 011 r/m, (address)
	rcr *reg16*,cl	11 011 reg
	shl/sal *mem16*,cl	mod 100 r/m, (address)
	shl/sal *reg16*,cl	11 100 reg
	shr *mem16*,cl	mod 101 r/m, (address)
	shr *reg16*,cl	11 101 reg
	sar *mem16*,cl	mod 111 r/m, (address)
	sar *reg16*,cl	11 111 reg
		(110 not used with 8088)
D4	aam	0A
D5	aad	0A
D6	(not used with 8088)	
D7	xlat	(none)
D8	esc 0	mod 000 r/m, (address)
D9	esc 1	mod 001 r/m, (address)
DA	esc 2	mod 010 r/m, (address)
DB	esc 3	mod 011 r/m, (address)
DC	esc 4	mod 100 r/m, (address)
DD	esc 5	mod 101 r/m, (address)
DE	esc 6	mod 110 r/m, (address)
DF	esc 7	mod 111 r/m, (address)
E0	loopnz/loopne	displacement byte
E1	loopz/loope	displacement byte
E2	loop	displacement byte
E3	jcxz	displacement byte
E4	in al,*port*	port byte
E5	in al,*port*	port byte

Figure 11.1 Continued.

Opcode	Instruction and Operands	Additional Bytes
E6	**out al,** *port*	port byte
E7	**out ax,** *port*	port byte
E8	**call** (near relative)	displacement word
E9	**jmp** (intra-segment relative)	displacement word
EA	**jmp** (inter-segment direct)	offset and segment number words
EB	**jmp** (intra-segment relative short)	displacement byte
EC	**in al,dx**	(none)
ED	**in ax,dx**	(none)
EE	**out al,dx**	(none)
EF	**out ax,dx**	(none)
F0	**lock** prefix byte	
F1	(not used with 8088)	
F2	**repne/repnz** prefix byte	
F3	**rep/repe/repz** prefix byte	
F4	**hlt**	(none)
F5	**cmc**	(none)
F6	**test** *mem8, imm8*	mod 000 r/m,(address),immediate byte
	test *reg8, imm8*	11 000 reg, immediate byte
	not *mem8*	mod 010 r/m, (address)
	not *reg8*	11 010 reg
	neg *mem8*	mod 011 r/m, (address)
	neg *reg8*	11 011 reg
	mul *mem8*	mod 100 r/m, (address)
	mul *reg8*	11 100 reg
	imul *mem8*	mod 101 r/m, (address)
	imul *reg8*	11 101 reg
	div *mem8*	mod 110 r/m, (address)
	div *reg8*	11 110 reg
	idiv *mem8*	mod 111 r/m, (address)
	idiv *reg8*	11 111 reg
F7	**test** *mem16, imm16*	mod 000 r/m,(address),immediate word
	test *reg16, imm16*	11 000 reg, immediate word
	not *mem16*	mod 010 r/m, (address)
	not *reg16*	11 010 reg
	neg *mem16*	mod 011 r/m, (address)
	neg *reg16*	11 011 reg

Figure 11.1 Continued.

Opcode	Instruction and Operands	Additional Bytes
	mul *mem16*	mod 100 r/m, (address)
	mul *reg16*	11 100 reg
	imul *mem16*	mod 101 r/m, (address)
	imul *reg16*	11 101 reg
	div *mem16*	mod 110 r/m, (address)
	div *reg16*	11 110 reg
	idiv *mem16*	mod 111 r/m, (address)
	idiv *reg16*	11 111 reg
F8	clc	(none)
F9	stc	(none)
FA	cli	(none)
FB	sti	(none)
FC	cld	(none)
FD	std	(none)
FE	inc *mem8*	mod 000 r/m, (address)
	inc *reg8*	11 000 reg
	dec *mem8*	mod 001 r/m, (address)
	dec *reg8*	11 001 reg
FF	inc *mem16*	mod 000 r/m, (address)
	dec *mem16*	mod 001 r/m, (address)
	call (far indirect)	mod 010 r/m, (address)
	call (near indirect)	mod 011 r/m, (address)
	jmp (intra-segment indirect)	mod 100 r/m, (address)
	jmp (inter-segment indirect)	mod 101 r/m, (address)
	push *mem16*	mod 110 r/m, (address)

For most instructions that have a register destination, the second byte is shown in Figure 11.1 (and other references on the Intel 8088) as "mod reg r/m." This byte has three fields, a 2-bit-long "mod" field, a 3-bit-long "reg" field, and a 3-bit-long "r/m" field.

The "reg" field contains a code for the destination register. The same codes are used any time information about a register is encoded in an instruction. Figure 11.2 shows how the eight possible register codes are assigned. Notice that the same code is used for, say, CX and CL. Distinct opcodes are always used for 8-bit and 16-bit operations, so 001 means CL for an 8-bit operation and CX for a 16-bit operation.

Figure 11.2 8088 Instruction Register Codes.

Code	Register 16	Register 8	Segment Register
000	AX	AL	ES
001	CX	CL	CS
010	DX	DL	SS
011	BX	BL	DS
100	SP	AH	
101	BP	CH	
110	SI	DH	
111	DI	BH	

Still considering instructions with a destination register, the "mod" and "r/m" fields work together to code the address mode of the source operand. A "mod" value of 11 means that the source for the operation is also a register. In this case, Figure 11.1 shows the "mod" field as 11, the "reg" field as "dest_reg" and the "r/m" field as "source_reg." The register codes shown in Figure 11.2 are used for both the source and destination register fields.

If mod = 00 and r/m = 110, then the source operand's addressing mode is memory direct. In this case the machine code contains two additional bytes for the offset of the operand.

All other combinations of "mod" and "r/m" correspond to some indirect memory addressing mode. These "mod" and "r/m" encodings for different addressing modes are shown in Figure 11.3. The register indirect modes are coded with mod=00 and "r/m" set to 100, 101 or 111. Indexed and based modes are shown to the right of the register indirect modes, with "r/m" codes of 100 and 101 for the indexed modes and 110 and 111 for the based modes. The first four rows of the table show the based and indexed modes.

Figure 11.3 8088 Effective Address Encoding.

r/m	mod = 00	mod = 01 or mod = 10
000	[BX + SI]	[BX + SI + displacement]
001	[BX + DI]	[BX + DI + displacement]
010	[BP + SI]	[BP + SI + displacement]
011	[BP + DI]	[BP + DI + displacement]
100	[SI]	[SI + displacement]
101	[DI]	[DI + displacement]
110	(direct mode)	[BP + displacement]
111	[BX]	[BX + displacement]

The "mod" field in these formats tells how many bytes there are in the displacement. A value of 00 means that there is no displacement byte in the machine code; that is, the addressing mode is register indirect or based and indexed without the optional displacement. A "mod" value of 10 means that there are two displacement bytes in the machine code; this word is added to the value that comes from the base register and/or index register. A value of 01 means that there is one displacement byte in the machine code; this byte is treated as a signed number and is extended to a word before it is added to the value from the base register and/or index register.

Notice that the operand [BP] does not appear in Figure 11.3—the logical combination of mod = 00 and r/m = 110 is the special pair that indicates memory direct mode. This means that there is really no register indirect addressing using the BP register. The assembler translates [BP] into [BP+0] and uses mod = 01, actually coding the zero byte.

The word address appears in parentheses in Figure 11.1 because not all memory operands require extra bytes of object code. If mod = 00 and r/m = 110 (direct addressing) there are two additional bytes, representing the offset of the operand. However, in other cases where mod=00, no additional bytes are used for address information. If mod = 01 or mod = 10, there are one or two bytes of additional object code present, displacements for indirect memory addressing modes that require them.

The preceding paragraphs started with the assumption that only instructions with a register destination were being discussed. However, most of the information is applicable to other instructions. For example, most instructions that have a memory destination and register source also use the "mod reg r/m" second byte. In such instructions, the "reg" field gives the source register, "mod" is never 11, and the usual combinations of "mod" and "r/m" indicate addressing mode of the memory operand.

There are some patterns to be found in the opcode bytes of the instructions. The 8088 instruction set has many instructions that have 8-bit and 16-bit versions. The opcodes for these instructions differ only in the last bit, with 0 used for the 8-bit operation, and 1 used for the 16-bit operation. For example, the comparison instructions with a register destination use opcode 3A($0011\ 1010_2$) for 8-bit comparisons and opcode 3B ($0011\ 1011_2$) for 16-bit comparisons.

Another set of patterns occurs in some single-byte instructions where the same instruction is available for each of the registers—the opcode ends in the appropriate register code. For instance, the inc instructions for *reg16*-operands have opcodes 40 through 47, and the last three bits are 000 through 111, the register codes for the registers to be incremented. Another way of looking at this is that the opcodes for this class of inc instructions are obtained by adding 40 and the register code.

Instructions with immediate operands must embed the immediate data in the machine code. Immediate data is always in the last one or bytes of the object code. Eight-bit operations with an immediate operand always have a single byte of immediate data. Sixteen-bit operations with an immediate operation often allow either a byte or a word of immediate data. If a byte is used, it is treated as a signed value and is extended to a word before the operation takes place. Many such instructions use the next-to-last bit of the object code byte to distinguish between a byte or a word of immediate data; 0 is used for a word and 1 is used for a byte.

The previous discussion describes several instances of 8088 instructions where a single opcode serves for several different versions of the same operation. In each such instance, the differences have been in the addressing mode of an operand—the basic operation was the same. In addition, the 8088 has 11 opcodes (80, 81, 83, D0, D1, D2, D3, F6, F7, FE, and FF), each of which is used for several distinct operations. When it is only necessary to encode information about one operand, the middle three bits of the second byte (used by the "reg" field in the "mod reg r/m" pattern) can be used to distinguish operations.

For example, for the opcode 80, the middle three bits of the second byte have the following meanings: **add**, 000; **or**, 001; **adc**, 010; **sbb**, 011; **and**, 100; **sub**, 101; **xor**, 110; and **cmp**, 111. The second operand of each instruction with opcode 80 is an immediate byte, so the "mod" and "r/m" fields in the second byte of machine code encode the first register or memory operand, using the same system as described before.

The 8088 instruction set includes a few instructions that duplicate the operations provided by other instructions, but are specific to the accumulator (AX or AL). For example, either opcode 05 or opcode 81 encodes **add ax, *imm16***. However, opcode 05 is specific to the AX register and the machine code requires only the immediate word in addition to the opcode. Opcode 81 requires a second byte to distinguish the **add** operation from the other possible operations, and to specify the register. Consequently the instruction with opcode 81 requires one more byte of object code than the instruction with opcode 05. For this pair of instructions, execution requires the same number of clock cycles. In some similar situations (such as opcodes A1 and 8B), the accumulator version of the instruction is faster as well as more compact. The accumulator version is chosen by MASM.

Recall that many 8088 instructions require only the opcode byte. Single bytes are also used to encode prefix operators that become part of the following instruction. For instance, a machine code byte containing 26 tells the 8088 to use the extra segment register ES in the following instruction rather than the default segment register (DS for most addressing modes). Similarly, an F3 byte says to apply the **rep** prefix to the primitive string operation encoded in the next byte, effectively producing a new instruction.

Machine code for the 8088 contains some peculiar patterns. For example, the **aad** and **aam** instructions have opcodes D4 and D5, respectively. No other instruction uses these opcodes and neither of them requires an operand to be encoded. However, both of these instructions have a second byte, always 0A. In general, 8088 instruction encodings are somewhat irregular compared to many other processors.

This section concludes with two examples of hand assembly. First consider the instruction **add cx,ax**. The alphabetical listing in Appendix A shows that any instruction with format **add *reg16,reg16*** has opcode 03 and a second byte with bits 11, followed by the destination register code, followed by the source register code. Figure 11.2 shows these codes to be 001 for CX and 000 for AX, so the second byte of the instruction is 11 001 000. Regrouping these bits gives C8 in hex. The machine code for the instruction is 03 C8.

Now consider the instruction **sub bx, [bx+si+10]**. The alphabetical listing shows that source format **sub *reg16,mem16*** has opcode 2B and additional parts "mod reg r/m, (address)." The "reg" field is easy; 011 encodes destination register BX. The memory operand has addressing mode based and indexed, with byte displacement. According to Figure 11.3, r/m = 000 for based and indexed, using a displacement. Recall that mod = 01 for byte displacement. Therefore the second byte of the instruction is 01 011 000, or 58 in hex. The (address) part of the instruction is simply the displacement 10, or $0A_{16}$. Therefore the machine code for this instruction is 2B 58 0A.

Exercises 11.2

1. Why can no 8088 assembly language instruction specify two memory operands?

2. Machine language for the Intel 80186, 80286, and 80386 processors is a superset of machine language for the Intel 8088 and 8086 processors; that is, each of the opcodes and machine code formats shown in Figure 11.1 is also correct for these more powerful processors. Most of the opcodes marked as "not used with 8088" in Figure 11.1 are assigned to 80186, 80286, and 80386 instructions. Using a source such as a library, find a reference for one or more of these processors and look up the instructions for which the unassigned opcodes are used. What additional capabilities do these new instructions provide?

3. Find the machine code for each of the following instructions. Make the assumption that

   ```
   value DW ?
   ```

   is at offset $1A9D_{16}$ in the data segment. Use Appendix A, Figure 11.1, Figure 11.2 and Figure 11.3 as needed.

   (a) `add    value, cx`
   (b) `add    dx, bx`
   (c) `push   ds`
   (d) `cmp    cx, value`

```
(e)   inc    cx
(f)   pop    ax
(g)   push   value
(h)   or     al, 35
(i)   sub    value, 2      (byte-size immediate operand)
(j)   and    bx, 0ff00h    (word-size immediate operand)
(k)   xchg   bx, cx
(l)   xchg   ax, cx        (note accumulator operand)
(m)   cwd
(n)   shl    dx, 1
(o)   neg    WORD PTR [bx]
(p)   imul   ch
(q)   div    value
(r)   dec    WORD PTR [bx+si]
```

11.3

Assorted Directives

Every directive commands an assembler to perform some action. Many MASM directives have been discussed in this book, and more will be introduced in subsequent chapters. This section reexamines the **ASSUME** directive, which is used in almost every program written for the Microsoft assembler. It also introduces the **ORG**, **EVEN**, and **ALIGN** directives, which affect the location counter. Finally, it discusses the two directives, **TITLE** and **SUBTTL**, which impact only the assembly listing.

Recall that the **address space** for the 8088 microprocessor, the range of legal addresses is 00000_{16} to $FFFFF_{16}$. Another way to say this is that each hardware address consists of five hex digits or 20 bits. However, each register in the 8088 is 16 bits long, so no register can hold a complete address. Section 2.1 described the way that each address has two 16-bit parts, a segment number and an offset, and how these are combined to produce a 20-bit address as the program executes.

The four segment registers, CS, DS, ES, and SS, are used to hold segment numbers. Offsets are stored in instructions or registers. For example, in an instruction where the operand has direct memory addressing mode, the operand's offset is embedded in the machine code. The offset of an operand that uses register indirect addressing will be in a register. The instruction pointer register IP always contains the offset of an instruction in the code segment. Some `call` and `jmp` instructions are assembled so that the machine code contains the offsets of other instructions.

The first section of this chapter described how an assembler uses the location counter to calculate offsets for data or instructions. A program written for the Microsoft Macro Assembler may contain multiple code segments or multiple data segments. MASM must be told which is *the* code segment (with segment number in CS) and which is *the* data segment (with segment number in DS) at any point of the assembly. This is the purpose of the **ASSUME** directive.

MASM's **ASSUME** directive has the format

```
ASSUME    segment_register:segment_name, ...
```

where ***segment_register*** can be any of CS, DS, ES, or SS and ***segment_name*** is the label on a segment directive.* If MASM encounters a symbol which is not located in a segment whose name is identified in an ASSUME directive, then the assembler generates an error message. Otherwise, MASM assumes that at runtime the segment number corresponding to the beginning of a segment will be in the segment register specified in the **ASSUME** directive, and it uses the offset of the symbol in the segment.

It is important to notice that when the assembler assumes the correct segment number will be in a segment register at runtime, it may be wrong. The **ASSUME** directive provides information for assembly; it is still necessary to get the correct values in segment registers at execution time. Recall that with DOS, part of this job is done by the operating system and part is the responsibility of the programmer. In particular, CS is initialized by DOS, using the segment number of the segment containing the symbol identified in the **END** directive. DOS also initializes SS, using the segment identified with the **SEGMENT STACK** directive. However, it is the job of the programmer to initialize DS and ES in order to fulfil the "promises" made by the **ASSUME** directive. As many examples have shown, a typical initialization sequence for DS is

```
mov    ax, SEG data
mov    ds, ax
```

One assembly language source code file may contain several **ASSUME** directives. This might be particularly appropriate with a long program that contained many procedures. As it scans a program, the assembler uses the most recent information for a given segment register. Sometimes it is desirable to tell MASM to ignore a previous assumption about a segment register even though no new assumption will take its place. In this case the syntax

```
segment_register: NOTHING
```

can be used in an ASSUME directive.

As has been illustrated, data can be defined in the data segment or the code segment—there is no actual difference between the two kinds of segments. Additionally, data could be defined in the extra segment or even in the stack segment. If a program has an **ASSUME** directive that identifies, say, the data segment,

---

* The Microsoft Macro Assembler also has a GROUP directive, which clusters several segments. A group name can be used instead of a segment name in the ASSUME directive.

code segment, and extra segment, then the programmer can use symbols that reference data in any of the three and MASM encodes the offset of each symbol in its own segment. Recall that the 8088 microprocessor normally combines the segment number in DS with an offset to get the 20-bit address of an operand. An exceptional situation occurs when the instruction is preceded by a segment override byte that tells the CPU to use another register instead of DS. If a program references a symbol defined in the segment that the **ASSUME** directive identifies as the extra segment, then MASM automatically includes the segment override byte; the programmer does not need to code **ES:** with the symbol. Similarly, **CS:** is not required for data defined in the code segment; MASM will generate the segment override byte as a result of information in the ASSUME directive.

An assembler normally starts the location counter at zero at the beginning of each segment and increments it by the number of bytes required for each statement as the statement is assembled. It is also possible to tell the assembler to use a particular value for the location counter. MASM and many other assemblers use an **ORG** directive for this purpose. The syntax of the **ORG** directive is

```
ORG value
```

where *value* specifies an offset. When MASM encounters an **ORG** directive, it sets the location counter to the indicated value.

Some operating systems require that the first instruction of the program be at a particular location. An **ORG** directive can be used to tell the assembler to begin assembly at the corresponding location. For example, DOS uses two types of executable programs, one type normally stored as an .EXE file and the other as a .COM file. The first instruction of a .COM program must start at offset 100_{16}, so the assembly language source code for such a program normally has the directive

```
ORG 100h
```

right after the **ASSUME** directive.[*]

The **ORG** directive can also be used in a data segment. In many computer systems, certain fixed memory locations are used by the operating system. In order to access these symbolically, the programmer can use an **ORG** directive specifying the offset of the location, followed by a data definition directive. With MASM, this might look like

```
        ORG   18
int9    DW    2 DUP (?)
```

in order to reference the interrupt vector for DOS interrupt 9. (For these locations to correspond to hardware addresses in the interrupt vector table, the segment register corresponding to the segment containing these directives must contain the segment number 0000 when the symbol `int 9` is used.) Other uses for **ORG**

---

[*] Other conditions must also be met for assembly language source code that will ultimately be a .COM program.

directives in data definition include moving the location counter forward to leave undefined blocks of storage or moving the location counter backward to redefine previously defined storage. Neither of these techniques is essential in assembly language programming.

MASM provides **EVEN** and **ALIGN***directives, which also affect the location counter. The Microsoft Macro Assembler can assemble source code for 8086, 80186, 80286, and 80386 processors in addition to the 8088 used in PCs. The first three of these microprocessors use a data bus that is 16 bits wide, so that a word of data can be transferred to or from memory in one memory access cycle *if* that word has an even address. If the word has an odd address, then the data can still be transferred, but two memory access cycles are required. The **EVEN** directive is generally used before a **DW** directive defining a word of storage. If the location counter is even, then the **EVEN** directive does nothing. If the location counter is odd, then MASM inserts a **nop** instruction (the single byte 90), so that the location counter will be even when the **DW** is assembled. This will force the word to be at an even address at execution time, assuring efficient accesses.

The **EVEN** directive has no operand, but **ALIGN** requires an operand that is a power of 2 (2, 4, 8, ...). The directive **ALIGN 2** is equivalent to **EVEN**. The 80386 microprocessor has a 32-bit data bus and can access a doubleword in memory in one read or write cycle *if* that doubleword has an address that is a multiple of four. The directive **ALIGN 4** causes MASM to insert from zero to three **nop** instructions, whatever number of instructions is needed to force the location counter to be a multiple of four.

Even for systems where **EVEN** or **ALIGN** directives can improve efficiency, it is not necessary to include such a directive before every word or doubleword definition. If, for example, a program for the 8086 uses several word-size variables, they can be grouped together preceded by a single **EVEN** directive. Once the location counter has an even value, it will continue to have even values as long as storage is reserved in word-size increments.

Almost every assembler has directives that only affect the assembly listing. One such directive is **PAGE**, which was introduced in Chapter 3. The **PAGE** directive, without an argument, causes a form feed character to be included in the listing file; it can also be used to tell the assembler how many lines per page and characters per line to put in the assembly listing.

The Microsoft Macro Assembler recognizes two directives that are designed to include title information in the listing file. Each source file can contain one **TITLE** directive. This directive has the syntax

 TITLE *text*

where *text* is any string of up to 60 characters. The character string specified in the **TITLE** directive is printed on the second line of each page of the assembly listing. A source file can contain many **SUBTTL** directives. The syntax of the **SUBTTL** directive is similar to that of the **TITLE** directive; the text given by the most recent **SUBTTL** directive is printed on the third line of an assembly listing page.

---

* **ALIGN** was introduced with version 5.0 of the MicroSoft Macro Assembler.

The purpose of directives like PAGE, TITLE, and SUBTTL is to contribute to good program documentation. Only a few years ago source code was punched on cards or paper tape, and an assembly listing gave the programmer his or her first good look at the entire program. Now programmers commonly enter code using video terminals. Comments in the source code provide documentation for code viewed on a monitor display. Nevertheless, assembly listings often make good debugging tools or hardcopy documentation of a program, so PAGE, TITLE, and SUBTTL are still worthwhile.

Exercises 11.3

1. Under certain circumstances, MASM will assemble an 8088 assembly program containing no ASSUME directive. What are these circumstances?

2. Suppose that data definitions are included along with instructions in the segment code. Give an appropriate ASSUME directive for CS and DS.

3. Given the segment

```
data     SEGMENT
         ORG    7h
value1   DW     ?
         EVEN
value2   DW     ?
data     ENDS
```

what is the offset of value1? What is the offset of value2?

11.4

Chapter Summary

This chapter has discussed the assembly process. The Microsoft Macro Assembler is a typical two-pass assembler. It reads an assembly language program twice, using a location counter to construct a symbol table during the first pass, and completing assembly during the second pass. The symbol table contains information about each identifier used in the program, including its type, size, and location.

The first byte of machine code for each 8088 instruction is its opcode. Some instructions are a single byte long, but most consist of multiple bytes. The second byte often has the format "mod reg r/m" where "reg" indicates a source or destination register, and the other two fields combine to describe the addressing mode. Other instruction bytes contain immediate data or the offset of a memory operand.

The **ASSUME** directive tells MASM what segment register will be associated at run-time with a program **SEGMENT**. The **ORG** directive gives the location counter a specified value. The **EVEN** and **ALIGN** directives insert **nop** instructions, if needed, to force the location counter to be even or a multiple of a power of 2, respectively. The **TITLE** and **SUBTTL** directives cause lines of descriptive text to be included in the assembly listing.

CHAPTER 12

Macros and Conditional Assembly

Many previous chapters have made extensive use of macros defined in the file IO.H. This chapter explains how to write macro definitions and tells how MASM uses these definitions to expand macros into their constituent statements.

Sometimes it is necessary to produce slightly different variants of an assembly language program or procedure. The Microsoft Macro Assembler can observe various conditions that can be tested at assembly time; MASM then chooses how to assemble the code on the basis of these conditions. For instance, a block of code may be assembled or skipped based on the definition of a constant. This ability to do conditional assembly is especially useful in macro definitions. This chapter describes some of the ways that conditional assembly can be used.

12.1

Macro Definition and Expansion

A macro was defined in Chapter 3 as a statement that is shorthand for a sequence of other statements. The assembler expands a macro to the statements it represents, and then assembles these new statements. A macro definition resembles a procedure definition in a high-level language. The first line gives the name of the macro being defined and a list of parameters; the main part of the definition consists of a collection of statements that describe the action of the macro in terms of the parameters. A macro is called much like a high-level language procedure, too—the name of the macro is followed by a list of arguments.

These similarities are superficial. A procedure call in a high-level language is compiled into a sequence of instructions to pass any parameters followed by a `call` instruction, whereas a macro call actually expands into statements given in the macro, with the arguments substituted for the parameters used in the macro definition. Code in a macro is repeated every time a macro is called, but there is just one copy of the code for a procedure. Macros often execute more rapidly than procedure calls since there is no overhead for passing parameters or for `call` and `ret` instructions, but this is usually at the cost of more bytes of object code.

Every macro definition is bracketed by **MACRO** and **ENDM** directives. The format of a macro definition is

```
name     MACRO     list of parameters
         assembly language statements
         ENDM
```

The parameters in the **MACRO** directive are ordinary symbols, separated by commas.* The assembly language statements may use the parameters as well as registers, immediate operands, or symbols defined outside the macro. These statements may even include macro calls.

A macro definition can appear anywhere in an assembly language source code file as long as the definition comes before the first statement that calls the macro. It is good programming practice to place macro definitions near the beginning of a source file.

The remainder of this section gives several examples of macro definitions and macro calls. Suppose that a program design requires several pauses where the user is prompted to press any key and the program waits for a key to be pressed. Rather than write this code every time or use a procedure, a macro **pause** can be defined. Figure 12.1 gives such a definition.

This **pause** macro has no parameter, so a call expands to almost exactly the same statements as are in the definition. If the statement

```
pause
```

---

* MASM also allows spaces or tabs as separators, but these can cause ambiguity in certain cases.

Figure 12.1 pause Macro.

```
pause   MACRO
; prompt user and wait for key to be pressed
        mov   dx, OFFSET wait_msg   ;; "Press any key ..."
        mov   ah, 09h               ;; display string function
        int   21h                   ;; call DOS

        mov   ah, 08h               ;; input character function
        int   21h                   ;; call DOS
        ENDM
```

is included in subsequent source code, then the assembler expands this macro call into the statements

```
; prompt user and wait for key to be pressed
        mov   dx, OFFSET wait_msg
        mov   ah, 09h
        int   21h

        mov   ah, 08h
        int   21h
```

How much of the macro expansion is actually shown in a listing file depends on MASM directives, mentioned at the end of this section. Comments starting with a pair of semicolons (called **macro comments**) are never listed. Notice that the **pause** macro is not self-contained; it references the label **wait_msg**, so an appropriate character string must be defined in the data segment.

The instructions executed in the expansion of the macro **pause** destroy the contents of the AX and DX registers; this may not be anticipated by the user if the macro definition and expansion are not shown. The **pause** macro could be made safer by adding the instructions

```
        push   ax            ;; save AX and DX
        push   dx
```

at the beginning of the definition, and

```
        pop    dx            ;; restore DX and AX
        pop    ax
```

at the end.

Note again that the definition and expansion for the **pause** macro contain no **ret** statement. Although macros look much like procedures, they generate in-line code when the macro call is expanded at assembly time.

Figure 12.2 Macro to Add Two Integers.

```
add2      MACRO  nbr1, nbr2
;; put sum of two word-size parameters in AX
          mov    ax, nbr1   ;; first number
          add    ax, nbr2   ;; second number
          ENDM
```

Figure 12.2 gives a definition of a macro **add2** that finds the sum of two parameters, putting the result in the AX register. The parameters used to define the macro are **nbr1** and **nbr2**. These labels are local to the definition. The same names could be used for other purposes in the program, although some human confusion might result.

The statements to which **add2** expands depends on the arguments used in a call. For example, the macro call

```
add2   value, 30    ; value + 30
```

expands to

```
mov    ax, value
add    ax, 30
```

The statement

```
add2   value1, value2    ; value1 + value2
```

expands to

```
mov    ax, value1
add    ax, value2
```

The macro call

```
add2   ax, bx       ; sum of two values
```

expands to

```
mov    ax, ax
add    ax, bx
```

(The instruction **mov ax, ax** is legal, even if it accomplishes nothing.)

In each of these examples the first argument is substituted for the first parameter **nbr1** and the second argument is substituted for the second parameter **nbr2**. Each macro results in two **mov** instructions, but since the types of arguments differ, the object code will vary.

If one of the parameters is missing the macro will still be expanded. For instance, the statement

```
add2 value
```

Figure 12.3 Macro to Swap Two Memory Words.

```
swap       MACRO  word1, word2
;; exchange two words in memory
        push   ax           ;; save AX
        mov    ax, word1    ;; 1st value to AX
        xchg   ax, word2    ;; 1st value to word2, 2nd to AX
        mov    word1, ax    ;; 2nd value to word1
        pop    ax           ;; restore AX
        ENDM
```

expands to

```
        mov    ax, value
        add    ax,
```

The argument **value** replaces **nbr1** and an empty string replaces **nbr2**. The assembler will report an error, but it will be for the illegal **add** instruction that results from the macro expansion, not for the missing argument.

Similarly, the macro call

```
        add  , value
```

expands to

```
        mov    ax,
        add    ax, value
```

The comma in the macro call separates the first missing argument from the second argument **value**. An empty argument replaces the parameter **nbr1**. The assembler will again report an error, for the illegal **mov** instruction, not for the missing argument.

Figure 12.3 shows the definition of a macro **swap** that will exchange the contents of two words in memory. It is very similar to the 8088 **xchg** instruction, that will not work with two memory operands.

As with the **add2** macro, the code generated by calling the **swap** macro depends on the arguments used. For example, the call

```
        swap   [bx], [bx+2]      ; swap adjacent words in array
```

expands to

```
        push   ax
        mov    ax, [bx]
        xchg   ax, [bx+2]
        mov    [bx], ax
        pop    ax
```

It might not be obvious to the user that the **swap** macro uses the AX register,

Figure 12.4 Macro to Find Smaller of Two Memory Words.

```
min2      MACRO  first, second
          LOCAL  end_if
;; put smaller of two words in the AX register
          mov    ax, first      ;; first value
          cmp    ax, second     ;; first  <= second ?
          jle    end_if         ;; exit if so
          mov    ax, second     ;; otherwise load second value
end_if:
          ENDM
```

so the **push** and **pop** instructions in the macro protect the user from accidentally destroying the contents of this register.

Figure 12.4 gives a definition of a macro **min2** that finds the minimum of two word-size signed integers, putting the smaller in the AX register. The code for this macro must implement a design with an **if** statement, and this requires at least one assembly language statement with a label. If an ordinary label were used, it would appear every time a **min2** macro call was expanded and the assembler would produce error messages because of duplicate labels. The solution is to use a **LOCAL** directive to define a symbol **end_if** that is local to the **min2** macro.

The **LOCAL** directive is used only within a macro definition and must be the first statement after the **MACRO** directive. (Not even a comment can separate the **MACRO** and **LOCAL** directives.) It lists one or more symbols, separated by commas, which are used within the macro definition. Each time the macro is expanded and one of these symbols is needed, it is replaced by a symbol starting with two question marks and ending with four hexadecimal digits (**??0000**, **??0001**, etc.) The same **??***dddd* symbol replaces the local symbol each place the local symbol is used in one particular expansion of a macro call.

The same symbols may be listed in **LOCAL** directives in different macro definitions or may be used as regular symbols in code outside of macro definitions.

The macro call

```
    min2    [bx], cx    ; find smaller of two values
```

might expand to the code

```
          mov    ax, [bx]
          cmp    ax, cx
          jle    ??0002
          mov    ax, cx
??0002:
```

Here **end_if** has been replaced in each of the two places it appears within the macro definition by **??0002** in the expansion. Another expansion of the same macro would use a different number after the question marks.

The MASM assembler has several directives that control how macros are listed in .LST files. The **.XALL** directive tells MASM to list only those statements that generate code or data, so that comments, **EQU**s, and some other statements are excluded. This is the default, which is in effect unless some other listing control directive is used. The **.LALL** directive instructs MASM to list all the statements in a macro expansion except for macro comments (starting with **; ;**). Finally, the **.SALL** directive tells MASM to suppress all macro expansion statements, showing only the macro call itself. The file IO.H contains an **.SALL** directive so that macro expansion listings do not obscure the programmer's code.

Exercises 12.1

1. Using the macro definition for **add2** given in Figure 12.2, show the sequence of statements to which each of the following macro calls expands.

    (a) **add2   25, bx**
    (b) **add2   cx, dx**
    (c) **add2   ; no argument**
    (d) **add2   value1, value2, value3**
        (Hint: The third argument is ignored since it has no matching parameter.)

2. Using the macro definition for **swap** given in Figure 12.3, show the sequence of statements to which each of the following macro calls expands.

    (a) **swap   value1, value2**
    (b) **swap   temp, [bx]**
    (c) **swap   value**

3. Using the macro definition for **min2** given in Figure 12.4, show the sequence of statements to which each of the following macro calls expands.

    (a) **min2   value1, value2**
        (Assume the local symbol counter is at 000A.)
    (b) **min2   cx, value**
        (Assume the local symbol counter is at 0019.)

Programming Exercises 12.1

1. Write a definition of a macro **add3** that has three word-size 2's complement integer parameters and that puts the sum of the three numbers in the AX register.

2. Write a definition of a macro **max2** that has two word-size 2's complement integer parameters and that puts the maximum of the two numbers in the AX register.

3. Write a definition of a macro **min3** that has three word-size 2's complement integer parameters and that puts the minimum of the three numbers in the AX register.

4. Write a definition of a macro **pause_for_key** with one parameter, an ASCII code (which may be an immediate operand or in a register half or byte of memory) for a printable character. The macro should implement the following design:

{ pause_for_key (*char*) }

display "Press *char* to continue";

until character entered at keyboard matches *char* loop
        input character without echoing it to display;
end until;

echo character to display;

5. Write a definition of a macro **upcase** with one parameter, a reference to a byte in memory. The code generated by the macro should examine the byte, and if it is the ASCII code for a lowercase letter, replace it by the ASCII code for the corresponding uppercase letter.

12.2

Conditional Assembly

There are times when a programmer wants to produce slightly different variants of a program or procedure. This might occur if a programmer were writing code to do machine level input or output where only port addresses changed for different machines (or for different devices attached to a single machine). Another situation might occur when the expansion of a macro needs to change depending on the number or type of arguments in the macro call. The Microsoft Macro Assembler's conditional assembly facility makes it possible to write source code that assembles differently depending on these or other conditions.

Figure 12.5 shows a definition for a macro **add_all**, which will add one to five word-size integers, putting the sum in the AX register. It employs the con-

Figure 12.5 `add_all` Macro Using Conditional Assembly.

```
add_all      MACRO  nbr1, nbr2, nbr3, nbr4, nbr5
;; add up to 5 word-size integers, putting sum in AX
             mov    ax, nbr1    ; first operand

             IFNB   <nbr2>
             add    ax, nbr2    ; second operand
             ENDIF

             IFNB   <nbr3>
             add    ax, nbr3    ; third operand
             ENDIF

             IFNB   <nbr4>
             add    ax, nbr4    ; fourth operand
             ENDIF

             IFNB   <nbr5>
             add    ax, nbr5    ; fifth operand
             ENDIF

             ENDM
```

ditional assembly directive **IFNB** (if not blank). This directive can be used only in macro definitions. When an **add_all** macro call is expanded and one of its **IFNB** directives is encountered, MASM examines the macro parameter whose name is enclosed between angle brackets (< and >). If that parameter has a corresponding argument passed to it, then it is "not blank" and the **add** instruction for that argument is included in the expansion of the macro. If a parameter does not have a corresponding argument, the **add** instruction is omitted from the macro expansion.

Given the macro call

```
add_all  bx, cx, dx, number, 1
```

each of the five macro parameters has a corresponding argument, so the macro expands to

```
mov    ax, bx      ; first operand
add    ax, cx      ; second operand
add    ax, dx      ; third operand
add    ax, number     ; fourth operand
add    ax, 1     ; fifth operand
```

The macro call

```
add_all  bx, cx, 45            ; value1 + value2 + 45
```

has only three arguments. The argument **bx** will become the value for parameter nbr1, cx will be substituted for nbr2, and 45 will be used for nbr3, but the parameters nbr4 and nbr5 will be blank. Therefore the macro expands to the statements

```
mov    ax, bx    ; first operand
add    ax, cx    ; second operand
add    ax, 45    ; third operand
```

Although it would be unusual to do so, arguments other than trailing ones can be omitted. For example, the macro call

```
add_all  bx, ,cx
```

has **bx** corresponding to **nbr1** and **cx** matched to **nbr3**, but all other parameters will be blank. Therefore the macro expands to

```
mov    ax, bx    ; first operand
add    ax, cx    ; third operand
```

If the first argument is omitted in an **add_all** macro call, the macro will still be expanded. However, the resulting statement sequence will contain a **mov** instruction with a missing operand, and this statement will cause MASM to issue an error message. For example, the macro call

```
add_all  , value1, value2
```

expands to

```
mov    ax,       ; first operand
add    ax, value1    ; second operand
add    ax, value2    ; third operand
```

An unusual and possibly creative use of the **add_all** macro is illustrated by the call

```
add_all  value, ax, ax, value, ax    ; 10 * value
```

which expands to

```
mov    ax, value    ; first operand
add    ax, ax    ; second operand
add    ax, ax    ; third operand
add    ax, value    ; fourth operand
add    ax, ax    ; fifth operand
```

The comment **10 * value** explains the purpose of this call.

The Microsoft assembler provides several conditional assembly directives. The **IFNB** directive has a companion **IFB** (if blank), which checks if a macro parameter is blank.

The **IF** and **IFE** directives can be used in any assembly language code, not just in macro definitions. These directives examine an expression *whose value can be determined at assembly time*. For **IF**, MASM assembles conditional code if the value of the expression is not zero. For **IFE**, MASM includes conditional code if the value is zero.

The **IFDEF** and **IFNDEF** are similar to **IF** and **IFE**. They examine a symbol and MASM assembles conditional code depending on whether or not the symbol has been defined in the program.

The **IF1** and **IF2** directives use no operand. Code that follows **IF1** is processed only during pass 1 of the assembly process, and code which follows IF2 is processed only during pass 2.

Each conditional assembly block is terminated by the **ENDIF** directive. An **ELSE** directive is also available to provide alternative code if the condition being checked is false. In general, blocks of conditional assembly code look like

```
IF...    [operands]
statements
ELSE
statements
ENDIF
```

Operands vary with the type of **IF** and are not used with all types. The **ELSE** directive and statements following it are optional.

The statements following **IF** or **ELSE** directives may include other **IF** directives; that is, conditional blocks may be nested.

Deeply nested conditional blocks are often difficult to code and confusing to read. The **EXITM** directive can be used to make some macro definitions simpler to write and understand. When MASM is processing a macro call and finds an **EXITM** directive, it immediately stops expanding the macro, ignoring any statements following **EXITM** in the macro definition. The design

```
if condition
then
        process assembly language statements for condition;
else
        process statements for negation of condition;
end if;
```

and the alternative design

```
if condition
then
        process assembly language statements for condition;
        terminate expansion of macro;
end if;
process statements for negation of condition;
```

are equivalent, assuming that there are no macro definition statements following those sketched in the designs. These alternative designs can be implemented using

```
IF... [operands]
assembly language statements for condition
ELSE
assembly language statements for negation of condition
ENDIF
```

and

```
IF... [operands]
assembly language statements for condition
EXITM
ENDIF
assembly language statements for negation of condition
```

Notice that the **EXITM** directive is not needed when the **ELSE** directive is used. A macro definition using **EXITM** appears in Figure 12.6.

Examples in this section and in Section 12.1 have shown macro calls that expanded to illegal statements as a result of missing arguments. Such illegal statements are detected by MASM during subsequent assembly rather than as the macro is expanded. The designer of a macro definition may wish to include safeguards to ensure that the correct number of arguments is included in a macro call, or that the call is valid in other ways. Conditional assembly directives make this possible. If, however, assembly errors are eliminated by avoiding generation of illegal statements, a user may not know when a macro call is faulty. It requires additional effort to inform the user of an error, displaying a console message and/or putting a message in the listing file.

The **%OUT** directive tells MASM to display a message on the standard output device, normally the monitor screen. This statement has the format

```
%OUT message
```

where **message** can be any collection of characters, including spaces and punctuation. Use of the **%OUT** directive is not restricted to macros or conditional assembly. However, it is logical to use it in a conditional block of a macro definition to display an error message if a macro call is missing a required argument. Such an application is shown in Figure 12.6 below.

It is somewhat more difficult to include a message in the listing file without generating an illegal statement. One option is to put the message in a **DB** directive. For instance, a conditional block might include

```
DB   "Missing second argument"
```

Such a statement would assemble correctly even if included in a code segment, but it would cause a run-time error if it were in an executable position in the program.

Of course, a comment can be used to produce a message in the listing file. In addition to allowing a semicolon to mark the beginning of a comment, the

Microsoft Macro Assembler has a **COMMENT** directive that can be used to put a comment in a source file and subsequent listing file. This directive is convenient in a conditional block for inserting a message in a listing file. It can be used to produce multiple-line comments. The **COMMENT** directive has the syntax

```
COMMENT delimiter
lines of comment text
delimiter
```

where *delimiter* is any nonblank character. The same character must be used at the beginning and end of the message, and must not appear within the comment text itself. In addition to text appearing in the middle lines, characters following the delimiter character on the first or last lines are also treated as comments. A **COMMENT** directive like

```
COMMENT + Warning
    -- missing first parameter in ADD_ALL macro
+ End of Warning
```

might be used in a macro definition.

The **min2** macro definition in Figure 12.6 incorporates safeguards to ensure that the macro is called with the correct number of parameters. The conditional block

```
        IFB     <value1>
        %OUT    first argument missing in min2 macro
COMMENT *
        min2 -- first argument missing
        *
        EXITM
        ENDIF
```

examines the first argument. If it is missing, then the **%OUT** directive displays the message "first argument missing in min2 macro." Actually, the **%OUT** directive will be encountered twice, during both passes of the assembly process, so that the same message is displayed two times. Assuming that a **.LALL** directive is in effect, the **COMMENT** directive puts "min2 - - first argument missing" in the listing file. Note that the conditional block ends with an **EXITM** directive, so that if the first argument is missing, no further expansion of the macro is done. An alternative way to suppress additional macro expansion would be to nest the rest of the macro definition between an **ELSE** directive and the **ENDIF** directive for this first conditional block.

The conditional block beginning with the directive

```
    IFB     <value2>
```

examines the second argument, generating messages if it is missing. The con-

Figure 12.6 Improved min2 Macro.

```
min2        MACRO   value1,value2,extra
            LOCAL   end_if
;; put smaller of value1 and value2 in AX

            IFB     <value1>
            %OUT    first argument missing in min2 macro
COMMENT     *
            min2 -- first argument missing
            *
            EXITM
            ENDIF

            IFB     <value2>
            %OUT    second argument missing in min2 macro
COMMENT     *
            min2 -- second argument missing
            *
            EXITM
            ENDIF

            IFNB    <extra>
            %OUT    more than two arguments in min2 macro
COMMENT     *
            min2 -- more than two arguments
            *
            EXITM
            ENDIF

            mov   ax, value1     ;; first value to AX
            cmp   ax, value2     ;; value1 <= value2?
            jle   end_if         ;; done if so
            mov   ax, value2     ;; otherwise value2 smaller
end_if:
            ENDM
```

ditional block beginning with the directive

```
        IFNB    <extra>
```

tells MASM to check to see if a third argument was listed in the macro call that is being expanded. Since there should be no third argument, messages are generated if the argument is not blank.

Figure 12.7 Recursive `add_all` Macro Definition.

```
add_all    MACRO   nbr1, nbr2, nbr3, nbr4, nbr5
;; add up to 5 word-size integers, putting sum in AX
           IFB     <nbr1>
           mov     ax, 0         ;; initialize sum
           ELSE
           add_all nbr2, nbr3, nbr4, nbr5    ;; add remaining arguments
           add     ax, nbr1    ;; add first argument
           ENDIF
           ENDM
```

A word of caution is needed at this point. If the third conditional block were

```
           IFNB     <extra>
           %OUT     extra argument(s) in min2 macro
COMMENT    *
           min2 -- extra argument(s)
           *
           EXITM
           ENDIF
```

and the macro call

```
     min2   bx, cx, dx
```

were coded, then the message displayed on the console would be

```
     dx argument(s) in min2 macro
```

and the comment would be

```
     COMMENT    *
                min2 -- dx argument(s)
                *
```

The word **extra** in the two messages would be taken as the symbol representing the third parameter, and would be replaced by the argument **dx**.

Recall that a macro definition can include macro calls. In fact, a macro definition may include a call to itself, that is, the definition of a macro may be recursive. Figure 12.7 gives a new definition of an **add_all** macro.

The basic idea of **add_all** is that the sum is zero if there are no arguments; otherwise the sum can be calculated by adding all arguments but the first and then adding the first argument. As an example, the macro call

```
     add_all   value1, value2, value3
```

expands to

```
     mov   ax, 0
     add   ax, value3
```

```
add   ax, value2
add   ax, value1
```

Only a limited number of parameters is possible in a recursive macro definition. The assembler maintains a stack that is used in processing such definitions, and this stack overflows if too many parameters and corresponding arguments are used.

Exercises 12.2

1. Using the macro definition for **add_all** given in Figure 12.5, show the sequence of statements to which each of the following macro calls expands.

   (a) `add_all   value, bx`
   (b) `add_all   cx, 1, value, dx`
   (c) `add_all   bx, cx, , , dx`

2. Using the macro definition for **min2** given in Figure 12.6, show the sequence of statements to which each of the following macro calls expands.

   (a) `min2   value1, value2`
       (Assume the local symbol counter is at 0004.)
   (b) `min2   , value`
       (Assume the local symbol counter is at 0011.)
   (c) `min2   cx`
       (Assume the local symbol counter is at 000B.)
   (d) `min2   value1, value2, value3`
       (Assume the local symbol counter is at 01D0.)

3. Using the macro definition for **add_all** given in Figure 12.7, show the sequence of statements to which each of the following macro calls expands.

   (a) `add_all   bx, cx`
   (b) `add_all   value1, value2, value3, value4, value5, value6`
   (c) `add_all   value, , dx`

Programming Exercises 12.2

1. Rewrite the macro definition for **swap** from Figure 12.3, so that a **swap** macro call must have exactly two arguments, and appropriate messages are sent to the console and put in the listing file if there are missing or extra arguments.

2. Write a definition of a macro `min3` that has exactly three word-size 2's complement integer parameters and that puts the minimum of the three numbers in the AX register. Generate appropriate messages for the console and the listing file if there are missing or extra arguments with a `min3` call.

3. Write a *nonrecursive* definition of a macro `min_all` that has six word-size 2's complement integer parameters and that puts the minimum of corresponding arguments in the AX register. The macro definition should generate appropriate error messages if the first argument is missing; however, no other argument is required and no special action should be taken if an argument after the first one is missing. Make sure the macro expansion would give the correct minimum in exceptional cases (such as if all argument values were negative.)

4. Write a *recursive* definition of a macro `min_all` that has six word-size 2's complement integer parameters and that puts the minimum of corresponding arguments in the AX register. Make sure the macro expansion would give the correct minimum in exceptional cases (such as if all argument values were negative.)

12.3

Macros in IO.H

Macros in the file IO.H are designed to provide simple, safe access to standard input and output devices. Figure 12.8 shows the contents of IO.H and the remainder of the section discusses the directives and macros in the file.

Most of the file IO.H consists of macro definitions, which, when used, generate code to call external procedures. However, the file does contain other directives. It begins with an `.XLIST` directive; this suppresses listing of all source code, in particular the contents of IO.H. It then has **EXTRN** directives, which identify the external procedures called by the macros. The file ends with an `.SALL` directive to suppress listing of any macro expansions and an `.LIST` directive so that the user's statements following the directive **INCLUDE io.h** will again be shown in the listing file.

The first macro defined is named **m_error**. This macro is called by the other macros if there are missing or excess arguments. It avoids repeating nearly identical code in the other macros. The **m_error** macro has one parameter, a message **msg** to be displayed on the console and included in a **COMMENT** directive in the listing file.

Figure 12.8 IO.H.

```
.XLIST        ; turn off listing

              EXTRN  itoa_proc:far, atoi_proc:far, out_proc:far
              EXTRN  ins_proc:far, inc_proc:far

m_error       MACRO  msg
              IF2
              %OUT msg
              .LALL
COMMENT *
        msg
* END COMMENT
              .ERR
              .SALL
              ENDIF
              ENDM

itoa          MACRO  dest,source,xtra    ;; convert integer to ASCII string

              IFB    <source>
              m_error <missing operand(s) in ITOA>
              EXITM
              ENDIF

              IFNB   <xtra>
              m_error <extra operand(s) in ITOA>
              EXITM
              ENDIF

              push   ax                   ;; save AX
              push   di                   ;; save DI
              mov    ax,source            ;; copy source to AX
              lea    di,dest              ;; destination address to DI
              call   itoa_proc            ;; call procedure
              pop    di                   ;; restore DI
              pop    ax                   ;; restore AX
              ENDM

atoi          MACRO  source,xtra          ;; convert ASCII string to integer in AX

              IFB    <source>
              m_error <missing operand in ATOI>
              EXITM
              ENDIF
```

Figure 12.8 Continued.

```
                IFNB    <xtra>
                m_error <extra operand(s) in ATOI>
                EXITM
                ENDIF

                push    si                  ;; save SI
                lea     si,source           ;; source address to SI
                call    atoi_proc           ;; call procedure
                pop     si                  ;; restore SI
                ENDM

   output       MACRO   string,length,xtra  ;; display macro

                IFB     <string>
                m_error <missing operand in OUTPUT>
                EXITM
                ENDIF

                IFNB    <xtra>
                m_error <extra operand(s) in OUTPUT>
                EXITM
                ENDIF

                push    ax                  ;; save AX
                push    si                  ;; save SI
                lea     si,string           ;; load address of source string

                IFB     <length>            ;; IF no length parameter
                mov     ax,0                ;;   set length to zero
                ELSE                        ;; ELSE
                mov     ax,length           ;;   copy length to AX
                ENDIF

                call    out_proc            ;; call procedure
                pop     si                  ;; restore SI
                pop     ax                  ;; restore AX
                ENDM


   inputs       MACRO   dest,length,xtra    ;; read string from keyboard

                IFB     <length>
                m_error <missing operand(s) in INPUTS>
                EXITM
                ENDIF
```

Figure 12.8 Continued.

```
                IFNB    <xtra>
                m_error <extra operand(s) in INPUTS>
                EXITM
                ENDIF

                push    di                  ;; save DX
                lea     di,dest             ;; destination address
                mov     cx,length           ;; length of buffer
                call    ins_proc            ;; call procedure
                pop     di                  ;; restore DX
                ENDM

inputc          MACRO   xtra                ;; read character from keyboard to AL
                IFNB    <xtra>
                m_error <extra operand(s) in INPUTC>
                EXITM
                ENDIF
                call    inc_proc            ;; call procedure
                ENDM

.SALL           ; suppress macro expansion listings
.LIST           ; begin listing
```

The body of the **m_error** macro is enclosed in an **IF2** conditional block. This restricts error messages to assembly pass 2, avoiding duplicate messages on the console. In fact, the **m_error** macro generates no statements other than the directives **IF2** and **ENDIF** during pass 1. During pass 2 the **%OUT** directive displays the message. Recall that an **.SALL** directive is in effect; the **m_error** macro generates an **.LALL** directive so that the **COMMENT** directive with its message are not suppressed. Another **.SALL** directive turns off listing of statements following the macro.

The **m_error** macro also includes an **.ERR** directive. This directive triggers a **forced error**. In addition to generating a generic error message, this directive causes MASM to discard the .OBJ file. Thus the user must correct the error and reassemble the source file before proceeding with linking.

The bulk of the file IO.H consists of definitions for **itoa**, **atoi**, **output**, **inputs**, and **inputc** macros. These definitions have similar structures. Each uses **IFB** and **IFNB** directives to check that a macro call has the correct number of arguments. The **m_error** macro is called with an error message if arguments are defective. Notice the < and > that surround the message. In this context, these characters serve to turn a multiword message into a single argument. Only error messages, no instructions, are generated if arguments are faulty. Actually, the checks are not quite complete. For instance, no error message would be generated with the macro call

```
itoa   , value
```

since the parameter **source** has a corresponding argument, and there is no argument corresponding to the parameter **xtra**. (See Exercise 1 in this section.)

Assuming that its arguments are correct, an input/output macro call expands to a sequence of instructions that copy argument values to registers and call the appropriate external procedure. To preserve their contents, **push** and **pop** instructions are generated for the registers used to pass parameters.

The **output** macro definition allows for an optional argument **length**. The value of the length argument is passed to the procedure **out_proc** in the AX register. The code

```
IFB     <length>              ;; IF no length parameter
mov     ax,0                  ;;    set length to zero
ELSE                          ;; ELSE
mov     ax,length             ;;    copy length to AX
ENDIF
```

ensures that AX contains the value 0 if the length argument is omitted. The statement **mov ax,length** will assemble in various ways, depending on the mode of the argument passed to the parameter **length**. The **out_proc** procedure examines the value in AX and if it is greater than zero, limits the number of characters displayed to this length.

Exercises 12.3

---

1. Rewrite the definition of **itoa** to provide complete argument checking. That is, check separately for missing **source** and **dest** arguments, generating specific messages for each missing argument. Allow for the possibility that both are missing.

2. Consider the following "enhancement" for the **output** macro.

```
IFB     <length>              ;; IF no length parameter
mov     ax,0                  ;;    set length to zero;
ELSE                          ;; ELSE
IF      length LE 80          ;;    IF length <= 80
mov     ax,length             ;;       copy length to AX;
ELSE                          ;;    ELSE
mov     ax,80                 ;;       set length to 80;
ENDIF                         ;;    END IF
ENDIF                         ;; END IF
```

where the relational operator **LE** returns –1 (nonzero) if the value of `length` is less than or equal to 80, and returns 0 otherwise. This code will only work if the length argument in an `output` macro call is a constant or a symbol representing a constant. Why?

12.4

Chapter Summary

Macros are defined using **MACRO** and **ENDM** directives. Macros may use parameters that are associated with corresponding arguments in macro calls. A call is expanded at assembly time. The statements in the expansion of a macro call appear in the macro definition, with arguments substituted for parameters. A macro definition may declare local labels, which MASM expands to different symbols for different macro calls.

Conditional assembly may be used in regular code or in macro definitions to generate different statements, based on conditions that can be checked at assembly time. The **IFB** and **IFNB** directives are used in macros to check for the absence or presence of arguments. Several other conditional assembly directives are also available, including **IF**, **IFE**, **IFDEF**, **IFNDEF**, **IF1**, and **IF2**. An **ELSE** directive may be used to provide two alternative blocks of code, and the **ENDIF** directive ends a conditional assembly block. If the assembler encounters an **EXITM** directive when expanding a macro definition, it immediately terminates expansion of the macro.

The **%OUT** directive causes a message to be displayed on the console at assembly time. The **COMMENT** directive can be used to generate a comment in a listing file. The **.ERR** directive triggers a forced error so that MASM displays an error message and does not produce an .OBJ file for the assembly.

The file IO.H contains definitions for a collection of input/output macros, and a few directives. These macro definitions use conditional assembly to check for missing or extra arguments, and generate code that calls external procedures.

CHAPTER 13

Decimal Arithmetic

Section 1.5 gave a brief introduction to the integer representation systems known as binary coded decimal (BCD). BCD representations are especially useful for storing integers with many digits, such as might be needed for financial records. BCD values are easier than 2's complement values to convert to or from ASCII format, but there are only a few 8088 instructions to facilitate arithmetic with BCD numbers.

This chapter describes BCD representation schemes and the 8088 instructions that are used with BCD numbers. It includes code to convert BCD representations for numbers to and from corresponding ASCII representations.

----- 13.1 -----

Packed BCD Representations

There are two major classifications of BCD schemes, packed and unpacked, and many variations with respect to the number of bytes used and how the sign of a value is represented. This section and Section 13.2 discuss packed BCD numbers. Section 13.3 tells about unpacked BCD numbers.

Packed BCD representations store two decimal digits per byte, one in the high-order four bits and one in the low-order four bits. For example, the bit pattern 0110 1001 represents the decimal number 69, using 0110 for 6 and 1001 for 9. One confusing thing about packed BCD is that this same bit pattern is written 69 in hexadecimal. However, this just means that if 0110 1001 is thought of as a BCD number, it represents the decimal value 69, but if it is taken as a signed or unsigned binary integer, the corresponding decimal value is 105. This again makes the point that a given pattern of bits can have several numeric interpretations, as well as nonnumeric meanings.

If single bytes were used for packed BCD representations, then decimal numbers from 0 to 99 could be stored. This would not be very useful, so typically several bytes are used to store a single number. There are many possible schemes; some use a fixed number of bytes and some have variable length, incorporating a field for length as part of the representation. The bit pattern for a number often includes one or more bits to indicate the sign of the number.

The Microsoft Macro Assembler provides a **DT** directive that may be used to define a 10-byte packed decimal number. Although other representation systems are equally valid, this book concentrates on this scheme. If the directive

```
DT  123456789
```

is included in an assembly language program, then MASM reserves ten bytes of storage with initial values (in hex)

    89 67 45 23 01 00 00 00 00 00

Notice that the bytes are stored backward, low-order to high-order, but within each byte the individual decimal digits are stored forward. This is consistent with the way that high-order and low-order bytes are reversed in word-length 2's complement integers. When programming with word-length 2's complement numbers, the programmer rarely needs to worry about how the bytes are stored. However, a programmer must know how packed BCD numbers are stored in order to process one byte at a time.

The tenth byte in this representation is used to indicate the sign of the entire number. This byte is 00 for a positive number and 80 for a negative number.

Therefore the **DT** directive

```
DT -1469
```

produces

69   14   00   00   00   00   00   00   00   80

Notice that only the sign indicator changes for a negative number; other digits of the representation are the same as they would be for the corresponding positive number.

Since an entire byte is used for the sign indicator, only nine bytes remain to store decimal digits. Therefore, the packed BCD scheme used by the **DT** directive stores a signed number up to decimal 18 digits long. MASM will indicate an error if more than 18 decimal digits are given in a **DT** directive.

Although **DT** directives can be used to initialize packed BCD numbers in an assembly language program and arithmetic can be done on these numbers with the aid of the instructions covered in the next section, packed BCD numbers are of little service unless they can be displayed for human use. Figure 13.1 gives the source code for a procedure **dtoa_proc** that converts a packed BCD number to the corresponding ASCII string. This procedure does the same job for packed BCD numbers as **itoa_proc** (Appendix G) does for 2's complement integers.

The procedure **dtoa_proc** has two parameters: a 10-byte-long packed BCD source and a 19-byte-long ASCII destination string. The destination is 19 bytes long to allow for a sign and 18 digits; the sign will be a space for a positive number and a minus (−) for a negative number. For the digits, leading zeros rather than spaces are produced. The offset in the data segment of each parameter is passed in an index register—the address of the BCD source in SI and the address of the ASCII destination in DI. The procedure implements the following design:

> save registers which will be altered;
> add 18 to DI to point at last byte of destination string;
>
> for count := 9 down to 1 loop
>   { process byte containing two digits }
>   copy next source byte to AL;
>   copy source byte to AH;
>   mask out high-order digit in AL;
>   convert low-order digit in AL to ASCII code;
>   store ASCII code for low-order digit in destination string;
>   decrement DI to point at next destination byte to left;
>   shift AH 4 bits to right to get only high-order digit;
>   convert high-order digit in AH to ASCII code;
>   store ASCII code for high-order digit in destination string;
>   decrement DI to point at next destination byte to left;

Figure 13.1 Packed BCD-to-ASCII Conversion.

```
dtoa_proc PROC NEAR          ; convert 10 byte BCD number at [SI]
                             ; to 19 byte long ASCII string at [DI]

          push di            ; save registers
          push si
          push ax
          push cx

          add  di, 18        ; point to last byte of destination
          mov  cx, 9         ; count of bytes to process
for1:     mov  al, [si]      ; byte with two bcd digits
          mov  ah, al        ; copy to high order byte of AX
          and  al, 00001111b         ; mask out higher order digit
          or   al, 30h       ; convert to ASCII character
          mov  [di], al      ; save lower order digit
          dec  di            ; point at next destination byte to left
          shr  ah, 1         ; shift out lower order digit
          shr  ah, 1
          shr  ah, 1
          shr  ah, 1
          or   ah, 30h       ; convert to ASCII
          mov  [di], ah      ; save higher order digit
          dec  di            ; point at next destination byte to left
          inc  si            ; point at next source byte
          loop for1          ; continue for 9 bytes

          mov  BYTE PTR [di], ' '   ; space for positive number
          and  BYTE PTR [si], 80h   ; check sign byte
          jz   non_neg              ; skip if not negative
          mov  BYTE PTR [di], '-'   ; minus sign
non_neg:

          pop  cx            ; restore registers
          pop  ax
          pop  si
          pop  di
          ret                ; return to caller

dtoa_proc ENDP
```

increment SI to point at next source digit to right;
end for;
move space to first byte of destination string;
if source number is negative
then
     move "-" to first byte of destination string;
end if;

restore registers which were altered;
return;

The most interesting part of the design and code is the portion that splits a single source byte into two destination bytes. Two copies of the source byte are made, one in AL and one in AH. The byte in AL is converted to the ASCII code for the low-order digit using an **and** to zero the left four bits and an **or** to put 0011 (hex 3) in their place.

```
and   al, 00001111b       ; mask out higher order digit
or    al, 30h   ; convert to ASCII character
```

The high-order digit takes a little more work. A sequence of four **shr** instructions discards the low-order digit in AH, moves the high-order digit to the right four bits and zeros the left four bits. Another **or** produces the ASCII code for the high order digit.

Once a packed BCD number is converted to an ASCII string it can be displayed using the **output** macro or a DOS function. Since BCD numbers are often used for financial calculations, some other ASCII representation may be more desirable than that generated by **dtoa_proc**. Some exercises at the end of this section specify alternatives.

Sometimes it is necessary to convert an ASCII string to a corresponding packed BCD value. Figure 13.2 shows a procedure **atod_proc** that accomplish-

Figure 13.2 ASCII-to-Packed BCD Conversion.

```
atod_proc PROC NEAR
; Convert ASCII string at [SI] to 10 byte BCD number at [DI].
; Source string must consist only of ASCII codes for digits,
;    terminated by a null byte.

          push si        ; save registers
          push di
          push cx
          push ax
```

Figure 13.2 Continued.

```
                mov   WORD PTR [di], 0        ; zero BCD destination
                mov   WORD PTR [di+2], 0
                mov   WORD PTR [di+4], 0
                mov   WORD PTR [di+6], 0
                mov   WORD PTR [di+8], 0

; find length of source string and move SI to trailing null
                mov   cx, 0       ; count := 0
while_1:    cmp   BYTE PTR [si], 0   ; while not end of string (null byte)
                jz    endwhile_1
                inc   cx          ; add 1 to count of characters
                inc   si          ; point at next character
                jmp   while_1     ; check again
endwhile_1:
; process source characters a pair at a time
while_2:    cmp   cx, 0       ; while count > 0
                jz    endwhile_2
                dec   si          ; point at next ASCII byte from right
                mov   al, BYTE PTR [si]    ; get byte
                and   al, 00001111b        ; convert to BCD digit
                mov   BYTE PTR [di], al    ; save BCD digit
                dec   cx          ; decrement count
                jz    endwhile_2  ; exit loop if out of source digits
                dec   si          ; point at next ASCII byte from right
                mov   al, BYTE PTR [si]    ; get byte
                shl   al, 1       ; shift to left and convert to digit
                shl   al, 1
                shl   al, 1
                shl   al, 1
                or    BYTE PTR [di], al    ; combine with other BCD digit
                dec   cx          ; decrement count
                inc   di          ; point at next destination byte
                jmp   while_2     ; repeat for all source characters
endwhile_2:
                pop   ax          ; restore registers
                pop   cx
                pop   di
                pop   si
                ret               ; return to caller
atod_proc ENDP
```

es this task in a restricted setting. The procedure has two parameters, an ASCII source string whose offset is in SI and a 10-byte BCD destination string whose offset is in DI. The ASCII source string is very limited. It can consist only of ASCII codes for digits terminated by a null byte; no sign, no space, or any other character code is permitted.

The design of procedure `atod_proc` is quite different from `atoi_proc` (Figure 9.7), which produces an integer from an ASCII string. The ASCII-to-integer routine scans source characters left to right one at a time, but the ASCII-to-packed BCD procedure scans the source string right to left, two characters at a time in order to pack two decimal digits into one byte. The procedure must begin by locating the right end of the string. If there is an odd number of source characters, then only one character will contribute to the last BCD byte. The design for `atod_proc` appears below.

```
save registers which will be altered;
initialize all 10 bytes of destination, each to 00;

counter := 0;
while SI is not pointing at trailing null byte of ASCII source loop
      add 1 to counter;
      increment SI to point at next byte of source string;
end while;

while counter > 0 loop
      decrement SI to point at next source byte from right;
      copy source byte to AL;
      convert ASCII code to digit by zeroing leftmost 4 bits;
      save low-order digit in destination string;
      subtract 1 from counter;

      if counter = 0
      then
            exit while loop;
      end if;

      decrement SI to point at next source byte from right;
      copy source byte to AL;
      shift AL 4 bits left to get digit in high-order 4 bits;
      or AL with destination byte to combine with low-order digit;
      subtract 1 from counter;
      increment DI to point at next destination byte;
end while;

restore registers that were altered;
return;
```

The first **while** loop in the design simply scans the source string left to right, counting digits preceding the trailing null byte. Although this design allows only ASCII codes for digits, an extra loop could be included to skip leading blanks and a leading minus or plus (– or +) could be noted. (These and other enhancements are specified in Exercise 5.)

The second `while` loop processes the ASCII codes for digits that have been counted in the first loop. Two digits, if available, must be packed into a single destination byte. Each time through the loop, there is at least one source byte, so the first is loaded into AL, changed from an ASCII code to a digit and stored in the destination string. (An alternative way to convert the ASCII code to a digit would be to subtract 30_{16}.) If source characters are exhausted, then the `while` loop is exited. Otherwise a second ASCII character is loaded into AL, `shl` instructions convert it to a digit in the left four bits of AL, and an `or` combines it with the right digit already stored in memory in the destination string.

The `atod_proc` could be used to convert a string obtained from the `inputs` macro. DOS function 10 could also be used to get a source string, although it would be necessary to put a trailing null byte after the digit codes.

Exercises 13.1

1. Find the initial values that MASM will generate for each `DT` directive below:
   (a) `DT   123456`
   (b) `DT   -123456`
   (c) `DT   345`
   (d) `DT   -345`
   (e) `DT   102030405060708090`
   (f) `DT   -102030405060708090`

2. Modify the code for the `dtoa_proc` procedure so that it produces leading spaces instead of zeros, and so that the minus sign, if any, is placed to the immediate left of the first nonzero digit. If the value of the entire number is zero, the final zero is not replaced by a space. The total string length should remain 19 characters.

3. Define a macro `dtoa` similar to the `itoa` macro described in Chapter 12. Use two parameters, `destination` and `source`, `destination` referencing a 19-byte-long ASCII string and `source` referencing a 10-byte packed BCD string in memory. Copy the offsets of these strings to DI and SI and call the procedure `dtoa_proc`. Push and pop the original values in DI and SI as appropriate. Include safeguards to ensure that the correct number of arguments are used in a call.

4. Modify the code for the `dtoa_proc` procedure so that it produces a 22-byte-long ASCII string giving a monetary representation of the source value. There should be leading spaces instead of zeros in the first 16 positions. In this representation, character 17 is always a decimal point. Characters 18 and 19 are always digits, even if they are zero. Character 20 is a space. Characters 21 and 22 are ASCII codes for CR if the value is positive and DB if the value is negative.

5. (a) Modify the code for the **atod_proc** procedure so that it will skip leading spaces in the source string, accept a leading plus or minus (+ or –) immediately before the first digit, and terminate scanning when any nondigit (rather than only a null byte) is encountered in the string. If a minus sign is encountered, the sign byte of the BCD representation is set to 80_{16}.

(b) Define a macro **atod** similar to the **atoi** macro described in Chapter 12. Use two parameters, **destination** and **source**, **destination** referencing a 10-byte packed BCD string and **source** referencing a 19-byte-long ASCII string in memory. Copy the offsets of these strings to DI and SI and call the procedure **atod_proc**. Save and restore the original values in DI and SI as appropriate. Include safeguards to ensure that the correct number of arguments are used in a call.

Programming Exercises 13.1

---

1. Write a procedure **dtoi_proc** to convert a 10-byte-long packed BCD number to a word-size 2's complement integer. The procedure should have one parameter, the offset of the source string in SI. Return the 2's complement value in AX. Flags should be set appropriately, including OF = 1 if the BCD number is too large to be stored as a word-size 2's complement integer.

2. Write a procedure **itod_proc** to convert a word-size 2's complement integer to a 10-byte-long packed BCD number. The procedure should have two parameters, the source value in AX and the offset of the BCD number in DI.

3. Write a procedure **edit_proc** that has two parameters, a pattern string with offset passed in DI and a 10-byte packed BCD value with offset in SI. The procedure selectively replaces some characters in the pattern string by spaces or by ASCII codes for digits extracted from the BCD value. Except for a terminating null byte, the only allowable characters in a pattern string are a pound sign (#), a comma (,) and a period (.). The procedure does not change a period. Each # is replaced by a digit. There should be at most 18 pound signs and, if there are fewer than 18, then lower-order digits from the BCD value are used. Leading zeros in the resulting string are changed to spaces unless they follow a period, in which case they remain zeros. A comma is unchanged unless it is adjacent to a space; such a comma is

changed to a space. The following examples (with ⌴ indicating a space) illustrate how **edit_proc** works. Note that the original pattern is destroyed by the procedure.

Before		*After* **edit_proc**	
pattern	##,###.##	pattern	⌴1,234.56
BCD value	123456		
pattern	##,###.##	pattern	⌴⌴⌴123.45
BCD value	12345		
pattern	##,###.##	pattern	⌴⌴⌴⌴⌴⌴.01
BCD value	1		

13.2

Packed BCD Instructions

Addition and subtraction operations for packed BCD numbers are similar to those for multiword 2's complement numbers (Section 4.5). Corresponding bytes of the two operands are added, and the carry from one addition is added to the next pair of bytes. There is no special addition instruction for BCD operands; the regular **add** and **adc** instructions are used. However, these instructions are designed for binary values, not BCD values, so for many operands they give the wrong sums.

The 8088 instruction set includes a **daa** (decimal adjust for addition) instruction, which is used after an addition instruction to correct the sum. This section explains the operation of the **daa** instruction and its counterpart **das** for subtraction. Procedures for addition and subtraction of 10-byte packed BCD numbers are developed, first for simple cases, then for general values, giving a complete addition, subtraction, and comparison package for this number representation.

A few examples illustrate the problem with using binary addition for BCD operands. The AF column gives the value of the auxiliary carry flag, the significance of which is discussed below.

Before		*After* **add al, bl**		
AL	*BL*	*AL*	*AF*	*CF*
34	25	59	0	0
37	25	SC	0	0
93	25	B8	0	0
28	39	61	1·	0
79	99	12	1	1

Although each answer is correct as the sum of two unsigned binary integers, only the first result is correct as a BCD value. The second and third sums contain bit patterns that are not used in BCD representations, C_{16} in the second example and B_{16} in the third. The last two sums contain no invalid digit—they are simply wrong as decimal sums.

The **daa** instruction is used after an addition instruction to convert a binary sum into a packed BCD sum. The instruction has no operand; the sum to be converted must be in the AL register half. A **daa** instruction examines and sets both the carry flag CF and the auxiliary carry flag AF. Recall that the carry flag is set to 1 during addition of two eight-bit numbers if there is a carry out of the left-most position. The AF flag similarly is set to 1 by **add** or **adc** instructions if there is a carry resulting from addition of the low-order four bits of the two operands. One way of thinking of this is that the sum of the two low-order hex digits is greater than F_{16}.

A **daa** first examines the right hex digit of the binary sum in AL. If this digit is over 9 (that is, A through F) then 6 is added to the entire sum and AF is set to 1. Notice that this would correct the result in the second example above since 5C + 6 = 62, the correct packed BCD sum of 37 and 25. The same correction is applied if AF = 1 when the **daa** is executed. Thus in the fourth example, 61 + 6 = 67.

After correcting the right digit, **daa** continues with the left digit in AL. The action is similar—if the left digit is over 9 or CF = 1, then 60_{16} is added to the entire sum. The carry flag CF is set to 1 in both cases. In the third example, B8 + 60 = 18 with a carry of 1.

Both digits must be corrected in the last example, 12 + 6 = 18 and 18 + 60 = 78 (CF = 1). The chart below completes the above examples, assuming that both of the following instructions are executed.

```
add    al, bl
daa
```

Before	After add		After daa	
AL: 34	AL: 59		AL: 59	
BL: 25	AF: 0	CF: 0	AF: 0	CF: 0
AL: 37	AL: 5C		AL: 62	
BL: 25	AF: 0	CF: 0	AF: 1	CF: 0
AL: 93	AL: B8		AL: 18	
BL: 25	AF: 0	CF: 0	AF: 0	CF: 1
AL: 28	AL: 61		AL: 67	
BL: 39	AF: 1	CF: 0	AF: 1	CF: 0
AL: 79	AL: 12		AL: 78	
BL: 99	AF: 1	CF: 1	AF: 1	CF: 1

The **das** instruction (decimal adjust for subtraction) is used after a **sub** or **sbb** instruction. It acts like the **daa** except that 6 or 60_{16} is subtracted rather than added to the value in AL. The following examples show how **das** works following **sub al,bl**. In the first example, both CF and AF are set to 1 since the subtraction requires borrows in both digit positions. When 6 and 60_{16} are subtracted from BC, the result is 56, and both CF and AF remain set to 1. This is the correct answer since $25 - 69 = 56$ (borrowing 1 to change 25 into 125.)

Before	*After* sub		*After* das	
AL: 25	AL: BC		AL: 56	
BL: 69	AF: 1	CF: 1	AF: 1	CF: 1
AL: 37	AL: 12		AL: 12	
BL: 25	AF: 0	CF: 0	AF: 0	CF: 0
AL: 93	AL: 6E		AL: 68	
BL: 25	AF: 1	CF: 0	AF: 1	CF: 0
AL: 92	AL: 59		AL: 53	
BL: 39	AF: 1	CF: 0	AF: 1	CF: 0
AL: 79	AL: E4		AL: 84	
BL: 95	AF: 0	CF: 1	AF: 0	CF: 1

The **daa** instruction takes a single byte of object code for its opcode 27. The **das** instruction has opcode 2F and no additional byte. Each requires four clock cycles to execute. In addition to modifying AF and CF, the **daa** or **das** instructions set or reset SF, ZF, and PF flags to correspond to the final value in AL. The overflow flag OF is undefined and other flags are not affected.

The first BCD arithmetic procedure in this section adds two nonnegative 10-byte numbers. Assume that SI points to one operand and DI points to the second operand, which is also the destination. This procedure is to be a building block for a complete set of packed BCD arithmetic procedures, so it should set flags in a fashion that is consistent with the **add** instruction. In particular, the sign flag SF should always be 0 when adding nonnegative numbers, the zero flag ZF should be 1 if the entire sum is zero, and the carry flag CF should be 1 if the sum is larger than 18 decimal digits. The overflow flag OF, auxiliary carry flag AF, and parity flag PF are all cleared to 0. A design for the procedure is given below.

```
save registers that will be modified;
set zero bit in flag byte, clear other bits;
clear carry flag in flag register;

for count := 1 to 9 loop
      copy destination byte to AL;
      add source byte to AL;
      use daa to convert sum to BCD;
      save AL in destination string;
      if AL is not zero
      then
            clear zero bit in flag byte;
      end if;
      increment DI and SI to point to next bytes;
end for;
```

if CF=1 from adding high order bytes
then

      set carry bit in flag byte;
end if;

store bits from flag byte in flag register;

restore registers that have been modified;
return;

This design is implemented in the procedure **add_bcd_1** (Figure 13.3). This procedure is **NEAR** since it is going to be part of a package of BCD procedures; it will only be called by other procedures in the same code segment. The processing of pairs of BCD bytes is done in a loop, with the instructions

```
mov   al, [di]   ; get one operand byte
adc   al, [si]   ; add other operand byte
daa              ; adjust to BCD
mov   [di], al   ; save sum
```

doing the work. A `clc` instruction zeros the carry flag prior to the loop so that addition of the low-order bytes does not need to be treated as a special case.

The flag values are handled using the AH register half as a collection of Boolean values, with bit 6 indicating a zero result. (This is the same bit position as is used in the flag register for the zero flag.) Initially this bit is set to 1, but it is changed to zero if the result of combining any pair of bytes is nonzero. No instruction in the loop after the **daa** changes the carry flag CF, so following the loop it still indicates whether or not a carry occurred in adding the high-order bytes of the two operands. If there was a carry, then bit 0 of AH is set to 1. To preserve original settings of the direction flag DF, the interrupt flag IF, and the trap flag TF, flag values are copied to CX using **pushf** and **pop** instructions. All bits except those for DF, IF, and TF are cleared. Then AH, with appropriate bits in the correct positions, is copied to CL. This leaves bit 11 corresponding to the overflow flag OF at zero, the bits for DF, IF, and TF (10, 9, and 8) unchanged, but ensures that the bits for SF, ZF, AF, PF, and CF (7, 6, 4, 2, and 0) get values from AH. Finally CX is copied back to the flag register using **push** and **popf** instructions.

A subtraction procedure for 10-byte packed BCD numbers is a little more difficult. Even with the operands restricted to nonnegative values, subtracting the source value (offset in SI) from the destination (offset in DI) will produce a negative result if the source is larger than the destination. The sign flag SF must be given an appropriate value, along with the zero flag ZF. However, the

Figure 13.3 Addition of Nonnegative Packed BCD Numbers.

```
add_bcd_1 PROC NEAR        ; add two nonnegative 10 byte packed BCD numbers
                           ; SI points to one number; DI to the other
; the sum replaces the operand to which DI points

          push si          ; save registers
          push di
          push cx
          push ax

          mov  ah, 01000000b  ; set zero bit in flag byte
          clc              ; clear carry flag in flag register
          mov  cx, 9       ; count of bytes to process
for_add:  mov  al, [di]    ; get one operand byte
          adc  al, [si]    ; add other operand byte
          daa              ; adjust to BCD
          mov  [di], al    ; save sum
          jz   next_add
          mov  ah, 0       ; clear "zero flag"
next_add: inc  di          ; point at next operand bytes
          inc  si
          loop for_add     ; repeat for all 9 bytes

          jnc  nc_add      ; skip if no carry from last daa
          or   ah, 1       ; set carry position in AH
nc_add:   pushf            ; copy flags to CX
          pop  cx
          and  cx, 0700h   ; zero all flag bits except DF, IF, TF
          or   cl, ah      ; ZF and CF from addition -- SF, AF, PF, OF each 0
          push cx          ; copy flags back to flag register
          popf

          pop  ax          ; restore registers
          pop  cx
          pop  di
          pop  si
          ret              ; return to caller

add_bcd_1 ENDP
```

carry flag will always be 0 since the difference is certain to fit in 18 decimal digits. A design for the procedure is below.

```
save registers that will be modified;
set zero bit in flag byte, clear other bits;
clear carry flag in flag register;

for count := 1 to 9 loop
        copy destination byte to AL;
        subtract source byte from AL;
        use das to convert difference to BCD;
        save AL in destination string;
        if AL is not zero
        then
                clear zero bit in flag byte;
        end if;
        increment DI and SI to point to next bytes;
end for;

if source > destination
then
        move DI back to first of destination;

        for count := 1 to 9 loop
                put 0 in AL;
                subtract destination byte from AL;
                use das to convert difference to BCD;
                save AL in destination string;
                increment DI;
        end for;

        move sign byte 80 to destination string;
        set sign bit in flag byte;
end if;

store bits from flag byte in flag register;

restore registers that have been modified;
return;
```

The first part of this design is almost the same as the design for addition. The condition (source > destination) is true if the carry flag is set after the first loop, and the difference is corrected by subtracting it from zero. If this were not done, then, for example, 3–7 would produce 999999999999999996 instead of –4. This design is implemented in the code for procedure **sub_bcd_1** in Figure 13.4.

Figure 13.5 shows a complete package for addition, subtraction and comparison of 10-byte packed BCD numbers. It is intended for separate assembly, with the procedures **add_bcd**, **sub_bcd**, and **cmp_bcd** accessible to other programs. It incorporates the special purpose procedures **add_bcd_1** and **sub_bcd_1**, which are utilized by the general procedures but are not listed in the **PUBLIC** directive. The general-purpose procedures are discussed below.

Figure 13.4 Subtraction of Nonnegative Packed BCD Numbers.

```
sub_bcd_1 PROC NEAR      ; subtract 2 nonnegative 10 byte packed BCD numbers
                         ; SI points to one number; DI to the other
; (destination - source) replaces destination

          push si        ; save registers
          push di
          push cx
          push ax

          mov  ah, 01000000b ; set zero bit in flag byte
          clc                ; clear carry flag in flag register
          mov  cx, 9     ; count of bytes to process
for_sub:  mov  al, [di]  ; get one operand byte
          sbb  al, [si]  ; subtract other operand byte
          das            ; adjust to BCD
          mov  [di], al  ; save difference
          jz   next_sub
          mov  ah, 0     ; clear "zero flag"
next_sub: inc  di        ; point at next operand bytes
          inc  si
          loop for_sub   ; repeat for all 9 bytes

          jz   setflags  ; done if result zero
          jnc  setflags  ; done if destination >= source

          sub  di, 9     ; point at beginning of destination
          mov  cx, 9     ; count of bytes to process
for_sub1: mov  al, 0     ; subtract destination from zero
          sbb  al, [di]
          das
          mov  [di], al
          inc  di        ; next byte
          loop for_sub1

          mov  BYTE PTR [di], 80h  ; negative result
          or   ah, 10000000b       ; sign bit
```

Figure 13.4 Continued.

```
setflags: pushf              ; copy flags to CX
          pop  cx
          and  cx, 0700h ; zero all flag bits except DF, IF, TF
          or   cl, ah    ; ZF and SF from subtraction -- CF, AF, PF, OF each 0
          push cx        ; copy flags back to flag register
          popf

          pop  ax        ; restore registers
          pop  cx
          pop  di
          pop  si
          ret            ; return to caller
sub_bcd_1 ENDP
```

Figure 13.5 General Packed BCD Procedures.

```
PUBLIC add_bcd, sub_bcd, cmp_bcd

bcd_code  SEGMENT
          ASSUME ds:bcd_code, cs:bcd_code

source    DT  ?              ; local copies of source and destination
dest      DT  ?

add_bcd_1 PROC NEAR
                            ; see Figure 13.3
add_bcd_1 ENDP


sub_bcd_1 PROC NEAR
                            ; see Figure 13.4
sub_bcd_1 ENDP


add_bcd   PROC FAR          ; add two 10 byte BCD numbers
                            ; SI points to one number; DI to the other
; the sum replaces the operand to which DI points

          push cx           ; save registers
          push bx
          push ax
          push es
          push ds
          push si
          push di
```

Figure 13.5 Continued.

```
            mov   ax, ds      ; copy original data segment number to ES
            mov   es, ax

            mov   ax, SEG bcd_code  ; load new segment number in DS
            mov   ds, ax

; copy source operand to local storage
            mov   bx, 0                    ; initial index
            mov   cx, 10                   ; bytes to copy
for_a1:     mov   al, es:[si]             ; get source byte
            mov   BYTE PTR source[bx], al  ; store
            inc   bx                       ; increment index
            inc   si                       ; increment source pointer
            loop  for_a1

; repeat to copy destination operand
            mov   bx, 0
            mov   cx, 10
for_a2:     mov   al, es:[di]
            mov   BYTE PTR dest[bx], al
            inc   bx
            inc   di
            loop  for_a2

            mov   al, BYTE PTR source+9  ; if both operands nonnegative
            or    al, BYTE PTR dest+9
            jnz   elseif_a1

            mov   si, OFFSET source     ; then use add_bcd_1 for operands
            mov   di, OFFSET dest
            call  add_bcd_1
            jmp   end_if_add

elseif_a1:
            mov   al, BYTE PTR source+9  ; elseif both operands negative
            and   al, BYTE PTR dest+9
            jz    elseif_a2
            mov   BYTE PTR source+9, 0   ; then change source
            mov   BYTE PTR dest+9, 0     ;    and dest to positive
            mov   si, OFFSET source      ; use add_bcd_1 for absolute values
            mov   di, OFFSET dest
            call  add_bcd_1
            jz    end_if_add             ; done if result zero
            mov   BYTE PTR dest+9, 80h   ; make result negative
            lahf                         ; set sign flag
            or    ah, 80h
            sahf
            jmp   end_if_add
```

Figure 13.5 Continued.

```
elseif_a2:
          cmp  BYTE PTR source+9, 80h ; elseif source negative
          jne  else_a3
          mov  BYTE PTR source+9, 0   ; then make source positive
          mov  si, OFFSET source      ; use sub_bcd_1 to subtract
          mov  di, OFFSET dest
          call sub_bcd_1
          jmp  end_if_add

else_a3:  mov  BYTE PTR dest+9, 0      ; change negative dest to positive
          mov  si, OFFSET dest         ; use sub_bcd_1 for source - dest
          mov  di, OFFSET source
          call sub_bcd_1
          pushf                        ; save flags
          mov  cx, 10                  ; copy source to destination
for_a3:   mov  al, [di]
          mov  [si], al
          inc  si
          inc  di
          loop for_a3
          popf                         ; restore flags

end_if_add:

; copy local destination back to original destination operand
          pop  di           ; offset in caller's data segment
          push di
          pushf             ; save flags
          mov  si, OFFSET dest
          mov  cx, 10        ; bytes to copy
          cld
          rep movsb
          popf              ; restore flags

          pop  di           ; restore registers
          pop  si
          pop  ds
          pop  es
          pop  ax
          pop  bx
          pop  cx

          ret               ; return to caller

add_bcd   ENDP
```

Figure 13.5 Continued.

```
sub_bcd   PROC FAR        ; subtract two 10 byte BCD numbers
                          ; SI points to one number; DI to the other
; difference (destination - source) replaces the operand to which DI points

          push cx         ; save registers
          push bx
          push ax
          push es
          push ds
          push si
          push di

          mov  ax, ds     ; copy original data segment number to ES
          mov  es, ax

          mov  ax, SEG bcd_code  ; load new segment number in DS
          mov  ds, ax

; copy source operand to local storage
          mov  bx, 0             ; initial index
          mov  cx, 10            ; bytes to copy
for_s1:   mov  al, es:[si]       ; get source byte
          mov  BYTE PTR source[bx], al ; store
          inc  bx               ; increment index
          inc  si               ; increment source pointer
          loop for_s1

; repeat to copy destination operand
          mov  bx, 0
          mov  cx, 10
for_s2:   mov  al, es:[di]
          mov  BYTE PTR dest[bx], al
          inc  bx
          inc  di
          loop for_s2

          mov  al, BYTE PTR source+9  ; if both operands nonnegative
          or   al, BYTE PTR dest+9
          jnz  elseif_s1

          mov  si, OFFSET source      ; then use sub_bcd_1 for operands
          mov  di, OFFSET dest
          call sub_bcd_1
          jmp  end_if_sub

elseif_s1:
          mov  al, BYTE PTR source+9  ; elseif both operands negative
          and  al, BYTE PTR dest+9
```

Figure 13.5 Continued.

```
            jz    elseif_s2
            mov   BYTE PTR source+9, 0   ; then change source
            mov   BYTE PTR dest+9, 0     ;     and dest to positive
            mov   di, OFFSET source      ; sub_bcd_1 -source,-dest
            mov   si, OFFSET dest
            call sub_bcd_1
            pushf                        ; save flags
            mov   cx, 10                 ; copy source to destination
for_s3:     mov   al, [di]
            mov   [si], al
            inc   si
            inc   di
            loop for_s3
            popf                         ; restore flags
            jmp   end_if_sub

elseif_s2:
            cmp   BYTE PTR source+9, 80h ; elseif source negative
            jne   else_s3
            mov   BYTE PTR source+9, 0   ; then make source positive
            mov   si, OFFSET source      ; use add_bcd_1 dest,-source
            mov   di, OFFSET dest
            call add_bcd_1
            jmp   end_if_sub

else_s3:    mov   BYTE PTR dest+9, 0     ; change negative dest to positive
            mov   di, OFFSET dest        ; use add_bcd_1 -dest,source
            mov   si, OFFSET source
            call add_bcd_1
            jz    end_if_sub             ; done if result zero
            mov   BYTE PTR dest+9, 80h   ; result is negative
            lahf                         ; set sign flag
            or    ah, 80h
            sahf

end_if_sub:

; copy local destination back to original destination operand
            pop   di        ; offset in caller's data segment
            push di
            pushf           ; save flags
            mov   si, OFFSET dest
            mov   cx, 10    ; bytes to copy
            cld
            rep movsb
            popf            ; restore flags
```

Figure 13.5 Continued.

```
            pop  di        ; restore registers
            pop  si
            pop  ds
            pop  es
            pop  ax
            pop  bx
            pop  cx

            ret            ; return to caller

sub_bcd     ENDP


cmp_bcd     PROC FAR       ; compare two 10 byte BCD numbers
                           ; SI points to one number; DI to the other
; no operand is changed -- flags set for difference (destination - source)

            push cx        ; save registers
            push bx
            push ax
            push es
            push ds
            push si
            push di

            mov  ax, ds    ; copy original data segment number to ES
            mov  es, ax

            mov  ax, SEG bcd_code  ; load new segment number in DS
            mov  ds, ax

; copy source operand to local storage
            mov  bx, 0                  ; initial index
            mov  cx, 10                 ; bytes to copy
for_c1:     mov  al, es:[si]            ; get source byte
            mov  BYTE PTR source[bx], al  ; store
            inc  bx                     ; increment index
            inc  si                     ; increment source pointer
            loop for_c1
```

Figure 13.5 Continued.

```
; repeat to copy destination operand
            mov   bx, 0
            mov   cx, 10
for_c2:     mov   al, es:[di]
            mov   BYTE PTR dest[bx], al
            inc   bx
            inc   di
            loop for_c2

            mov   al, BYTE PTR source+9  ; if both operands nonnegative
            or    al, BYTE PTR dest+9
            jnz   elseif_c1

            mov   si, OFFSET source      ; then use sub_bcd_1 for operands
            mov   di, OFFSET dest
            call sub_bcd_1
            jmp   end_if_cmp
elseif_c1:
            mov   al, BYTE PTR source+9  ; elseif both operands negative
            and   al, BYTE PTR dest+9
            jz    elseif_c2
            mov   BYTE PTR source+9, 0   ; then change source
            mov   BYTE PTR dest+9, 0     ;     and dest to positive
            mov   di, OFFSET source      ; sub_bcd_1 -source,-dest
            mov   si, OFFSET dest
            call sub_bcd_1
            jmp   end_if_cmp
elseif_c2:
            cmp   BYTE PTR source+9, 80h ; elseif source negative
            jne   else_c3
            mov   BYTE PTR source+9, 0   ; then make source positive
            mov   si, OFFSET source      ; use add_bcd_1 dest,-source
            mov   di, OFFSET dest
            call add_bcd_1
            jmp   end_if_cmp

else_c3:    mov   BYTE PTR dest+9, 0     ; change negative dest to positive
            mov   di, OFFSET dest        ; use add_bcd_1 -dest,source
            mov   si, OFFSET source
            call add_bcd_1
            jz    end_if_cmp             ; done if result zero
            lahf                         ; set sign flag
            or    ah, 80h
            sahf
end_if_cmp:
```

Figure 13.5 Continued.

```
            pop  di          ; restore registers
            pop  si
            pop  ds
            pop  es
            pop  ax
            pop  bx
            pop  cx
            ret              ; return to caller

cmp_bcd   ENDP

bcd_code  ENDS
          END
```

Each of the procedures add_bcd, sub_bcd, and cmp_bcd uses two parameters, a destination operand with offset passed to the procedure in DI and a source operand with offset in SI. The addition and subtraction procedures replace the destination by (destination+source) and (destination −source), respectively. They also set flags corresponding to the result of the operation: the sign flag SF and the zero flag ZF are given customary values, the carry flag CF is set to 1 if the sum or difference is larger than 18 decimal digits, and each of the overflow flag OF, auxiliary carry flag AF, and parity flag PF are cleared to zero. Other flags are unchanged. The cmp_bcd does not change the destination; it just sets flags identically as set by sub_bcd.

All procedures are contained in a segment bcd_code. This segment begins with two DT directives that provide local storage for the caller's packed BCD values. Each procedure first copies the caller's destination and source values to this local storage. The add_bcd and sub_bcd procedures (but not cmp_bcd) copy the local destination back to the caller's destination before exiting. Copying to a procedure involves using DS to hold the segment number of bcd_code and ES to hold the segment number of the caller's data segment. The loop

```
; copy source operand to local storage
            mov   bx, 0                     ; initial index
            mov   cx, 10                    ; bytes to copy
for_s1:     mov   al, es:[si]               ; get source byte
            mov   BYTE PTR source[bx], al   ; store
            inc   bx                        ; increment index
            inc   si                        ; increment source pointer
            loop for_s1
```

copies the source operand. Note the use of the segment override in es:[si] to get a source byte from the caller's data segment.

A **rep movsb** makes it easier to copy the local destination back to the caller's storage at the end of a procedure. A similar instruction is not used at the beginning of a procedure since DS contains the segment number for the destination and ES contains the segment number for the source, the opposite of the arrangement needed for string instructions. Another complication is that both SI and DI are in use with the caller's offsets.

Basically each procedure chooses one of four actions depending on the signs of the operands. In each case, the operation is translated to a sum or difference of non-negative numbers that is handled by **add_bcd_1** or **sub_bcd_1**. Some cases then require a changed sign in the result, a flag to be set, or the local source value to be copied to the local destination value if source and destination roles were reversed. A complete design for **add_bcd** is below.

```
    save registers that will be modified;
    copy caller's parameters to local 10-byte storage areas;

    if both destination and source are nonnegative
    then
            add_bcd_1 (destination, source);

    elseif both destination and source are negative
    then { use – [-destination + (-source)] }
            destination := -destination;
            source := -source;
            add_bcd_1 (destination, source);
            if sum is not zero
            then
                    destination := –destination;
                    SF := 1;
            end if;

    elseif destination nonnegative and source negative
    then { use destination – (–source) }
            source := -source;
            sub_bcd_1 (destination, source);

    else { destination negative and source nonnegative }
            { use source – (-destination) }
            destination := -destination;
            sub_bcd_1 (source, destination);
            destination := source;
    end if;

    copy local destination back to caller's storage;
    restore registers that were altered;
    return;
```

In the second case (both operands negative), the corresponding positive values are added. Unless the result is zero (from adding two negative 0's), the correct answer is the negation of the sum, so 80_{16} is appended to the destination string and the sign flag SF is set to 1. The sign flag SF is altered using the `lahf` and `sahf` instructions. The `lahf` instruction copies the low-order byte from the flag register into AH and the `sahf` copies AH to the low-order byte of the flag register. The instructions

```
lahf
or    ah, 80h
sahf
```

therefore make SF = 1 without changing other flag bits. The `or` instruction does clear OF to 0 in the high-order byte of the flag register, but that is no problem since 0 is the desired value in all cases.

The `lahf` instruction has opcode 9F and `sahf` has opcode 9E. Each takes 1 byte of object code and requires four clock cycles to execute. Neither is frequently used. In **add_bcd** the sign flag could be set using the same techniques as were used in **add_bcd_1** and **sub_bcd_1**.

The general subtraction algorithm is similar to the one for addition. The following design shows what is done in each of the four cases.

if both destination and source are nonnegative
then
    sub_bcd_1 (destination, source);

elseif both destination and source are negative
then { use -source – (-destination) }
    destination := -destination;
    source := -source;
    sub_bcd_1 (source, destination);
    destination := source;

elseif destination nonnegative and source negative
then { use destination + (-source) }
    source := -source;
    add_bcd_1 (destination, source);

else { destination negative and source nonnegative }
    { use – (-destination + source) }
    destination := -destination;
    add_bcd_1 (destination, source);
    if sum not zero
    then
        destination := -destination;
        SF := 1;
    end if;
end if;

Since comparison of two operands involves setting flags exactly as a subtraction operation would set them, the code for **cmp_bcd** is very similar to that for **sub_bcd**. In fact, **cmp_bcd** actually calculates the difference of the local copies of the operands, but omits the instructions used to get the result back to the caller.

The procedures in this section effectively extend the 8088 instruction set. This section concludes with an example of a simple program that finds the sum and maximum of a collection of large positive integers entered at the terminal. This example (in Figure 13.6) points out the uses and the limitations of the new "instructions." The exercises suggest a variety of ways in which the package for 10-byte packed BCD arithmetic can be further enhanced.

Figure 13.6 Sum and Maximum Using BCD Numbers.

```
; program to find the sum and maximum of a collection of large integers

INCLUDE io.h

EXTRN add_bcd:FAR, sub_bcd:FAR, cmp_bcd:FAR

cr          EQU 13
Lf          EQU 10

stack       SEGMENT STACK
            DW      256 DUP (?)
stack       ENDS

data        SEGMENT
prelim      DB      cr,Lf,'This program will find the sum and maximum of a', cr, Lf
            DB      'of positive integers.  Enter values one at a time,', cr, Lf
            DB      'using 9999999999 (10 9''s) to terminate input.', cr, Lf, 0
prompt      DB      cr, Lf, 'Value?  ', 0
str_in      DB      20 DUP (?)
value       DT      ?
sentinel    DT      9999999999
max         DT      0
sum         DT      0
results     DB      cr, Lf, Lf, 'Sum:'
sum_out     DB      19 DUP (?)
            DB      '        Maximum:'
max_out     DB      19 DUP (?), cr, Lf, 0
data        ENDS
```

Figure 13.6 Continued.

```
code      SEGMENT
          ASSUME ds:data, cs:code

dtoa_proc PROC NEAR
                            ; see Figure 13.1
dtoa_proc ENDP


atod_proc PROC NEAR
                            ; see Figure 13.2
atod_proc ENDP


start:    mov  ax, SEG data  ; initialize data segment number
          mov  ds, ax
          mov  es, ax        ; data segment = extra segment

          output prelim      ; display instructions

while:    output prompt      ; prompt for value
          inputs str_in, 20  ; input value in ASCII format

          mov  di, OFFSET value  ; convert to BCD
          mov  si, OFFSET str_in
          call atod_proc

          mov  si, OFFSET value  ; compare value and sentinel
          mov  di, OFFSET sentinel
          call cmp_bcd
          je   end_while     ; exit loop if equal

          mov  di, OFFSET sum     ; add value to sum
          call add_bcd

          mov  di, OFFSET max      ; compare value to maximum so far
          call cmp_bcd
          jnle end_if

          ; new value is larger -- copy to max
          mov  di, OFFSET max    ; destination
          mov  si, OFFSET value  ; source
          cld                    ; copy forward
          mov  cx, 10            ; 10 bytes to copy
          rep movsb              ; move 10 bytes of string
end_if:
          jmp  while             ; repeat
end_while:
```

Figure 13.6 Continued

```
        mov     di, OFFSET sum_out ; convert sum to ASCII
        mov     si, OFFSET sum
        call    dtoa_proc

        mov     di, OFFSET max_out ; convert maximum to ASCII
        mov     si, OFFSET max
        call    dtoa_proc

        output results

exit:   mov  ax, 4c00h              ; function 4C, error code 0
        int  21h                    ; call DOS to exit

code    ENDS
        END  start
```

Exercises 13.2

1. In each part below, assume that the instructions

   ```
   add    al, bl
   daa
   ```

   are executed. Give the values in the register half AL, carry flag CF and auxiliary flag AF: (1) after the **add** and before the **daa** and (2) after the **daa**.

(a)	AL:	35	BL:	42	(b)	AL:	27	BL:	61
(c)	AL:	35	BL:	48	(d)	AL:	47	BL:	61
(e)	AL:	35	BL:	92	(f)	AL:	27	BL:	69
(g)	AL:	75	BL:	46	(h)	AL:	00	BL:	61
(i)	AL:	85	BL:	82	(j)	AL:	89	BL:	98
(k)	AL:	76	BL:	89	(l)	AL:	27	BL:	00

2. Repeat each of the parts of Exercise 1 for the instructions

   ```
   sub    al, bl
   das
   ```

Programming Exercises 13.2

---

1. Write a **neg_bcd** procedure that has one parameter, a 10-byte packed BCD value whose offset is passed to the procedure in DI. The procedure should negate (reverse the sign of) the BCD value. Values of the AF, CF, OF, PF, SF, and ZF flags should be set or cleared appropriately. In particular, SF should be 1 if the result is negative and ZF should be 1 if the result is zero. Watch out for negative zero, 00 00 00 00 00 00 00 00 00 80.

2. Although the procedures in this section effectively add new functions to the 8088 instruction set, the procedure calls are more awkward to use than normal instructions. Remedy this situation by defining **add_d**, **sub_d**, and **cmp_d** macros. Each macro should have two parameters, referencing 10-byte packed BCD values in memory. The order of the parameters should be consistent with 8088 **add**, **sub**, and **cmp** instructions. A macro call should generate code to preserve and restore registers, load the offsets of the arguments into DI and SI, and call the appropriate procedure.

3. It takes several instructions to copy a 10-byte packed BCD value from one address to another. Define a **mov_d** macro to do this job. The macro should have two parameters, referencing 10-byte-long storage areas. A macro call should generate code to preserve and restore registers, and copy the contents of the second area to the first.

4. Write a complete program that implements the following design to keep accounts for a firm with large credits and debits. Store all values internally in 10-byte packed BCD format.

   balance := 0;

   forever loop
           display "[C]redit, [D]ebit, [Q]uit ?";
           input choice;
           if choice="q" or "Q" then exit loop;

           display "Amount? ";
           input amount;
           convert amount from ASCII to BCD;
           if choice="c" or "C"
           then
                   add amount to balance;
           else
                   subtract amount from balance;
           end if;

           convert balance to ASCII;
           display "New balance", balance;

   end loop;

5. This section has said nothing about multiplication of 10-byte packed BCD numbers. Develop an algorithm for multiplication of two such numbers and implement it in a `mul_bcd` procedure.

6. This section has said nothing about division of 10-byte packed BCD numbers. Develop an algorithm for division of two such numbers and implement it in a `div_bcd` procedure.

13.3

Unpacked BCD Representations and Instructions

Unpacked BCD numbers differ from packed representations by storing one decimal digit per byte instead of two. The bit pattern in the left half of each byte is 0000. This section describes how to define unpacked BCD numbers, how to convert this representation to and from ASCII, and how to use 8088 instructions to do some arithmetic operations with unpacked BCD numbers.

There is no standard length for unpacked BCD representations. In this section each value will be stored in eight bytes, with high-order digits on the left and low-order digits on the right (the reverse of the way a DT directive stores packed BCD numbers). No sign byte will be used, son only non-negative numbers will be represented. An ordinary DB directive can be used to initialize an unpacked BCD value. For example, the statement

```
DB   0,0,0,5,4,3,2,8
```

reserves eight bytes of storage containing 00 00 00 05 04 03 02 08, the unpacked BCD representation for 54328. The directive

```
DB   8 DUP (?)
```

establishes an eight-byte-long area which can be used to store an unpacked BCD value.[*]

It is simple to convert an unpacked BCD value to or from ASCII. Suppose that the data segment of a program includes the directives

```
ascii      DB   8 DUP (?)
unpacked   DB   8 DUP (?)
```

If **unpacked** already contains an unpacked BCD value, the following code fragment will produce the corresponding ASCII representation at `ascii`.

---

[*] The DQ (define quadword) directive could also be used to reserve an eight-byte-long storage area. A DQ can only be used to reserve space for a BCD value, not to initialize a BCD value. If a numeric operand is specified with a DQ, storage is initialized to either a floating point value or a 2's complement integer, depending on the presence or absence of a decimal point in the operand.

```
                mov    di, OFFSET ascii        ; destination
                mov    si, OFFSET unpacked     ; source
                mov    cx, 8                   ; bytes to process
        for:    mov    al, [si]                ; get digit
                or     al, 30h                 ; convert to ASCII
                mov    [di], al                ; store ASCII character
                inc    di                      ; increment pointers
                inc    si
                loop   for                     ; repeat for all bytes
```

Converting from an ASCII string to an unpacked BCD representation is equally easy. The same loop structure can be used with the roles of DI and SI reversed, and with the **or** instruction replaced by

```
        and    al, 0fh         ; convert ASCII to unpacked BCD
```

Conversions between ASCII and unpacked BCD are even simpler if they are done in place (see Exercise 3).

The 8088 instruction set includes four instructions to facilitate arithmetic with unpacked BCD representations. Each mnemonic begins with **aa** for "ASCII adjust"—Intel uses the word *ASCII* to describe unpacked BCD representations, even though the ASCII representation for a digit has 0011 in the left half-byte and the unpacked representation has 0000. The four instructions are **aaa**, **aas**, **aam**, and **aad**. Information about these instructions is given in Figure 13.7.

The **aaa** and **aas** instructions are similar to their packed BCD counterparts **daa** and **das**. For addition, bytes containing unpacked BCD operands are combined using an **add** or **adc** instruction, yielding a sum in the AL register half. An **aaa** instruction then corrects the value in AL, if necessary. An **aaa** instruction sets flags and may also affect AH; recall that a **daa** affects only AL and flags. The following algorithm describes how **aaa** works.

```
        if (right digit in AL > 9) or (AF=1)
        then
              add 6 to AL;
              increment AH;
              AF := 1;
        end if;

        CF := AF;
        left digit in AL := 0;
```

The action of an **aas** instruction is similar. The first two operations inside the **if** are replaced by

```
        subtract 6 from AL;
        decrement AH;
```

The OF, PF, SF, and ZF flags are left undefined by **aaa** and **aas** instructions.

Figure 13.7 Unpacked BCD Instructions.

Instruction	Mnemonic	Clock Cycles	Number of Bytes	Opcode
ASCII adjust for addition	**aaa**	4	1	37
ASCII adjust for subtraction	**aas**	4	1	3F
ASCII adjust for multiplication	**aam**	83	2	D4 0A
ASCII adjust for division	**aad**	60	2	D5 0A

Here are some examples of showing how **add** and **aaa** work together. In each example, assume that the following pair of instructions is executed.

```
add   al, ch
aaa
```

Before	*After* **add**	*After* **aaa**
AX: 00 04	AX: 00 07	AX: 00 07
CH: 03	AF: 0	AF: 0 CF: 0
AX: 00 04	AX: 00 0B	AX: 01 01
CH: 07	AF: 0	AF: 1 CF: 1
AX: 0 08	AX: 00 11	AX: 01 07
CH: 09	AF: 1	AF: 1 CF: 1
AX: 05 05	AX: 05 0C	AX: 06 02
CH: 07	AF: 0	AF: 1 CF: 1

Another set of examples illustrates how **sub** and **aas** find differences of single-byte unpacked BCD operands. This time, assume that the following instructions are executed.

```
sub   al, dl
aas
```

Before	*After* **sub**	*After* **aas**
AX: 00 08	AX: 00 05	AX: 00 05
DL: 03	AF: 0	AF: 0 CF: 0
AX: 00 04	AX: 00 FD	AX: FF 07
DL: 07	AF: 1	AF: 1 CF: 1
AX: 05 02	AX: 05 F9	AX: 04 03
DL: 09	AF: 1	AF: 1 CF: 1

Figure 13.8 Addition of Two Eight-byte Unpacked BCD Numbers.

```
add_unp     PROC FAR        ; add two 8 byte unpacked BCD numbers
                            ; SI points to one number; DI to the other
; the sum replaces the operand to which DI points

            push cx         ; save registers
            push ax

            add  si, 8      ; point at byte after source
            add  di, 8      ; byte after destination
            clc             ; clear carry flag
            mov  cx, 8      ; count of bytes to process
for_add:    dec  di         ; point at operand bytes to left
            dec  si
            mov  al, [di]   ; get one operand byte
            adc  al, [si]   ; add other operand byte
            aaa             ; adjust to unpacked BCD
            mov  [di], al   ; save sum
            loop for_add    ; repeat for all 9 bytes

            pop  ax         ; restore registers
            pop  cx
            ret             ; return to caller

add_unp     ENDP
```

Figure 13.8 displays a procedure add_unp that can be used for addition of eight-byte unpacked BCD numbers. This procedure is simpler than the similar add_bcd_1 procedure in Figure 13.3. In particular, no effort is made to produce significant flag values; only the value of the carry flag CF is meaningful after the procedure is executed. Since low-order digits are stored to the right, the bytes are processed right to left. It is not necessary to push and pop SI and DI since 8 is added to each before the loop that decrements them eight times. (Programming Exercise 1 specifies the corresponding procedure for subtraction.)

One interesting thing about the procedure add_unp is that it will give the correct unpacked BCD sum of eight-byte *ASCII* (not unpacked BCD) numbers—Intel's use of "ASCII" in the unpacked BCD mnemonics is not as unreasonable as it first seems. The procedure is successful for ASCII strings since the action of the aaa instruction depends only on what add does with low-order digits, and aaa always sets the high-order digit in AL to zero. However, even if the operands are true ASCII strings, the sum is not ASCII, it is unpacked BCD.

Two single byte unpacked BCD operands are multiplied using an ordinary mul instruction, resulting in a product in the AX register. Since single digits have value at most 9, the product in AX is at most 81_{10} (51_{16}). A byte can hold an binary number up to 127_{10}, so AH will contain leading zeros. The **aam** instruction converts the product in AX to two unpacked BCD digits in AH and AL. In effect, an **aam** instruction divides the number in AL by 10, putting the quotient in AH and the remainder in AL. The following examples assume that the instructions

```
mul   bh
aam
```

are executed.

Before	*After* **mul**	*After* **aam**
AX: 00 09		
BH: 09	AX: 00 51	AX: 08 01
AX: 00 05		
BH: 06	AX: 00 1E	AX: 03 00
AX: 00 06		
BH: 07	AX: 00 2A	AX: 04 02

Some flags are affected by an **aam** instruction. The PF, SF, and ZF flags are given values corresponding to the final value in AX; the AF, CF, and OF flags are undefined. Most programs are not concerned with flag settings following an **aam**.

Multiplication of single-digit numbers is not very useful. Figure 13.9 gives a procedure **mul_unp_1** to multiply an eight-byte unpacked BCD number by a single-digit unpacked BCD number. The offset of the eight-byte operand is in SI and the single-digit operand is in BL. The DI register contains the offset of an eight-byte destination field—instead of replacing one operand, the product is stored as a third parameter.

The algorithm that is implemented is essentially the same one as used by grade-school children. The single digit is multiplied times the low-order digit of the multidigit number, the units digit is stored and the tens digit is recorded as a carry to add to the next product. All eight products can be treated the same by initializing a last_carry variable to zero prior to beginning a loop. Here is the design that is actually implemented.

{ multiply $X_7X_6X_5X_4X_3X_2X_1X_0$ times Y giving $Z_7Z_6Z_5Z_4Z_3Z_2Z_1Z_0$}

```
last_carry := 0;
for i := 0 to 7 loop
      multiply X_i times Y;
      add last_carry;
      Z_i := units digit;
      last_carry := tens digit;
end for;
```

In the code for **mul_unp**, the value for last_carry is stored in the BH register half. After a digit from the eight-byte BCD value is multiplied by the single digit

Figure 13.9 Multiplication of Unpacked BCD Numbers.

```
mul_unp_1 PROC FAR         ; multiply 8 byte and 1 byte unpacked BCD numbers
                           ; SI points to 8 byte number, single byte in BL
; DI contains offset of destination field

          push cx          ; save registers
          push bx
          push ax

          add  si, 8       ; point at byte after source
          add  di, 8       ; byte after destination
          mov  bh, 0       ; last_carry := 0
          mov  cx, 8       ; count of bytes to process
for_mul:  dec  si          ; point at operand byte to left
          dec  di          ; and at destination byte
          mov  al, [si]    ; digit from 8 byte number
          mul  bl          ; multiply by single byte
          aam              ; adjust to unpacked BCD
          add  al, bh      ; add last_carry
          aaa              ; adjust to unpacked BCD
          mov  [di], al    ; store units digit
          mov  bh, ah      ; store last_carry
          loop for_mul     ; repeat for all 9 bytes

          pop  ax          ; restore registers
          pop  bx
          pop  cx
          ret              ; return to caller

mul_unp_1 ENDP
```

in BL, the product is adjusted to unpacked BCD and last_carry is added. It is then necessary to adjust the sum to unpacked BCD. Actually, the sequence

```
          mul  bl          ; multiply by single byte
          add  al, bh      ; add last_carry
          aam              ; adjust to unpacked BCD
```

could replace the four instructions used, saving four clock cycles per iteration of the loop. This change simply involves adding last_carry in binary rather than decimal.

The **aad** instruction essentially reverses the action of the **aam** instruction. It combines a two-digit unpacked BCD value in AH and AL into a single binary value in AX, multiplying the digit in AH by 10 and adding the digit in AL. The AH register half is always cleared to 00. The PF, SF, and ZF flags are given values corresponding to the result; AF, CF, and OF are undefined.

The **aad** instruction is used *before* a **div** instruction, contrary to the other

"ASCII adjust" instructions, which are used after the corresponding arithmetic instructions. The examples below assume that the instructions

```
aad
div   dh
```

are executed.

Before	*After* **aad**	*After* **div**
AX: 07 05	AX: 00 4B	AX: 03 09
DH:108	DH: 08	
AX: 06 02	AX: 00 3E	AX: 02 0F
DH: 04	DH: 04	
AX: 09 03	AX: 00 5D	AX: 01 2E
DH: 02	DH: 02	

In the first example, the quotient and remainder are in BCD format in AL and AH, respectively, following the **div** instruction. However, the second and third examples show that this is not always the case. The remainder is correct in AH because it is a binary remainder following division by a number 9 or smaller. The remainder must be 0 through 8, and for numbers in this range a single-byte binary value agrees with the unpacked BCD representation. The quotient in AL is obviously a binary number, not a BCD representation. To convert it to unpacked BCD, an **aam** instruction needs to follow the **div**. In the second example, this would change AX to 01 05, the correct quotient for 62/4. In the third example, **aam** would yield 04 06 in AX, again the correct quotient. Notice that the remainder from the division is lost, so if it is needed, it must be copied from AH before **aam** is executed.

Notice that the problems illustrated by the above examples cannot occur when the digit in AH is smaller than the divisor in DH. The elementary-school algorithm for dividing a single-digit into a multidigit number works left to right through the dividend, dividing a two-digit number by the divisor. The first of the two digits is the remainder from the previous division, which must be smaller than the divisor. The following design formalizes the grade-school algorithm.

{ divide $X_7X_6X_5X_4X_3X_2X_1X_0$ by Y giving $Z_7Z_6Z_5Z_4Z_3Z_2Z_1Z_0$ }

```
last_remainder := 0;
for i := 7 downto 0 loop
      dividend := 10 * last_remainder + X_i;
      divide dividend by Y getting quotient & last_remainder;
      Z_i := quotient;
end for;
```

Code that implements this design is given in Figure 13.10. The AH register is ideally suited to store last_remainder since that is where the remainder ends up following division of a 16-bit binary number by an 8-bit number.

Figure 13.10   Division of Unpacked BCD Numbers.

```
div_unp_1 PROC FAR          ; divide 8 byte unpacked BCD number by 1 byte number
                            ; SI points to 8 byte number, single byte in BL
; DI contains offset of destination field

                push cx          ; save registers
                push ax
                push si
                push di

                mov   ah, 0    ; last_remainder := 0
                mov   cx, 8    ; count of bytes to process
for_div:        mov   al, [si] ; digit from 8 byte number
                aad            ; adjust to binary
                div   bl       ; divide by single byte
                mov   [di], al ; store quotient
                inc   si       ; point at next digit of dividend
                inc   di       ; and at next destination byte
                loop for_div   ; repeat for all 9 bytes

                pop   di       ; restore registers
                pop   si
                pop   ax
                pop   cx
                ret            ; return to caller

div_unp_1 ENDP
```

It is possible to multiply or divide two multibyte numbers. Programming Exercises 3 and 4 invite the ambitious student to develop and implement algorithms to do these jobs.

――――― **Exercises 13.3** ――――――――――――――――――――――――――

1. In each part below, assume that the instructions

    ```
    add   al, bl
    aaa
    ```

    are executed. Give the values in the AX register, carry flag CF and auxiliary flag AF: (1) after the **add** and before the **aaa** and (2) after the **aaa**.

(a) AX: 00 05   BL: 02   (b) AX: 02 06   BL: 03
(c) AX: 03 05   BL: 08   (d) AX: 00 07   BL: 06
(e) AX: 00 09   BL: 08   (f) AX: 02 07   BL: 09
(g) AX: 04 01   BL: 09   (h) AX: 00 00   BL: 01

2. Repeat each of the parts of Exercise 1 for the instructions

```
sub    al, bl
aas
```

3. Both parts of this problem assume the definition

```
value    DB    8 DUP(?)
```

(a) Assume that **value** contains ASCII codes for digits 0 through 9. Write a code fragment to replace these bytes "in place" by the corresponding unpacked BCD values.
(b) Assume that **value** contains an eight-byte-long unpacked BCD value. Write a code fragment to replace these bytes "in place" by the corresponding ASCII codes for digits 0 through 9.

4. In each of the following parts, assume that the instructions

```
mul    ch
aam
```

are executed. Give the values in the AX register: (1) after the **mul** and before the **aam** and (2) after the **aam**.

(a) AL: 05   CH: 02   (b) AL: 06   CH: 03
(c) AL: 03   CH: 08   (d) AL: 07   CH: 06
(e) AL: 09   CH: 08   (f) AL: 07   CH: 09
(g) AL: 04   CH: 09   (h) AL: 08   CH: 01

5. In each of the following parts, assume that the instructions

```
aad
div    dl
aam
```

are executed. Give the values in the AX register: (1) after the **aad** and before the **div**, (2) after the **div** and before the **aam** and (3) after the **aam**.

(a) AX: 07 05   DL: 08   (b) AX: 05 06   DL: 09
(c) AX: 02 07   DL: 08   (d) AX: 04 07   DL: 06
(e) AX: 05 09   DL: 06   (f) AX: 03 07   DL: 07
(g) AX: 07 04   DL: 03   (h) AX: 05 00   DL: 04

Programming Exercises 13.3
---

1. Write a procedure **sub_unp** to find the difference of two eight-byte unpacked BCD numbers. The offsets of the two operands will be passed to the procedure in DI and SI. The source operand should be subtracted from the destination operand; store the difference in the eight-byte field to which DI points. The procedure should set CF to 1 if the source is larger than the destination and clear it to 0 otherwise.

2. Here is a possible variable-length representation for multibyte unpacked BCD numbers. An unsigned binary value in the first byte tells how many decimal digits there are in the number. Then digits are stored right to left (low-order to high-order). For example, the decimal number 1234567890 could be stored 0A 00 09 08 07 06 05 04 03 02 01. This system allows for decimal numbers up to 255 digits long to be stored.

   Write a procedure **add_var** that adds two unpacked BCD numbers stored in this variable length format. The DI and SI registers will point to the numbers; return the sum in the field whose offset is in DI. The two numbers are not necessarily the same length. The sum may be the same length as the longer operand, or one byte longer. Assume that sufficient space has been reserved in the destination field for the sum, even if DI points to the shorter operand.

3. Develop an algorithm to find the product of two eight-byte unpacked BCD numbers. Implement this algorithm in a procedure **mul_unp**.

4. Develop an algorithm to find the quotient of two eight-byte unpacked BCD numbers. Implement this algorithm in a procedure **div_unp**.

13.4

Chapter Summary

Integers may be stored in a computer in binary coded decimal form instead of unsigned or 2's complement binary form. There are two basic BCD systems, packed and unpacked. Packed BCD values store two decimal digits per byte, and unpacked BCD values store a single decimal digit per byte.

Binary representations are much more compact than BCD representations and the 8088 processor has more instructions for doing arithmetic with binary numbers. However, BCD representations can easily store very large integers and are simple to convert to or from ASCII.

BCD systems may use a variable or a fixed number of bytes, and may or may not store a sign indicator. The MASM assembler provides a **DT** directive that can produce a ten-byte signed, packed BCD number. Unpacked BCD numbers can be initialized using DB directives.

Arithmetic is done with BCD numbers by combining pairs of bytes from two operands using ordinary binary arithmetic instructions. The binary results are then adjusted to BCD. Packed decimal representations use **daa** (decimal adjust for addition) and **das** (decimal adjust for subtraction) instructions. Using these instructions along with binary arithmetic instructions, a complete arithmetic package for packed BCD numbers can be developed.

Four instructions are used for unpacked BCD arithmetic: **aaa** (ASCII adjust for addition), **aas** (ASCII adjust for subtraction), **aam** (ASCII adjust for multiplication), and **aad** (ASCII adjust for division). The **aad** instruction is different from the others in that it is applied to a BCD result to convert it to binary before applying a **div** instruction.

CHAPTER 14

Floating Point Arithmetic

This book has concentrated on integer representations of numbers, primarily the 2's complement representation since the 8088 microprocessor has a variety of instructions for byte-length and word-length 2's complement numbers. Chapter 13 discussed the BCD systems of representing integers and the small collection of instructions designed to work with them.

Section 1.5 described the IEEE format used to store floating point values in 32 bits. The MASM assembler has directives that accept decimal operands and initialize storage using the IEEE format. However, the 8088 microprocessor does not have instructions to do arithmetic with floating point values. This chapter shows two methods to do floating point arithmetic with a PC. The first is to employ a collection of procedures that implement arithmetic operations such as addition and multiplication. The other option is to install an Intel 8087 Math Coprocessor that executes basic and advanced mathematical instructions. Most PCs have a socket to accept an 8087 but do not have this chip installed.

The first two sections of this chapter develop basic floating point arithmetic procedures that require only an 8088 CPU. Addition, subtraction, multiplication, division, negation and comparison operations are implemented in the first section. Section 14.2 covers procedures for converting floating point values to and from integer and ASCII formats. The procedures in Sections 14.1 to 14.2 serve as examples of assembly language implementation of moderately complex, useful algorithms and also illustrate some techniques not covered earlier in this book. Looking at this code makes one appreciate why programs that use floating point arithmetic are usually so much less efficient than those that require only integer arithmetic.

The next two sections of the chapter provide an introduction to the 8087 coprocessor and some of the instructions it executes. Section 14.3 describes the architecture of the 8087, which has its own internal registers and communicates with the main 8088 processor only through memory. Finally, Section 14.4 shows how to write programs using 8087 instructions.

14.1

Floating Point Operations Using Only 8088 Instructions

The Microsoft Macro Assembler has three directives that can be used to reserve storage for floating point (real or decimal) values and, optionally, to initialize storage to floating point values. They are DD (define doubleword), DQ (define quadword), and DT (define ten-byte). The DD directive reserves four bytes of storage and the DQ directive reserves eight bytes; either of these directives can be used to initialize storage to 2's complement integer values or to floating point values. To determine which format to use, MASM examines a directive's operand; an integer operand yields a 2's complement value and a real operand (written with a decimal point or in "E notation") gives a floating point value. The DT directive (first discussed in Section 13.1) initializes storage to a 10-byte BCD values when an integer operand is used, or to a 10-byte floating point value when a real operand is coded.

The DD directive produces floating point values in the IEEE **single format**.[*] Recall from Section 1.5 that this scheme includes the pieces that describe a number in "base-two scientific notation:"

- a sign bit
- an 8-bit **biased exponent** which is the actual exponent (characteristic) plus 127
- a 23-bit fraction, which is the mantissa of the number with the leading 1 and binary point of the fraction removed

The remainder of this chapter will concentrate on this 32-bit format. The DQ directive produces floating point values in the 64-bit **double format** specified by IEEE. The DT directive produces floating point values in the same 80-bit for-

---

[*] Versions of MASM prior to version 5.0 used an alternative floating point format by default. However, if MASM was executed using the /R option, then IEEE floating point formats were used.

mat that the 8087 coprocessor uses internally.

Figure 14.1 sketches a package for floating point arithmetic. Procedures for multiplication, division, addition, subtraction, negation, and comparison are declared public so that they can be used by other programs or procedures. Most of the procedures begin by using the **expand** macro to break each floating point parameter into sign, exponent, and fraction components. These are stored in separate fields of the **fp** structures **fp1** and **fp2**. The **sign** field contains 00_{16} to represent a plus sign or 80_{16} to represent a minus sign. The actual (unbiased) exponent is stored as a 2's complement word in the **expnt** field. The 24-bit fraction (with the leading 1 in place) is placed in two words in the **f_hi** and **f_lo** fields. Initially **fp1.f_hi** and **fp2.f_hi** fields contain eight leading 0 bits.

Each procedure combines the components of its parameters to yield a result in the structure **fp3**. Often this result is not **normalized**, that is, there are not exactly 24 significant fraction bits. The **NEAR** procedure **normalize** adjusts the fraction and exponent to recover the standard format

$$\text{sign } f_{23} . f_{22} \cdots f_0 \times 2^{\text{expnt}}, \qquad \text{where } f_{23} = 1$$

The macro **combine** is used to merge the fields of **fp3** into a IEEE single floating point value that is returned on the stack in place of the destination parameter.

The remainder of this section examines the code used in the various macros and procedures in this package. Several of the procedures employ moderately complex algorithms; these algorithms are also detailed.

Notice that there is a problem representing the number 0.0 using the normal IEEE scheme. There is no "binary scientific notation" zero with a 1 bit preceding the binary point of the fraction. The best that can be done is 1.0×2^{-127}, which is small, but nonzero. According to the rules given previously, this value would have IEEE representation consisting of 32 zero-bits. However, the two bit patterns that end with 31 zeros are considered special cases, and each is interpreted as 0.0 instead of plus or minus 1.0×2^{-127}. It will be necessary to consider these special cases in subsequent code.

In addition to a special bit pattern to represent 0.0, the IEEE standard describes three other distinctive situations. The pattern

s 11111111   00000000000000000000000

(sign bit s, biased exponent 255, and fraction 0) represents plus or minus infinity. These values are used, for example, as quotients when a nonzero number is divided by zero. Another special case is called NaN (not a number) and is represented by any bit pattern with a biased exponent of 255 and a nonzero fraction. The quotient 0/0 should result in NaN, for example. The final special case is a denormalized number—when the biased exponent is zero and the fraction is nonzero, then no leading 1 is assumed for the fraction. This allows for representation of extra small numbers.

Figure 14.1 Sketch of Floating Point Operations Package.

```
; This code provides multiplication, division, subtraction,
; negation and comparison operations for floating point operands in
; IEEE single (32 bit) format.

PUBLIC fp_mul, fp_div, fp_add, fp_sub, fp_neg, fp_cmp

fp_ops    SEGMENT
          ASSUME ds:fp_ops, cs:fp_ops

fp        STRUC              ; structure for parts of fp numbers
          sign    DB    ?
          expnt   DW    ?
          f_hi    DW    ?    ; high order part of fraction
          f_lo    DW    ?    ; low order part of fraction
fp        ENDS

fp1       fp      <>
fp2       fp      <>
fp3       fp      <>

expand    MACRO   dest, source

combine   MACRO   dest

normalize PROC NEAR          ; normalize fp3

fp_mul    PROC FAR           ; product of two floating point numbers

fp_div    PROC FAR           ; quotient of two floating point numbers

fp_add    PROC FAR           ; sum of two floating point numbers
fp_sub    LABEL FAR          ; entry point for subtraction

fp_neg    PROC FAR           ; change sign of floating point number

fp_cmp    PROC FAR           ; compare two floating point numbers

fp_ops    ENDS

          END
```

Code in this section's floating point package looks for the special zero representations wherever needed. It does not recognize or generate any NaN. It produces plus or minus infinity upon division by zero. The code does not recognize or generate denormalized numbers. Although useful, this package falls short of the standard specified by IEEE.

Figure 14.2 gives the definition for the **expand** macro. Floating point parameters will have been pushed on the stack as two words, the high-order word

Figure 14.2 expand Macro.

```
expand    MACRO   dest, source
          LOCAL   non_zero, endif_e
;; take the floating point value with low order word at [BP+source]
;; and high order word at [BP+source+2] and expand it into separate pieces:
;; sign in byte dest.sign, fraction (with leading 1) in words dest.f_hi
;; and dest.f_lo, and unbiased exponent in word dest.expnt
          mov   ax, [bp+source] ;; low order word of destination
          mov   dest.f_lo, ax   ;; save 16 low order fraction bits
          mov   ax, [bp+source+2]  ;; high order word of destination
          mov   bx, ax          ;; make copy
          test  ax, 7fffh       ;; exponent and high-order fraction zero?
          jnz   non_zero        ;; skip if non-zero
          cmp   WORD PTR [bp+source], 0  ;; is low order word also zero?
          jnz   non_zero
          mov   dest.f_hi, 0    ;; value is zero—use zero fraction
          mov   dest.expnt, 0   ;; and zero exponent
          mov   dest.sign, 0    ;; and plus sign
          jmp   SHORT endif_e
non_zero:
          and   ax, 007fh       ;; clear all but last 7 bits
          or    al, 80h         ;; add leading 1 of fraction
          mov   dest.f_hi, ax   ;; save 8 high order fraction bits
          mov   ax, bx          ;; get high order word again
          and   ah, 80h         ;; zap all but sign bit in AH
          mov   dest.sign, ah   ;; save sign
          shl   bx, 1           ;; 8 bit exponent to BH
          mov   al, bh          ;; make 16 bit value in AX
          xor   ah, ah
          sub   ax, 127         ;; subtract bias
          mov   dest.expnt, ax  ;; save actual exponent
endif_e:
          ENDM
```

before the low-order word. The typical macro call **expand fp1,10** is used to break apart the floating point parameter on the stack at [BP+10] and [BP+12], storing the pieces in the fields of **fp1**. For this example, the low-order word is at [BP+10], and since it contains just the low-order 16 bits of the fraction, it can be immediately copied to **fp1.f_lo**. The high-order word at [BP+12] contains the bits needed for the sign, exponent, and high order part of the fraction. These bits are copied to AX and a second copy is made to BX. This word is tested to see if the exponent and fraction bits are all zero. If so, the low-order word of the value is tested to see if it contains all zeros. If both tests succeed, then the floating value is zero; the structure is loaded with 00 for plus, zero exponent, and zero fraction.

If the floating point value is not zero, then the seven high-order fraction bits are extracted by masking off the leading nine bits and the leading 1 is appended using an **or** instruction. Another **and** operation isolates the sign bit. A single left shift moves the biased exponent into BH; it is turned into a 16-bit unsigned number in AX before the bias 127 is subtracted to give the actual exponent.

Figure 14.3 gives the definition for the **combine** macro. The job of **combine** is to piece together the two words of the floating point result from the fields of **fp3**—it reverses what **expand** does. This macro requires no source parameter since each procedure that generates a floating point result puts the pieces of the result in the structure **fp3**. The corresponding floating point value is always returned on the stack. With the binary operations (addition, subtraction, multiplication, and division) the result replaces the first parameter value at [BP+10] and [BP+12]. With the negation operation, the result replaces the single parameter at [BP+6] and [BP+8]. The destination parameter **dest** gives the offset where the result will be placed.

The **combine** macro first copies the low-order word of the fraction to **[bp+dest]**. Then the high-order word of the fraction is copied into AX and shifted left one bit to move the leading 1 into AH. The biased exponent is calculated in BX, and the low-order eight bits are copied from BL into AH replacing the leading 1 from the expanded fraction. A right shift of one bit puts the exponent and fraction bits in the correct positions in AX. Finally, **or ah,fp3.sign** appends the leading sign bit. The resulting high-order word of the floating point result is stored at **[bp+dest+2]** on the stack.

Multiplication is the easiest floating point operation to implement. It is based on the usual method of multiplying numbers in scientific notation:

- multiply the fractions to get the fraction of the result
- add the exponents to get the exponent of the result
- follow customary rules of signs to get the sign of the result

The only problem with this method is that the product must have a normalized fraction, that is $1.f_{22}f_{21}\cdots f_0$, so that the leading 1 can be dropped. The product

Figure 14.3 combine Macro.

```
combine   MACRO  dest
;; combine sign byte, fraction words, and exponent word stored in
;; structure fp3 into one floating point value with low order word
;; at [BP+dest] and high order word at [BP+dest+2]
          mov  ax, fp3.f_lo    ;; low order part of fraction
          mov  [bp+dest], ax   ;;   on stack to return
          mov  ax, fp3.f_hi    ;; prepare high order word of result
          shl  ax, 1           ;; shift leading 1 of fraction into AH
          mov  bx, fp3.expnt   ;; get exponent
          add  bx, 127         ;; add bias
          mov  ah, bl          ;; copy 8 bit fraction to AH
          shr  ax, 1           ;; move exponent and fraction to right
          or   ah, fp3.sign    ;; attach sign
          mov  [bp+dest+2], ax ;; put high order word on stack
          ENDM
```

of two normalized fractions is not necessarily normalized; for example 1.1 * 1.1 is 10.01. The following design describes the entire procedure.

> expand destination operand into sign_1, expnt_1 and frctn_1;
> expand source operand into sign_2, expnt_2 and frctn_2;
> sign_3 := sign_1 **xor** sign_2;
> expnt_3 := expnt_1 + expnt_2;
> frctn_3 := frctn_1 * frctn_2;
> normalize result in sign_3, expnt_3 and frctn_3;
> combine sign_3, expnt_3 & frctn_3 into destination location;

The **xor** and + operations in this design are easily performed on the fields stored in **fp** structures. The **xor** on byte-length operations corresponds to usual sign rules. The exponents are word-length 2's complement values, so the 8088 has instructions to add them.

Unfortunately each fraction is 24 bits long and the 8088 has no instruction for multiplying operands over 16 bits long. Consequently the multiplication must be performed using another algorithm. This scheme is very similar to the ordinary decimal multiplication algorithm—the first number is multiplied by each digit of the second number in turn, products other than the first one are shifted left one position, and these products are added. The process is easier for binary numbers than for decimal numbers since the product of the first number by one of the bits in the second number is either 0 or a copy of the first number. In general, the product will have approximately as many significant digits as the sum of the digits in the two factors.

The design below gives some of the details of the multiplication algorithm. Since two 24-bit numbers with leading 1's are being multiplied, the product will have 47 or 48 significant bits. However, since only 24 bits will be retained in the floating point result, the algorithm is written to generate only the high-order 24 bits of the product. Instead of shifting partial products to the left one bit each iteration to get a 48-bit product, the 24 low-order bits are shifted off to the right one at a time as the product is generated.

```
product := 0;
for count := 1 to 24 loop
        shift product right 1 bit;
        if bit 0 of multiplier = 1
        then
                add multiplicand to product;
        end if;
        shift multiplier right 1 bit;
    end for;
```

There are still minor problems implementing this algorithm since the product, multiplier, and multiplicand in the floating point multiplication are 24-bit fractions, each stored in two words. Each time one of the above shifts is performed, it involves shifting the rightmost bit of the high-order word into the carry flag CF and from there into the leftmost bit of the low-order word as its rightmost bit is shifted right and discarded. Figure 14.4 shows all of the code for the floating point multiplication procedure.

Procedure **normalize** takes care of adjusting the exponent and fraction of the result to ensure that the fraction has exactly 24 significant bits. The fraction is stored in two 16-bit words, and it is conceivable that there are as many as 32 significant bits. If there are over 24 bits, the fraction is shifted right to produce exactly 24 significant bits and the exponent is increased by the number of places that had to be shifted. If there are fewer than 24 bits, the fraction is shifted left and the exponent is decreased. The special case of a zero fraction is handled by setting the sign to "plus" and the exponent to –127; when the bias of 127 is added to the exponent as the parts are combined, the resulting floating point representation will consist of 32 zero-bits. The algorithm for the normalization procedure is given below; the code that implements the algorithm is in Figure 14.5.

Figure 14.4 Floating Point Multiplication Procedure.

```
fp_mul    PROC FAR              ; product of two floating point numbers

; Two floating point parameters are passed on the stack.
; The destination is pushed first, then the source.
; For each, high order word (sign, exponent, 7 fraction bits) pushed first,
;   then low order word (low order 16 fraction bits).
; The destination is replaced on the stack by the product destination*source.

          push bp               ; save and reload BP
          mov  bp, sp

          push ax               ; save other registers
          push bx
          push cx
          push dx
          push ds

          mov  ax, SEG fp_ops   ; establish new data segment number
          mov  ds, ax
; separate destination into sign, exponent and fraction parts in fp1
          expand fp1, 10

; separate source into sign, exponent and fraction parts in fp2
          expand fp2, 6

          mov  al, fp1.sign     ; get destination sign
          xor  al, fp2.sign     ; calculate sign of product
          mov  fp3.sign, al     ; save in fp3

          mov  ax, fp1.expnt    ; exponent of destination
          add  ax, fp2.expnt    ; calculate exponent of product
          mov  fp3.expnt, ax    ; save in fp3

; multiply fractions using add and shift algorithm
; product in fp3.f_hi and fp3.f_lo; fraction in fp2 is destroyed

          mov  fp3.f_hi, 0      ; product := 0
          mov  fp3.f_lo, 0
          mov  dx, fp1.f_hi     ; copy fraction of multiplicand to DX and AX
          mov  ax, fp1.f_lo
          mov  cx, 24           ; 24 bits to process
for_1m:   shr  fp3.f_hi, 1      ; shift product right 1 bit
          rcr  fp3.f_lo, 1
          test fp2.f_lo, 1      ; low order bit of multiplier = 1 ?
          jz   end_if2m
          add  fp3.f_lo, ax     ; add multiplicand to product
          adc  fp3.f_hi, dx
```

Figure 14.4 Continued.

```
end_if2m:
            shr   fp2.f_hi, 1     ; shift multiplier right 1 bit
            rcr   fp2.f_lo, 1
            loop for_1m

            call normalize        ; normalize result

            combine 10            ; result replaces destination operand on stack

exit_m:     pop ds                ; restore registers
            pop dx
            pop cx
            pop bx
            pop ax
            pop bp

            ret 4                 ; return, discarding source operand

fp_mul      ENDP
```

if frctn = 0
then
    sign := "+";
    expnt := -127;
    return;
end if;

if fraction $>= 1\ 00\ 00\ 00_{16}$
then { more than 24 bits }

    until frctn $< 1\ 00\ 00\ 00_{16}$ loop
        shift frctn right 1 bit;
        add 1 to expnt;
    end until;
else { 24 or fewer bits }
    while frctn $< 80\ 00\ 00_{16}$ loop
        shift frctn left 1 bit;
        subtract 1 from expnt;
    end while;
end if;

Figure 14.5 Floating Point Normalization Procedure.

```
normalize PROC NEAR            ; normalize fp3
if_1n:    cmp  fp3.f_hi, 0     ; fraction = 0 ?
          jnz  endif_1n
          cmp  fp3.f_lo, 0
          jnz  endif_1n
          mov  fp3.expnt,-127  ; exponent for zero result
          mov  fp3.sign, 0     ; sign for zero result
          ret                  ; exit
endif_1n:

if_2n:    test fp3.f_hi,0ff00h ; more than 24 significant bits in fraction?
          jz   else_2n
until_1n: shr  fp3.f_hi, 1     ; shift fraction right 1 bit
          rcr  fp3.f_lo, 1
          inc  fp3.expnt       ; add 1 to exponent
          test fp3.f_hi,0ff00h
          jnz  until_1n        ; continue until exactly 24
          jmp SHORT endif_2n
else_2n:
while_1n: test fp3.f_hi,0ff80h ; fewer than 24 significant bits in fraction?
          jnz  endwhile_1n
          shl  fp3.f_lo, 1     ; shift fraction left 1 bit
          rcl  fp3.f_hi, 1
          dec  fp3.expnt       ; subtract 1 from exponent
          jmp  while_1n
endwhile_1n:
endif_2n:
          ret                  ; return

normalize ENDP
```

The division procedure computes the quotient of the destination (first) parameter by the source (second) parameter. The basic algorithm is almost as simple as the one for multiplication. In order to avoid division by zero, a special case is needed to check for zero source.

> if source = 0
> then
>   quotient := [sign of source] infinity;
> else
>   separate destination into sign_1, expnt_1 and frctn_1;
>   separate source into sign_2, expnt_2, and frctn_2;
>   sign_3 := sign_1 xor sign_2;

```
            expnt_3 := expnt_1 - expnt_2;
            frctn_3 := frctn_1 / frctn_2;
            normalize result in expnt_3 and frctn_3;
            combine sign_3, expnt_3 and frctn_3 into destination;
        end if;
```

As in the multiplication algorithm, 24-bit fractions stored in two words must be combined. Since the 8088 cannot divide 24-bit operands, an additional algorithm is required. The following design shows how to generate the high-order 24 bits of the quotient, all that will be kept for the fraction.

```
            quotient := 0;
            for count := 1 to 24 loop
                shift quotient left 1 bit;
                if dividend >= divisor
                then
                        bit 0 of quotient := 1;
                        subtract divisor from dividend;
                end if;
                shift dividend left 1 bit;
            end for;
```

Figure 14.6 shows the code for the division procedure. Note that every operation involving the 24-bit quotients is complex, involving two comparisons, two shifts, two subtractions, etc.

Figure 14.6 Floating Point Division Procedure.

```
fp_div      PROC FAR                ; quotient of two floating point numbers

; Two floating point parameters are passed on the stack.
; The destination is pushed first, then the source.
; For each, high order word (sign, exponent, 7 fraction bits) pushed first,
;   then low order word (low order 16 fraction bits).
; The destination is replaced on the stack by the quotient destination/source.

            push bp                 ; save and reload BP
            mov  bp, sp

            push ax                 ; save other registers
            push bx
            push cx
            push dx
            push ds
```

Figure 14.6 Continued.

```
              mov   ax, SEG fp_ops   ; establish new data segment number
              mov   ds, ax

              ; check for source=0 (division by zero, infinity result)
              mov   ax, [bp+8]       ; high order word of source
              and   ax, 7fffh        ; delete sign bit
              or    ax, [bp+6]       ; both parts zero?
              jnz   endif_2d
              mov   ax, [bp+8]       ; high order word of source
              xor   ax, [bp+12]      ; set sign of result
              and   ax, 8000h        ; zero all but sign
              or    ax, 7f80h        ; exponent 255 for infinity
              mov   [bp+12], ax      ; save high order word
              mov   WORD PTR [bp+10], 0  ; rest of fraction is zero
              jmp   exit_d           ; skip other steps
endif_2d:

; separate destination into sign, exponent and fraction parts in fp1
              expand fp1, 10

; separate source into sign, exponent and fraction parts in fp2
              expand fp2, 6

              mov   al, fp1.sign     ; get destination sign
              xor   al, fp2.sign     ; calculate sign of quotient
              mov   fp3.sign, al     ; save in fp3

              mov   ax, fp1.expnt    ; exponent of destination
              sub   ax, fp2.expnt    ; calculate exponent of quotient
              mov   fp3.expnt, ax    ; save in fp3

; divide fractions using subtract and shift algorithm
; quotient in fp3.f_hi and fp3.f_lo; fraction in fp1 is destroyed

              mov   fp3.f_hi, 0      ; quotient := 0
              mov   fp3.f_lo, 0
              mov   dx, fp2.f_hi     ; copy fraction of divisor to DX and AX
              mov   ax, fp2.f_lo
              mov   cx, 24           ; 24 bits to process
for_1d:       shl   fp3.f_lo, 1      ; shift quotient left 1 bit
              rcl   fp3.f_hi, 1
              cmp   fp1.f_hi, dx     ; dividend >= divisor ?
              ja    then_3d          ; yes, if high order part greater
              jb    endif_3d         ; no, if high order part less
              cmp   fp1.f_lo, ax     ; high order equal, test low order parts
              jnae  endif_3d
```

Figure 14.6 Continued.

```
then_3d:   or    fp3.f_lo, 1      ; bit 0 of quotient := 1
           sub   fp1.f_lo, ax     ; subtract divisor from dividend
           sbb   fp1.f_hi, dx
endif_3d:
           shl   fp1.f_lo, 1      ; shift dividend left 1 bit;
           rcl   fp1.f_hi, 1
           loop  for_1d           ; continue for 24 bits

           call  normalize        ; normalize result

           combine 10             ; result replaces destination operand on stack

exit_d:    pop   ds               ; restore registers
           pop   dx
           pop   cx
           pop   bx
           pop   ax
           pop   bp

           ret 4                  ; return, discarding source operand

fp_div     ENDP
```

Floating point addition and subtraction are more complicated than multiplication or division. Subtraction does not require a separate procedure since it can be handled by negating the second parameter and then adding. The design for the addition/subtraction procedure is given in Figure 14.7.

Code for the addition/subtraction procedure is in Figure 14.8. An interesting feature of the code is that it has two **entry points**, one identified by the **PROC** directive and one identified by the **LABEL** directive. If **fp_add** is called, then procedure execution begins with the **clc** instruction first and then the **jmp** skips the **stc** following the **LABEL** directive. However, if **fp_sub** is called, then procedure execution begins with the **stc** instruction. Thus the carry flag will be 0 for addition and 1 for subtraction. This flag value is not destroyed by the various **push** and **mov** instructions in the common code starting at **add_sub:** and after the preliminaries are finished, the carry flag is rotated into the high-order bit of CL to record whether the operation is addition or subtraction. The CL register can later be used to reverse the sign of the second operand for a subtraction operation.

Figure 14.7   Addition/Subtraction Algorithm.

```
separate destination operand into sign_1, expnt_1, and frctn_1;
separate source operand into sign_2, expnt_2, and frctn_2;

if operation is subtraction
then
     reverse sign_2;
end if;

if expnt_1 < expnt_2
then { make first exponent the larger }
     swap sign_1 and sign_2;
     swap expnt_1 and expnt_2;
     swap frctn_1 and frctn_2;
end if;

if frctn_1 = 0
then  { non-zero operand gives the result }
     sign_3 := sign_2;
     expnt_t := expnt_2;
     frctn_3 := frctn_2;
else  { make adjust smaller exponent to match larger and add }
     while expnt_1 > expnt_2 loop
          shift frctn_2 right 1 bit;
          add 1 to expnt_2;
     end while;

     expnt_3 := expnt_1;
     if sign_1 = sign_2
     then  { same sign }
          sign_3 := sign_1;}
          frctn_3 := frctn_1 + frctn_2;
     else  { opposite signs }
          if frctn_1 ≥ frctn_2
          then
               frctn_3 := frctn_1 - frctn_2;
               sign_3 := sign_1;
          else
               frctn_3 := frctn_2 - frctn_1;
               sign_3 := sign_2;
          end if;
     end if;
end if;

normalize result in sign_3, expnt_3 and frctn_3;
combine sign_3, expnt_3 and frctn_3 into destination location;
```

Figure 14.8 Floating Point Addition Procedure.

```
fp_add     PROC FAR            ; sum of two floating point numbers

; Two floating point parameters are passed on the stack.
; The destination is pushed first, then the source.
; For each, high order word (sign, exponent, 7 fraction bits) pushed first,
;   then low order word (low order 16 fraction bits).
; The destination is replaced on the stack by the sum destination+source.
; The same code serves for subtraction; the second parameter is negated.

           clc                 ; carry=0 to show addition
           jmp SHORT add_sub

fp_sub     LABEL FAR           ; entry point for subtraction
           stc                 ; carry=1 to show subtraction
add_sub:   push bp             ; save and reload BP
           mov  bp, sp

           push ax             ; save other registers
           push bx
           push cx
           push dx
           push ds

           mov  ax, SEG fp_ops ; establish new data segment number
           mov  ds, ax

           mov  cl, 0          ; CL will negate source for subtraction
           rcr  cl, 1          ; carry flag to high order bit of CL

; separate destination into sign, exponent and fraction parts in fp1
           expand fp1, 10

; separate source into sign, exponent and fraction parts in fp2
           expand fp2, 6

           xor  fp2.sign, cl   ; change sign for subtraction
           mov  ax, fp1.expnt  ; ensure that fp1.expnt >= fp2.expnt
           cmp  ax, fp2.expnt
           jge  endif_a
           xchg fp2.expnt, ax  ; finish swap of exponents
           mov  fp1.expnt, ax
           mov  al, fp1.sign   ; swap signs
           xchg fp2.sign, al
           mov  fp1.sign, al
           mov  ax, fp1.f_hi   ; swap high order parts of fractions
```

Figure 14.8 Continued.

```
        xchg fp2.f_hi, ax
        mov  fp1.f_hi, ax
        mov  ax, fp1.f_lo    ; swap low order parts of fractions
        xchg fp2.f_lo, ax
        mov  fp1.f_lo, ax
endif_a:

        mov  ax, fp1.f_lo    ; is fraction of larger number zero?
        or   ax, fp1.f_hi
        jnz  endif_0a        ; regular case if nonzero
        mov  al, fp2.sign    ; copy smaller number to result
        mov  fp3.sign, al
        mov  ax, fp2.expnt
        mov  fp3.expnt, ax
        mov  ax, fp2.f_hi
        mov  fp3.f_hi, ax
        mov  ax, fp2.f_lo
        mov  fp3.f_lo, ax
        jmp  exit_a          ; quit
endif_0a:

; make two exponents equal
        mov  ax, fp1.expnt   ; get exponent of fp1
while_1a: cmp ax, fp2.expnt  ; exponents equal?
        je   endwhile_1a
        shr  fp2.f_hi, 1     ; shift fraction2 right 1 place
        rcr  fp2.f_lo, 1
        inc  fp2.expnt       ; add 1 to exponent2
        jmp  while_1a
endwhile_1a:
        mov  fp3.expnt, ax   ; save common exponent

; add fractions if signs same, else subtract
        mov  al, fp1.sign    ; get destination sign
        xor  al, fp2.sign    ; calculate sign of quotient
        jnz  else_1a         ; not zero means signs different

; both signs same
        mov  al, fp1.sign    ; use common sign
        mov  fp3.sign, al
        mov  ax, fp1.f_lo    ; add fractions, low order part
        add  ax, fp2.f_lo
        mov  fp3.f_lo, ax
        mov  ax, fp1.f_hi    ; high order part
        adc  ax, fp2.f_hi
        mov  fp3.f_hi, ax
        jmp  SHORT endif_1a
```

Figure 14.8 Continued.

```
else_1a:                        ; opposite signs
        mov     ax, fp1.f_hi    ; fraction 1 > fraction 2 ?
        cmp     ax, fp2.f_hi
        ja      then_2a         ; yes if high order part greater
        jb      else_2a         ; no if high order part less
        mov     ax, fp1.f_lo    ; if equal, check low order parts
        cmp     ax, fp2.f_lo
        jb      else_2a
then_2a: mov    al, fp1.sign    ; fraction 1 >= fraction 2—use sign of fp1
        mov     fp3.sign, al
        mov     ax, fp1.f_lo    ; subtract fractions, low order part
        sub     ax, fp2.f_lo
        mov     fp3.f_lo, ax
        mov     ax, fp1.f_hi    ; high order part
        sbb     ax, fp2.f_hi
        mov     fp3.f_hi, ax
        jmp     SHORT endif_1a
else_2a: mov    al, fp2.sign    ; f2 larger—use its sign
        mov     fp3.sign, al
        mov     ax, fp2.f_lo    ; subtract fractions, low order part
        sub     ax, fp1.f_lo
        mov     fp3.f_lo, ax
        mov     ax, fp2.f_hi    ; high order part
        sbb     ax, fp1.f_hi
        mov     fp3.f_hi, ax
endif_1a:

exit_a: call    normalize       ; normalize result
        combine 10              ; result replaces destination operand on stack

        pop ds                  ; restore registers
        pop dx
        pop cx
        pop bx
        pop ax
        pop bp
        ret 4                   ; return, discarding source operand

fp_add  ENDP
```

When adding two floating point numbers, one cannot simply add fractions; the numbers must have the same exponent. Digits in the number with the smaller exponent are less significant than those in the number with the larger exponent. In the procedure, the two values are swapped if necessary to ensure that the second value has the smaller exponent. If the number with the larger exponent is zero, then there is nothing further to do—the result is the other number. Otherwise the second exponent is incremented as the fraction is shifted right to make the exponents match. The common exponent is then the exponent expnt_3 of the result (possibly changed later by normalization).

Once the exponents of the operands match, addition is done following normal rules for signed numbers. If the two numbers have the same sign, the fractions are added and the common sign is used for sign_3. If the numbers have opposite signs, the smaller fraction is subtracted from the larger, and the sign of the larger is used for the result.

Floating point negation involves only a single parameter. The code is given in Figure 14.9. It expands the parameter, reverses the sign, normalizes the result, and uses the result, to replace the parameter. A more efficient alternative would be to simply code

```
xor   [BP+8], 8000h    ; flip sign in high order word
```

However, this risks producing the result 80000000_{16}, that is –0. The **normalize** procedure eliminates this possibility. All procedures in this package correctly use –0 operands and avoid –0 results.

The floating point comparison procedure assigns appropriate values to the zero flag ZF and the sign flag SF. In addition, the OF, CF, AF, and PF flags are cleared. Therefore, following a call to **fp_cmp**, the appropriate conditional jump instructions are the same as those used following comparison of signed integers.

In order to compare two floating point operands, this package subtracts the values and then examines the difference. The following algorithm is used.

```
use fp_sub to calculate fp_1 - fp_2;
OF := 0;
CF := 0;
AF := 0;
PF := 0;
ZF := 0;
SF := 0;

if the difference fp_1 - fp_2 = 0
then
        ZF := 1;
end if;

if the difference fp_1 - fp_2 < 0
then
        SF := 1;
end if;
```

Figure 14.9 Floating Point Negation Procedure.

```
fp_neg      PROC FAR            ; change sign of floating point number

; Floating point parameter passed on the stack.
; High order word (sign, exponent, 7 fraction bits) pushed first,
;    then low order word (low order 16 fraction bits).
; The parameter is replaced on the stack by value -(parameter).

            push bp             ; save and reload BP
            mov  bp, sp
            push ax             ; save other registers
            push bx
            push ds

            mov  ax, SEG fp_ops ; establish new data segment number
            mov  ds, ax

            expand   fp3, 6     ; expand source parameter
            xor  fp3.sign, 80h  ; flip sign
            call normalize      ; normalize
            combine 6           ; combine, replacing source parameter

            pop  ds             ; restore registers
            pop  bx
            pop  ax
            pop  bp
            ret
```

The code that implements this design is given in Figure 14.10. This code also shows a typical floating point procedure call, in this case to **fp_sub**. Four **push** instructions are needed to pass the two floating point operands on the stack. The difference is returned on the stack, and the two **pop** instructions following **call fp_sub** retrieve this result from the stack. The flag values are stored in AH and an **sahf** instruction puts them in the flag register.

Figure 14.10 Floating Point Comparison Procedure.

```
fp_cmp    PROC FAR              ; compare two floating point numbers

; Two floating point parameters are passed on the stack.
; For each, high order word (sign, exponent, 7 fraction bits) pushed first,
;   then low order word (low order 16 fraction bits).
; Flags are set as follows:
;   ZF = 1 iff parameter1 = parameter2
;   SF = 1 iff parameter1 < parameter2
;   OF=0, CF = 0, AF = 0 and PF = 0

          push bp               ; save and reload BP
          mov  bp, sp

          push ax               ; save other registers
          push bx
          push cx
          push ds

          mov  ax, SEG fp_ops   ; establish new data segment number
          mov  ds, ax

          push [bp+12]          ; push destination
          push [bp+10]
          push [bp+8]           ; push source
          push [bp+6]
          call fp_sub           ; subtract operands
          pop  cx               ; low order word of difference
          pop  bx               ; high order word
          mov  ah, 0            ; "flags" <-- 0
          cmp  cx, 0            ; zero result?
          jnz  else_c
          cmp  bx, 0
          jnz  else_c
          or   ah, 01000000b    ; ZF <-- 1
          jmp  SHORT endif_c
else_c:   and  bh, 10000000b    ; isolate sign of difference
          or   ah, bh           ; use sign in "flags"
endif_c:
          sahf                  ; copy "flags" into flag register
                                ; (OF = 0 from "or" instructions)
exit_c:   pop  ds               ; restore registers
          pop  cx
          pop  bx
          pop  ax
          pop  bp

          ret 8                 ; return, discarding both operands

fp_cmp    ENDP
```

———— *Exercises 14.1* ————————————————————————————

1. Find the initial value that MASM will generate for each of these DD directives.

(a) fp1   DD   0.0   (b)   fp2   DD   1.0
(c) fp3   DD   -1.0   (d)   fp4   DD   -8.0
(e) fp5   DD   1000.0   (f)   fp6   DD   65000.0
(g) fp7   DD   19.5   (h)   fp8   DD   23.75
(i) fp9   DD   -105.625   (j)   fp10   DD   -0.625

———— *Programming Exercises 14.1* ————————————————————

1. The `fp_cmp` implementation in this section (Figure 14.10) calls **fp_sub**. Write an alternative implementation that is self-contained. After expanding the operands, consider signs of the operands first, then exponent sizes if the operands have the same sign, and finally fraction sizes if the operands had identical signs and exponents.

2. In the code for **fp_add** and **fp_sub**, the fraction of the operand with the smaller exponent is shifted right as many places as are necessary to make exponents match. Notice that if the difference in exponents is at least 24, all bits of the fraction will be shifted off, so that the resulting fraction is zero. Add code that checks to see if expnt_1 – expnt_2 ≥ 24, and simply returns the first operand if it is. This check should come after the operands have been swapped to make the first operand the larger one.

3. The procedures in this section's floating point package all use 24-bit fractions stored in two 16-bit words. More accurate results could be obtained if more fraction bits were maintained as the various algorithms are carried out, even though only 24 bits are kept in the IEEE format. Implement the addition/subtraction procedure using 28-bit fractions instead of 24 bit fractions. Notice that the **expand** and **combine** macros will also have to be modified.

———— 14.2 ————————————————————————————————————

Converting Floating Point Numbers to Other Formats

In the previous section a package of procedures for floating point operations was developed. Those procedures are sufficient for implementing most algorithms involving floating point computations. However, it is also frequently necessary to convert floating point numbers to or from other formats. This section develops procedures that convert a floating point number to an integer, an integer to a floating point number, a floating point number to an ASCII string, and an ASCII string to a floating point number. The procedures involving ASCII strings make it possible to do input and output of floating point values.

These four procedures are included in a package **fp_conv**. A sketch of the entire package is given in Figure 14.11. This package uses one segment for code and data. Data which is specific to particular procedures is defined just before the procedure code, rather than at the beginning of the entire package. Structure **fp** and procedure **normalize** are identical to the corresponding components in the floating point operations package developed in Section 14.1; they are not described again in this section.

Procedure **ftoi** converts a floating point operand to an equivalent word-length 2's complement value, if one exists. It works by carrying out the same sort of operation one does to convert scientific notation to ordinary notation—the radix point is moved according to the value of the exponent. This algorithm "moves the radix point" by shifting the appropriate number of leading fraction bits into the low-order bits of the AX register. If the exponent is 0, then the leading 1 bit is shifted into the AX register; if the exponent is 1, then first two bits are shifted, and so on. A negative exponent corresponds to a floating point number that has absolute value under 1; no bits are shifted into AX and a result of 0 is returned. The algorithm used is described by the following pseudocode.

```
clear AX;
for count:=0 to expnt loop
        shift leftmost fraction bit into AX;
end for;
if sign = "-"
then
        negate value in AX;
end if;
```

The code for procedure **ftoi** is given in Figure 14.12. Since this is the only procedure in this package that needs to expand a floating point parameter, it does not employ the **expand** macro used by the procedures in Section 14.1;

Figure 14.11 Sketch of Floating Point Conversions Package.

```
; This code provides procedures to convert IEEE single (32 bit) floating
; point numbers to and from 16 bit 2's complement integers, and to and
; from ASCII strings.

PUBLIC  itof, ftoi, ftoa, atof
EXTRN   fp_add:FAR, fp_sub:FAR, fp_mul:FAR, fp_div:FAR, fp_neg:FAR, fp_cmp:FAR

fp_conv   SEGMENT
          ASSUME ds:fp_conv, cs:fp_conv

fp        STRUC                   ; structure for parts of fp numbers
```

Figure 14.11 Continued.

```
fp1        fp      <>
fp3        fp      <>

normalize PROC NEAR              ; normalize fp3

ftoi       PROC FAR              ; convert floating point number to integer

itof       PROC FAR              ; convert integer to floating point number

value      DD  ?
ten        DD  10.0
one        DD  1.0
round      DD  0.000005
fdigit     DD  ?
exponent   DW  ?

ftoa       PROC FAR              ; convert floating point number to
                                 ; 12 byte long ASCII string

false      EQU  0
true       EQU  1
point      DB   ?
minus      DB   ?
digits     DD   0.0, 1.0, 2.0, 3.0, 4.0, 5.0, 6.0, 7.0, 8.0, 9.0
divisor    DD   ?

atof       PROC FAR              ; convert ASCII string to floating point number

fp_conv    ENDS

           END
```

similar code is built into `ftoi`. In addition, in procedure `ftoi` it is not necessary to check for a zero value when expanding the parameter. Treating a pattern of all zero bits as 1.0×2^{-127} results in returned integer 0 without the extra code for the check.

In order to shift bits efficiently, the 24 bits of the fraction are copied into the BX and DX registers. The CX register is used as a loop counter. One shift and two rotate-through-carry instructions serve to shift a leading fraction bit into AX. After all appropriate bits are shifted into AX, the result is negated if the original floating point parameter was negative.

Notice that this procedure fails without any error indication if the floating point parameter is too large. Exercise 1 at the end of this section invites the reader to correct this fault. The `ftoi` procedure also truncates any fractional part, it does not round to the nearest integer. Exercise 2 suggests a way to modify

Figure 14.12 Floating Point-to-Integer Conversion Procedure.

```
ftoi        PROC FAR             ;  convert floating point number to integer

; Floating point source parameter passed on the stack.
; High order word (sign, exponent, 7 fraction bits) pushed first,
;   then low order word (low order 16 fraction bits).
; The fractional part of the source is truncated,
;   and the equivalent integer (if any) is returned in AX.

            push bp              ; save and reload BP
            mov  bp, sp

            push bx              ; save other registers
            push cx
            push dx
            push ds

            mov  ax, SEG fp_conv ; establish new data segment number
            mov  ds, ax

; separate source into sign, exponent and fraction parts in fp1
            mov  ax, [bp+6]      ; low order word
            mov  fp1.f_lo, ax    ; save 16 low order fraction bits
            mov  ax, [bp+8]      ; high order word
            mov  bx, ax          ; make copy
            and  ax, 007fh       ; clear all but last 7 bits
            or   al, 80h         ; leading 1 of fraction
            mov  fp1.f_hi, ax    ; save 8 high order fraction bits
            mov  ax, bx          ; copy back
            and  ah, 80h         ; zap all but sign bit
            mov  fp1.sign, ah    ; and save
            shl  bx, 1           ; 8 bit exponent to BH
            mov  al, bh          ; make 16 bit value in AX
            xor  ah, ah
            sub  ax, 127         ; subtract bias
            mov  fp1.expnt, ax   ; save actual exponent

            mov  ax, 0           ; start to build integer
            mov  bx, fp1.f_hi    ; use BX and DX for fraction
            mov  dx, fp1.f_lo
            mov  cx, 0           ; for loop index
for_1i:     cmp  cx, fp1.expnt   ; count <= exponent?
            jnle endfor_1i
            shl  dx, 1           ; shift high order bit of fraction into AX
            rcl  bl, 1
            rcl  ax, 1
            inc  cx              ; increment count
            jmp  for_1i
```

Figure 14.12 Continued.

```
endfor_1i:
           and  fp1.sign, 80h   ; negative?
           jz   endif_1i
           neg  ax                ; negate integer for negative sign
endif_1i:
           pop ds                 ; restore registers
           pop dx
           pop cx
           pop bx
           pop bp

           ret 4                  ; return, discarding source operand

ftoi    ENDP
```

the procedure to get a rounded result.

The algorithm for converting a word-length 2's complement integer parameter to a floating point value is in some ways the opposite of the floating point-to-integer algorithm. After noting the sign of the integer and ensuring that it is nonnegative, the number's significant bits are counted as they are shifted one at a time into the floating point fraction. Note that an integer value of 1 should have an exponent of 0. Starting the count at –1 makes it correspond to the exponent. The `itof` procedure implements the following design.

```
if integer < 0
then
      sign := minus;
      integer := - integer;
else
      sign := plus;
end if;

exponent := –1;
fraction := 000000₁₆;
while integer > 0 loop
      shift right bit of integer into left of fraction;
      add 1 to exponent;
end while;

normalize result;
store result at offset given by destination parameter;
```

The code for procedure `itof` is given in Figure 14.13. This procedure differs from most others in this chapter in that it returns its floating point result in the caller's data segment rather than on the stack. The reason for this is that an integer parameter uses only a single word on the stack and the floating point result requires two words. Consequently, the integer parameter cannot simply be replaced by the floating point result. This procedure uses a second parameter giving the offset in the caller's data segment of the destination for the result.

The integer parameter value −32768 requires special attention. Since it is 8000_{16}, it cannot be negated like other negative values. Instead, the corresponding unsigned value is also 8000_{16}.

Figure 14.13   Integer-to-Floating Point Conversion Procedure.

```
itof      PROC FAR              ;  convert integer to floating point number

; Two parameters passed on the stack.
; (1) 16 bit integer source.
; (2) offset of floating point destination.
; A floating point value equivalent to the source integer is stored
;    at the destination address.

          push bp               ; save and reload BP
          mov  bp, sp

          push ax               ; save other registers
          push bx
          push cx
          push dx
          push ds

          mov  ax, SEG fp_conv ; establish new data segment number
          mov  ds, ax

          mov  ax, [bp+8]       ; integer source

          cmp  ax, 0            ; integer < 0
          jge  else_1j
          mov  fp3.sign, 80h    ; minus sign
          cmp  ax, 8000h        ; integer = -32768?
          je   endif_1j         ; if so, 8000h is the correct unsigned form
          neg  ax               ; otherwise, negate to get unsigned integer
          jmp SHORT endif_1j
else_1j:  mov  fp3.sign, 0      ; plus sign
endif_1j:
          mov  fp3.expnt, -1    ; start exponent at -1
          mov  bx, 0            ; generate fraction in BX and DX
          mov  dx, 0
```

Figure 14.13 Continued.

```
                while_1j:  or   ax,  ax        ;   integer <> 0?
                           jz   endwhile_1j
                           shr  ax,  1          ;   shift rightmost bit of integer
                                                    into fraction
                           rcr  bl,  1
                           rcr  dx,  1
                           inc  fp3.expnt       ;   add 1 to exponent
                           jmp  while_1j
                endwhile_1j:

                mov  fp3.f_hi, bx     ; store fraction in fp3
                mov  fp3.f_lo, dx
                call normalize       ; normalize result

; put result in caller's data segment

                mov  dx, fp3.f_lo    ; low order part of fraction
                mov  ax, fp3.f_hi    ; prepare high order word of result
                shl  ax, 1           ; remove leading 1 from fraction
                mov  bx, fp3.expnt   ; get exponent
                add  bx, 127         ; add bias
                mov  ah, bl          ; copy 8 bits to AH
                shr  ax, 1           ; move exponent and fraction to right
                or   ah, fp3.sign    ; attach sign

                mov  bx, [bp+6]      ; get address for result
                pop  ds              ; restore DS
                mov  [bx], dx        ; store low order word
                mov  [bx+2], ax      ; store high order word

                pop  dx              ; restore remaining registers
                pop  cx
                pop  bx
                pop  ax
                pop  bp

                ret 4                ; return, discarding both operands

itof      ENDP
```

The end of the code is somewhat unusual in that not all registers are restored at the same time. The result is put in the AX and DX registers and then the destination offset is copied from the stack to BX. Next the caller's data segment number is popped into DS. With the result in registers, local data no longer needs to be accessed and the two words of the floating point number are copied into the caller's data segment. Finally the remaining registers are restored.

The remaining two procedures are for conversions of floating point values to and from ASCII strings. These procedures and the algorithms for them are more "high-level" than for other components presented in Sections 14.1 and 14.2. Instead of dealing with the bit fields that make up IEEE floating point representations, they treat real numbers as entities to be manipulated with addition, subtraction, multiplication, division, negation, and comparison procedures. The algorithms are just as suitable for implementation in a high-level language as in assembly language.

The `ftoa` procedure converts a floating point parameter to "E notation." The procedure generates a 12-byte-long ASCII string consisting of

- a leading minus sign (–) or a blank
- a digit
- a decimal point (.)
- five digits
- the letter *E*
- a plus sign (+) or a minus sign (–)
- two digits

This string represents the number in base-10 scientific notation. For example, for the decimal value 145.8798, the procedure would generate the string "␣1.45880E+02". Notice that the ASCII string gives a rounded value.

Figure 14.14 displays the design for the `ftoa` procedure. After the leading space or minus sign is generated, most of the work necessary to get the remaining characters is done before they are actually produced. The value is repeatedly multiplied or divided by 10 until it is at least 1.0 but less than 10.0. Multiplication is used if the value is initially less than 1; the number of multiplications gives the negative power of 10 required for scientific notation. Division is used if the value is initially 10.0 or more; the number of divisions gives the positive power of 10 required for scientific notation.

Only five digits are going to be displayed after the decimal point. The value between 1.0 and 10.0 is rounded by adding 0.000005; if the sixth digit after the decimal point is 5 or greater, this will be reflected in the digits that are actually displayed. It is possible that this addition gives a sum of 10.0 or more; if this happens, the value is divided by 10 again and the exponent is incremented.

With a value at least 1.0 but under 10.0, truncating to an integer gives the digit to go before the decimal point. This digit and the decimal point are generated. Then the remaining five digits can be generated by repeatedly subtracting the whole part from the value, multiplying the remaining fraction by 10, and truncating the new value to an integer.

After the "fraction" of the ASCII string is generated, the letter E, a + or –, and the exponent digits are generated. The exponent will contain at most two digits—the single IEEE notation provides for numbers as large as 2^{128}, which is less than 10^{39}.

Figure 14.15 shows the code for the `ftoa` procedure. Data values that are used by this procedure are defined after the previous procedure and just before

Figure 14.14 Floating Point-to-ASCII Conversion Algorithm.

```
point at first destination byte;

if value ≥ 0
then
      put blank in destination string;
else
      put "-" in destination string;
      value := - value;
end if;
point at next destination byte;

exponent := 0;
if value not zero
then
      if value ≥ 10
      then
            until value < 10 loop
                  divide value by 10;
                  add 1 to exponent;
            end until;
      else
            while value < 1 loop
                  multiply value by 10;
                  subtract 1 from exponent;
            end while;
      end if;
end if;

add 0.000005 to value; { for rounding }
if value > 10
then
      divide value by 10;
      add 1 to exponent;
end if;

digit := int(value);
convert digit to ASCII and store in destination string;
point at next destination byte;
store "." in destination string;
point at next destination byte;
```

Figure 14.14 Continued.

```
                    for i := 1 to 5 loop
                            value := 10 * (value - float(digit));
                            digit := int(value);
                            convert digit to ASCII and store in destination string;
                            point at next destination byte;
                    end for;

                    store "E" in destination string;
                    point at next destination byte;
                    if exponent ≥ 0
                    then
                            put "+" in destination string;
                    else
                            put "-" in destination string;
                            exponent := - exponent;
                    end if;
                    point at next destination byte;
                    convert exponent to two decimal digits;
                    convert two decimal digits of exponent to ASCII;
                    store high order character of exponent in destination string;
                    point at next destination byte;
                    store low order character of exponent in destination string;
```

this one begins. The code implements the algorithm in a fairly straightforward fashion. It repeatedly uses calls to procedures in the previous section's floating point operations package. It also uses **ftoi** in this package to truncate the floating point value to an integer, as well as **itof** to get a corresponding floating point "integer" to subtract from the value, yielding the fractional part of the number.

An unusual feature in the **ftoa** procedure is the method of converting the two exponent digits to ASCII. With the exponent in the AX register, an **aam** instruction yields the corresponding two BCD digits in AH and AL. These are easily converted to ASCII codes using the instruction **or ax,3030h**. This technique only works when exactly two digits are needed.

Figure 14.15 Floating Point-to-ASCII Conversion Procedure.

```
    value       DD    ?
    ten         DD    10.0
    one         DD    1.0
    round       DD    0.000005
    fdigit      DD    ?
    exponent    DW    ?
```

Figure 14.15 Continued.

```
ftoa       PROC FAR              ; convert floating point number to
                                 ; 12 byte long ASCII string

; Two parameters passed on the stack
;    (1) offset of destination string in caller's data segment
;    (2) floating point value
;        High order word (sign, exponent, 7 fraction bits) pushed first,
;        then low order word (low order 16 fraction bits).
; ASCII string with format [blank/-]d.dddddE[+/-]dd is generated.
           push bp               ; save and reload BP
           mov  bp, sp

           push ax               ; save other registers
           push bx
           push cx
           push ds
           push es
           push di

           mov  ax, ds           ; caller's data segment number
           mov  es, ax
           mov  ax, SEG fp_conv  ; establish new data segment number
           mov  ds, ax

           mov  ax, [bp+6]       ; low order part of fp parameter
           mov  WORD PTR value, ax
           mov  ax, [bp+8]       ; high order part
           mov  WORD PTR value+2, ax
           mov  di, [bp+10]      ; offset of destination

if_1a:     push WORD PTR value+2              ; value >= 0?
           push WORD PTR value
           mov  ax, 0           ; compare with 0
           push ax
           push ax
           call fp_cmp
           jnge else_1a
then_1a:   mov  BYTE PTR es:[di], ' '        ; blank for positive value
           jmp  SHORT endif_1a
else_1a:   mov  BYTE PTR es:[di], '-'        ; minus sign for negative value
           push WORD PTR value+2             ; change value to positive
           push WORD PTR value
           call fp_neg
           pop  WORD PTR value
           pop  WORD PTR value+2
```

Figure 14.15 Continued.

```
     endif_1a:
                inc  di                        ; point at next destination byte
                mov  exponent, 0               ; exponent := 0

     if_2a:     push WORD PTR value+2          ; value = 0?
                push WORD PTR value
                mov  ax, 0
                push ax
                push ax
                call fp_cmp
                jne  then_2a
                jmp  endif_2a
     then_2a:
     if_3a:     push WORD PTR value+2          ; value >= 10?
                push WORD PTR value
                push WORD PTR ten+2
                push WORD PTR ten
                call fp_cmp
                jnge else_3a
     then_3a:
     until_a:   push WORD PTR value+2          ; value := value / 10.0
                push WORD PTR value
                push WORD PTR ten+2
                push WORD PTR ten
                call fp_div
                pop  WORD PTR value            ; pop quotient off stack
                pop  WORD PTR value+2
                inc  exponent                  ; add 1 to exponent
                push WORD PTR value+2          ; value < 10 ?
                push WORD PTR value
                push WORD PTR ten+2
                push WORD PTR ten
                call fp_cmp
                jnl  until_a
     enduntil_a:
                jmp  SHORT endif_3a


     else_3a:
     while_a:   push WORD PTR value+2          ; value < 1 ?
                push WORD PTR value
                push WORD PTR one+2
                push WORD PTR one
                call fp_cmp
                jnl  endwhile_a
                push WORD PTR value+2          ; value := value * 10.0
                push WORD PTR value
```

Figure 14.15 Continued.

```
        push WORD PTR ten+2
        push WORD PTR ten
        call fp_mul
        pop  WORD PTR value            ; pop product off stack
        pop  WORD PTR value+2
        dec  exponent                  ; subtract 1 from exponent
        jmp  while_a
endwhile_a:
endif_3a:

; at this point 1.0 <= value < 10.0

        push WORD PTR value+2          ; add rounding value
        push WORD PTR value
        push WORD PTR round+2
        push WORD PTR round
        call fp_add
        pop  WORD PTR value
        pop  WORD PTR value+2

if_4a:  push WORD PTR value+2          ; ensure value still < 10
        push WORD PTR value
        push WORD PTR ten+2
        push WORD PTR ten
        call fp_cmp
        jnge endif_4a
then_4a: push WORD PTR value+2         ; value >= 10-divide by 10 again
        push WORD PTR value
        push WORD PTR ten+2
        push WORD PTR ten
        call fp_div
        pop  WORD PTR value
        pop  WORD PTR value+2
        inc  exponent                  ; and increment exponent
endif_4a:
endif_2a:

        push WORD PTR value+2          ; convert value to integer
        push WORD PTR value
        call ftoi
        mov  bx, ax                    ; copy integer to BX
        or   ax, 30h                   ; convert digit to character
        mov  BYTE PTR es:[di], al      ; store character in destination
        inc  di                        ; point at next destination byte
        mov  BYTE PTR es:[di], '.'     ; decimal point
        inc  di                        ; point at next destination byte
```

Figure 14.15 Continued.

```
        mov  cx, 5                      ; count of remaining digits
for_a:  push bx                         ; convert digit to floating point
        mov  ax, OFFSET fdigit
        push ax
        call itof
        push WORD PTR value+2           ; value := value - digit
        push WORD PTR value
        push WORD PTR fdigit+2
        push WORD PTR fdigit
        call fp_sub
; it is not necessary to pop difference off stack since it would just
; have to be pushed back on to multiply by 10
        push WORD PTR ten+2             ; value := value * 10
        push WORD PTR ten
        call fp_mul
; it IS necessary to pop product off stack since it is needed for the
; new value in the next iteration of the loop
        pop  WORD PTR value
        pop  WORD PTR value+2
        push WORD PTR value+2           ; convert value to integer
        push WORD PTR value
        call ftoi
        mov  bx, ax                     ; copy integer to BX
        or   ax, 30h                    ; convert digit to character
        mov  BYTE PTR es:[di], al       ; store character in destination
        inc  di                         ; point at next destination byte
        loop for_a

        mov  BYTE PTR es:[di], 'E'      ; exponent indicator
        inc  di                         ; point at next destination byte

        mov  ax, exponent               ; get exponent
if_5a:  cmp  ax, 0                      ; exponent >= 0 ?
        jnge else_5a
then_5a: mov  BYTE PTR es:[di], '+'     ; nonnegative exponent
        jmp  SHORT endif_5a
else_5a: mov  BYTE PTR es:[di], '-'     ; negative exponent
        neg  ax                         ; change exponent to positive
endif_5a:
        inc  di                         ; point at next destination byte

        aam                             ; convert exponent to 2 digits
        or   ax, 3030h                  ; convert both digits to ASCII
        mov  BYTE PTR es:[di], ah       ; store characters in destination
        inc  di                         ; point at next destination byte
        mov  BYTE PTR es:[di], al
```

Figure 14.15 Continued.

```
        pop  di          ; restore registers
        pop  es
        pop  ds
        pop  cx
        pop  bx
        pop  ax
        pop  bp

        ret  6

ftoa    ENDP
```

The `atof` procedure finds the floating point value that corresponds to an ASCII string in memory. As implemented, it is restricted to an ASCII string with an optional leading minus sign; leading blanks or a plus sign are not allowed. It accepts any number of digits and decimal points; a decimal point after the first one is effectively ignored. Any character other than a leading minus sign, a digit, or a decimal point terminates the string. Consequently "E notation" is not acceptable.

The design for this `atof` procedure is given in Figure 14.16. As digits are encountered, the value is accumulated in much the same way as was used for ASCII to integer conversion—the old value is multiplied by 10 and the new digit is added to the product. If there are digits after a decimal point, this procedure will yield a value that is too large. To get the correct result, the accumulated value must be divided by 10 for each digit after the decimal point. To do this, the Boolean variable point is set to true when a decimal point is encountered, and the floating point variable divisor (initialized to 1.0) is multiplied by 10 each time point is true and a digit is processed. The variable divisor is then used to scale the result to the correct magnitude.

The code for procedure `atof` is given in Figure 14.17. The data that are needed only for this procedure are defined just before the procedure. (The doubleword **value**, defined before `ftoa` is also used.) Most of the code in procedure `atof` is unexceptional. One interesting feature is the use of a **lookup table** to convert a single digit to floating point. The ten doublewords starting at **digits** contain the floating point values 0.0 through 9.0. The value 0.0 is at offset 0 in this block, 1.0 is at offset 4, 2.0 is at offset 8, etc. The floating point value equivalent to a single-digit integer is obtained by multiplying the digit by four (using shifts), and utilizing the result to select the correct value from the table. This is much more efficient than calling the `itof` procedure.

Figure 14.16 ASCII-to-Floating Point Conversion Algorithm.

```
value := 0.0;
divisor := 1.0;
point := false;
minus := false;

point at first character of source string;
if source character = "-"
then
      minus := true;
      point at next character of source string;
end if;

while (source character is a digit or a decimal point) loop
      if source character = "."
      then
            point := true;
      else
            convert ASCII digit to 2's complement digit;
            digit_value := float(digit);
            value := 10 * value + digit_value;
            if point
            then
               multiply divisor by 10;
            end if;
      end if;
      point at next character of source string;
end while;

if point
then
      value := value/divisor;
end if;

if minus
then
      value := – value;
end if;
```

Figure 14.17 ASCII-to-Floating Point Conversion Procedure.

```
false       EQU  0
true        EQU  1
point       DB   ?
minus       DB   ?
digits      DD   0.0, 1.0, 2.0, 3.0, 4.0, 5.0, 6.0, 7.0, 8.0, 9.0
divisor     DD   ?


atof        PROC FAR            ; convert ASCII string to floating point number

; Two parameters passed on the stack
;   (1) offset of destination floating point number in caller's data segment
;   (2) offset of source string
; The string must consist of an optional minus sign, followed by a digits
; and (optionally) a decimal point. Any other character terminates
; the string.

            push bp             ; save and reload BP
            mov  bp, sp

            push ax             ; save other registers
            push bx
            push ds
            push es
            push si

            mov  ax, ds         ; caller's data segment number
            mov  es, ax
            mov  ax, SEG fp_conv ; establish new data segment number
            mov  ds, ax

            mov  WORD PTR value+2, 0  ; value := 0.0
            mov  WORD PTR value, 0
            mov  ax, WORD PTR one+2   ; divisor := 1.0
            mov  WORD PTR divisor+2, ax
            mov  ax, WORD PTR one
            mov  WORD PTR divisor, ax
            mov  point, false   ; no decimal point found yet
            mov  minus, false   ; no minus sign found yet
            mov  si, [bp+6]     ; offset of first source character

if_1f:      cmp  BYTE PTR es:[si], '-'    ; leading minus sign?
            jne  endif_1f
then_1f:    mov  minus, true    ; minus sign found
            inc  si
endif_1f:

while_f:    mov  bl, es:[si]    ; get next character
```

Figure 14.17 Continued.

```
            cmp  bl, '.'            ; decimal point?
            jne  digit
            mov  point, true        ; found decimal point
            jmp  SHORT next_ch
  digit:    cmp  bl, '0'            ; digit?
            jl   endwhile_f
            cmp  bl, '9'
            jg   endwhile_f
            and  bx, 000fh          ; convert ASCII to integer value
            push WORD PTR value+2      ; value := value * 10
            push WORD PTR value
            push WORD PTR ten+2
            push WORD PTR ten
            call fp_mul
; it is not necessary to pop product off stack since it would just
; have to be pushed back on to add digit
            shl  bx, 1              ; multiply digit by 4
            shl  bx, 1
            push WORD PTR digits[bx]+2  ; look up floating point digit in table
            push WORD PTR digits[bx]
            call fp_add                 ; value := value + digit
            pop  WORD PTR value
            pop  WORD PTR value+2
  if_2f:    cmp  point, true        ; already found a decimal point?
            jne  endif_2f
  then_2f:  push WORD PTR divisor+2     ; divisor := divisor * 10
            push WORD PTR divisor
            push WORD PTR ten+2
            push WORD PTR ten
            call fp_mul
            pop  WORD PTR divisor
            pop  WORD PTR divisor+2
  endif_2f:
  next_ch:  inc  si                 ; point at next source character
            jmp  while_f
  endwhile_f:

  if_3f:    cmp  point, true             ; was there a decimal point?
            jne  endif_3f
  then_3f:  push WORD PTR value+2        ; value := value / divisor
            push WORD PTR value
            push WORD PTR divisor+2
            push WORD PTR divisor
            call fp_div
            pop  WORD PTR value
            pop  WORD PTR value+2
  endif_3f:
```

Figure 14.17 Continued.

```
if_4f:      cmp   minus, true          ; was there a minus sign?
            jne   endif_4f
then_4f:    push  WORD PTR value+2     ; value := -value
            push  WORD PTR value
            call  fp_neg
            pop   WORD PTR value
            pop   WORD PTR value+2
endif_4f:

            mov   bx, [bp+8]           ; offset of destination value
            mov   ax, WORD PTR value   ; copy value to user's data segment
            mov   es:[bx], ax
            mov   ax, WORD PTR value+2
            mov   es:[bx+2], ax

            pop   si                   ; restore registers
            pop   es
            pop   ds
            pop   bx
            pop   ax
            pop   bp

            ret   4

atof        ENDP
```

───── Exercises 14.2 ─────

1. The `ftoi` procedure fails without any error indication if the floating point parameter is too large. Correct this situation by making the overflow flag OF zero if the truncated real value is in the range −32,768 to 32,767, and 1 if the value is not in this range. Also, assign the sign flag SF, the zero flag ZF and the parity flag PF appropriate values. Clear the carry flag CF. Other flags should remain unchanged.

2. The `ftoi` procedure truncates any fractional part—it does not round. Rewrite `ftoi` so that it rounds to the nearest integer. Hint: After shifting the bits into AX, the next bit of the fraction will be 1 if the remaining fraction is 0.5 or larger; add this next bit to the value in AX.

3. Improve the `atof` procedure so that it skips leading blanks in the source string, accepts a leading plus sign, and uses a second decimal point as a string terminator instead of just ignoring it.

--------- *Programming Exercises 14.2* --

1. Write a complete program that will prompt for and input a decimal value for the radius of a circle, and will calculate and display (appropriately labeled) the circumference and the area of the circle. Use any convenient method to input and output character strings, `atof` and `ftoa` procedures to convert between floating point and ASCII, and floating point procedures from Section 14.1 to implement arithmetic operations.

2. The following algorithm efficiently approximates the square root of a nonnegative number x

   ```
   root := 1.0;
   until (abs(root – old_root) < small_value) loop
         old_root := root;
         root := (root + x/root)/2.0;
   end until;
   ```

   Implement this design in a procedure `sqrt`, using 0.001 for small_value. The procedure should pass one floating point parameter on the stack and should return the square root on the stack, replacing the parameter.

   Write a main program to prompt for and input a positive integer value, and generate square roots of all integers from 1 through the chosen value. Display the results in a two-column table with appropriate column headers; put the integers in the first column and their square roots in the second column.

--------- 14.3 --

8087 Coprocessor Architecture

A **math coprocessor** is an integrated circuit that is used to extend the instruction set of a central processing unit so that a computer system with both processors can execute floating point instructions as well as ordinary instructions. The Intel 8087 Math Coprocessor is designed specifically to work with Intel 8088 and 8086 CPUs. It has its own internal registers, completely separate from the familiar 8088 registers. It executes instructions to do floating point arithmetic operations, including commonplace operations such as addition or multiplication, and more complicated operations such as evaluation of some transcendental functions. Not only can it transfer floating point operands data to or from memory, it can also transfer integer or BCD operands to or from the coprocessor. Nonfloating formats are always converted to floating point when moved to the 8087; a number in internal floating point format can be converted to integer or BCD format as it is moved to memory.

The 8087 coprocessor has eight **data registers**, each 80 bits long. A ten-byte IEEE floating point format is used for values stored in these registers. The registers are basically organized as a stack—for example, when the `fld` (floating load) instruction is used to transfer a value from memory to the 8087, the value is loaded into the register at the top of the stack, and data stored in the stack top and other registers are pushed down one register. However, some instructions can access any of the eight registers, so that the organization is not a "pure" stack.

The names of the eight 8087 data registers are

- ST, the stack top, also called ST(0),
- ST(1), the register just below the stack top,
- ST(2), the register just below ST(1),
- ST(3), ST(4), ST(5), ST(6), and
- ST(7), the register at the bottom of the stack.

In addition to the eight data registers, the 8087 has seven 16-bit **control registers**. These are called the **control word**, the **status word**, the **tag word**, the **instruction pointer** (two registers), and the **operand pointer** (also two registers). The status word is the only control register that will be considered in this book. Some of its bits are assigned values by floating point comparison instructions, and these bits must be examined in order for the 8088 to execute conditional jump instructions based on floating point comparison.

Before considering the 8087 instructions, a few notes are in order. Each 8087 mnemonic starts with the letter *F*, which is not used as the first character of any 8088 instruction. Most 8087 instructions act on the 8087 stack top ST and one other operand in another 8087 register or in memory. No 8087 instruction can access an internal 8088 register—any data to be transmitted between the 8088 and 8087 must be stored in memory by one processor and loaded by the other.

Figure 14.18 8087 Data Load Instructions.

Mnemonic	Operand	Action
fld	st (*num*)	contents of 8087 register pushed onto stack
fld	*memory* (real)	real value from memory pushed onto stack
fild	*memory* (integer)	integer value from memory converted to floating point and pushed onto stack
fbld	*memory* (BCD)	BCD value from memory converted to floating point and pushed onto stack
fld1	(none)	1.0 pushed onto stack
fldz	(none)	0.0 pushed onto stack
fldpi	(none)	π (pi) pushed onto stack
fldl2e	(none)	$\log_2(e)$ pushed onto stack
fldl2t	(none)	$\log_2(10)$ pushed onto stack
fldlg2	(none)	$\log_{10}(2)$ pushed onto stack

The 8087 instructions will be examined in groups, starting with instructions to push operands onto the stack. Figure 14.18 lists these mnemonics.

Some examples will illustrate how these instructions work. Suppose that the 8087 register stack contains

1.0	ST
2.0	ST(1)
3.0	ST(2)
	ST(3)
	ST(4)
	ST(5)
	ST(6)
	ST(7)

with values shown in decimal rather than IEEE floating point format. Suppose also that the data segment contains

```
fp_value    DD   10.0
int_value   DW   20
bcd_value   DT   30
```

If the instruction **fld fp_value** is executed, the register stack will contain

10.0	ST
1.0	ST(1)
2.0	ST(2)
3.0	ST(3)
	ST(4)
	ST(5)
	ST(6)
	ST(7)

Starting with these values, if the instruction `fld st(2)` is executed, the register stack will contain

2.0	ST
10.0	ST(1)
1.0	ST(2)
2.0	ST(3)
3.0	ST(4)
	ST(5)
	ST(6)
	ST(7)

Notice that the value 2.0 from ST(2) is pushed onto the top of the stack, but not removed from the stack. Starting with these values, assume that the instruction `fild int_value` is executed. The new contents of the register stack will be

20.0	ST
2.0	ST(1)
10.0	ST(2)
1.0	ST(3)
2.0	ST(4)
3.0	ST(5)
	ST(6)
	ST(7)

What is not obvious here is that the 16-bit value 00 14 is converted to an 80-bit floating point value. An integer operand must be word length or doubleword length; neither byte length nor quadword length integer operands are allowed.

If the instruction **fbld bcd_value** is executed, the stack values will become

30.0	ST
20.0	ST(1)
2.0	ST(2)
10.0	ST(3)
1.0	ST(4)
2.0	ST(5)
3.0	ST(6)
	ST(7)

where the 80-bit BCD value is converted to the very different 80-bit floating point format. Finally, if the instruction **fldz** is executed, the register stack will contain

0.0	ST
30.0	ST(1)
20.0	ST(2)
2.0	ST(3)
10.0	ST(4)
1.0	ST(5)
2.0	ST(6)
3.0	ST(7)

The stack is now full. No further value can be pushed onto the stack unless some value is popped from the stack, or the stack is cleared. The instruction **finit** initializes the 8087 and clears the contents of all eight registers. Normally a program that uses the 8087 will include the instruction

```
finit     ; initialize the math coprocessor
```

near the beginning of the code. It may be desirable to reinitialize the 8087 at

Figure 14.19 8087 Data Store Instructions.

Mnemonic	Operand	Action
fst	st(*num*)	replaces contents of ST(*num*) by copy of value from ST; only ST(*num*) is affected
fstp	st(*num*)	replaces contents of ST(*num*) by copy of value from ST; ST popped off the stack
fst	*memory* (real)	copy of ST stored as real value in memory; the stack is not affected
fstp	*memory* (real)	copy of ST stored as real value in memory; ST popped off the stack
fist	*memory* (integer)	copy of ST converted to integer and stored in memory
fistp	*memory* (integer)	copy of ST converted to integer and stored in memory; ST popped off the stack
fbstp	*memory* (BCD)	copy of ST converted to BCD and stored in memory; ST popped off the stack

points in the code, but normally this is not required since values will be popped from the stack, not allowed to accumulate on the stack.

Figure 14.19 lists the 8087 instructions that are used to copy data from the stack top to memory, or to another 8087 register. These instructions are mostly paired—one instruction of each pair copies ST to its destination and pops ST off the 8087 stack and the other instruction is identical except that ST is not popped off the stack. Note, however, the final instruction comes only in a "P-version", so that when a BCD destination is specified, ST must be popped off the stack.

A few examples will illustrate the actions of and the differences between these instructions. Suppose that at execution time the 8087 register stack contains

1.0	ST
2.0	ST(1)
3.0	ST(2)
4.0	ST(3)
	ST(4)
	ST(5)
	ST(6)
	ST(7)

The left diagram that follows shows the resulting stack if **fst st(2)** is executed and the right diagram shows the resulting stack if **fstp st(2)** is executed.

1.0	ST
2.0	ST(1)
3.0	ST(2)
4.0	ST(3)
	ST(4)
	ST(5)
	ST(6)
	ST(7)

2.0	ST
3.0	ST(1)
4.0	ST(2)
	ST(3)
	ST(4)
	ST(5)
	ST(6)
	ST(7)

Assume that the directive

```
int_value   DW   ?
```

is coded in the data segment. Suppose that the 8087 register stack contains

10.0	ST
20.0	ST(1)
30.0	ST(2)
40.0	ST(3)
	ST(4)
	ST(5)
	ST(6)
	ST(7)

The left diagram that follows shows the resulting stack if `fist int_value` is executed and the right diagram shows the resulting stack if

```
fistp int_value
```

is executed. In both cases, the contents of `int_value` will be 00 0A, the word-length 2's complement integer version of the floating point number 10.0.

10.0	ST
20.0	ST(1)
30.0	ST(2)
40.0	ST(3)
	ST(4)
	ST(5)
	ST(6)
	ST(7)

20.0	ST
30.0	ST(1)
40.0	ST(2)
	ST(3)
	ST(4)
	ST(5)
	ST(6)
	ST(7)

In addition to the load and store instructions listed above, the 8087 has an `fxch` instruction that will exchange the contents of two 8087 registers. With no operand,

```
fxch            ; exchange ST and ST(1)
```

will exchange the contents of the stack top and ST(1) just below ST on the stack. With a single operand, for example,

```
fxch  st(3) ; exchange ST and ST(3)
```

will interchange ST with the specified register.

Figure 14.20 shows the 8087 addition instructions. There are versions for adding the contents of ST to another register, contents of any register to ST, a real number from memory to ST or an integer number from memory to ST. There is *not* a version that uses a BCD number. The `faddp` instruction pops the stack top after adding it to another register, so that both operands are destroyed.

A few examples illustrate how the 8087 addition instructions work. Suppose that the data segment contains the directives

```
fp_value    DD   5.0
int_value   DW   1
```

and that the 8087 register stack contains

Figure 14.20 8087 Addition Instructions.

Mnemonic	Operands	Action
fadd	(none)	pops both ST and ST(1); adds these values; pushes sum onto the stack
fadd	st(num),st	adds ST(num) and ST; replaces ST(num) by the sum
fadd	st,st(num)	adds ST and ST(num); replaces ST by the sum
fadd	memory (real)	adds ST and real number from memory; replaces ST by the sum
fiadd	memory (integer)	adds ST and integer from memory; replaces ST by the sum
faddp	st(num),st	adds ST(num) and ST; replaces ST(num) by the sum; pops ST from stack

10.0	ST
20.0	ST(1)
30.0	ST(2)
40.0	ST(3)
	ST(4)
	ST(5)
	ST(6)
	ST(7)

After the instruction

    fadd   st,st(3)

is executed, the stack contains

50.0	ST
20.0	ST(1)
30.0	ST(2)
40.0	ST(3)
	ST(4)
	ST(5)
	ST(6)
	ST(7)

Starting with these stack values, after the two instructions

```
fadd    fp_value
fiadd   int_value
```

are executed, the contents of the stack are

56.0	ST
20.0	ST(1)
30.0	ST(2)
40.0	ST(3)
	ST(4)
	ST(5)
	ST(6)
	ST(7)

Finally, if the instruction

```
faddp   st(2)
```

is executed, the stack will contain

20.0	ST
86.0	ST(1)
40.0	ST(2)
	ST(3)
	ST(4)
	ST(5)
	ST(6)
	ST(7)

Subtraction instructions are displayed in Figure 14.21. The first six instructions are very similar to the corresponding addition instructions. The second six subtraction instructions are the same except that the operands are subtracted in the opposite order. This is sometimes convenient since subtraction is not a commutative operation.

Figure 14.21 8087 Subtraction Instructions.

Mnemonic	Operands	Action
fsub	(none)	pops ST and ST(1); calculates ST(1) – ST; pushes difference onto the stack
fsub	st(*num*),st	calculates ST(*num*) – ST; replaces ST(*num*) by the difference
fsub	st,st(*num*)	calculates ST – ST(*num*); replaces ST by the difference
fsub	*memory* (real)	calculates ST – real number from memory; replaces ST by the difference
fisub	memory (integer)	calculates ST – integer from memory; replaces ST by the difference
fsubp	st(*num*),st	calculates ST(*num*) – ST; replaces ST(*num*) by the difference; pops ST from the stack

Figure 14.21 Continued.

Mnemonic	Operands	Action
fsubr	(none)	pops ST and ST(1); calculates ST – ST(1); pushes difference onto the stack
fsubr	st(*num*),st	calculates ST – ST(*num*); replaces ST(*num*) by the difference
fsubr	st,st(*num*)	calculates ST(*num*) – ST; replaces ST by the difference
fsubr	*memory* (real)	calculates real number from memory – ST; replaces ST by the difference
fisubr	*memory* (integer)	calculates integer from memory – ST; replaces ST by the difference
fsubpr	st(*num*),st	calculates ST – ST(*num*); replaces ST(*num*) by the difference; pops ST from the stack

An example illustrates the difference between the parallel subtraction instructions. Suppose that the 8087 stack contains

15.0	ST
25.0	ST(1)
35.0	ST(2)
45.0	ST(3)
55.0	ST(4)
	ST(5)
	ST(6)
	ST(7)

The two diagrams that follow show the results after executing the instructions `fsub st,st(3)` and `fsubr st,st(3)`.

after `fsub st,st(3)`

–30.0	ST
25.0	ST(1)
35.0	ST(2)
45.0	ST(3)
55.0	ST(4)
	ST(5)
	ST(6)
	ST(7)

after `fsubr st,st(3)`

30.0	ST
25.0	ST(1)
35.0	ST(2)
45.0	ST(3)
55.0	ST(4)
	ST(5)
	ST(6)
	ST(7)

Multiplication and division instructions are listed in Figures 14.22 and 14.23, respectively. Multiplication instructions have the same forms as the addition instructions in Figure 14.20. Division instructions have the same forms as subtraction instructions in Figure 14.20, that is, the "R versions" reverse the operands' dividend and divisor roles.

Figure 14.22 8087 Multiplication Instructions.

Mnemonic	Operands	Action
fmul	(none)	pops ST and ST(1); multiplies these values; pushes product onto the stack
fmul	st(*num*),st	multiplies ST(*num*) and ST; replaces ST(*num*) by the product
fmul	st,st(*num*)	multiplies ST and ST(*num*); replaces ST by the product
fmul	*memory* (real)	multiplies ST and real number from memory; replaces ST by the product
fimul	*memory* (integer)	multiplies ST and integer from memory; replaces ST by the product
fmulp	st(*num*),st	multiplies ST(*num*) and ST; replaces ST(*num*) by the product; pops ST from stack

Figure 14.23 8087 Division Instructions.

Mnemonic	Operands	Action
fdiv	(none)	pops ST and ST(1); calculates ST(1) / ST; pushes quotient onto the stack
fdiv	st(*num*),st	calculates ST(*num*) / ST; replaces ST(*num*) by the quotient
fdiv	st,st(*num*)	calculates ST / ST(*num*); replaces ST by the quotient
fdiv	memory (real)	calculates ST / real number from memory; replaces ST by the quotient
fidiv	memory (integer)	calculates ST / integer from memory; replaces ST by the quotient
fdivp	st(*num*),st	calculates ST(*num*) / ST; replaces ST(*num*) by the quotient; pops ST from the stack
fdivr	(none)	pops ST and ST(1); calculates ST/ST(1); pushes quotient onto the stack
fdivr	st(*num*),st	calculates ST / ST(*num*); replaces ST(*num*) by the quotient
fdivr	st,st(*num*)	calculates ST(*num*) / ST; replaces ST by the quotient
fdivr	memory (real)	calculates real number from memory / ST; replaces ST by the quotient
fidivr	memory (integer)	calculates integer from memory / ST; replaces ST by the quotient
fdivpr	st(*num*),st	calculates ST / ST(*num*); replaces ST(*num*) by the quotient; pops ST from the stack

Figure 14.24 describes four miscellaneous 8087 instructions. Additional instructions that calculate tangent, arctangent, exponent, and logarithm functions are not covered in this book.

The 8087 provides a collection of instructions to compare the stack top ST to a second operand. These are listed in Figure 14.25. Recall that the 8087 has seven 16-bit control register. The comparison instructions assign values to bits 11, 10, and 8 in the control register called the status word; these **condition code** bits are named C3, C2, and C0, respectively. These flags are set as follows:

	C3	*C2*	*C0*
ST > second operand	0	0	0
ST < second operand	0	0	1
ST = second operand	1	0	0

Another possibility is that the operands are not comparable. This can occur

Figure 14.24 Miscellaneous 8087 Instructions.

Mnemonic	*Operands*	*Action*
`fabs`	(none)	ST := | ST | (absolute value)
`fchs`	(none)	ST := – ST (reverse sign)
`frndint`	(none)	rounds contents of ST to an integer
`fsqrt`	(none)	replaces contents of ST by its square root

if one of the operands is the IEEE representation for infinity or not a number. In this case, all three bits are set to 1. If a comparison is made in order to determine program flow, simply setting flags in the 8087 status word is no help. Conditional jump instructions look at bits in the flag register in the 8088, not the status word in the 8087. Consequently, the status word must be copied to memory before its bits can be examined by an 8088 instruction, perhaps with a `test` instruction. The 8087 has an `fstsw` instruction that stores the status word in a word in memory. For example, if the data segment contains the directive

```
status_word    DW    ?
```

then a program might use the instruction

```
fstsw    status_word    ; store status word
```

The 8087 also has instructions for loading or storing other control registers.
Because the 8087 chip is a coprocessor, its operations must be synchronized with the 8088 CPU. The 8087 constantly monitors the instructions that are being

Figure 14.25 8087 Comparison Instructions.

Mnemonic	*Operands*	*Action*
`fcom`	(none)	compares ST and ST(1)
`fcom`	`st (`*num*`)`	compares ST and ST(*num*)
`fcom`	*memory* (real)	compares ST and real number in memory
`ficom`	*memory* (integer)	compares ST and integer in memory
`ftst`	(none)	compares ST and 0
`fcomp`	(none)	compares ST and ST(1); then pops stack
`fcomp`	`st (`*num*`)`	compares ST and ST(*num*); then pops stack
`fcomp`	*memory* (real)	compares ST and real number in memory; then pops stack
`ficomp`	*memory* (integer)	compares ST and integer in memory; then pops stack
`fcompp`	(none)	compares ST and ST(1); then pops stack twice

executed. If the 8087 recognizes a floating point instruction for it to execute, then it signals the 8088 that it wants to carry out the instruction by putting a request signal on the 8088 TEST input pin. The 8087 does not, however, begin execution of the instruction while the 8088 is still busy. To become idle the 8088 must execute an 8088 `wait` instruction at the same time as the request is asserted on the TEST pin.

The Microsoft assembler inserts a `wait` instruction prior to each 8087 instruction. When the 8088 executes the `wait` instruction, the 8087 recognizes that the 8088 is idle and begins to execute the floating point instruction that was deferred. At the same time, the 8087 drops its request signal to the 8088. The 8088 `wait` instruction is really a "wait for test," and when the TEST line changes, the 8088 resumes normal operation, carrying out instructions at the same time the 8087 works on its operation. This is usually desirable, but can cause difficulty if the 8087 is storing data in memory that is to be accessed immediately by 8088 instructions; the 8087 may not finish storing the data before the 8088 fetches it from memory. An `fwait` instruction following the store instruction solves the problem, forcing the 8088 to wait until the 8087 completes its operation. An `fwait` is only needed following store instructions, not after other 8087 instructions.

Exercises 14.3

1. Suppose that a program's data segment contains

```
fp_value    DD    0.5
int_value   DW    6
```

and that code executed so far by the program has not changed these values. Suppose also that the 8087 stack contains

9.0	ST
12.0	ST(1)
23.0	ST(2)
24.0	ST(3)
35.0	ST(4)
	ST(5)
	ST(6)
	ST(7)

Assume that these values are correct before each instruction below is executed; do NOT use the "after" state of one problem as the "before" state of the next problem. Give the contents of the 8087 stack, of `fp_value` and of `int_value` following execution of the instruction.

(a)	`fld`	`st(2)`	(b)	`fld`	`fp_value`	
(c)	`fild`	`int_value`	(d)	`fldpi`		
(e)	`fst`	`st(4)`	(f)	`fstp`	`st(4)`	
(g)	`fst`	`fp_value`	(h)	`fistp`	`int_value`	
(i)	`fxch`	`st(3)`	(j)	`fadd`		
(k)	`fadd`	`st(3),st`	(l)	`fadd`	`st,st(3)`	
(m)	`faddp`	`st(3),st`	(n)	`fsub`	`fp_value`	
(o)	`fisub`	`int_value`	(p)	`fisubr`	`int_value`	
(q)	`fsubp`	`st(3),st`	(r)	`fmul`	`st, st(4)`	
(s)	`fmul`		(t)	`fmul`	`fp_value`	
(u)	`fdiv`		(v)	`fdivr`		
(w)	`fidiv`	`int_value`	(x)	`fdivp`	`st(2),st`	
(y)	`fchs`		(z)	`fsqrt`		

2. Suppose that a program's data segment contains

```
fp_value    DD    1.5
int_value   DW    9
```

and that code executed so far by the program has not changed these values. Suppose also that the 8087 stack contains

9.0	ST
12.0	ST(1)
23.0	ST(2)
24.0	ST(3)
35.0	ST(4)
	ST(5)
	ST(6)
	ST(7)

Assume that these values are correct before each instruction below is executed. Give the contents of the 8087 status word flags C3, C2, and C0 following execution of the instruction. For parts (e) and (f), also give the contents of the stack following execution of the instructions.

(a) `fcom`

(b) `fcom  st(3)`

(c) `fcom  fp_value`

(d) `ficom  int_value`

(e) `fcomp`

(f) `fcompp`

14.4

Programming with the 8087 Coprocessor

This section gives a single example of a procedure coded with 8087 instructions. The example is an implementation of the ASCII-to-floating point conversion algorithm given in Figure 14.16 (Section 14.2). Using the 8087, it is not as important to avoid an unessential division, so the **if**

```
if point
then
        value := value/divisor;
end if;
```

has been eliminated, leaving only the assignment statement

value := value/divisor;

Code for this new implementation is given in Figure 14.26.

The original implementation of the **atof** algorithm (Figure 14.17) used doublewords in memory to store divisor and value. This implementation uses ST(1) for divisor and ST for value except for one short segment where they are reversed in order to modify "divisor." After the preliminary busy work, the instructions

```
fld1            ; divisor := 1.0
fldz            ; value := 0.0
```

initialize these two variables. Note that the value 1.0 for "divisor" ends up in ST(1) since it is pushed down by the **fldz** instruction.

The code is the same as the previous implementation until it is time to realize the design

value := 10*value + digit_value

This is accomplished by the instructions

```
mov  digit, bx      ; put integer in memory
fmul ten            ; value := value * 10
fiadd digit         ; value := value + digit
```

Figure 14.26 8087 Implementation of atof Procedure.

```
ten        DD   10.0
false      EQU  0
true       EQU  1
point      DB   ?
minus      DB   ?
digit      DW   ?


atof       PROC FAR             ; convert ASCII string to floating point number

; Two parameters passed on the stack
;    (1) offset of destination floating point number in caller's data segment
;    (2) offset of source string
; The string must consist of an optional minus sign, followed by a series
; of digits and at most one decimal point. Invalid characters are skipped.
; The string is terminated by a null byte.

           push bp              ; save and reload BP
           mov  bp, sp

           push ax              ; save other registers
           push bx
           push ds
           push es
           push si

           mov  ax, ds          ; caller's data segment number
           mov  es, ax
           mov  ax, SEG fp_conv ; establish new data segment number
           mov  ds, ax

           fld1                 ; divisor := 1.0
           fldz                 ; value := 0.0
           mov  point, false    ; no decimal point found yet
           mov  minus, false    ; no minus sign found yet
           mov  si, [bp+6]      ; offset of first source character

if_1f:     cmp  BYTE PTR es:[si], '-'    ; leading minus sign?
           jne  endif_1f
then_1f:   mov  minus, true     ; minus sign found
           inc  si
endif_1f:

           while_f: mov  bl, es:[si]      ; get next character
           cmp  bl, '.'         ; decimal point?
           jne  digit?
           mov  point, true     ; found decimal point
           jmp  SHORT next_ch
```

Figure 14.26 Continued.

```
digit?:     cmp  bl, '0'          ; digit?
            jl   endwhile_f
            cmp  bl, '9'
            jg   endwhile_f
            and  bx, 000fh         ; convert ASCII to integer value
            mov  digit, bx         ; put integer in memory
        .   fmul ten               ; value := value * 10
            fiadd digit            ; value := value + digit
if_2f:      cmp  point, true       ; already found a decimal point?
            jne  endif_2f
            fxch                   ; put divisor in ST and value in ST(1)
            fmul ten               ; divisor := divisor * 10
            fxch                   ; value back to ST; divisor back to ST(1)
endif_2f:
next_ch:    inc  si                ; point at next source character
            jmp  while_f
endwhile_f:

            fdivr                  ; value := value / divisor

if_4f:      cmp  minus, true       ; was there a minus sign?
            jne  endif_4f
            fchs                   ; value := -value
endif_4f:
            mov  bx, [bp+8]        ; offset of destination value
            fstp DWORD PTR es:[bx]  ; store value in user's data segment
            fwait                  ; wait to be sure transfer done

            pop  si                ; restore registers
            pop  es
            pop  ds
            pop  bx
            pop  ax
            pop  bp

            ret  4

atof        ENDP
```

Note that a word-length 2's complement version of `digit` is stored in memory. The 8087 takes care of converting it to floating point as part of the **fiadd** instruction.

To implement "multiply divisor by 10," the number that is to be multiplied must be in ST. The instructions

```
        fxch              ; put divisor in ST and value in ST(1)
        fmul ten          ; divisor := divisor * 10
        fxch              ; value back to ST; divisor back
```

take care of swapping divisor and value, carrying out the multiplication in ST, and then swapping back.

When it is time to execute "value := value / divisor" the instruction

```
        fdivr     ; value := value / divisor
```

pops value from ST and "divisor" from ST(1), computes the quotient and pushes it back to ST. After this instruction, ST(1) is no longer in use by this procedure.

The instruction **fchs** changes the sign of value if a leading minus sign was noted in the ASCII string. Finally, the instructions

```
        fstp DWORD PTR es:[bx]   ; store value in user's data segment
        fwait                    ; wait to be sure transfer done
```

store the result at the address provided by the procedure's caller, waiting to execute further 8088 instructions until the transfer to memory is complete. Note that the **fstp** pops the result off the stack, so that no floating point numbers generated by this procedure are left on the 8087 stack. This ensures that repeated calls to the procedure will not overflow the stack.

Programming Exercises 14.4

---

1. An algorithm for converting a 32-bit IEEE floating point number to an ASCII string was given in Figure 14.14. Figure 14.15 displayed an implementation using the floating point emulation procedures developed earlier in the chapter. Rewrite procedure **ftoa** to use 8087 instructions instead of the emulation procedures.

2. Write a complete program that will prompt for and accept as input a decimal value for the radius of a circle, and will calculate and display (appropriately labeled) the circumference and the area of the circle. Use any convenient method to input and output character strings, **atof** and **ftoa** procedures to convert between floating point and ASCII, and 8087 instructions for floating point operations.

3. The following algorithm approximates the cube root of a real number x

   root := 1.0;
   until (abs(root - old_root) < small_value) loop
         old_root := root;
         root := (2.0 * root + x/root^2)/3.0;
   end until;

Implement this design in a procedure `cuberoot`, using 0.001 for small_value. Assume there are two parameters passed on the stack, the first the address for the result and the second the address of x. (Both addresses are offsets in the caller's data segment.) Use 8087 instructions to implement floating point operations in the design.

Write a main program to prompt for and input a positive integer value, and generate cube roots of all integers from 1 through the chosen value. Display the results in a two-column table with appropriate column headers; put the integers in the first column and their cube roots in the second column.

14.5

Chapter Summary

The Microsoft assembler uses the DD directive to reserve space for a 32-bit floating point number. If a decimal operand is specified, it is stored in IEEE "single" format.

There are two ways to manipulate floating point numbers stored in the 32-bit IEEE format. The first method is to use only 8088 instructions to code procedures to operate on floating point numbers. This involves separating out the bit patterns for exponents and fractions and using them to build sums, products, etc. Section 14.1 developed a set of procedures to do basic floating point operations, multiplication, division, addition, subtraction, negation, and comparison. Section 14.2 crafted a package of procedures to convert between floating point format and other formats, to word-length 2's complement integer, from integer, to ASCII string, and from ASCII.

Floating point numbers can also be manipulated using an 8087 numeric coprocessor. The 8087 has eight 80-bit registers that are organized basically as a stack. It executes a variety of instructions using floating point operands. It can also load and store operands in 2's complement and BCD formats, converting such representations to and from floating point as needed. Section 14.4 presented an implementation of the ASCII-to-floating point conversion algorithm that used the 8087 for floating point calculations, resulting in a much shorter and more efficient procedure than was given in Section 14.2.

8088/8086 Instructions

aaa ASCII adjust for addition

Operation: adjust AL and AH after addition of unpacked BCD numbers
Flags affected: AF, CF set/reset. OF, PF, SF, ZF undefined.
Reference: Section 13.3

Source Format	Opcode	Other Bytes	Clock Cycles
aaa	37	(none)	4

aad ASCII adjust for division

Operation: adjust AL and AH before division of unpacked BCD numbers
Flags affected: PF, SF, ZF set/reset. AF, CF, OF undefined.
Reference: Section 13.3

Source Format	Opcode	Other Bytes	Clock Cycles
aad	D5	0A	60

aam ASCII adjust for multiplication

Operation: adjust AL and AH after multiplication of unpacked BCD numbers
Flags affected: PF, SF, ZF set/reset. AF, CF, OF undefined.
Reference: Section 13.3

Source Format	Opcode	Other Bytes	Clock Cycles
aam	D4	0A	83

aas **ASCII adjust for subtraction**

Operation: adjust AL and AH after subtraction of unpacked BCD numbers
Flags affected: AF, CF set/reset. OF, PF, SF, ZF undefined.
Reference: Section 13.3

Source Format	Opcode	Other Bytes	Clock Cycles
aas	3F	(none)	4

adc **add with carry**

Operation: destination := destination + source + carry
Flags affected: AF, CF, OF, PF, SF, ZF set/reset.
Reference: Section 4.5

Source Formats	Opcode	Other Bytes	Clock Cycles
adc *mem8,reg8*	10	mod reg r/m, (address)	16+
adc *mem16,reg16*	11	mod reg r/m, (address)	24+
adc *reg8,mem8*	12	mod reg r/m, (address)	9+
adc *reg8,reg8*	12	11 dest_reg source_reg	3
adc *reg16,mem16*	13	mod reg r/m, (address)	13+
adc *reg16,reg16*	13	11 dest_reg source_reg	3
adc *al,imm8*	14	immediate byte	4
adc *ax,imm16*	15	immediate word	4
adc *mem8,imm8*	80	mod 010 r/m,(address), immediate byte	17+
adc *reg8,imm8*	80	11 010 reg, immediate byte	4
adc *mem16,imm16*	81	mod 010 r/m,(address), immediate word	25+
adc *reg16,imm16*	81	11 010 reg, immediate word	4
adc *mem16,imm8*	83	mod 010 r/m,(address), immediate byte	25+
adc *reg16,imm8*	83	11 010 reg, immediate byte	4

add **addition**

Operation: destination := destination + source
Flags affected: AF, CF, OF, PF, SF, ZF set/reset.
Reference: Section 4.2

Source Formats	Opcode	Other Bytes	Clock Cycles
add *mem8, reg8*	00	mod reg r/m, (address)	16+
add *mem16,reg16*	01	mod reg r/m, (address)	24+

Source Formats	Opcode	Other Bytes	Clock Cycles
add *reg8,mem8*	02	mod reg r/m, (address)	9+
add *reg8,reg8*	02	11 dest_reg source_reg	3
add *reg16,mem16*	03	mod reg r/m, (address)	13+
add *reg16,reg16*	03	11 dest_reg source_reg	3
add *al,imm8*	04	immediate byte	4
add *ax,imm16*	05	immediate word	4
add *mem8,imm8*	80	mod 000 r/m,(address), immediate byte	17+
add *reg8,imm8*	80	11 000 reg, immediate byte	4
add *mem16,imm16*	81	mod 000 r/m,(address), immediate word	25+
add *reg16,imm16*	81	11 000 reg, immediate word	4
add *mem16,imm8*	83	mod 000 r/m,(address), immediate byte	25+
add *reg16,imm8*	83	11 000 reg, immediate byte	4

and **logical and**

Operation: destination := destination and source
Flags affected: PF, SF, ZF set/reset. CF=0, OF=0. AF undefined.
Reference: Section 9.1

Source Formats	Opcode	Other Bytes	Clock Cycles
and *mem8,reg8*	20	mod reg r/m, (address)	16+
and *mem16,reg16*	21	mod reg r/m, (address)	24+
and *reg8,mem8*	22	mod reg r/m, (address)	9+
and *reg8,reg8*	22	11 dest_reg source_reg	3
and *reg16,mem16*	23	mod reg r/m, (address)	13+
and *reg16,reg16*	23	11 dest_reg source_reg	3
and *al,imm8*	24	immediate byte	4
and *ax,imm16*	25	immediate word	4
and *mem8,imm8*	80	mod 100 r/m,(address), immediate byte	17+
and *reg8,imm8*	80	11 100 reg, immediate byte	4
and *mem16,imm16*	81	mod 100 r/m,(address), immediate word	25+
and *reg16,imm16*	81	11 100 reg, immediate word	4

and *mem16,imm8*	83	mod 100 r/m,(address), immediate byte	25 +
and *reg16,imm8*	83	11 100 reg, immediate byte	3

call **call procedure**

Operation: save return address on stack, transfer control to procedure
Flags affected: none
Reference: Section 6.1

Source Formats	Opcode	Other Bytes	Clock Cycles
call *label* (near)	E8	displacement word	23
call *label*(far)	9A	offset and segment number words	36
call *mem32* (far)	FF	mod 010 r/m, (address)	53+
call *mem16* (near)	FF	mod 011 r/m, (address)	29+
call *reg16* (near)	FF	mod 011 r/m	24

cbw **convert byte to word**

Operation: extend sign bit of AL into AH
Flags affected: none
Reference: Section 4.4

Source Format	Opcode	Other Bytes	Clock Cycles
cbw	98	(none)	2

clc **clear carry flag**

Operation: CF := 0
Flags affected: CF = 0
Reference: Section 4.5

Source Format	Opcode	Other Bytes	Clock Cycles
clc	F8	(none)	2

cld **clear direction flag**

Operation: DF := 0
Flags affected: DF = 0
Reference: Section 7.1

Source Format	Opcode	Other Bytes	Clock Cycles
cld	FC	(none)	2

cli   **clear interrupt flag**

Operation: IF := 0
Flags affected: IF = 0
Reference: none

Source Format	Opcode	Other Bytes	Clock Cycles
cli	FA	(none)	2

cmc   **complement carry flag**

Operation: CF := 1 - CF
Flags affected: CF
Reference: Section 4.5

Source Format	Opcode	Other Bytes	Clock Cycles
cmc	F5	(none)	2

cmp   **compare**

Operation: flags set for (destination - source)
Flags affected: AF, CF, OF, PF, SF, ZF set/reset.
Reference: Section 5.2

Source Formats	Opcode	Other Bytes	Clock Cycles
cmp *mem8,reg8*	38	mod reg r/m, (address)	9+
cmp *mem16,reg16*	39	mod reg r/m, (address)	13+
cmp *reg8,mem8*	3A	mod reg r/m, (address)	9+
cmp *reg8,reg8*	3A	11 dest_reg source_reg	3
cmp *reg16,mem16*	3B	mod reg r/m, (address)	13+
cmp *reg16,reg16*	3B	11 dest_reg source_reg	3
cmp *al,imm8*	3C	immediate byte	4
cmp *ax,imm16*	3D	immediate word	4
cmp *mem8,imm8*	80	mod 111 r/m,(address), immediate byte	10+
cmp *reg8,imm8*	80	11 111 reg, immediate byte	4
cmp *mem16,imm16*	81	mod 111 r/m,(address), immediate word	14+
cmp *reg16,imm16*	81	11 111 reg, immediate word	4
cmp *mem16,imm8*	83	mod 111 r/m,(address), immediate byte	10+
cmp *reg16,imm8*	83	11 111 reg, immediate byte	4

cmps **compare string elements**

Operation: set flags for (destination - source); adjust SI and DI
Flags affected: AF, CF, OF, PF, SF, ZF set/reset.
Reference: Section 7.2

Source Formats	Opcode	Other Bytes	Clock Cycles
cmpsb	A6	(none)	22
cmpsw	A7	(none)	30

cwd **convert word to double**

Operation: extend sign bit of AX into DX
Flags affected: none
Reference: Section 4.4

Source Format	Opcode	Other Bytes	Clock Cycles
cwd	99	(none)	5

daa **decimal adjust for addition**

Operation: adjust AL after addition of packed BCD numbers
Flags affected: AF, CF, PF, SF, ZF set/reset. OF undefined.
Reference: Section 13.2

Source Format	Opcode	Other Bytes	Clock Cycles
daa	27	(none)	4

das **decimal adjust for subtraction**

Operation: adjust AL after subtraction of packed BCD numbers
Flags affected: AF, CF, PF, SF, ZF set/reset. OF undefined.
Reference: Section 13.2

Source Format	Opcode	Other Bytes	Clock Cycles
das	2F	(none)	4

dec **decrement**

Operation: operand := operand - 1
Flags affected: AF, OF, PF, SF, ZF set/reset.
Reference: Section 4.2

Source Formats	Opcode	Other Bytes	Clock Cycles
dec ax	48	(none)	2
dec cx	49	(none)	2
dec dx	4A	(none)	2

Source Formats	Opcode	Other Bytes	Clock Cycles
dec bx	4B	(none)	2
dec sp	4C	(none)	2
dec bp	4D	(none)	2
dec si	4E	(none)	2
dec di	4F	(none)	2
dec *mem8*	FE	mod 001 r/m, (address)	15+
dec *reg8*	FE	11 001 reg	3
dec *mem16*	FF	mod 001 r/m, (address)	23+

div   **unsigned division**

Operation: dividend divided by divisor yields quotient and remainder
Flags affected: AF, CF, OF, PF, SF, ZF undefined.
Reference: Section 4.4

Source Formats	Opcode	Other Bytes	Clock Cycles
div *mem8*	F6	mod 110 r/m, (address)	86–96+
div *reg8*	F6	11 110 reg	80–90
div *mem16*	F7	mod 110 r/m, (address)	154–172+
div *reg16*	F7	11 110 reg	144–162

esc   **escape**

Operation: put operand on bus for coprocessor
Flags affected: none
Reference: none

Source Formats	Opcode	Other Bytes	Clock Cycles
esc 0, *mem8*	D8	mod 000 r/m, (address)	12+
esc 0, *reg8*	D8	11 000 reg	2
esc 1, *mem8*	D9	mod 000 r/m, (address)	12+
esc 1, *reg8*	D9	11 000 reg	2
esc 2, *mem8*	DA	mod 000 r/m, (address)	12+
esc 2, *reg8*	DA	11 000 reg	2
esc 3, *mem8*	DB	mod 000 r/m, (address)	12+
esc 3, *reg8*	DB	11 000 reg	2
esc 4, *mem8*	DC	mod 000 r/m, (address)	12+
esc 4, *reg8*	DC	11 000 reg	2
esc 5, *mem8*	DD	mod 000 r/m, (address)	12+
esc 5, *reg8*	DD	11 000 reg	2
esc 6, *mem8*	DE	mod 000 r/m, (address)	12+
esc 6, *reg8*	DE	11 000 reg	2
esc 7, *mem8*	DF	mod 000 r/m, (address)	12+
esc 7, *reg8*	DF	11 000 reg	2

hlt   **halt**

Operation: stop CPU execution pending interrupt or reset
Flags affected: none
Reference: none

Source Format	Opcode	Other Bytes	Clock Cycles
hlt	F4	(none)	2

idiv   **signed division**

Operation: dividend divided by divisor yields quotient and remainder
Flags affected: AF, CF, OF, PF, SF, ZF undefined.
Reference: Section 4.4

Source Formats	Opcode	Other Bytes	Clock Cycles
idiv *mem8*	F6	mod 111 r/m, (address)	107–118+
idiv *reg8*	F6	11 111 reg	101–112
idiv *mem16*	F7	mod 111 r/m, (address)	175–194+
idiv *reg16*	F7	11 111 reg	165–184

imul   **signed multiplication**

Operation: multiply operands
Flags affected: CF, OF set/reset. AF, PF, SF, ZF undefined.
Reference: Section 4.3

Source Formats	Opcode	Other Bytes	Clock Cycles
imul *mem8*	F6	mod 101 r/m, (address)	86–104+
imul *reg8*	F6	11 101 reg	80–98
imul *mem16*	F7	mod 101 r/m, (address)	138–164+
imul *reg16*	F7	11 101 reg	128–154

in   **input from port**

Operation: transfer data from port to accumulator
Flags affected: none
Reference: Section 10.4

Source Formats	Opcode	Other Bytes	Clock Cycles
in al,*port*	E4	port byte	10
in ax,*port*	E5	port byte	14
in al,dx	EC	(none)	8
in ax,dx	ED	(none)	12

inc   increment operand

Operation: operand := operand + 1
Flags affected: AF, OF, PF, SF, ZF set/reset.
Reference: Section 4.2

Source Formats	Opcode	Other Bytes	Clock Cycles
inc ax	40	(none)	2
inc cx	41	(none)	2
inc dx	42	(none)	2
inc bx	43	(none)	2
inc sp	44	(none)	2
inc bp	45	(none)	2
inc si	46	(none)	2
inc di	47	(none)	2
inc *mem8*	FE	mod 000 r/m, (address)	15 +
inc *reg8*	FE	11 000 reg	3
inc *mem16*	FF	mod 000 r/m, (address)	23 +

int   interrupt

Operation: save flags, call interrupt handler
Flags affected: IF=0, TF=0.
Reference: Section 10.1

Source Formats	Opcode	Other Bytes	Clock Cycles
int 3	CC	(none)	72
int *imm8*	CD	immediate byte	71

into   interrupt on overflow

Operation: save flags, call interrupt handler if CF=1
Flags affected: IF, TF.
Reference: Section 10.1

Source Formats	Opcode	Other Bytes	Clock Cycles
into	CE	(none)	73 or 4

iret   interrupt return

Operation: return from interrupt
Flags affected: all
Reference: Section 10.1

Source Formats	Opcode	Other Bytes	Clock Cycles
iret	CF	(none)	44

jcxz   jump if CX = 0

Operation: jump if CX register contains zero
Flags affected: none
Reference: Section 5.4

Source Format	Opcode	Other Bytes	Clock Cycles
jcxz	E3	displacement byte	18 or 6

jmp   jump unconditionally

Operation: jump depending on flag values
Flags affected: none
Reference: Section 5.1

Source Formats	Opcode	Other Bytes	Clock Cycles
jmp label	E9	displacement word	15
jmp label	EA	offset and segment number words	15
jmp label	EB	displacement byte	15
jmp mem16	FF	mod 101 r/m, (address)	18 +
jmp mem32	FF	mod 100 r/m	24 +
jmp reg16	FF	11 101 reg	11

jcondition   jump conditionally

Operation: jump depending on flag values
Flags affected: none
Reference: Section 5.2
Other Bytes: displacement byte
Clock Cycles: 16 or 4

Source Formats	Opcode	Jump if	Description
ja/jnbe	77	CF=0 and ZF=0	jump above (unsigned)
jae/jnb	73	CF=0	jump above or equal (unsigned)
jb/jnae	72	CF=1	jump below (unsigned)
jbe/jna	76	CF=0 or ZF=1	jump below or equal (unsigned)
jc	72	CF=1	jump carry
jnc	73	CF=0	jump no carry
jl/jnge	7C	SF≠OF	jump less (signed)
jle/jng	7E	SF≠OF or ZF=1	jump less or equal (signed)
jg/jnle	7F	SF=OF and ZF=0	jump greater (signed)
jge/jnl	7D	SF=OF	jump greater or equal (signed)
je/jz	74	ZF=1	jump equal (zero)
jne/jnz	75	ZF=0	jump not equal (zero)
jo	70	OF=1	jump overflow

Source Formats	Opcode	Jump if	Description
jno	71	OF=0	jump no overflow
jp/jpe	7A	PF=1	jump parity/parity even
jnp/jpo	7B	PF=0	jump no parity/parity odd
js	78	SF=1	jump sign
jns	79	SF=0	jump no sign

lahf   load flags from AH

Operation: AH := SF, ZF, -, AF, -, PF, -, CF
Flags affected: none
Reference: Section 13.2

Source Format	Opcode	Other Bytes	Clock Cycles
lahf	9F	(none)	4

l*segment_register*   load far pointer

Operation: load segment register and destination register from memory
Flags affected: none
Reference: none

Source Formats	Opcode	Other Bytes	Clock Cycles
lds *reg16,mem*	C5	mod reg r/m, (address)	24+
les *reg16,mem*	C4	mod reg r/m, (address)	24+

lea   load effective address

Operation: load effective address of source into destination register
Flags affected: none
Reference: Section 5.5

Source Format	Opcode	Other Bytes	Clock Cycles
lea *reg16,mem*	8D	mod reg r/m, (address)	2+

lock   lock the bus

Operation: locks out other processors during execution of next instruction
Flags affected: none
Reference: none

Source Format	Opcode	Clock Cycles
lock (prefix byte)	F0	2

`lods` **load string element**

Operation: copy source element to AH or AX; adjust SI
Flags affected: none
Reference: Section 7.2

Source Formats	Opcode	Other Bytes	Clock Cycles
`lodsb`	AC	(none)	12
`lodsw`	AD	(none)	16

`loop` **loop**

Operation: decrement CX; jump if CX ≠ 0
Flags affected: none
Reference: Section 5.4

Source Format	Opcode	Other Bytes	Clock Cycles
`loop`	E2	displacement byte	17 or 5

`loopcondition` **loop conditionally**

Operation: decrement CX; jump if CX ≠ 0 and ZF set/reset
Flags affected: none
Reference: Section 5.4

Source Formats	Opcode	Other Bytes	Clock Cycles
`loopz`/`loope`	E1	displacement byte	18 or 6
`loopnz`/`loopne`	E0	displacement byte	19 or 5

`mov` **move byte or word**

Operation: destination := source
Flags affected: none
Reference: Section 4.1

Source Formats	Opcode	Other Bytes	Clock Cycles
`mov` *mem8,reg8*	88	mod reg r/m, (address)	9 +
`mov` *reg8,reg8*	88	11 dest_reg source_reg	2
`mov` *mem16,reg16*	89	mod reg r/m, (address)	13 +
`mov` *reg16,reg16*	89	11 dest_reg source_reg	2
`mov` *reg8,mem8*	8A	mod reg r/m, (address)	8 +
`mov` *reg16,mem16*	8B	11 dest_reg source_reg, (address)	12 +
`mov` *mem16,sreg*	8C	mod reg r/m, (address)	13 +
`mov` *reg16,sreg*	8C	11 reg r/m	2
`mov` *sreg,mem16*	8E	mod reg r/m, (address)	12 +
`mov` *sreg,reg16*	8E	11 reg r/m	2

Source Formats	Opcode	Other Bytes	Clock Cycles
mov al,*mem8*	A0	offset word (direct addressing)	10
mov ax,*mem16*	A1	offset word	14
mov *mem8*,al	A2	offset word	10
mov *mem16*,ax	A3	offset word	14
mov al,*imm8*	B0	immediate byte	4
mov cl,*imm8*	B1	immediate byte	4
mov dl,*imm8*	B2	immediate byte	4
mov bl,*imm8*	B3	immediate byte	4
mov ah,*imm8*	B4	immediate byte	4
mov ch,*imm8*	B5	immediate byte	4
mov dh,*imm8*	B6	immediate byte	4
mov bh,*imm8*	B7	immediate byte	4
mov ax,*imm16*	B8	immediate word	4
mov cx,*imm16*	B9	immediate word	4
mov dx,*imm16*	BA	immediate word	4
mov bx,*imm16*	BB	immediate word	4
mov sp,*imm16*	BC	immediate word	4
mov bp,*imm16*	BD	immediate word	4
mov si,*imm16*	BE	immediate word	4
mov di,*imm16*	BF	immediate word	4
mov *mem8*,*imm8*	C6	mod 000 r/m,(address), immediate byte	10 +
mov *reg8*,*imm8*	C6	11 000 r/m, immediate byte	4
mov *mem16*,*imm16*	C7	mod 000 r/m,(address), immediate word	14 +
mov *reg16*,*imm16*	C7	11 000 r/m, immediate word	4

movs **move string element**

Operation: copy source element destination; adjust SI and DI
Flags affected: none
Reference: Section 7.1

Source Formats	Opcode	Other Bytes	Clock Cycles
movsb	A4	(none)	18
movsw	A5	(none)	26

mul **unsigned multiplication**

Operation: multiply operands
Flags affected: CF, OF set/reset. AF, PF, SF, ZF undefined.
Reference: Section 4.3

Source Formats	Opcode	Other Bytes	Clock Cycles
mul *mem8*	F6	mod 100 r/m, (address)	76–83 +
mul *reg8*	F6	11 100 reg	70–77
mul *mem16*	F7	mod 100 r/m, (address)	128–143 +
mul *reg16*	F7	11 100 reg	118–133

neg **negation**

Operation: 2's complement negation
Flags affected: AF, CF, OF, PF, SF, ZF set/reset.
Reference: Section 4.2

Source Formats	Opcode	Other Bytes	Clock Cycles
neg *mem8*	F6	mod 011 r/m, (address)	16+
neg *reg8*	F6	11 011 reg	3
neg *mem16*	F7	mod 011 r/m, (address)	24+
neg *reg16*	F7	11 011 reg	3

nop **no operation**

Operation: none
Flags affected: none
Reference: Section 5.1

Source Format	Opcode	Other Bytes	Clock Cycles
nop	90	(none)	3

not **logical not**

Operation: 1's complement
Flags affected: none
Reference: Section 9.1

Source Formats	Opcode	Other Bytes	Clock Cycles
not *mem8*	F6	mod 010 r/m, (address)	16+
not *reg8*	F6	11 010 reg	3
not *mem16*	F7	mod 010 r/m, (address)	24+
not *reg16*	F7	11 010 reg	3

or **logical or**

Operation: destination := destination or source
Flags affected: PF, SF, ZF set/reset. CF=0, OF=0. AF undefined.
Reference: Section 9.1

Source Formats	Opcode	Other Bytes	Clock Cycles
or *mem8,reg8*	08	mod reg r/m, (address)	16 +
or *mem16,reg16*	09	mod reg r/m, (address)	24 +
or *reg8,mem8*	0A	mod reg r/m, (address)	9 +
or *reg8,reg8*	0A	11 dest_reg source_reg	3
or *reg16,mem16*	0B	mod reg r/m, (address)	13 +
or *reg16,reg16*	0B	11 dest_reg source_reg	3
or *al,imm8*	0C	immediate byte	4
or *ax,imm16*	0D	immediate word	4
or *mem8,imm8*	80	mod 001 r/m,(address), immediate byte	17 +
or *reg8,imm8*	80	11 001 reg, immediate byte	4
or *mem16,imm16*	81	mod 001 r/m,(address), immediate word	25 +
or *reg16,imm16*	81	11 001 reg, immediate word	4
or *mem16,imm8*	83	mod 001 r/m,(address), immediate byte	25 +
or *reg16,imm8*	83	11 001 reg, immediate byte	3

out **output to port**

Operation: transfer data from accumulator to port
Flags affected: none
Reference: Section 10.4

Source Formats	Opcode	Other Bytes	Clock Cycles
out *al,port*	E6	port byte	10
out *ax,port*	E7	port byte	14
out *al,dx*	EE	(none)	8
out *ax,dx*	EF	(none)	12

pop **pop**

Operation: pop word from stack to destination
Flags affected: none
Reference: Section 6.2

Source Formats	Opcode	Other Bytes	Clock Cycles
pop *es*	07	(none)	12
pop *ss*	17	(none)	12
pop *ds*	1F	(none)	12
pop *ax*	58	(none)	12
pop *cx*	59	(none)	12
pop *dx*	5A	(none)	12
pop *bx*	5B	(none)	12

Source Formats	Opcode	Other Bytes	Clock Cycles
pop sp	5C	(none)	12
pop bp	5D	(none)	12
pop si	5E	(none)	12
pop di	5F	(none)	12
pop *mem16*	8F	mod 000 r/m, (address)	25 +

popf   **pop flags**

Operation: pop word from stack to flags register
Flags affected: all
Reference: Section 6.2

Source Format	Opcode	Other Bytes	Clock Cycles
popf	9D	(none)	12

push   **push**

Operation: push source word onto stack
Flags affected: none
Reference: Section 6.2

Source Formats	Opcode	Other Bytes	Clock Cycles
push es	06	(none)	14
push cs	0E	(none)	14
push ss	16	(none)	14
push ds	1E	(none)	14
push ax	50	(none)	15
push cx	51	(none)	15
push dx	52	(none)	15
push bx	53	(none)	15
push sp	54	(none)	15
push bp	55	(none)	15
push si	56	(none)	15
push di	57	(none)	15
push *mem16*	FF	mod 110 r/m, (address)	24 +

pushf   **push flags**

Operation: push flags register onto stack
Flags affected: none
Reference: Section 6.2

Source Format	Opcode	Other Bytes	Clock Cycles
pushf	9C	(none)	14

rcdirection **rotate through carry**

Operation: rotate operand through carry flag
Flags affected: CF, OF set/reset.
Reference: 9.2

Source Formats	Opcode	Other Bytes	Clock Cycles
rcl *mem8*,1	D0	mod 010 r/m, (address)	15+
rcl *reg8*,1	D0	11 010 reg	2
rcl *mem16*,1	D1	mod 010 r/m, (address)	23+
rcl *reg16*,1	D1	11 010 reg	2
rcl *mem8*,cl	D2	mod 010 r/m, (address)	4/bit+20+
rcl *reg8*,cl	D2	11 010 reg	4/bit+8
rcl *mem16*,cl	D3	mod 010 r/m, (address)	4/bit+28+
rcl *reg16*,cl	D3	11 010 reg	4/bit+8
rcr *mem8*,1	D0	mod 011 r/m, (address)	15+
rcr *reg8*,1	D0	11 011 reg	2
rcr *mem16*,1	D1	mod 011 r/m, (address)	23+
rcr *reg16*,1	D1	11 011 reg	2
rcr *mem8*,cl	D2	mod 011 r/m, (address)	4/bit+20+
rcr *reg8*,cl	D2	11 011 reg	4/bit+8
rcr *mem16*,cl	D3	mod 011 r/m, (address)	4/bit+28+
rcr *reg16*,cl	D3	11 011 reg	4/bit+8

rep/repcondition **repeat prefix**

Operation: repeat string operation
Flags affected: none
Reference: Section 7.2

Source Formats	Opcode
rep/repe/repz prefix	F3
repne/repnz prefix	F2

ret **return from procedure**

Operation: pop return address from stack; optionally increment SP
Flags affected: none
Reference: Section 6.1

Source Formats	Opcode	Other Bytes	Clock Cycles
ret (near)	C3	(none)	20
ret (far)	CB	(none)	34
ret *imm16* (near)	C2	immediate word	24
ret *imm16* (far)	CA	immediate word	33

rodirection **rotate**

Operation: rotate operand
Flags affected: CF, OF set/reset.
Reference: 9.2

Source Formats	Opcode	Other Bytes	Clock Cycles
rol *mem8*,1	D0	mod 000 r/m, (address)	15 +
rol *reg8*,1	D0	11 000 reg	2
rol *mem16*,1	D1	mod 000 r/m, (address)	23 +
rol *reg16*,1	D1	11 000 reg	2
rol *mem8*,cl	D2	mod 000 r/m, (address)	4/bit+20 +
rol *reg8*,cl	D2	11 000 reg	4/bit+8
rol *mem16*,cl	D3	mod 000 r/m, (address)	4/bit+28 +
rol *reg16*,cl	D3	11 000 reg	4/bit+8
ror *mem8*,1	D0	mod 001 r/m, (address)	15 +
ror *reg8*,1	D0	11 001 reg	2
ror *mem16*,1	D1	mod 001 r/m, (address)	23 +
ror *reg16*,1	D1	11 001 reg	2
ror *mem8*,cl	D2	mod 001 r/m, (address)	4/bit+20 +
ror *reg8*,cl	D2	11 001 reg	4/bit+8
ror *mem16*,cl	D3	mod 001 r/m, (address)	4/bit+28 +
ror *reg16*,cl	D3	11 001 reg	4/bit+8

sahf **store AH into flags**

Operation: SF, ZF, -, AF, -, PF, -, CF := AH
Flags affected: AF, CF, PF, SF, ZF set/reset.
Reference: Section 13.2

Source Format	Opcode	Other Bytes	Clock Cycles
sahf	9E	(none)	4

sadirection/ **shift**
shdirection

Operation: shift operand; for right arithmetic shift, fill with sign bit
Flags affected: CF, OF, PF, SF, ZF set/reset. AF undefined.
Reference: 9.2

Source Formats	Opcode	Other Bytes	Clock Cycles
sar *mem8*,1	D0	mod 111 r/m, (address)	15 +
sar *reg8*,1	D0	11 111 reg	2
sar *mem16*,1	D1	mod 111 r/m, (address)	23 +
sar *reg16*,1	D1	11 111 reg	2
sar *mem8*,cl	D2	mod 111 r/m, (address)	4/bit+20 +

Source Formats	Opcode	Other Bytes	Clock Cycles
sar *reg8*,cl	D2	11 111 reg	4/bit+8
sar *mem16*,cl	D3	mod 111 r/m, (address)	4/bit+28 +
sar *reg16*,cl	D3	11 111 reg	4/bit+8
shl/sal *mem8*,1	D0	mod 100 r/m, (address)	15 +
shl/sal *reg8*,1	D0	11 100 reg	2
shl/sal *mem16*,1	D1	mod 100 r/m, (address)	23 +
shl/sal *reg16*,1	D1	11 100 reg	2
shl/sal *mem8*,cl	D2	mod 100 r/m, (address)	4/bit+20 +
shl/sal *reg8*,cl	D2	11 100 reg	4/bit+8
shl/sal *mem16*,cl	D3	mod 100 r/m, (address)	4/bit+28 +
shl/sal *reg16*,cl	D3	11 100 reg	4/bit+8
shr *mem8*,1	D0	mod 101 r/m, (address)	15 +
shr *reg8*,1	D0	11 101 reg	2
shr *mem16*,1	D1	mod 101 r/m, (address)	23 +
shr *reg16*,1	D1	11 101 reg	2
shr *mem8*,cl	D2	mod 101 r/m, (address)	4/bit+20 +
shr *reg8*,cl	D2	11 101 reg	4/bit+8
shr *mem16*,cl	D3	mod 101 r/m, (address)	4/bit+28 +
shr *reg16*,cl	D3	11 101 reg	4/bit+8

sbb   **subtract with borrow**

Operation: destination := destination - source - carry
Flags affected: AF, CF, OF, PF, SF, ZF set/reset.
Reference: Section 4.5

Source Formats	Opcode	Other Bytes	Clock Cycles
sbb *mem8,reg8*	18	mod reg r/m, (address)	16 +
sbb *mem16,reg16*	19	mod reg r/m, (address)	24 +
sbb *reg8,mem8*	1A	mod reg r/m, (address)	9 +
sbb *reg8,reg8*	1A	11 dest_reg source_reg	3
sbb *reg16,mem16*	1B	mod reg r/m, (address)	13 +
sbb *reg16,reg16*	1B	11 dest_reg source_reg	3
sbb al,*imm8*	1C	immediate byte	4
sbb ax,*imm16*	1D	immediate word	4
sbb *mem8,imm8*	80	mod 011 r/m,(address), immediate byte	17 +
sbb *reg8,imm8*	80	11 011 reg, immediate byte	4
sbb *mem16,imm16*	81	mod 011 r/m,(address), immediate word	25 +
sbb *reg16,imm16*	81	11 011 reg, immediate word	4

Source Formats	Opcode	Other Bytes	Clock Cycles
sbb *mem16,imm8*	83	mod 011 r/m,(address), immediate byte	25 +
sbb *reg16,imm8*	83	11 011 reg, immediate byte	4

scas   scan string element

Operation: set flags for (AL/AX - source); adjust DI
Flags affected: AF, CF, OF, PF, SF, ZF set/reset.
Reference: Section 7.2

Source Formats	Opcode	Other Bytes	Clock Cycles
scasb	AE	(none)	15
scasw	AF	(none)	19

segment override prefix bytes

Operation: modify segment register choice
Flags affected: none
Reference: Section 11.3

Source Formats	Opcode
cs:	2E
ds:	3E
es:	26
ss:	36

stc   set carry flag

Operation: CF := 1
Flags affected: CF = 1
Reference: Section 4.5

Source Format	Opcode	Other Bytes	Clock Cycles
stc	F9	(none)	2

std   set direction flag

Operation: DF := 1
Flags affected: DF = 1
Reference: Section 7.1

Source Format	Opcode	Other Bytes	Clock Cycles
std	FD	(none)	2

sti **set interrupt flag**

Operation: IF := 1
Flags affected: IF = 1
Reference: none

Source Format	Opcode	Other Bytes	Clock Cycles
sti	FB	(none)	2

stos **store string element**

Operation: copy AH or AX to source element; adjust DI
Flags affected: none
Reference: Section 7.2

Source Formats	Opcode	Other Bytes	Clock Cycles
stosb	AA	(none)	11
stosw	AB	(none)	15

sub **subtraction**

Operation: destination := destination - source
Flags affected: AF, CF, OF, PF, SF, ZF set/reset.
Reference: Section 4.2

Source Formats	Opcode	Other Bytes	Clock Cycles
sub mem8,reg8	28	mod reg r/m, (address)	16 +
sub mem16,reg16	29	mod reg r/m, (address)	24 +
sub reg8,mem8	2A	mod reg r/m, (address)	9 +
sub reg8,reg8	2A	11 dest_reg source_reg	3
sub reg16,mem16	2B	mod reg r/m, (address)	13 +
sub reg16,reg16	2B	11 dest_reg source_reg	3
sub al,imm8	2C	immediate byte	4
sub ax,imm16	2D	immediate word	4
sub mem8,imm8	80	mod 101 r/m,(address), immediate byte	17 +
sub reg8,imm8	80	11 101 reg, immediate byte	4
sub mem16,imm16	81	mod 101 r/m,(address), immediate word	25 +
sub reg16,imm16	81	11 101 reg, immediate word	4
sub mem16,imm8	83	mod 101 r/m,(address), immediate byte	25 +
sub reg16,imm8	83	11 101 reg, immediate byte	4

test **logical test**

Operation: flags set for (destination and source)
Flags affected: PF, SF, ZF set/reset. CF=0, OF=0. AF undefined.
Reference: Section 9.1

Source Formats	Opcode	Other Bytes	Clock Cycles
test *reg8,mem8*	84	mod reg r/m, (address)	9+
test *reg8,reg8*	84	11 dest_reg source_reg	3
test *reg16,mem16*	85	mod reg r/m, (address)	13+
test *reg16,reg16*	85	11 dest_reg source_reg	3
test *al,imm8*	A8	immediate byte	4
test *ax,mem16*	A9	immediate word	4
test *mem8,imm8*	F6	mod 000 r/m,(address), immediate byte	11+
test *reg8,imm8*	F6	11 000 reg, immediate byte	5
test *mem16,imm16*	F7	mod 000 r/m,(address), immediate word	15+
test *reg16,imm16*	F7	11 000 reg, immediate word	5

wait **wait**

Operation: suspend CPU execution
Flags affected: none
Reference: Section 14.3

Source Format	Opcode	Other Bytes	Clock Cycles
wait	9B	(none)	4

xchg **exchange**

Operation: destination ↔ source
Flags affected: none
Reference: Section 4.1

Source Formats	Opcode	Other Bytes	Clock Cycles
xchg *reg8,mem8*	86	mod reg r/m, (address)	17+
xchg *reg8,reg8*	86	11 dest_reg source_reg	4
xchg *reg16,mem16*	87	mod reg r/m, (address)	25+
xchg *reg16,reg16*	87	11 dest_reg source_reg	4
xchg ax,cx	91	(none)	3
xchg ax,dx	92	(none)	3
xchg ax,bx	93	(none)	3
xchg ax,sp	94	(none)	3
xchg ax,bp	95	(none)	3

Source Formats	Opcode	Other Bytes	Clock Cycles
xchg ax,si	96	(none)	3
xchg ax,di	97	(none)	3

xlat **translate**

Operation: translate byte in AL using table to which BX points
Flags affected: none
Reference: Section 7.3

Source Format	Opcode	Other Bytes	Clock Cycles
xlat	D7	(none)	11

xor **logical exclusive or**

Operation: destination := destination xor source
Flags affected: PF, SF, ZF set/reset. CF=0, OF=0. AF undefined.
Reference: Section 9.1

Source Formats	Opcode	Other Bytes	Clock Cycles
xor mem8,reg8	30	mod reg r/m, (address)	16+
xor mem16,reg16	31	mod reg r/m, (address)	24+
xor reg8,mem8	32	mod reg r/m, (address)	9+
xor reg8,reg8	32	11 dest_reg source_reg	3
xor reg16,mem16	33	mod reg r/m, (address)	13+
xor reg16,reg16	33	11 dest_reg source_reg	3
xor al,imm8	34	immediate byte	4
xor ax,imm16	35	immediate word	4
xor mem8,imm8	80	mod 110 r/m,(address), immediate byte	17+
xor reg8,imm8	80	11 110 reg, immediate byte	4
xor mem16,imm16	81	mod 110 r/m,(address), immediate word	25+
xor reg16,imm16	81	11 110 reg, immediate word	4
xor mem16,imm8	83	mod 110 r/m, (address), ´immediate byte	25+
xor reg16,imm8	83	11 110 reg, immediate byte	3

8087 Instructions

Mnemonic	Operand(s)	Operation
f2xm1	(none)	$Y = 2^x - 1$; X from ST, Y to ST
fabs	(none)	ST := | ST | (absolute value)
fadd	(none)	pops both ST and ST(1); adds these values; pushes sum onto the stack
fadd	st(num),st	adds ST(num) and ST; replaces ST(num) by the sum
fadd	st,st(num)	adds ST and ST(num); replaces ST by the sum
fadd	memory (real)	adds ST and real number from memory; replaces ST by the sum
faddp	st(num),st	adds ST(num) and ST; replaces ST(num) by the sum; pops ST from stack
fbld	memory (BCD)	BCD value from memory converted to floating point and pushed onto stack
fbstp	memory (BCD)	copy of ST converted to BCD and stored in memory; ST popped off the stack
fclex/ fnclex	(none)	clear exception flags
fchs	(none)	ST := − ST (reverse sign)
fcom	(none)	compares ST and ST(1)
fcom	st(num)	compares ST and ST(num)
fcom	memory (real)	compares ST and real number in memory
fcomp	(none)	compares ST and ST(1); then pops stack
fcomp	st(num)	compares ST and ST(num); then pops stack
fcomp	memory (real)	compares ST and real number in memory; then pops stack
fcompp	(none)	compares ST and ST(1); then pops stack twice
fdecstp	(none)	decrement stack pointer
fdisi/ fndisi	(none)	disable interrupts
fdiv	(none)	pops ST and ST(1); calculates ST(1) / ST; pushes quotient onto the stack

Mnemonic	Operand(s)	Operation
fdiv	st(num),st	calculates ST(num) / ST; replaces ST(num) by the quotient
fdiv	st,st(num)	calculates ST / ST(num); replaces ST by the quotient
fdiv	memory (real)	calculates ST / real number from memory; replaces ST by the quotient
fdivp	st(num),st	calculates ST(num) / ST; replaces ST(num) by the quotient; pops ST from the stack
fdivpr	st(num),st	calculates ST / ST(num); replaces ST(num) by the quotient; pops ST from the stack
fdivr	(none)	pops ST and ST(1); calculates ST / ST(1); pushes quotient onto the stack
fdivr	st(num),st	calculates ST / ST(num); replaces ST(num) by the quotient
fdivr	st,st(num)	calculates ST(num) / ST; replaces ST by the quotient
fdivr	memory (real)	calculates real number from memory / ST; replaces ST by the quotient
feni/ fneni	(none)	enable interrupts
ffree	st(num)	free register
fiadd	memory (integer)	adds ST and integer from memory; replaces ST by the sum
ficom	memory (integer)	compares ST and integer in memory
ficomp	memory (integer)	compares ST and integer in memory; then pops stack
fidiv	memory (integer)	calculates ST / integer from memory; replaces ST by the quotient
fidivr	memory (integer)	calculates integer from memory / ST; replaces ST by the quotient
fild	memory (integer)	integer value from memory converted to floating point and pushed onto stack
fimul	memory (integer)	multiplies ST and integer from memory; replaces ST by the product
fincstp	(none)	increment stack pointer
finit/ fninit	(none)	initialize the 8087
fist	memory (integer)	copy of ST converted to integer and stored in memory
fistp	memory (integer)	copy of ST converted to integer and stored in memory; ST popped off the stack
fisub	memory (integer)	calculates ST – integer from memory; replaces ST by the difference
fisubr	memory (integer)	calculates integer from memory – ST; replaces ST by the difference
fld	st(num)	contents of 8087 register pushed onto stack
fld	memory (real)	real value from memory pushed onto stack
fld1	(none)	1.0 pushed onto stack
fldcw	mem32	load control doubleword
fldenv	mem	load 14-byte coprocessor state

Mnemonic	Operand(s)	Operation
`fldl2e`	(none)	$\log_2(e)$ pushed onto stack
`fldl2t`	(none)	$\log_2(10)$ pushed onto stack
`fldlg2`	(none)	$\log_{10}(2)$ pushed onto stack
`fldln2`	(none)	$\log_e(2)$ pushed onto stack
`fldpi`	(none)	π(pi) pushed onto stack
`fldz`	(none)	0.0 pushed onto stack
`fmul`	(none)	pops ST and ST(1); multiplies these values; pushes product onto the stack
`fmul`	`st(`*num*`),st`	multiplies ST(*num*) and ST; replaces ST(*num*) by the product
`fmul`	`st,st(`*num*`)`	multiplies ST and ST(*num*); replaces ST by the product
`fmul`	*memory* (real)	multiplies ST and real number from memory; replaces ST by the product
`fmulp`	`st(`*num*`),st`	multiplies ST(*num*) and ST; replaces ST(*num*) by the product; pops ST from stack
`fnop`	(none)	no operation
`fpatan`	(none)	partial arctangent; Z = arctan(Y/X); X from ST, Y from ST(1), Z to ST
`fprem`	(none)	partial remainder of ST/ST(1)
`fptan`	(none)	partial tangent; Y/X = tan(Z); Z from ST, Y to ST(1), X to ST
`frndint`	(none)	rounds contents of ST to an integer
`frstor`	*mem*	restore 94-byte coprocessor state
`fsave/` `fnsave`	*mem*	save 94-byte coprocessor state
`fscale`	(none)	$Y = Y * 2^x$; Y from/to SP, X from SP(1)
`fsqrt`	(none)	replaces contents of ST by its square root
`fst`	`st(`*num*`)`	replaces contents of ST(*num*) by copy of value from ST; only ST(*num*) is affected
`fst`	*memory* (real)	copy of ST stored as real value in memory; the stack is not affected
`fstcw/` `fnstcw`	*mem16*	store control word
`fstenv/` `fnstenv`	*mem*	store 14-byte coprocessor state
`fstp`	`st(`*num*`)`	replaces contents of ST(*num*) by copy of value from ST; ST popped off the stack
`fstp`	*memory* (real)	copy of ST stored as real value in memory; ST popped off the stack
`fstsw/` `fnstsw`	*mem16*	store status word

Mnemonic	Operand(s)	Operation
fsub	(none)	pops ST and ST(1); calculates ST(1) – ST; pushes difference onto the stack
fsub	st(num),st	calculates ST(num) – ST; replaces ST(num) by the difference
fsub	st,st(num)	calculates ST – ST(num); replaces ST by the difference
fsub	memory (real)	calculates ST – real number from memory; replaces ST by the difference
fsubp	st(num),st	calculates ST(num) – ST; replaces ST(num) by the difference; pops ST from the stack
fsubpr	st(num),st	calculates ST – ST(num); replaces ST(num) by the difference; pops ST from the stack
fsubr	(none)	pops ST and ST(1); calculates ST – ST(1); pushes difference onto the stack
fsubr	st(num),st	calculates ST – ST(num); replaces ST(num) by the difference
fsubr	st,st(num)	calculates ST(num) – ST; replaces ST by the difference
fsubr	memory (real)	calculates real number from memory – ST; replaces ST by the difference
ftst	(none)	compares ST and 0
fwait	(none)	suspend processor (same as 8088 wait)
fxam	(none)	reports contents of ST in condition flags
fxch	(none)	exchange contents of ST and ST(1)
fxch	st(num)	exchange contents of ST and ST(num)
fxtract	(none)	extract exponent and significant fields of ST; exponent to ST(1), significant to ST
fyl2x	(none)	$Z = Y \log_2(X)$; X from ST, Y from ST(1), Z to ST
fyl2xp1	(none)	$Z = Y \log_2(X + 1)$; X from ST, Y from ST(1), Z to ST

Differences Between Intel 80286 and 80386 Microprocessors

The Intel Corporation has manufactured microprocessors for several years. The original IBM PCs were
built around the Intel 8088 that is the primary subject of this book. However, prior to IBM's entry into
the microcomputer market, the Intel 8080 and
8085 microprocessors were popular choices in other
manufacturers' personal computers.

Intel made the 8086 available at approximately
the same time as the 8088. Since that time, Intel
has introduced increasingly more powerful microprocessors, including the 80186, 80286, 80386, and
80486. The 8086 and 80186 microprocessors have
been used in relatively few microcomputers. IBM
adopted the 80286 as the CPU in its PC AT series
of computers, and the 80286 has been a popular
choice for many other microcomputers. The 80386
has also been adopted for many microcomputer systems, including the IBM System 2/Model 80. The
80486 was recently introduced, and few systems
have been announced to date.

This appendix discusses some of the features of
the newer, more powerful Intel microprocessors,
concentrating on the 80286 and 80386. It is important to note that the more powerful microprocessors are upward compatible from the 8088; that is,

each is capable of executing a program written for an 8088. This means that an assembly language program written for the 8088 can be assembled and run on an 80286 system or an 80386 system, or can even be assembled on an 8088 system and then executed on one of the other microprocessors. The opposite is not true—the 80286 and 80386 have advanced capabilities, including the ability to execute instructions not recognized by the 8088.

Operating Modes

The 8088 microprocessor was designed to be the CPU for a computer system used by a single user to execute a single task. The 80286 and 80386 microprocessors were designed to be CPUs for computer systems that can handle more than one task and/or more than one user.

The 80286 has two operating modes, *real-address mode* and *protected mode*. When in real-address mode, the 80286 is effectively a fast 8088/8086 that can execute some additional instructions. In this mode, only a single task can be executed. The 80286 has 24 address lines, as compared to 20 in the 8088. This means that it can address 16 megabytes of memory, but in real-address mode, only one megabyte is used, the same as with the 8088.

In protected mode, the 80286 uses not only the 16 megabytes of memory made possible by its 24 address lines, it also has memory management features that allow it to address up to one gigabyte (2^{30} bytes) of virtual memory. The 80286 has the same registers as the 8088, plus several new registers for task and memory management. These additional registers are normally manipulated by an operating system, not an applications program. The PC-DOS and MS-DOS operating systems do not provide for virtual memory management, multiple users, or multiple tasks.

The 80386 has three operating modes: *real-address mode*, *protected mode*, and *virtual 8086 mode*. Real-address mode on the 80386 is similar to real-address mode on the 80286; the microprocessor acts like a very fast 8088/8086 that can execute additional instructions. A programmer can also take advantage of the fact that registers in the 80386 hold 32 bits, rather than 16 as in the 8088 and 80286.

Protected mode on the 80386 is similar to protected mode on the 80286, but its memory management features are more sophisticated. The 80386 has 32 address lines, so that it can address up to four gigabytes (2^{32} bytes) of physical memory, and its memory management features make it possible to address up to 64 terabytes (2^{46} bytes) of virtual memory.

Virtual 8086 mode on the 80386 is used to execute an 8088/8086 program without switching to real-address mode. Real-address mode allows execution of only one task, but several tasks can be running at the same time in virtual 8086 mode or in protected mode. This requires support from an operating system, of course. A virtual 8086 task is not limited to 8088/8086 instructions; it can use the additional instructions and 32-bit register width available on the 80386.

Speed

Several things affect the speed at which a computer system operates. One of these is the *data bus width*, the number of lines connecting the CPU to memory. The table below shows the data bus widths for several Intel microprocessors.

Microprocessor	Data Bus Width
8086	16
8088	8
80286	16
80386	32
80386-SX	16
80486	32

A system with an 8-bit data bus can transfer one byte of data in a single memory-access cycle, whereas a system with a 16-bit data bus can transfer two bytes of data in one memory-access cycle and a system with a 32-bit data bus can transfer four bytes of data in one memory-access cycle

The 8088 and 8086 microprocessors have the same internal structure and execute exactly the same instructions set. However, the 8086 is faster because it can execute memory-access operations quicker. The 80386 and 80386-SX microprocessors also have the same internal structure and execute a common instruction set (larger than the 8088/8086 set), but the 80386 is faster because its 32-bit data bus transfers data more rapidly than the 16-bit data bus of the 80386-SX.

The second factor affecting the speed of a microcomputer system is its *clock rate*. Every microcomputer system has a system clock whose pulses are used to time all system activities. Original IBM PCs used a 4.77 MHz clock, that is, a clock generating 4,770,000 cycles per second. Many later 8088 systems use higher clock rates, with 8 Mhz being fairly common; an 8 MHz system runs about 1.68 (8/4.77) times faster than a 4.77 MHz system. Systems with an 80286 CPU often have clock rates of 8 to 12 MHz. "Slow" 80386 systems use 16 MHz clocks; some 80386 systems use clocks as fast as 33 MHz. A 33-MHz system would execute instructions almost seven times faster than a 4.77 MHz system, even if no other factors were involved.

A third factor affecting execution times is that 80286 and 80386 microprocessors execute many instructions in fewer clock cycles than the 8088, and they do not require extra clock cycles to execute instructions with a memory operand. Figure 4.3 in Chapter 4 lists the number of additional clock cycles and additional operand bytes required for each 8088 memory addressing mode. The "additional clock cycles" column does not apply to 80286 and 80386 microprocessors, although one additional clock cycle is required for the most complicated addressing mode, based and indexed with a displacement.

As an example, the instruction

```
mov bx, number
```

where **number** is a direct mode memory operand, requires 18 clock cycles on an 8088 system, 14 clock cycles on an 8086 system (because of the 16-bit address bus), 5 clock cycles on an 80286 system, and 4 clock cycles on an 80386 system. For a particular instruction, 80286 and 80386 microprocessors typically require approximately the same number of clock cycles, and this number is much smaller than the number of clock cycles needed for the 8088 to execute the same instruction. The 80486 is significantly faster than the 80386; it executes most instructions in one clock cycle.

The internal registers of an 80386 microprocessor are 32 bits long rather than 16 bits long in the 8088 and 80286. This speeds operations with 32-bit operands since such operations can be carried out with single instructions rather than sequences of instructions. The 80486 also has 32-bit registers.

One can measure computing speed just by looking at the CPU of a computer, but other system components also affect it. If "slow" memory chips are used in a computer, then each memory access may be delayed by one or more *wait states*. Also, computer programs typically involve many read and write operations to disk drives. Most 80286 and 80386 systems include hard disk drives which are much faster than floppy disk drives. Hard disk drives vary also, and the hard disk drives used with more powerful CPUs typically are faster than those used with less powerful microprocessors.

Instruction Sets

The instruction set recognized by the 80286 microprocessor includes all 8088 instructions and more. Similarly, the instruction set recognized by the 80386 microprocessor includes all 80286 instructions and more. Some of the added instructions are familiar, but are applicable to additional operand types. Other new instructions perform operations that are not even possible on an 8088. Some of the additional 80286 and 80386 instructions are discussed below.

The 80286 and 80386 have **pusha** (push all) and **popa** (pop all) instructions that push and pop the AX, CX, DX, BX, SP, BP, SI, and DI registers with a single instruction. The 80386 also has **pushad** and **popad** instructions that push and pop the 32-bit 80386 registers. The **push** instruction, limited to register and memory operands with the 8088, allows an immediate operand on the 80286 and 80386.

The 8088 **imul** instruction specifies only one register or memory operand—the other is always in AX or AL. The 80286 **imul** has two additional formats. Two operands can be used, the first a register and the second immediate.

    imul register, immediate

In this version, the value in the register is multiplied by the immediate value, with the product stored in the register. Another 80286 format uses three operands

    imul register, source, immediate

where the operand **source** can be a register or memory reference. With this format, the source value is multiplied by the immediate value, and the result is stored in the register specified by the first operand. The products in these 80286 formats are not double-length; if the result will not fit in the specified register, the carry and overflow flags are set.

The 80386 has yet another `imul` format. It specifies a register and a source operand, which can be a register or memory reference.

```
imul register, source
```

The values in the register and at the specified source location are multiplied to get a single-length product that is stored in the register. The carry and overflow flags are set if the result is too large to fit in the register.

These new formats apply only to `imul` instructions. There are no comparable formats for `mul` instructions. The only new division instructions are 80386 versions with two operands; a first operand of EAX (the 32-bit extended AX register) means to divide the 64-bit 2's complement number in EDX and EAX by a 32-bit number specified as the second operand.

Shift and rotate instructions on the 8088 allow only 1 and CL as the second operand, specifying a shift/rotate of 1 position or the number of positions specified in the CL register. 80286 and 80386 shift and rotate instructions allow an immediate operand specifying a number other than 1.

The 80386 has a collection of double precision shift instructions using the mnemonics `shld` and `shrd`. Each has three operands, two registers and a third operand which is either CL or immediate. The number of bits specified by the third operand are shifted from the second register to the first.

Conditional jumps on the 8088 and 80286 are limited to a destination between 128 bytes before and 127 bytes after the instruction following the jump. The 80386 allows the destination to be between 32768 bytes before and 32767 bytes after the next instruction. The source code syntax of the instruction is the same, but the machine code is different.

The 80286 and 80386 provide `enter` and `leave` instructions to facilitate implementation of procedures. The `enter` instruction creates a stack frame by pushing BP, setting BP to a reference point in the stack, allocating stack space for local variables, and copying frame pointers from procedures in which this one is nested. Several 8088 instructions are required to accomplish the same tasks. The `leave` instruction reverses the actions of the enter instruction.

A `bound` instruction is available on the 80286 and 80386 to check if an index value for an array is within specified limits. The index to be checked is in a register and the limits are stored in consecutive memory locations. The instruction

```
bound register, memory
```

then checks the value in the register against the values in memory. If the register value is less than the first memory value or greater than the second memory value, an Interrupt 5 is generated.

The 80386 has a variety of new move instructions. The `movzx` instruction copies data from a register or memory location to a register with twice as many bits, filling the left half of the destination with zero bits. The **movsx** instruction is similar, except that the left half of the destination is filled with copies of the sign bit from the source operand. This is similar to the action of the 8088 **cbw** and **cwd** instructions. The 80386 has a **cwde** instruction which converts a signed word in AX to a signed doubleword in EAX by copying the sign bit of AX into all bits of EAX, and a **cdq** instruction which converts a signed doubleword in EAX to a signed quadword (64 bits) in EDX and EAX by copying the sign bit of EAX into all bits of EDX.

The 80386 has two additional segment registers, FS and GS, which are used like DS and ES to designate data segments. 80386 **lfs** and **lgs** instructions copy a segment number value from memory to FS and GS, respectively.

There are several new 80286 and 80386 instructions which are not discussed here. Most of these are used in systems programming rather than applications programming.

The 80486 microprocessor has a built-in floating point unit (FPU). This FPU executes the same instructions as the 80387 math coprocessor.

MASM Directives

This is a partial listing of directives available in MASM 5.1.

Directive	Action	Reference
ALIGN	align next variable or instruction to byte which is multiple of operand	11.3
ASSUME	select segment register(s) to be the default for all symbols in segment(s)	3.2, 11.3
COMMENT	indicates a comment	12.2
DB	allocate and optionally initialize bytes of storage	3.4
DW	allocate and optionally initialize words of storage	3.4
DD	allocate and optionally initialize doublewords of storage	3.4, 14.1
DQ	allocate and optionally initialize quadwords of storage	3.4, 14.1
DT	allocate and optionally initialize 10-byte-long storage units	3.4, 13.1, 14.1
ELSE	mark beginning of alternative code within conditional assembly block	12.2
END	terminate assembly; optionally indicate program entry point	3.2
ENDIF	terminate a conditional assembly block	12.2
ENDM	terminate a macro definition	12.1
ENDP	mark end of procedure definition	6.1
ENDS	mark end of segment or structure	3.2, 8.3
EQU	assign expression to name	3.2
.ERR	generate an error	12.3

Directive	Action	Reference
.ERR1	generate an error on pass 1 only	none
.ERR2	generate an error on pass 2 only	none
.ERRB	generate an error if argument blank	none
.ERRDEF	generate an error if argument is defined	none
.ERRE	generate an error if argument false (0)	none
.ERRNB	generate an error if argument not blank	none
.ERRNDEF	generate an error if argument not defined	none
.ERRNZ	generate an error if argument true (not 0)	none
EVEN	align next variable or instruction to even byte	11.3
EXITM	terminate macro expansion	12.2
EXTRN	indicate externally defined symbols	6.1
IF	assemble statements if argument is true (not 0)	12.2
IF1	assemble statements on pass 1 only	12.2
IF2	assemble statements on pass 2 only	12.2
IFB	assemble statements if argument blank	12.2
IFDEF	assemble statements if argument defined	12.2
IFE	assemble statements if argument is false (0)	12.2
IFNB	assemble statements if argument not blank	12.2
IFNDEF	assemble statements if argument not defined	12.2
INCLUDE	insert source code from named file into source file being assembled	3.2
LABEL	create a new label with specified type and current location counter	14.1
.LALL	list all statements in macros	3.3
.LIST	list all statements	3.2
LOCAL	declare local variables in macro definition	12.1
MACRO	start macro definition	12.1
ORG	set location counter to argument	11.3
%OUT	display text on monitor	12.2
PAGE	set length and width of program listing; generate page break	3.3
PROC	start procedure definition	6.1
PUBLIC	identify symbols to be visible outside module	6.1
.RADIX	set default radix for numeric values	3.4
.SALL	list no statements in macro expansions	3.3
STRUC	start structure definition	8.3
SUBTTL	define a program listing subtitle	11.3
TITLE	define the program listing title	11.3
.XALL	list statements in macro expansions which generate code or data	12.1
.XLIST	list no program statement	none

Microsoft's DEBUG and CodeView Debuggers

A **debugger** is a utility that enables a programmer to trace the execution of a program. Typically the programmer can either step through the program one instruction at a time or set **breakpoints** where execution pauses. Between execution of instructions, the user can examine the contents of registers and/or memory to see they are affected by program execution.

Microsoft distributes two debuggers. The DEBUG utility is included with DOS operating systems. The CodeView program is included with MASM and with Microsoft high-level language compilers. With DEBUG the user sees the program in an assembly language format that is equivalent to the source program, but which lacks the original symbols for data and code references. CodeView is the more powerful tool; it allows tracing to be done using the original source code. This appendix briefly describes how to use these products for tracing programs. In addition to their program-tracing ability, each of these products provides many aditional functions; these aditional capabilities are not discussed.

Figure E.1 DEBUG commands.

Command	Operand	Function
U		unassemble next 32 bytes
U	address	unassemble next 32 bytes at *address*
T		trace execution of one instruction; display register contents and next instruction
T	count	trace execution of next *count* instructions
P		like trace, except for `call`, `loop`, `int`, and repeated string instructions, which execute as atomic operations
D	address	dump 128 bytes starting at *address*
G		execute program
G	address	execute program, pausing at breakpoint specified by *address*
L		reload program after termination
Q		quit; exit to DOS

DEBUG

To use DEBUG, first assemble and link the program in the usual way. As MASM is used, specify a listing (.LST) file for the program—it will be needed for debugging.

DEBUG is started using the command

```
DEBUG  program.EXE
```

For the example program discussed in Section 3.2, the command to DOS would be

```
A> debug example.exe
```

(DEBUG or the program to be traced might be on a disk in a drive other than the A drive.) This command loads DEBUG, which in turn loads EXAMPLE.EXE. DEBUG displays a single dash (-) as a prompt. At this prompt, the user can enter a variety of commands; some of these are summarized in Figure E.1.

Each DEBUG command is a single letter. If a command has an operand, it is typed immediately after the command letter; no space is allowed. Figure E.2 shows a sample session with DEBUG. This session was initiated by typing using the DOS command `debug example.exe`. User input is underlined.

The session begins with a u command that *unassembles* (or *disassembles*) 32 bytes of source code, beginning with the first instruction in the data segment. Disassembly translates object code to corresponding source code. For this particular run the data segment number was 174D, the first instruction was at offset 0000, and the object code of the first instruction was B84517. One way to write

Figure E.2 Using DEBUG with EXAMPLE.EXE.

```
-u

174D:0000 B84517        MOV     AX,1745
174D:0003 8ED8          MOV     DS,AX
174D:0005 50            PUSH    AX
174D:0006 56            PUSH    SI
174D:0007 8D360400      LEA     SI,[0004]
174D:000B B80000        MOV     AX,0000
174D:000E 9ACF005617    CALL    1756:00CF
174D:0013 5E            POP     SI
174D:0014 58            POP     AX
174D:0015 57            PUSH    DI
174D:0016 8D3E3300      LEA     DI,[0033]
174D:001A B92800        MOV     CX,0028
174D:001D 9A4A015617    CALL    1756:014A
-ucs:005d

174D:005D A10000        MOV     AX,[0000]
174D:0060 03060200      ADD     AX,[0002]
174D:0064 50            PUSH    AX
174D:0065 57            PUSH    DI
174D:0066 8BC0          MOV     AX,AX
174D:0068 8D3E6800      LEA     DI,[0068]
174D:006C 9A00005617    CALL    1756:0000
174D:0071 5F            POP     DI
174D:0072 58            POP     AX
174D:0073 50            PUSH    AX
174D:0074 56            PUSH    SI
174D:0075 8D365B00      LEA     SI,[005B]
174D:0079 B80000        MOV     AX,0000
174D:007C 9ACF005617    CALL    1756:00CF
-g005d


Enter first number:  50


Enter second number:  -20


AX=FFEC  BX=0000  CX=0003  DX=0000  SP=0200  BP=0000  SI=0000  DI=0000
DS=1745  ES=1715  SS=1725  CS=174D  IP=005D   NV UP EI NG NZ NA PO NC
174D:005D A10000        MOV     AX,[0000]                    DS:0000=0032
-dds:0000


1745:0000  32 00 EC FF 45 6E 74 65-72 20 66 69 72 73 74 20   2...Enter first 1745:0010
6E 75 6D 62 65 72 3A 20-20 00 0D 0A 45 6E 74 65   number:  ...Ente
1745:0020  72 20 73 65 63 6F 6E 64-20 6E 75 6D 62 65 72 3A   r second number:
1745:0030  20 20 00 2D 32 30 00 00-00 00 00 00 00 00 00 00   .-20..........
```

500 | Appendix E

Figure E.2 Continued.

```
1745:0040  00 00 00 00 00 00 00 00-00 00 00 00 00 00 00 00   ................
1745:0050  00 00 00 00 00 00 00 00-00 00 00 0D 0A 54 68 65   ...........The
1745:0060  20 73 75 6D 20 69 73 20-00 00 00 00 00 00 0D 0A    sum is ........
1745:0070  00 00 00 00 00 00 00 00-00 00 00 00 00 00 00 00   ................
-t


AX=0032  BX=0000  CX=0003  DX=0000  SP=0200  BP=0000  SI=0000  DI=0000
DS=1745  ES=1715  SS=1725  CS=174D  IP=0060   NV UP EI NG NZ NA PO NC
174D:0060 03060200       ADD      AX,[0002]                          DS:0002=FFEC
-t


AX=001E  BX=0000  CX=0003  DX=0000  SP=0200  BP=0000  SI=0000  DI=0000
DS=1745  ES=1715  SS=1725  CS=174D  IP=0064   NV UP EI PL NZ NA PE CY
174D:0064 50             PUSH     AX
-g


The sum is      30


Program terminated normally
-g
```

the source code for B84517 is MOV AX,1745. The listing file in Figure 3.5 shows the first instruction of the code segment as

```
        0000  B8 ---- R              start:   mov   ax,SEG data
```

At assembly time the segment number could only be referenced symbolically as SEG data. Its actual value is known at execution time, and DEBUG shows the segment number 1745 that was used for this program run.

The next line of the DEBUG display

```
        174D:0003 8ED8              MOV       DS,AX
```

corresponds exactly to the next line of the listing file

```
        0003   8E D8                 mov       ds,ax
```

The next lines in the source file are

```
prompt:  output prompt1          ; prompt for first number
         inputs string,40        ; read ASCII characters
```

These macro calls expand to several instructions that are not shown in the listing file because of an .SALL directive in IO.H. The instructions from PUSH AX through POP AX are the expansion of the output macro. The remaining lines in the DEBUG display show part of the expansion of the inputs macro.

Without symbols in the disassembled machine code it can be difficult to relate DEBUG's listing the to the original source code. However, with the assembly options used in this book, offsets shown in the listing file will correspond to off-sets shown in the machine code, so that the listing file can be used to locate instructions and data while using DEBUG.

Suppose that the user wants to trace the actual addition of the two values. The interesting instructions are shown in the assembly listing at offsets 005D and 0060.

```
005D  A1 0000 R          mov     ax,number1      ; first number to AX
0060  03 06 0002 R       add     ax,number2      ; add second number
```

The next command `ucs:005d` shows disassembly of these and additional instructions. (The prefix `cs:` is optional here.) Notice that the machine code at run-time is identical to the object code shown by MASM, except for the rever-sal of low-order and high-order bytes in the word 0002.

```
174D:005D A10000          MOV     AX,[0000]
174D:0060 03060200        ADD     AX,[0002]
```

The symbol **number1** is referenced as [0000] (the value stored at offset 0000), and the symbol **number2** is referenced as [0002]. Although this code is descrip-tive, it is not quite equivalent to the original source code—MASM treats an operand like [0000] or [0002] as immediate, not direct.

To execute the program to this point, the command g005d is used. Instructions are then executed up to, but not including the one at offset 005D. Execution is suspended at the breakpoint and DEBUG displays the contents of the registers, the flag values (**NV UP EI NG NZ NA PO NC**), the object code and disassembled source code for the next instruction to be executed, and the value of the memory operand for the next instruction (**DS:0000=0032**). The flags are in mnemonic form; for example, **NC** means "no carry," that is, CF=0. The notation **DS:0000=0032** means that 0032 is stored at offset 0000 in the data segment, and that this is the memory operand for the **mov** instruction to be executed next.

To have a look at a larger portion of memory, a dump instruction is used. The command **dds:0000** dumps 128 bytes of memory starting at offset 0000 in the data segment. (The prefix **ds:** is optional here.) The memory dump dis-plays eight lines. The first number on each line is the segment number:offset address for the first byte. Then the contents of 16 bytes of memory are shown, first in hex and then in character format. The characters correspond to the inter-pretation the bytes as ASCII codes; a period is used for an unprintable character or for a hex value larger than 7F, the largest ASCII code.

The dump verifies that the memory at offset 0000 contains 32 00, the word 0032 with the bytes stored in reverse order. The next two bytes of memory (at offsets 0003 and 0004) are EC FF, that is, the word FFEC. The words 0032 and FFEC are the word-length 2's complement representations for 50 and −20, respectively, the numbers that were entered as earlier instructions in the program executed. Notice that part of the dump that follows is easily readable; it contains ASCII codes for the various labels.

The trace instruction T causes the program to execute one instruction. This instruction, mov ax,number1 (MOV AX, [0000]), is not shown by the trace command, but the results of executing the instruction are shown. The contents of the AX register have changed to be 0032. The next instruction to be executed is also displayed, as well as the memory operand referenced by [0002].

Another T command executes the instruction add ax,number2 (ADD AX, [0002]). The word in the AX register then becomes 001E. Notice that the flags also change. In particular CY means that CF=1, as one would expect from adding 0032 and FFEC.

The next instruction to be executed is push ax, the first instruction in the expansion of the macro itoa sum,ax. To continue execution of the program without tracing individual instructions a G command with no operand is used. The program completes execution and DEBUG displays Program terminated normally. A Q command exits DEBUG, returning to DOS.

DEBUG displays Program terminated normally as a result of the int instruction which requests DOS to terminate the program. If additional program tracing is desired, it is necessary to reload the program. The L command is used for this purpose.

DEBUG has many additional capabilities. Some of the above commands allow additional operands. There are several additional commands. One other command, the A command, allows the user to enter or modify an assembly language program by giving assembly language source code—DEBUG actually has a rudimentary assembler built in. Other commands allow DEBUG to read specified sectors from a disk, to modify the bytes, and to write the results back to the disk, a very dangerous but occasionally useful practice.

CodeView

Before tracing a program with CodeView, special preliminary steps are required. These steps are shown below for the example program discussed in Section 3.2, and then a sample CodeView session with that program is presented.

The first preliminary step is to slightly modify the source code. The directive for the code segment must have an operand that specifies the *class name* CODE in apostrophes. The expanded form of the directive is

```
code          SEGMENT  'CODE'
```

(It is acceptable to include class name CODE on code segment directives in any assembly language source program.)

Next, the assembler MASM and the linker LINK must be told to generate .OBJ and .EXE files which contain the symbolic information required by CodeView. One one way to do this is to add /zi to the source filename when invoking MASM and /co to the object module name when running LINK. Assembling and linking EXAMPLE.ASM then looks like

```
A>masm
Microsoft (R) Macro Assembler Version 5.10
Copyright (C) Microsoft Corp 1981, 1988. All rights reserved.

Source filename [.ASM]: example/zi
Object filename [example.OBJ]:
Source listing  [NUL.LST]: example
Cross-reference [NUL.CRF]:

  47576 + 383009 Bytes symbol space free

      0 Warning Errors
      0 Severe  Errors

A>link

Microsoft (R) Overlay Linker  Version 3.61
Copyright (C) Microsoft Corp 1983-1987. All rights reserved.

Object Modules [.OBJ]: example/co+io
Run File [EXAMPLE.EXE]:
List File [NUL.MAP]:
Libraries [.LIB]:

A>
```

CodeView is started using the command

    CV *program*

For the example program, the command to DOS would be

    A> cv example

(CodeView does not require the .EXE extension.) This command loads CodeView, which in turn loads EXAMPLE.EXE.

CodeView displays a screen separated into several windows. Figure E.3 shows an initial screen display. The top line of the screen is called the menu bar. The entries **F8=Trace** and **F5=Go** indicate keys that substitute for dialog commands (discussed below). Other entries in the menu bar are names of other menus. These other menus are activated by holding the Alt key while pressing the first (highlighted) character in the name. For example, Alt-W brings up the watch menu. If a computer has a mouse, an alternative is to point at the desired command and click the left mouse button.

The display window, the largest window on the screen, is below the menu bar. It presents the program currently being traced. In Figure E.3, it shows lines

Figure E.3 Initial CodeView Display.

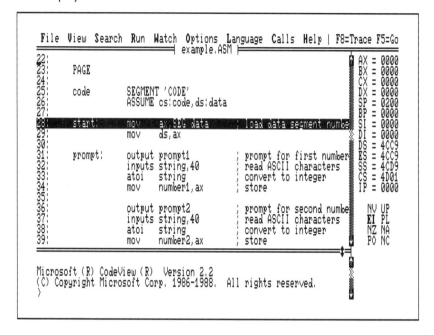

22 through 39 of the original source code. The next instruction to be executed is highlighted. In Figure E.3, line 28 is highlighted since the program has just been loaded and **mov ax, SEG** data is the first instruction to be executed.

The dialog window is at the bottom of the screen below the display window. Initially the dialog window shows Microsoft's copyright notice and a > prompt. Commands for CodeView are entered in the dialog window.

The register window is to the right of the display window and the dialog window. The register window shows the current contents of all the 8088's registers. The contents of the flag register are shown as a set of eight mnemonics; for example, NC means "no carry," that is, CF=0. When relevant, the bottom of the register window displays the memory operand of the next instruction.

Requests for CodeView are communicated by typing commands in the dialog window, by pressing a function key or some key combination, or by using a mouse. Figure E.4 shows how to invoke some Codeview actions using the dialog window or keys.

Figure E.5 shows the CodeView display for the example program after two trace (**T**) commands have been entered in the dialog window. Line 31 is now the next to be executed. The values in the AX and DS registers change when the immediate operand **SEG data** was loaded into AX and then copied to DS; the data segment number for this program run was 4CF9.

As additional **T** instructions are entered in the dialog box, the statements of the example program are executed one at a time. With default CodeView options, the **output** and **inputs** macros are executed with single **T** commands;

Figure E.4 Selected CodeView Commands.

Command	Dialog/key	Function
F2	key	makes the register window disappear or appear
F4	key	displays the program's output screen; press any key to return to the CodeView display
F5	key	execute program to the next breakpoint or to the end of the program
G	dialog	same as F5 key
F6	key	moves the cursor between the display and dialog windows
Ctrl-G	key	enlarge the display or dialog window (whichever contains the cursor); the other window gets smaller
F8	key	trace execution of one instruction; if the instruction is a `call` or `int` and the corresponding code has been assembled and linked with symbolic data for CodeView, tracing will continue within the procedure
T	dialog	same as F8 key
F9	key	set or remove a breakpoint at the current program line in the display window
BP	dialog	set a breakpoint at a specified program line; for example, `BP .40`
BC	dialog	remove a specified breakpoint; `BC *` clears all breakpoints
F10	key	like trace, except for `call` and `int` instructions, which execute as atomic operations
P	dialog	same as F10 key
Ctrl-W	key	add watch expression to the watch window
? *symbol*	dialog	show value of *symbol*
L	dialog	load (restart) the current program
Q	dialog	quit; exit to DOS

Figure E.5 CodeView Display After Two **T** Commands.

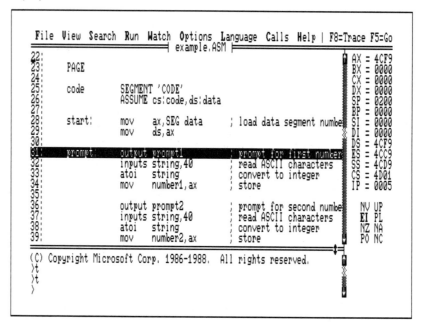

Figure E.6 Output Screen During Program Execution.

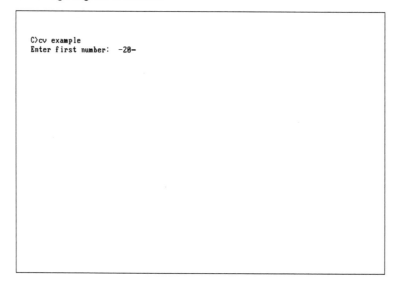

Figure E.7 Entering a Watch Variable, 1.

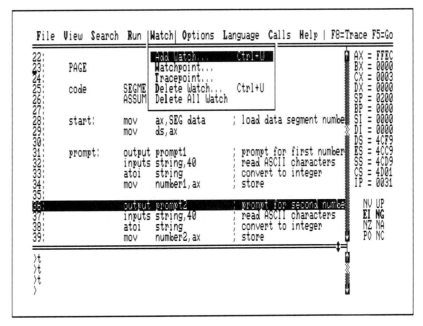

individual statements which make up the macros are not traced. When the **inputs** macro is executed, the CodeView display disappears and is replaced by an ordinary display which shows the screen the way it appeared when CodeView was executed, with the addition of the prompt generated by the example program. Figure E.6 shows this screen as it appeared on the author's system; the number –20 has been typed, but Return has not yet been pressed.

As soon as Return is pressed, the CodeView display returns. Figure E.7 shows the display a little later in the CodeView session; two more trace (**T**) commands have been entered and Alt-W has been pressed. The next statement to be executed is line 36, with the instruction **output prompt2**. CX contains 0003, the number of characters read by the **inputs** macro. AX contains FFEC, the word-length 2's complement version of –20 generated by the **atoi** macro.

CodeView has several ways to examine data stored in the data segment. One way is to declare a watch expression for each variable of interest. In Figure E.7 Alt-W has opened the watch menu window. The **Add Watch** line is highlighted, and pressing Return produces the new window shown in Figure E.8. The name **number1** has been typed in this window, indicating that this symbol is to be watched. When Return is pressed, the display changes to the one shown in Figure E.9. A watch window has been opened between the menu bar and the display window. The watch window shows the symbol **number1** and its current value **0xffec**. (The prefix **0x** indicates a hexadecimal value.) Any time **number1** changes, the value in the watch window will be updated.

Figure E.8 Entering a Watch Variable, 2.

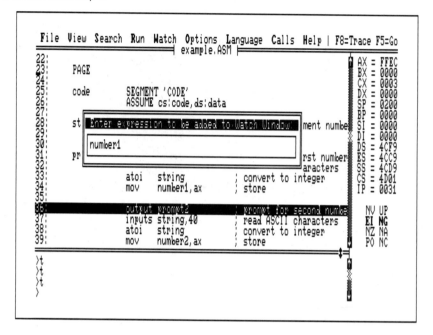

Figure E.9 CodeView Display with Watch Window.

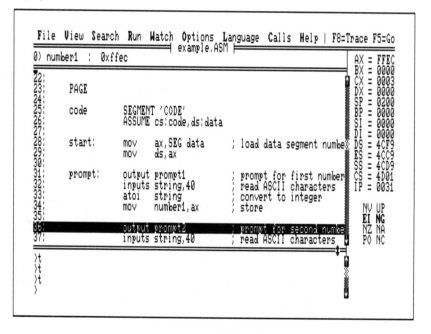

Figure E.10 CodeView Display in Middle of Program.

```
 File  View  Search  Run  Watch  Options  Language  Calls  Help | F8=Trace F5=Go
                           example.ASM
0) number1 :   0xffec                                              AX = 0023
1) number2 :   0x0023                                              BX = 0000
                                                                  CX = 0002
32:              inputs string,40        ; read ASCII characters  DX = 0000
33:              atoi   string           ; convert to integer     SP = 0200
34:              mov    number1,ax        ; store                  BP = 0000
35:                                                                SI = 0000
36:              output prompt2           ; prompt for second numbe DI = 0000
37:              inputs string,40         ; read ASCII characters  DS = 4CF9
38:              atoi   string            ; convert to integer     ES = 4CC9
39:              mov    number2,ax        ; store                  SS = 4CD9
40:                                                                CS = 4D01
41:              mov    ax,number1        ; first number to AX     IP = 005D
42:              add    ax,number2        ; add second number
43:                                                                NV UP
44:              itoa   sum,ax            ; convert to ASCII charac EI PL
45:                                                                NZ NA
46:              output label1            ; output label and sum   PO NC

>t                                                                DS:0000
>t                                                                    FFEC
>t
>
```

Figure E.10 shows the CodeView display later in the same debugging session. Four more trace (T) instructions have been given, the number 35 has been entered for the value of the second number, and the variable **number2** has been added to the watch window. Line 41 is the next statement to be executed, the instruction **mov ax, number1**. The bottom of the register window shows the location and value of the symbol **number1**.

```
DS:0000
    FFEC
```

Tracing two more instructions results in the display shown in Figure E.11. The addition operation has put the sum 000F in AX. Flag values PE and CY are highlighted to show that PF=1 and CF=1, both as a result of the addition. The next statement to be executed is on line 44.

At this point, the user decided to execute the program to its end and entered a **G** command. The resulting CodeView display is shown in Figure E.12. It looks almost like Figure E.11 except that no line is highlighted as the next to be executed, and the dialog window reports **Program terminated normally (0)**. This is somewhat unsatisfying, since the output of the program cannot be seen. Pressing F4 switches to the output screen shown in Figure E.13. Pressing any key goes back to the CodeView display for further actions. Once back at the CodeView display, the **L** command would reload the program for further tracing, or a **Q** command would exit to DOS.

Figure E.11 CodeView Display near End of Program.

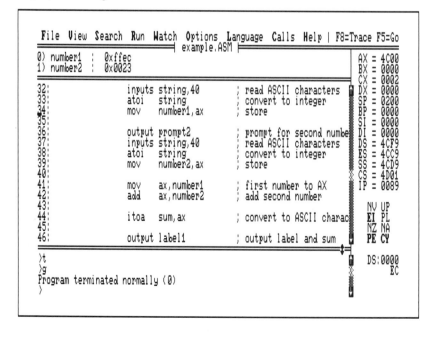

Figure E.12 CodeView Display After Program Terminates.

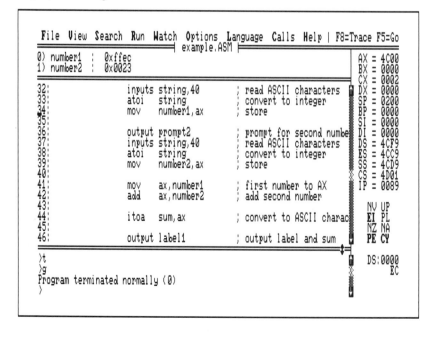

Figure E.13 Output Screen After Program Terminates.

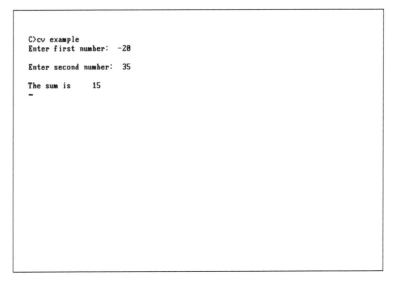

```
C>cv example
Enter first number:  -20

Enter second number:  35

The sum is     15
_
```

CodeView supports many other features. One of the most useful is the ability to set breakpoints, flagging statements at which execution will pause after a G command is given. When tracing a long program, setting a breakpoint just before a suspected problem area will be more efficient than getting to that point through a long sequence of **T** instructions.

To set a breakpoint, the F6 key is used to move the cursor to the display window. The Up arrow, down arrow, Page Up, or Page Down key can be used to scroll through the source code to locate the line at which a breakpoint is to be set. With the cursor on that line, the F9 key sets the breakpoint, and the entire line is highlighted to indicate the breakpoint. If a line is already a breakpoint, the F9 key removes the breakpoint. Pushing F6 again moves the cursor back to the dialog window for command entry.

Listing of IO.H

```
;   header file for assembly language programs
;   contains macro definitions for itoa, atoi, output, inputs and inputc
;   author:  R. Detmer

.XLIST          ; turn off listing

                EXTRN   itoa_proc:far, atoi_proc:far, out_proc:far
                EXTRN   ins_proc:far, inc_proc:far

m_error         MACRO   msg
                IF2
                %OUT msg
                .LALL
COMMENT *
        msg
* END COMMENT
                .ERR
                .SALL
                ENDIF
                ENDM

itoa            MACRO   dest,source,xtra     ;; convert integer to ASCII string

                IFB     <source>
                m_error <missing operand(s) in ITOA>
                EXITM
                ENDIF

                IFNB    <xtra>
                m_error <extra operand(s) in ITOA>
                EXITM
                ENDIF
```

```
                push    ax              ;; save AX
                push    di              ;; save DI
                mov     ax,source       ;; copy source to AX
                lea     di,dest         ;; destination address to DI
                call    itoa_proc       ;; call procedure
                pop     di              ;; restore DI
                pop     ax              ;; restore AX
                ENDM

atoi    MACRO   source,xtra     ;; convert ASCII string to integer in AX

                IFB     <source>
                m_error <missing operand in ATOI>
                EXITM
                ENDIF

                IFNB    <xtra>
                m_error <extra operand(s) in ATOI>
                EXITM
                ENDIF

                push    si              ;; save SI
                lea     si,source       ;; source address to SI
                call    atoi_proc       ;; call procedure
                pop     si              ;; restore SI
                ENDM

output  MACRO   string,length,xtra  ;; display macro

                IFB     <string>
                m_error <missing operand in OUTPUT>
                EXITM
                ENDIF

                IFNB    <xtra>
                m_error <extra operand(s) in OUTPUT>
                EXITM
                ENDIF

                push    ax              ;; save AX
                push    si              ;; save SI
                lea     si,string       ;; load address of source string

                IFB     <length>        ;; IF no length parameter
                mov     ax,0            ;;   set length to zero
                ELSE                    ;; ELSE
                mov     ax,length       ;;   copy length to AX
                ENDIF
```

```
            call    out_proc            ;; call procedure
            pop     si                  ;; restore SI
            pop     ax                  ;; restore AX
            ENDM

inputs      MACRO   dest,length,xtra    ;; read string from keyboard

            IFB     <length>
            m_error <missing operand(s) in INPUTS>
            EXITM
            ENDIF

            IFNB    <xtra>
            m_error <extra operand(s) in INPUTS>
            EXITM
            ENDIF

            push    di                  ;; save DX
            lea     di,dest             ;; destination address
            mov     cx,length           ;; length of buffer
            call    ins_proc            ;; call procedure
            pop     di                  ;; restore DX
            ENDM

inputc      MACRO   xtra                ;; read character from keyboard to AL
            IFNB    <xtra>
            m_error <extra operand(s) in INPUTC>
            EXITM
            ENDIF
            call    inc_proc            ;; call procedure
            ENDM

.SALL       ; suppress macro expansion listings
.LIST       ; begin listing
```

Listing of IO.ASM

```
; external procedures called by itoa, atoi, output, inputs and inputc
; author:  R. Detmer

          NAME    io
          PUBLIC itoa_proc, atoi_proc, out_proc, ins_proc, inc_proc

dosint    MACRO   function            ;; Call the DOS interrupt
          mov     ah,function         ;; Put function number in AH
          int     21h
          ENDM

io        SEGMENT
          ASSUME cs:io, ds:io          ; only ins_proc has local data

; Procedure to convert integer in AX to string of 6 characters at (DI)
itoa_proc PROC    FAR
          push    ax                  ; Save registers
          push    bx                  ;    used by
          push    cx                  ;    procedure
          push    dx
          push    di
          push    es
          pushf                       ; save flags

          cmp     ax,8000h            ; special case -32,768?
          jne     normal              ; if not, then normal case
          mov     BYTE PTR [di],'-'    ; manually put in ASCII codes
          mov     BYTE PTR [di+1],'3' ;    for -32,768
          mov     BYTE PTR [di+2],'2'
          mov     BYTE PTR [di+3],'7'
          mov     BYTE PTR [di+4],'6'
```

```
                mov     BYTE PTR [di+5],'8'
                jmp     SHORT finish            ; done with special case

normal:         mov     dx,ax                   ; save number
                mov     ax,ds                   ; copy data segment
                mov     es,ax                   ;   number to extra segment

                mov     al,' '                  ; put blanks in
                mov     cx,5                    ;   first five
                cld                             ;   bytes of
                rep stosb                       ;   destination field

                mov     ax,dx                   ; restore number
                mov     cl,' '                  ; default sign (blank for +)
                cmp     ax,0                    ; check sign of number
                jge     setup                   ; skip if not negative
                mov     cl,'-'                  ; sign for negative number
                neg     ax                      ; number in AX now >= 0

setup:          mov     bx,10                   ; divisor

divloop:        mov     dx,0                    ; extend number to doubleword
                div     bx                      ; divide by 10
                add     dl,30h                  ; convert remainder to character
                mov     [di],dl                 ; put character in string
                dec     di                      ; move forward to next position
                cmp     ax,0                    ; check quotient
                jne     divloop                 ; continue if quotient not zero

                mov     [di],cl                 ; insert blank or "-" for sign

finish:         popf                            ; restore flags
                pop     es                      ; restore registers
                pop     di
                pop     dx
                pop     cx
                pop     bx
                pop     ax
                ret                             ;exit
itoa_proc       ENDP


; Procedure to scan data segment starting at offset in SI, interpreting
; ASCII characters as an integer value which is returned in AX.

; Leading blanks are skipped. A leading - or + sign is acceptable.
; Digit(s) must immediately follow the sign (if any).
; Memory scan is terminated by any non-digit, and the address of
; the terminating character is in SI.
```

```
; The following flags are affected:
;   AC is undefined
;   PF, SF and ZF reflect sign of number returned in AX.
;   CF reset to 0
;   OF set to indicate error. Possible error conditions are:
;     - no digits in input
;     - more than 5 digits in input
;     - value outside range -32,768 to 32,767
;   (AX) will be 0 if OF is set.

atoi_proc    PROC    FAR
             push    bx               ; Save registers
             push    cx
             push    dx
             pushf                    ; save flags

while_blank:cmp      BYTE PTR [si],' '  ; space?
             jne     end_while_blank    ; exit if not
             inc     si                 ; increment character pointer
             jmp     while_blank        ; and try again
end_while_blank:

             mov     ax,1             ; default sign multiplier
if_plus:     cmp     BYTE PTR [si],'+'  ; leading + ?
             je      skip_sign          ; if so, skip over
if_minus:    cmp     BYTE PTR [si],'-'  ; leading - ?
             jne     save_sign          ; if not, save default +
             mov     ax,-1              ; -1 for minus sign
skip_sign:   inc     si                 ; move past sign

save_sign:   push    ax               ; push sign multiplier on stack
             mov     ax,0             ; number being accumulated
             mov     cx,0             ; count of digits so far

while_digit:cmp      BYTE PTR [si],'0'  ; compare next character to '0'
             jl      end_while_digit    ; not a digit if smaller than '0'
             cmp     BYTE PTR [si],'9'  ; compare to '9'
             jg      end_while_digit    ; not a digit if bigger than '9'
             mov     bx,10            ; multiplier
             mul     bx               ; multiply old number by 10
             jo      overflow         ; exit if product too large
             mov     bl,[si]          ; ASCII character to BL
             and     bx,000Fh         ; convert to single-digit integer
             add     ax,bx            ; add to sum
             jc      overflow         ; exit if sum too large
             inc     cx               ; increment digit count
             inc     si               ; increment character pointer
             jmp     while_digit      ; go try next character
end_while_digit:
```

```
            cmp     cx,0                    ; no digits?
            jz      overflow                ; if so, set overflow error flag
            cmp     cx,5                    ; more than 5 digits?
            jg      overflow                ; if so, set overflow error flag

; if value is 8000h and sign is '-',  want to return 8000h (-32,768)

            cmp     ax,8000h                ; 8000h ?
            jne     too_big?
            pop     bx                      ; retrieve multiplier
            cmp     bx,-1                   ; -1 ?
            je      ok1                     ; return 8000h
            push    bx                      ; save multiplier again

too_big?:   test    ax,ax                   ; check sign flag
            jns     ok                      ; will be set if number > 32,767

overflow:   pop     bx                      ; discard multiplier
            pop     ax                      ; get flags
            or      ax,0000100001000100B  ; set overflow, zero & parity flags
            and     ax,1111111101111110B  ; reset sign and carry flags
            push    ax                      ; push new flag values
            mov     ax,0                    ; return value of zero
            jmp     atoi_exit               ; quit

ok:         pop     bx                      ; sign
            imul    bx                      ; make signed number
ok1:        popf                            ; get original flags
            test    ax,ax                   ; set flags for new number
            pushf                           ; save flags

atoi_exit:  popf                            ; get flags
            pop     dx                      ; restore registers
            pop     cx
            pop     bx
            ret                             ;exit
atoi_proc   ENDP

; Procedure to display string with starting address in SI
; Null character terminates display in all cases
; If (AX) > 0, this value limits the number of characters displayed
; No registers are changed; flags are not affected.

out_proc    PROC    FAR
            push    ax                      ; Save registers
            push    bx
            push    cx
```

```
            push    si
            push    dx
            pushf                           ; save flags

            mov     cx,ax                   ; copy count to CX

out_loop:   mov     dl,[si]                 ; character to print
            test    dl,dl                   ; check character to be printed
            jz      end_out                 ; exit if null character
            test    ax,ax                   ; see if counter should be checked
            jle     show_it                 ; if not positive, don't check counter
            cmp     cx,0                    ; check count of remaining characters
            jle     end_out                 ; quit if not positive
show_it:    push    ax                      ; save flag AX
            dosint  2                       ; display character
            pop     ax                      ; restore AX
            inc     si                      ; increment string pointer
            dec     cx                      ; decrement count
            jmp     out_loop                ; repeat

end_out:    popf                            ; restore flags
            pop     dx                      ; restore registers
            pop     si
            pop     cx
            pop     bx
            pop     ax
            ret                             ;exit
out_proc    ENDP

; Procedure to input string from keyboard.

; CX contains the length of the user's buffer. It is assumed that this
; length is between 1 and 81.

; DI contains the offset in DS of the user's buffer where the string will
; be stored.
; The string will be terminated by a null character (00h).

; The actual number of characters (not counting the null) is returned in CX.
; This number will be between 0 and 80.

; Flags are unchanged.

buffer      DB      83 DUP (?)              ; local buffer for string

ins_proc    PROC    FAR
            push    ax                      ; Save registers
            push    dx
            push    di
            push    si
```

```
                push   ds
                push   es
                pushf                          ; save flags

                mov    ax,ds                   ; copy data segment number to ES
                mov    es,ax

                mov    ax,cs                   ; copy code segment number to DS
                mov    ds,ax

                cmp    cx,80                   ; buffer length <= 80 ?
                jle    ins1
                mov    cx,80                   ; reduce buffer length to 80
ins1:           cmp    cx,2                    ; buffer length >= 2 ?
                jge    ins2
                mov    cx,2                    ; increase buffer length to 2

ins2:           dec    cx                      ; maximum number of characters
                mov    buffer,cl
                mov    dx,OFFSET buffer        ; local buffer address
                dosint 0ah                     ; DOS function A does the input

                mov    cl,buffer+1             ; actual number of characters
                mov    ch,0                    ; convert to word
                jcxz   end_in                  ; skip if no characters

                push   cx                      ; save count to return
                mov    si,OFFSET buffer+2      ; start in local buffer
                cld                            ; ensure forward copy
                rep movsb                      ; copy string from local to user buffer
                pop    cx                      ; restore count

end_in:         mov    BYTE PTR es:[di],0      ; null character terminator
                mov    dl,10                   ; output linefeed
                dosint 2                       ;   using DOS call

                popf                           ; restore flags
                pop    es                      ; restore registers
                pop    ds
                pop    si
                pop    di
                pop    dx
                pop    ax
                ret                            ; exit

ins_proc        ENDP
```

```
; Procedure to wait for, input and echo character from keyboard.
; Character returned in AL. AH set to zero.
; No other registers are affected.
; Flags are not affected.

inc_proc      PROC    FAR                 ; input character from keyboard
              dosint 1                    ; DOS interrupt 1 does the job
              mov     ah,0                ; clear AH
              ret                         ; exit
inc_proc      ENDP
io            ENDS
              END
```

Index